MEDJUGORJE:
A TIME FOR TRUTH AND
A TIME FOR ACTION

MEDJUGORJE:
A TIME FOR TRUTH AND
A TIME FOR ACTION

Denis Nolan

The publisher recognizes and accepts that the final authority regarding the apparitions at Medjugorje rests with the Holy See of Rome, to whose judgment we willingly submit

The Publisher

Cover Art & Design
Janet Schaefer

Copyright ©1993 Queenship Publishing

Library of Congress Catalogue No. 93-83221

ISBN: 1-882972-05-8

Printed in the United States of America

Dedication

To our beautiful Mother, Mary, the Queen of Peace in Medjugorje – *our life, our sweetness and our hope* – and to the priests and sisters of St. James Church and the visionaries and families of the parish who have so generously responded to her call:

Dearest Mother we your children
Come from all the world before you.
We come bringing you our problems
And with them our hearts desires.

The entire Church looks to you,
The last star of our salvation.
Purify us and embrace us,
Fervently we pray, sweet Mother.

The small town of Bijakovici
And all nearby Medjugorje
They both spread your special glory
And exalt your holy name.

Because of the love, dear Mother,
Which you have poured out upon us here,
We now vow to be more faithful
To the will of God our Father.

Look upon us, console us.
Lay your loving hands upon us.
Intercede for us to Jesus;
Mary Queen of Peace, pray for us

Kraljici mira

From a Sermon by Saint Anselm

(Oratio 52: 158, 955-956)

Virgin Mary, all nature is blessed in you!

Blessed Lady, sky and stars, earth and rivers, day and night - everything that is subject to the power or use of man - rejoice that through you they are in some sense restored to their lost beauty and are endowed with inexpressible new grace. All creatures were dead, as it were, useless for men or for the praise of God, who made them. The world, contrary to its true destiny, was corrupted and tainted by the acts of men who served idols. Now all creation has been restored to life and rejoices that it is controlled and given splendor by men who believe in God.

The universe rejoices with new and indefinable loveliness. Not only does it feel the unseen presence of God himself, its Creator, it sees him openly, working and making it holy. These great blessings spring from the blessed fruit of Mary's womb.

Through the fullness of the grace that was given you, dead things rejoice in their freedom, and those in heaven are glad to be made new. Through the Son who was the glorious fruit of your virgin womb, just souls who died before his life-giving death rejoice as they are freed from captivity, and the angels are glad at the restoration of their shattered domain.

Lady, full and overflowing with grace, all creation receives new life from your abundance. Virgin, blessed above all creatures, through your blessing all creation is blessed, not only creation from its Creator, but the Creator himself has been blessed by creation.

To Mary, God gave his only-begotten Son, whom he loved as himself. Through Mary, God made himself a Son, not different but the same, by nature Son of God and Son of Mary. The whole universe was created by God, and God was born of Mary. God created all things, and Mary gave birth to God. The God who made all things gave himself form through Mary, and thus he made his own creation. He who could create all things from nothing would not remake his ruined creation without Mary.

God, then, is the Father of the created world and Mary the mother of the re-created world. God is the Father by whom all things were given life, and Mary the mother through whom all things were given new life. For God begot the Son, through whom all things were made, and Mary gave birth to him as the Savior of the world. Without God's Son, nothing could exist; without Mary's Son, nothing could be redeemed.

Truly the Lord is with you, to whom the Lord granted that all nature should owe as much to you as to himself.

"Tell Medjugorje that I am with you. I bless you. I beg you: protect Medjugorje! Protect Our Lady's message!" [6/17/92]

Pope John Paul II

"In a society brutalized by a scorn for God reaching even to the destruction of human beings...God reveals the power of the motherly heart! **HE IS SENDING THE MOST HOLY VIRGIN MARY RIGHT INTO SUCH A TIME AND SUCH A WORLD** to draw people anew to the only Redeemer."

"Many in the world believe that the Mother of God has established herself also in the highlands of Hercegovina and as **Queen of Peace has called in Medjugorje** for conversion and peace... In her messages in the Church and in the world the Blessed Virgin Mary calls Jesus' call to awareness: 'The time is fulfilled!'"

"Whoever entrusts himself to her will surely find the Redeemer! She leads each one with her motherly hand on the way of salvation! With this confidence we now want to entrust, devote and consecrate ourselves to her, the **QUEEN OF PEACE!**" [1/15/92]

"People who believe and are convinced in conscience that with these messages [the messages of Medjugorje] they can stimulate people to the good - to conversion, to peace - **they should do it. This is a matter of conscience.**" [9/27/92]

Cardinal Franjo Kuharic

[His Eminence Cardinal Franjo Kuharic is Primate of Croatia and President of the Yugoslavian Bishops' Conference which is responsible for investigating the apparitions in Medjugorje for the Church.]

"I feel immense gratitude towards the Lord. He is always capable of communicating His messages to us men, in particular through His mother." [11/92]

Bishop Ratko Peric

[Response given by Msgr. Peric, the new Bishop of Mostar, the diocese to which Medjugorje belongs, to the question, "Do you believe in the apparitions of the Blessed Mother in Medjugorje?"]

"I am deeply convinced of the apparitions in Medjugorje and am deeply grateful. ...Step by step the Immaculate Heart of Mary will triumph. And I am also deeply convinced that Medjugorje is a sign for this."

Cardinal Frantizek Tomasek

"The cruelties that are happening daily in former Yugoslavia encourage us to direct this appeal to all the faithful in the Church, so that more than ever we become aware of the importance of the messages of Medjugorje... The war that has been raging for a year in this area shows us more deeply how very much we share responsibility for these horrible events when we take these messages with too little seriousness or even reject them."

Bishop Paolo Hnilica, S.J.

"Some would gladly silence the Blessed Mother after ten years of apparitions in Medjugorje so that no one hears her...I experience this war as a kind of Satanism... I consider this terrible war as God's warning for us all to convert [reconcile] - for our Croatian people and the other peoples of Yugoslavia, Europe and the whole world to be saved!"

Archbishop Frane Franic

"The good fruit of Medjugorje is unparalleled in the history of the Church."

Fr. Michael O'Carroll C.S.S.P.

"We have more conversions from Medjugorje than any place in the world! ...I don't recall in history anything comparable to the Medjugorje events. Could it be as has happened in the past, God wants to exalt the humble and put down the proud with the rallying cry 'Vox populi, vox Dei' ('The voice of the people, the voice of God')?"

Bishop Nicholas D'Antonio

"And they would not accept him. But Jesus said to them, 'A prophet is only despised in his own country and in his own house.'" Matthew 13: 57-58

"The Jews took up stones again to stone him. Jesus answered them, 'I have shown you many good works from the Father; for which of these do you stone me?'" John 10:31

"He [Satan] is a liar and the father of lies." John 8:44

"At that time Jesus declared, 'I thank thee, Father, Lord of heaven and of earth, that thou hast hidden these things from the wise and the understanding and revealed them to babes; yes, Father, for such was thy gracious will.'" Matthew 11: 25

"And when he drew near and saw the city, he wept over it, saying, 'Would that even today you knew the things that make for peace! But now they are hid from your eyes. For the days shall come upon you, when your enemies will cast up a bank about you and surround you, and hem you in on every side, and dash you to the ground, you and your children within you, and they will not leave one stone upon another in you, because you did not recognize the time of your visitation.'" Luke 19:41-44

Table of Contents

Medjugorje:
A Chronology of Coincidences

- On June 27, 1991, the Bishops' Conference of the former Yugoslavia was scheduled to meet in Mostar in Bosnia-Herzegovina. It was rumored that the Conference, at this meeting, would prohibit any further public dissemination of the messages of Our Lady from Medjugorje; and in fact a team of bishops and theologians from the Bishops' Conference had come to Medjugorje on June 17th to discuss this proposed prohibition. Then on June 25, 1991, the tenth anniversary of the Medjugorje apparitions, Croatia declared independence and proceeded to secede from Yugoslavia. On June 27th, the Serbian army invaded Croatia and multi-ethnic Yugoslavia exploded in a thunderous surge of Balkan barbarism. The palace and cathedral of Medjugorje's chief antagonist — the host of the proposed meeting in Mostar — would in succeeding months literally go up in flames and the Bishops' Conference could never meet again to issue the rumored condemnation.

Coincidence or not, this was only the latest episode in a continuing series of conveniently timed events and circumstances that mysteriously seemed to protect Medjugorje from its many enemies. Consider this:[1]

- When the apparitions were first reported in June 1981, the claims of the visionaries were summarily rejected by Fr. Jozo Zovko, the pastor

---

[1] We are not suggesting here that the war that tore Yugoslavia asunder is in any sense a sort of divine punishment. We note, however, that Providence in Its Infinite Wisdom honors human free will to the extent that the rejection of a special grace brings not condemnation but deprivation of the special protection offered by such a grace. Moreover, the exercise of human free will often results in the triumph of evil — but God tolerates the evil that men do only because he makes even such evil serve His ultimate Plan and Purpose. Protection offered by Providence in response to acceptance of a spoecial grace is clearly illustrated in the case of Fatima and Portugal.

It is well known that Portugal was preserved from the Second World War. According to Sister Lucia of Fatima this preservation came about because the bishops of Portugal consecrated their country to the Immaculate Heart of Mary on May 13, 1938 (the anniversary of Fatima) and renewed this act on December 8, 1940 at her request. Writing to Pope Pius XII on December 2, 1940, Sister Lucia said, "Most Holy Father ... Our Lord promises to give a special protection to our country during this war, in consideration of the consecration which the Reverend Bishops of Portugal have made of the nation to the Immaculate Heart of Mary. And this protection will be the proof of the graces which God would give to the other nations, if like Portugal, they were to consecrate themselves to it." In this section, we make no claim of infallibly discerning the workings of Providence. We are simply drawing attention to the complex interplay of factors and events that has amazingly kept Medjugorje alive.

of the parish of Medjugorje. Bishop Pavao Zanic, the Bishop of Mostar, the diocese to which Medjugorje belonged, came to the defense of the visionaries in the face of both their skeptical pastor and the suspicious Communist authorities of the region.

- When the authorities decided to move in and "shut down" Medjugorje, Fr. Zovko reportedly received a private revelation that he should "protect the children." As a result of his help, the children managed to escape their Communist persecutors. Fr. Zovko himself was sent to prison for his actions.

- As the Bishop of Mostar too came under pressure from the Communists, his support for the visionaries began to wane. Gradually, the Bishop became actively hostile to Medjugorje. At this time, the visionaries found a new champion in Archbishop Frane Franic, the bishop of neighboring Split.

- Claims of apparitions usually come under the jurisdiction of the local bishop, and it is he who has the initial authority for determining the legitimacy of such claims. Accordingly, Bishop Zanic instituted a commission to investigate Medjugorje. One of the first investigators that the bishop sent to Medjugorje was Fr. Slavko Barbaric, O.F.M., a psychologist. Although Fr. Barbaric was initially skeptical, he was so impressed with the veracity of the visionaries that he stayed on in Medjugorje and became their spiritual director.

- It soon became clear that Bishop Zanic's commission was not interested in getting "all the facts". It appeared that the commission had already decided what kind of verdict it would issue - a negative one. Then, once again, the mysterious shield protecting Medjugorje went up: before the bishop's commission could issue its verdict, the Vatican suddenly intervened and took the whole investigation out of the hands of the bishop. This was reportedly the first time in modern history that the Vatican directly intervened in a local investigation of this kind. Jurisdiction over further investigation into Medjugorje was turned over to the Bishops' Conference of Yugoslavia.

- Medjugorje, meanwhile, had long since ceased to be a local affair. Millions of pilgrims from every corner of the world were streaming into this hamlet seeking the Mother of God. Modern technology deployed to study the visionaries during the apparitions indicated that no natural explanation could be found for the phenomena. Global communications media amplified the message of Medjugorje.

- At the Vatican, it gradually became obvious to visiting bishops that Pope John Paul II had a very positive view of Medjugorje. An incredible incident in this context is recounted by no less a source than Bishop Angelo Kim, President of the Korean Episcopal Conference, in the *Korean Catholic* weekly, 11 November 1990: "During the recent synod in Rome, the Korean bishops were invited to lunch with the Pope. In particular Mgr. Kim said to the Pope, 'Thanks to you, Poland has now been freed from communism.' The Pope replied, 'No, not me, **but by the works of the Blessed Virgin, according to her affirmations at Fatima and Medjugorje.'** "(1) Six years earlier, in March, 1984, just after consecrating Russia to the Immaculate Heart of Mary, the Holy Father sent his long time friend and confidant, Bishop Paolo Hnilica, S.J., to Medjugorje: **"You must go to Medjugorje. Medjugorje is the fulfillment of Fatima!"**

- As a campaign of disinformation and slander was launched against Medjugorje, two of the greatest Catholic theologians in Europe, Fr. Rene Laurentin and Fr. Hans Urs Von Balthasar, came to its defense. Fr. Laurentin, one of the greatest living Mariologists and the Church's most prominent expert on apparitions, began a painstaking investigation into Medjugorje that ended in a positive verdict (backed with exhaustive evidence) on the phenomenon. Fr. Balthasar, a thinker who has been ranked among the greatest theologians of this century, became an ardent champion of the authenticity of Medjugorje. To a great extent, the labors of Frs. Laurentin and Balthasar counteracted the vigorous campaign of disinformation on Medjugorje that could have killed it in the eyes of Church authorities.

- The ball was now in the court of the Yugoslavian Bishops' Conference. It was popularly known that Bishop Zanic was making every effort to bring about a negative verdict from the Conference. In the bishops' meeting on Medjugorje in November 1990, Bishop Zanic came close to persuading the Conference to declare the apparitions fraudulent. Archbishop Franic's efforts, however, prevented this outcome and the Conference concluded only that "on the basis of inquiries conducted up until the present time, one cannot affirm that we are dealing here with supernatural apparitions or revelations." This carefully neutral statement was neither an affirmation nor a denial of the authenticity of the apparitions.[2] Significantly, the bishops recognized the importance of Medjugorje by affirming that "the constant concourse in Medjugorje of faithful coming from different parts of the

---

[2] An article quoting the President of the Doctrinal Commission of the Yugoslavian Bishops Conference, Archbishop Frane Franic, in the January 6, 1991 issue of *Siobodna Dalmacija* has not been widely reported in the English speaking world: "The bishops used this ambiguous sentence because they did not want to humiliate Bishop Pavao Zanic of Mostar, who constantly claimed that Our Lady did not appear to the seers. ...When the Yugoslav bishops discussed the Medjugorje issue, they told Bishop Zanic that the Church was not giving a final decision on Medjugorje and consequently his opposition was without any foundation. Hearing this, Bishop Zanic began to cry and to shout, and the rest of the bishops then quit any further discussion." Worth noting is Our Lady's subsequent message from Medjugorje (following the worldwide dissimination of the resulting press release, *Yugoslavian Bishops Say Medjugorje Not Supernatural*): "I stay among you as long as it is God's will. Thank you that you will not betray my presence here and I thank you because your response is serving God and peace," [January 25, 1991].

Eighteen months after Our Lady warned in her following September 25th message, "Now as never before Satan wants to show the world his shameful face by which he wants to seduce as many people as possible onto the way of death and sin. Therefore, dear children, help my Immaculate Heart to triumph..."

- The **Holy Father** wrote the Secretary General of the United Nations: **"Death, torture, rape and expulsion are the many faces of hatred** setting one people against another [in Bosnia-Hercegovina] ... Life, so precious for each and every one, no longer has value." [*L'Osservatore Romano*, March 17, 1993 p.1.]

- **Bishop Franjo Komarica**, head of the commission investigating Medjugorje for the Bishop's Conference of Yugoslavia, declared: **"If the international community allows strict etnic partitioning [in Bosnia] that's the beginning of the end of the civilized world! We are nailed to the cross and hang without hope!** ... The unprovoked total destruction of [my] diocese is continuing unabated, where the church has been present for over 17 centuries! ... We beg all who consider themselves human beings — those who can constructively help us: Do not burden your conscience with indifference due to our misfortunes and downfall! **We do not want our downfall (for which we are not to blame), to become your downfall on the day of judgment before God Almighty, before whom we will all have to stand. Protect us and help us while there is still time!"** [*Mary's People*, March 28, 1993, p. 8; *Glas Koncila* (Croation National Catholic weekly) March 7, 1993].

- To question: "Do you believe that we have neglected to listen to this call, this voice of peace — from the Queen of PEace in Medjugorje — and **if it would have been recognized that the Mother of God comes,** maybe the graces would have been spread over the people in much greature measure?" **Cardinal Franjo Kuharic**, President of the Episcopal Conference of (former) Yugoslavia, replied: **"This will remain an open question."** [Medjugorje Gebetsaktion, #25, p. 11]. [Regarding this "open question" note Fr. Grafenauer's testimony: pp 409-413].

world and animated by motives of faith calls for the bishops' attention and care."

- Then came the decision by the Bishops' Conference to hold a meeting on Medjugorje in Mostar on June 27, 1991; and the rest, as they say, is history.

- As we reflect on the mysterious events protecting Medjugorje, our thoughts turn to the inferno that swept through Yugoslavia, the unthinkable nightmare endured by millions of Croatians, Serbs and Bosnians throughout the former republic. What is remarkable is that Medjugorje was left physically unscathed even in the midst of destruction all around it. As a postscript, we add here a report on Medjugorje that appeared on the front page of *The Wall Street Journal* on November 9, 1992; "The war has enhanced Medjugorje's fame as an oasis of peace and mystery. At one point, the war front was only three miles away - so close that Easter Mass was held in a sandbagged cellar. Planes and artillery ravaged nearby towns. But only six shells hit Medjugorje. The casualties: one cow, one chicken, one dog. The sole air raid on the town ended with a few bombs exploding harmlessly. ...Dragan Kozina, the town's mayor and military commander, is struck by another seeming miracle. Of 150 local men who have gone off to war, two have been injured slightly and none have been killed. 'You have to believe that either we are very lucky,' he says, 'or that someone is protecting us.'" To those who have meditated on the series of fortunate coincidences that protected Medjugorje, this final report will come as no surprise. [For the record, it must be stated that the Virgin has taken no sides in the savage war. Visionary Marija Pavlovic is quoted on this matter by the Journal: "The Virgin is wiser than us. For her, there is no Serbia or Croatia. She says Satan is present on all sides in this war."]

It is worth remembering too that the timing of Medjugorje is, to say the least, thought-provoking.

It came at the eve of the end of Communism just as Fatima came at the eve of the onset of Communism.

Medjugorje came as an affirmation — almost a celebration — of the teachings of the Second Vatican Council with a corresponding rejection of doctrinal abuses that followed the Council.

It came during the pontificate of one of the most Marian popes in history - just six weeks after he had called upon Our Lady, "Mary, come! Mary, come!"[3] immediately following the assassination attempt on his life.

The intersection of the Fatima and the Medjugorje "coincidences" are of particular interest.

- On May 5, 1917, Pope Benedict XV sent an official letter to Catholics around the world requesting them to pray to the Queen of Peace to obtain "peace ... for our agitated world." The apparitions of Fatima began eight days later, on May 13, and continued on the 13th of each month until October — with the exception of the August apparition, which took place on the 19th.

- In the July 13th apparitions, Our Lady said she would be asking for the consecration of Russia to her Immaculate Heart so that Russia could be converted. During an apparition on June 13th, 1929, to Sister Lucia, the only surviving Fatima visionary, Mary said: "The moment has come for God to ask the Holy Father to make, in union with all the bishops of the world, the consecration of Russia to my Immaculate Heart. He promises to save Russia by this means." She also prophesied that, "In the end, my Immaculate Heart will triumph. The Holy Father will consecrate Russia to me, and it will be converted and a certain period of peace will be granted to the world." On May 29, 1930, Sister Lucia noted that the beginning of the conversion of Russia would be signaled by the official approval of freedom of religion by the Russian state.

- Pope John Paul II attributed his escape from death, on May 13, 1981, to Our Lady of Fatima. During his stay in the hospital, the Pope studied the documents on Fatima provided him by Bishop Paolo Hnilica and told him, "Paolo, in these three months I have come to understand that the only solution to all the problems of the world, the deliverance from atheism and rebellion against God is the conversion of Russia. The conversion of Russia is the content and meaning of the message of

---

[3] Andre Frossard reported: "As he was being rushed to the hospital John Paul II said, more and more feely as the moments passsed, only Our Lady's name, Mary, and none of the things the nespapers attributed to him," [*Portrait of John Paul II*, Ignatius, 1990, p. 55].

Fatima. Not until then will the triumph of Mary come." [*Mary's People*, December 27, 1992]. After he left the hospital, top priority would be given to consecrating Russia to the Immaculate Heart of Mary so as to bring about the conversion of Russia.

- A little over a month after the attempt on the life of the Holy Father, Mary began her apparitions at Medjugorje. [She chose Medjugorje, she said, because of the faith of the people there. In 1933, after considerable sacrifice and expense, the villagers had constructed a huge concrete cross on the highest mountain overlooking the village in honor of the 1900th anniversary of the death of Christ.] In one of her early messages at Medjugorje, she said, "Russia is the people where God will be most glorified."

- On March 25, 1984, in union with a moral totality of Catholic bishops, Pope John Paul II consecrated the world and Russia to the Immaculate Heart of Mary. Sister Lucia confirmed to the Papal Nuncio of Lisbon that the March, 1984 consecration met the conditions requested by Our Lady. [In a letter to the present author, Sister Lucia said, "Yes, the consecration of the world is well accomplished."]

- In July 1989, Sister Lucia announced through the *Fatima Family Messenger* that God had accepted the collegial consecration of Russia requested by Our Lady, the consecration "has been accomplished" and "God will keep his word." By the end of 1989, the Communist regimes of Eastern Europe began to collapse in domino fashion; and the Soviet Union itself began to experiment with Mikhail Gorbachev's *glasnost*. In a meeting with Pope John Paul II on December 1, 1989, Gorbachev pledged to protect religious freedom in the Soviet Union.

- On August 19, 1991, the Communists in the Soviet Union staged a coup. This date was the 74th anniversary of Mary's August 19, 1917 apparition at Fatima. The coup failed on August 22, 1991, the feast of the Queenship of Mary. In her message of August 25, 1991 at Medjugorje, the Blessed Mother made her first direct reference to Fatima: "I invite you to renunciation for nine days so that with your help, everything I wanted to realize through the secrets I began in Fatima may be fulfilled." In hindsight, the failure of the August coup was a crucial milestone in the conversion of Russia and in the fulfillment of "the secrets I began in Fatima." In the same August 25 message, Our Lady warned that "Satan is strong and wants to sweep away plans of peace and joy." In her next message, [September 25, 1991] she warned, "Now as never before, Satan wants to show the world his shameful face by which he plans to seduce as many people as possible onto the way of death and sin. Therefore, dear children, help my Immaculate Heart to triumph." Pope John Paul II has remarked "that the collapse of communism in Eastern Europe 'compel[s] us to think in a special way about Fatima.' " [*Wall Street Journal*, September 27, 1991.] And, as previously mentioned, to the President of the Korean Episcopal Conference, Msgr. Angelo Kim, the Holy Father had given credit for communism's demise "to the works of the Blessed Virgin, according to her affirmations at Fatima and Medjugorje." [*Korean Catholic*, November 11, 1990.]

- On December 25, 1991, Soviet dictator Mikhail Gorbachev resigned and paved the way for a new democratic commonwealth of countries.

- With prophetic vision, in 1984 Pope John Paul II had introduced Medjugorje to Bishop Hnilica as "the fulfillment of Fatima."

- At Medjugorje we have been promised a Great Sign some time in the future. For those who have "eyes to see," the entire history of Medjugorje — as we have seen here — is a series of "great signs."

A Message from Mother Teresa

MISSIONARIES OF CHARITY
54A ACHARYA J. CHANDRA BOSE
CALCUTTA 700016, INDIA

J.M.J.   8/4/92

Dear Mr Denis Nolan,

Thank you for your kind letter of 4-4-92.

I am afraid I will not be able to come for the National Conference, due to my health – though I will be with you with my prayer. We are all praying one hail Mary before Holy Mass to Our Lady of Medjugorje asking Her to give us the medicine for Aids patients – up to now we have nothing – Ask Our Lady to answer our prayers.

Try to have one hour of Adoration during the Conference.

Please keep praying for our Society, our Poor and for me.

God bless you
Mc Teresa mc

A Message from Sister Lucia of Fatima

In response to the author's request presented by Fr. John De Marchi, I.M.C. to Sr. Lucia, the sole surviving visionary of Fatima that she pray for the intentions of the 1992 National Conference on Medjugorje and the unity of Our Lady's family in America — specifically the unity of the Fatima and Medjugorje Movements in America — Sr. Lucia, on February 12, 1992, sent a letter from her convent to Coimbra, Portugal, stating that she "prays for your intentions." Also, in answer to the question, "In your opinion, Sr. Lucia, has Our Lady accepted the consecration of the Holy Father? Has the consecration Our Lady asked for taken place?" she responded, "Yes, the consecration of the world is well established."

Foreword:

Most Reverend Michael D. Pfeifer, O.M.I.
Bishop of San Angelo, Texas

Medjugorje: A Time for Truth and a Time for Action is a remarkable collage of commentaries on a phenomenon that has dramatically influenced the life and thought of Catholics and other Christians for over a decade. The book gives a comprehensive but concise overview of the phenomenon of Medjugorje and includes the analyses and perspectives of bishops and scientists, scholars and sages, journalists and laypersons.

A Time for Truth and a Time for Action performs a valuable service for Catholics who have read or heard about Medjugorje but do not know what to make of it in the context of the Church's teachings. On the one hand, the book addresses the critiques and critics of Medjugorje by methodically answering the objections to the reported apparitions. On the other, it explores the question of whether Catholics can believe in the apparitions before the Church has reached a formal verdict. In my own pastoral letter on Medjugorje ("The Gospel, Mary and Medjugorje"), I noted that "in the past, the faithful began to act upon the contents of private revelations before the Church's approval was given. For example, the Church only approved the apparition at Fatima thirteen years after the events. Medjugorje, therefore, remains open for acceptance and integration by an individual as the Church continues her official investigation."

The chapter on Pope John Paul II and Mother Teresa on Medjugorje will be of special interest to most readers in view of the influence that both have had not just on Catholics but on the world. The study of the relationship of Fatima to Medjugorje and the testimonies of Bishops and prominent Mariologists will be welcomed by Marian devotees. In this book we see too that Medjugorje in its theology and teaching mirrors Vatican II and Pope John Paul II.

The significance of Medjugorje lies, above all, in its message for the modern world. The constant miracle of Medjugorje is a spiritual one: the miracle of converted hearts and changed lives. This constant miracle is available to anyone willing to live the Medjugorge messages of Faith, Prayer, Fasting, Penance and Peace.

Mary, our Mother, wants us to focus our lives on Christ — our way, our life, and our truth — and to teach us how to actively and effectively live the Gospel for our day and time.

March, 1993

"I have received your book, MEDJUGORJE: A TIME FOR CHANGE AND A TIME FOR ACTION. Please be assured of my every best wish that Our Blessed Lady will use your work for the good which the world so desperately needs."

Bishop Carl A. Fisher, S.S.J.

AN APPEAL TO THE BISHOPS OF THE CATHOLIC CHURCH

Your Excellencies!

It is now over eleven years since six peasant children in the tiny village of Medjugorje in Bosnia-Hercegovina have reported witnessing ongoing apparitions of the Blessed Virgin Mary. Over 15 million pilgrims from every corner of the globe have journeyed to Medjugorje drawn by the renewed preaching of the Gospel message in this humble hamlet. Among these pilgrims, there were over 30,000 priests and numerous bishops who came to Medjugorje and celebrated Holy Mass there.

Today the world knows that Bosnia-Hercegovina has turned into a battlefield and a graveyard. But Medjugorje and its message live on. By a great grace of God, the village and its church were spared the devastation suffered by the rest of the country. Pilgrims continue to come to Medjugorje — although in smaller numbers. The visionaries continue to report daily apparitions of the Blessed Mother.

The question for the faithful is this: is the Blessed Virgin Mary indeed appearing in Medjugorje? As their shepherds, as successors of the Holy Apostles, they look to Your Excellencies for an answer.

As your humble servants, we wish to submit here to you the evidence in favor of the affirmation that Medjugorje is indeed an authentic apparition of the Blessed Virgin.

As Your Excellencies no doubt remember, two of the greatest apparitions of the Blessed Mother in history, Guadalupe and Fatima, had a profound impact not just on the Church but on human history. From Guadalupe came a birth of the Catholic Faith in the New World and the conversion of millions. From Fatima came prophecies of world wars and of the spread of militant atheism along with the conversion of multitudes and a battle plan laid out by Our Lady for the Church's final victory through the triumph of her Immaculate Heart.

We believe that Medjugorje is a Marian apparition on the same scale as Guadalupe and Fatima. As even non-believers acknowledge, Medjugorje has produced mass conversions and a remarkable renewal of the sacraments in the life of the faithful. Just as Fatima came as a harbinger of the rise of Communism, Medjugorje came as the harbinger of its fall. In effect, Medjugorje has been called the fulfillment of Fatima and the Fatima peace plan in action. Medjugorje might also be called a Second Vatican Council apparition — so perfectly does its message reflect and amplify the teachings of this Council.

It is well known that the authenticity of Medjugorje is still being investigated by the Catholic Church through various bodies vested with the authority to make judgments on the matter. Caution on matters of such great moment is understandable and advisable. In this process of investigation and judgment,the *sensus fidelium,* the testimony of the belief and devotion of the faithful, is part of the data that merits consideration and requires explanation. All the great apparitions in history were recognized and approved by the Church only after the faithful took up the cause and persevered in presenting their case to the authorities. As with everything else pertaining to Church discipline, the faithful have an absolute obligation to submit to the verdict of the Church when this verdict has finally been reached. Until that time, however, the faithful have a duty to present their case to the Church — a duty that springs from their conviction that God continues to reveal His salvific scheme in history through various means including apparitions of the Blessed Virgin Mary.

When a particular phenomenon impresses itself on the consciousness of the faithful as an authentic apparition of the Blessed Virgin, the faithful must present their testimony to the Church with serene submission to the Church's ruling. Just as important as submission to the Church is the duty of presenting the evidence to proper authorities. This is how Fatima and Lourdes were approved by the Church. If not for the fervor and perseverance of the faithful, these apparitions would never have been investigated by the Church. The Church cannot possibly investigate every claim to an apparition. Only those claims that evoke enduring devotion in a growing body of believers can be considered worthy of investigation by the Church. Such is the case, we contend, with Medjugorje. The sheer number of reported miracles and conversions and the power and the glory that have drawn multitudes to the confessional and the Eucharist can only be compared to Lourdes, Fatima and Guadalupe.

The *sensus fidelium* has been a significant litmus test in the development even of fundamental doctrines of the Church. The Second Vatican Council recognizes and applauds the *sensus fidelium*. Inspired by the commendations of the Council and the precedents in the history of the apparitions, we present here to you the *sensus fidelium* as it applies to Medjugorje and to the faithful who have experienced there the love and presence of the Mother of God.

We note here that the verdict of the Church on Medjugorje may be delayed because a judgment is generally issued only after the phenomenon under review has ceased. This is the case partially because all the data required for such a judgment will be available only when the apparitions have ceased. The Medjugorje apparitions, of course, are still in progress, but it is still possible that the Church could choose to make a judgment even before the apparitions are over. We have, for instance, the example of Our Lady's apparitions in Betania, Venezuala which began on March 25, 1976, and were given official Church approval on November 21, 1987, although they had not yet ceased. While formal Church approval can only be given after an official pronouncement on the apparition as "worthy of belief," historically the faithful have not withheld assent to the authenticity of a given apparition when they had reasonable grounds for accepting it as authentic. Neither Lourdes nor Fatima would have been officially approved if the faithful had withheld assent to the authenticity of those apparitions before they were approved. The Church launched an investigation of the apparitions, on the basis of which they were approved, only because of the fervent and persistent conviction of the faithful. Both St. Catherine Labouré and Don Bosco gave their hearty assent to the apparition at Lourdes before it was officially recognized. In fact, the final verdict on Lourdes cited "the throng of people" it had attracted as one of the criteria in favor of its authenticity. Fatima, it must be remembered, was approved by the Church only after thirteen years of investigation.

We, who are sincerely trying to respond to Our Lady's call, are deeply encouraged by the recent consecration of Croatia to the Queen of Peace by His Eminence Cardinal Franjo Kuharic, the Primate of Croatia and the head of the Yugoslavian Bishops' Conference (the body responsible for investigating Medjugorje). The Queen of Peace is the title by which the Blessed Virgin is reported to have revealed herself in the Medjugorje apparitions. It is significant, then, that the Primate of Croatia has chosen to consecrate his country to the Blessed Virgin under this title. If it is indeed Mary who is appearing at Medjugorje, then it is fitting that she be welcomed by the shepherds of the Church of which she is the Mother.

We realize that our solemn conviction that the Mother of God is appearing in Medjugorje to the six young visionaries is a belief that belongs (and will always belong) to the arena of private revelation. A belief in a private revelation — and this includes Fatima and Lourdes — will never carry the certainty and the authority of the public revelation preserved by the Church: the Gospel and the dogmas of faith. Furthermore, this belief in a private revelation is held in a spirit of total obedience to the Church with all associated activity being governed by the discipline of the Church.

By their very nature, claims of supernatural intervention and activity in human history lie beyond the purview of the scientific method. The very birth of the Christian Gospel is rooted in claims of supernatural intervention in history: the life of Our Lord with all its miracles and His miraculous resurrection from the dead. Science cannot verify or falsify these claims, but we can legitimately conclude that the testimony provided by the first witnesses to these events provide a reasonable basis for faith. Reliable testimony is the critical factor. While affirming that the public revelation — the Gospel — cannot be compared to any private revelation, we note that "reliable testimony" is also the criterion by which a private revelation is accepted as authentic by the Church. In addition, the content of the private revelation must conform to the public revelation if it is to be judged "worthy of belief." We believe in Medjugorje, as we do in Lourdes, Fatima and Guadalupe, because we believe that it conforms to these two criteria.

It has been said that the truths that God wishes approved by the Church will be approved regardless of the human response. This is most definitely the case. It is equally true, however, that the abuse of human free will can cause delays and unnecessary obstacles in the process of defining a doctrine or approving an apparition. To take but one example, we point to the doctrine of the Assumption of the Blessed Virgin. The doctrine of the Assumption was widely accepted by the faithful in the early Church. Unfortunately, in the ninth century, the Abbot of Corbie, Paschase Radbert, published a letter that was spuriously attributed to St. Jerome and that seemed to doubt the doctrine. During this period, another monk, Usuard, published a martyrology that relegated the doctrine to the realm of superstition. Both publications threw a cloud over the doctrine. The falsity of the publications was established only after seven centuries during which time they continued to do damage. By the immeasurable grace of God, the doctrine was finally defined as a dogma of the Church in this century. Misrepresentations and other abuses of human free will similarly delayed official approval of most of the major apparitions of the Blessed Virgin.

It is with great sorrow that we point, in this context, to the campaign of disinformation and slander that has been launched against Medjugorje by its enemies. This campaign has thrown a cloud over Medjugorje in the same way that false accusations have obscured the truth in the past. Since we believe that the Blessed Virgin is appearing in Medjugorje, we consider it our responsibility to refute the charges and allegations hurled at Medjugorje. Our objective in this volume is to answer every one of the major criticisms directed at Medjugorje. It is our contention that these criticisms are demonstrably false and that they are the result either of misunderstanding or of malice. This is all that we the faithful can do. It is our humble request to Your Excellencies that you study our case. If you find this case to be compelling, we implore you to add your voice to the defense of Medjugorje to ensure the swift triumph of the truth. If the Mother of God is appearing at Medjugorje, then her ablest champions will be her beloved Shepherds.

Finally, two key issues associated with Medjugorje must be brought to view. The first is the question of the "secrets." As with many of the major apparitions, the visionaries at Medjugorje believe that they will be entrusted with ten secrets that are of great import for the world. Two of the visionaries have received all ten secrets and no longer experience daily apparitions. The four other visionaries have received nine of the secrets and the apparitions will cease for them when they receive the tenth secret. The significance of such secrets can be understood with reference to Fatima. The first secret of Fatima concerned a vision of hell while the second secret predicted the Second World War. The secrets of Medjugorje are believed to be eschatological in nature and will be revealed shortly before the events they predict unfold. Nevertheless, the public messages of Medjugorje are immensely more important than the secrets. The primary purpose of Medjugorje is to lead the faithful to lives of prayer and holiness - and this comes only from living the message of Medjugorje and not from the secrets.

Secondly, we mention the promise of a "great sign." The visionaries report that the Blessed Virgin has promised a "great sign" at the end of the apparition that will convince skeptics and critics. The concept of a "great sign" that remained for future generations is again found in other apparitions: the holy tilma at Guadalupe, the healing spring at Lourdes, the miracle of the sun at

Fatima. We believe that a clear sign comparable to the signs given at other apparitions will be given at Medjugorje. We believe, however, that the Blessed Virgin does not wish us to wait until the "great sign" to affirm her appearance at Medjugorje and to live her message.

In closing, we will quote three public messages of Medjugorje [intended for the world and not just the visionaries] that may explain our sense of urgency:

"Let them [visitors to Medjugorje and those who hear about Medjugorje] believe as if they see; believe firmly." [1981]

[I wish] "people to know what is happening in Medjugorje. Speak about it so that all will be converted. Tell the whole world, tell it without delay, 'Be converted and do not wait.' "

"Dear children! You are responsible for the messages. The source of grace is here, but you, dear children, are the vehicles transmitting the gifts. Therefore, dear children, I am calling you to work responsibly. Everyone will be responsible according to his own measure. Dear children, I am calling you to give the gift to others with love, and not to keep it for yourselves." [May 8, 1986]

On January 25, 1993 Our Lady called us to, *"...Discern the signs of this time. I am with you and I guide you into a new time, a time which God gives you as grace..."*

If the evidence we assemble in this volume seems sufficiently weighty, we humbly request Your Excellencies to submit your testimonies in favor of Medjugorje to the Holy Father, to the Prefect of the Sacred Congregation for the Doctrine of the Faith and to Cardinal Franjo Kuharic, President of the Yugoslavian Bishops' Conference.

Respectfully submitted,

I PROLOG

1. INTRODUCTION

Mysterium tremendum et fascinans: the Mystery tremendous and fascinating. Throughout the centuries, across continents and cultures and entire civilizations, the sense of a transcendent order of being underlying the here-and-now has pervaded the collective consciousness of the human race.

But that was yesterday. With the advent of the modern metropolis and the possibility of pandering to every mode of sensory stimulation, we were anaesthetized and locked up in the padded cells of our own minds. Though some of us were lobotomized, most of us just suffered from amnesia. But the sense of a great Mystery unfolding both behind the scenes and on the stage of human history simply receded from the modern mind.

"The sacred," said Harvard sociologist Daniel Bell, "is the space of wonder and awe, of the noumenal which remains a mystery and the numinous which is its aura. Until contemporary times this principle has been observed by almost every human group we know. Ours is the first to annul the boundaries which maintained the preciousness of the principle of life itself." [*Bulletin of the American Academy of Arts and Sciences*, March 1978.] In the Scriptures we were told, "Now we see, as in a glass, darkly." With the onset of the modern era, we learnt that there was only darkness and that we could never see.

And then came Medjugorje. Like a meteor hurtling out of Heaven, like dawn breaking through the darkness, she came, the Lady in white. "I have come to show the world that God exists. I have come to convert and reconcile all people ... Tell the whole world, tell it without delay. Be converted and do not wait!" The Lady in white appeared to six peasant children in Medjugorje, Yugoslavia, in June of 1981, and identified herself as the Blessed Virgin Mary, venerated as the Mother of God not just by Catholic and Eastern Orthodox Christians but by Luther, Calvin and Zwingli. She was to come again and again, day after day, year after year with a message of peace and reconciliation and of the infinite unconditional love of God.

Thus began the phenomenon that drew millions of people of every race and religion to a remote village in a country which was, for a generation, the meeting point of East and West. This was not a passing fad for with each passing month the pilgrims multiplied; 20 million pilgrims had travelled to Medjugorje by the time that war broke out in Bosnia-Herzegovina. Least of all was Medjugorje a creation of the media. On the contrary, the purveyors of prime time entertain-

1

ment with their constant craving for novelty and sensation were bewildered by the inner dynamic of a phenomenon that would not submit to their fickle formulae. Before their pens and cameras, in this little hamlet, millions of men and women continued to testify to the reality of the Transcendent in their lives, in the world and in history. And once again, the **Mysterium tremendum et fascinans** was manifested on the horizon of human history.

"No one believes in such things in this day and age," we were told from the beginning of this century. And that was that. But no "day and age" can lock out the Ground of Being or lock in our ineluctable yearning for the Plenitude of Perfection. In one respect, it was a shock to the modern psyche. In another respect, it was a shock that shook us out of our slumber and brought us face to face with ourselves and with the infinite Lover who brought us into being.

(i) How It All Began

By now, the broad outlines of the mysterious happenings at Medjugorje are familiar to the public at large. The sequence of events that culminated in the Medjugorje phenomenon have been lucidly recreated by Wayne Weible, in his **Medjugorje: The Message.**

Ivanka Ivankovic, 15, and her friend, Mirjana Dragicevic, 16, having finished their field chores had gone for a walk on the dirt road that wound from their hamlet of Bijakovici, along the base of the hill known as Podbrdo. On their way home, Ivanka happened to glance up and was startled to see the shimmering figure of a woman up on the hill, bathed in a brilliant light. 'Mirjana, look, it's Gospa!' (Our Lady) she exclaimed without really thinking about what she was saying. 'Come on,' replied her friend with a wave of disgust, not even bothering to look, 'Why would Gospa appear to us?' and she continued down the road towards her home. But Ivanka in a high state of excitement pleaded with her to believe that she really had seen something. When they came near the home of Milka Pavlovic, 13, she was just coming out to bring in the family sheep. Ivanka begged the two of them to return with her to see if the figure was still there; and when they reached the place where Ivanka had seen her, now Mirjana and Milka also saw her.

They were soon joined by Vicka Ivankovic, 17, a close companion of the two who had gone looking for them. Seeing them waving excitedly to her from the road, she hurried to join them. When they told her they were seeing the Madonna, she was too scared to look and ran away, wondering how her friends could tease about something so sacred.

But driven by curiosity she returned a short while later with two boys who had been picking apples along the roadside, Ivan Dragicevic, 16, and Ivan Ivankovic, 20. (None of the youths involved were closely related; many of the villagers had the same last names.) The younger Ivan ran away, but the other stayed and also saw what he would later describe as 'something completely white, turning.'

Vicka, having clearly seen the apparition upon returning, was more explicit. She described the figure as wearing a silver-grey gown, having dark hair and a pale white complexion. She stated that the figure, who appeared to be holding a baby in her arms, beckoned for them to come up the hill, closer; but they were too frightened to move. (With the exception of Christmas, this would be the only time that the apparition would appear with her Son.)

Some of the youths began to cry; others prayed. They stayed until dusk and a light mist began to fall. Returning to their homes, they told their families what had happened — and were scolded and teased, the parents fearful that the neighbors would call them liars. Vicka's sister playfully teased her saying, 'Maybe they saw a flying saucer!'

The next day, after completing their work in the fields, they felt an inner urge to return to the hillside, although not all of them were able to do so. Milka's mother, not really believing her daughter, had taken her to a distatnt field to work that day; and when she, too, felt the urge to return, it was too far. When the others stopped by Milka's house to get her, they were told by her older sister, Marija, 17, that she wasn't home. So they asked Marija to come with them. Jakov Colo, only 10 years of age and a cousin of Milka and Marija, was also at the house; at the urging of Marija, he decided to go with them.

Ivan Ivankovik who was several years older than the others decided that going to see 'visions' was for children, and he declined to return. (A few days later he would become a staunch believer and regret not having returned; shortly thereafter, he would be arrested and jailed for two months for going up on the hill against a police order forbidding the young visionaries and their followers to do so.) The other Ivan did go, possibly embarrassed at having run away the day before. A number of villagers followed at a distance, curious to see if the 'rumor' of the Madonna's appearance was true.

Shortly after 6:00 p.m. the figure appeared again, gesturing to them to come to her. This time they did. In fact, they ran up the hill at an astonishing rate of speed; and when they reached the figure, they fell to their knees. Some of the onlookers tried to follow but could not keep up. They reported that the six young people seemed to be looking up at something slightly above them and a few feet away. The youths began praying the Lord's Prayer, because, as Vicka would later explain, 'We didn't know what else to do.' This second-day visit lasted approximately fifteen minutes, during which the figure identified herself as 'The Blessed Virgin Mary.'

Again there was some teasing when they returned to their homes; but with the witness of other villagers, it was mild. They knew these children were not given to fanciful exaggeration or playing pranks, and they definitely would not lie about something so sacred to them. If they said they'd seen something, then they had seen it — even if no one else could.

Word traveled fast among the five hamlets that made up the parish of Medjugorje — especially word of the most extraordinary occurrence in common memory. The following afternoon several thousand people gathered on the hill with the children. They seemed to have come from everywhere — some from as far away as the town of Ljubuske and even from the city of Mostar, more than a half-hour's drive away.

On this third day a glowing light appeared on the hillside, and it guided the six seers to the site of their next encounter with the Gospa. Others could see the light but could not see what was inside of it. Milka was also present, her mother realizing after Marija's experience the second day that her younger daughter had actually been telling the truth. She allowed Milka to go, at Marija's insistence that she, too, would see. But sadly, she did not see the Gospa — that day or since.

This time the six, having gained courage from the previous day's experience, asked the figure several questions: why had she come to their village? And why to them? And what did she want of the people?

'I have come here, because there are many devout believers here,' was her response. 'I have come to tell you that God exists, and He loves you. Let the others who do not see me, believe as you do.'

Jakov reported it a little differently. According to him, her reason for coming was that all might be at peace and be reconciled one to another. (I found it more credible that the six young visionaries did not repeat verbatim the same story; in fact given the natural independence of young people that age, I would have found it suspicious if all their reports were word-for-word identical.)

By the fourth day, the government authorities at their regional headquarters in nearby Citluk had become alarmed; the situation was getting out of control. They summoned the six young people to the police station where they were intensively interrogated and examined by a doctor — who pronounced them perfectly normal, healthy teenagers." [Wayne Weible, *Medjugorje: The Message* (Orleans, Massachusetts: Paraclete Press, 1989), 9-13]

The six visionaries are in many ways representative of the various flavors of human nature. Vicka, always bursting with joy, is a "Martha" at the service of pilgrims and those who need her. Even at the height of the war in Bosnia, she ministered to the needs of the suffering. Marija is a contemplative spirit who exudes an aura of quiet and profound spirituality. Ivan is shy and melancholic; Jakov, restless and mischievous. Mirjana is considered the most mature and intelligent of the visionaries and is the only one who has attended a university. Ivanka is a balanced, down to earth girl, the first to marry; her days are now filled with the responsibilities of motherhood. It was this many-splendored mosaic of human nature that was granted a glimpse into the beyond.

(ii) The Meaning of Medjugorje

Their glimpse was not to be a private experience. In different degrees and different ways, millions of people became participants in the ethereal adventure of the visionaries. Medjugorje seemed to rip away the shroud that the modern world had wrapped around itself. In an instant, we were wrenched from our TV sets and our concrete cornucopias and shown the Real World — a world in which Good and Evil were locked in mortal combat with no one neutral, a world in which history is a supernatural drama of choices that bless or condemn, a world in which we live on the very brink of eternity.

At one level, the Mystery of Medjugorje is simply another reminder of the Mystery manifested most fully on Calvary. At another level, Medjugorje addresses the spiritual blindness and the suffocating suppression of the spiritual impulse that is uniquely characteristic of the modern age. To a world spinning out of control, Medjugorje emerged not just as a light in the spiritual darkness but as an echo of the Love that incarnated Itself in Galilee and that alone can quench the thirst of our souls.

As at Galilee and at almost every other manifestation of the supernatural in history, the Mystery of Medjugorje unfolded in the everyday, in a poor and lowly setting. There are signs and wonders in the Gospels but no pomp or material grandeur. So it was to be in Medjugorje. To appreciate the Eternal one must first lose one's fascination with the ephemeral.

As at Galilee, too, the manifestation of the supernatural in Medjugorje was greeted with hostility by the paradigmatic Pharisees and Sadducees. Arrayed against Medjugorje, on the one side, were the ultra-Traditionalists who cannot believe in the God Who loves all men and women of every religion [a message proclaimed not only at Medjugorje but also at the Second Vatican Council] and Who can reveal His will through peasants. On the other side were the Modernists, Liberals and unbelievers who cannot believe in the God Who demands total fidelity to the absolutes of faith and morals [a message again that comes from both Medjugorje and Vatican II]. In the middle, free of arrogant preconceptions, were the common people who responded joyfully with their hearts to a phenomenon that was as obviously authentic as it was astounding.

Responding to Medjugorje on its own terms means viewing it in the light of time and of eternity. On the plane of time, we are startled by its striking significance in salvation history.

- Ever since the supreme revelation of God in the Incarnation, history has reverberated with echoes of the salvific drama going on behind the scenes. The most powerful and effective such "reminders" of the Good News have been apparitions of the Blessed Virgin Mary that have taken place in various places at various times. The three best known apparitions of Mary were at Guadalupe, Lourdes and Fatima. Each one of these three focused ultimately on the Divine plan of salvation and led to the conversions of millions. Medjugorje's relation to these three apparitions is well described by John DeMers: Medjugorje is "a maturing and perhaps even the fulfillment of the unconditional love at Guadalupe, the reminder of our need for penance at Lourdes and the urgent plea for change at Fatima. All these elements can be found in the nine years of messages given to six young people in the tiny Yugoslav village of Medjugorje." [*Mary's People*, 1990]. Medjugorje too has led to the conversion of millions of people.

- Medjugorje stands in particularly close relation to Fatima and has been widely described as the fulfillment of Fatima. In Fatima we were given a prophecy concerning the rise and eventual fall of Communism — a prophecy which reached its fulfillment during the Medjugorje apparitions. At Fatima, the Blessed Mother said, "In the end, my Immaculate Heart will triumph. The Holy Father will consecrate Russia to me, and it will be converted and a certain period of grace will be granted to the world."[4] Early on, at Medjugorje, she said, "Russia is the people where God will be most glorified." As we will see, Pope John Paul II has not been oblivious to the Fatima-Medjugorje connection and attributes the fall of Communism to "the works of the Blessed Virgin, according to her affirmations at Fatima and Medjugorje." In her message of August 25, 1991, the Blessed Mother said, "I invite you to renunciation for nine days so that with your help, everything I wanted to realize through the secrets I began in Fatima may be fulfilled." The connections between Fatima and Medjugorje are explored further in "Medjugorje, the Fulfillment of Fatima."

• Just as Medjugorje "makes sense" in the light of Fatima, Medjugorje is also a supernatural testimony to the truth of the Second Vatican Council. As noted later in this book, Marian apparitions do not preempt the teachings of the Church. Only after the Church has defined a doctrine or clarified its teachings on an issue will the Mother of the Church speak about it in an apparition. This was the case at Lourdes where Mary introduced herself as the Immaculate Conception shortly after the doctrine of the Immaculate Conception had been defined. Thematically, Medjugorje is pre-eminently a Vatican II apparition. The Second Vatican Council did not change any of the fundamental teachings of the Church. But the Council did help us make "progress" in deepening our understanding of certain truths, in enabling us to grasp the previously obscured implications of certain other truths, in helping us see some truths in a new light, and in changing some of our attitudes of mind. For instance, the Council offered dramatic new perspectives on the role of the laity and the nature of marital love. As for "attitudes of mind," we have been told by the Council that sin must be seen not just in terms of losing Heaven and suffering the pains of Hell but also in terms of negating our love for the Blessed Lord and causing Him added suffering. The Second Vatican Council

---

[4] And from Medjugorje on September 25, 1991 she called to us, "Help my Immaculate Heart to triumph...I beseech all of you to offer prayers and sacrifices for my intentions so I can present them to God for what is most necessary...Thank you for having responded to my call."

reiterated all the great Marian doctrines while presenting them to us in a Christocentric/Theocentric context. Likewise Mary presents herself to us at Medjugorje in Christocentric and Theocentric terms while emphasizing her role as Mediatrix. The Second Vatican Council also gave us a new perspective on the various world religions. The Council saw all things, including the religions of the world, in the light of God's infinite love for humanity. In His infinite love, God seeks "the salvation of all men." Ultimately, our salvation depends on whether we say Yes or No to God — and He will do everything to get us to say Yes. The world religions are manifestations of humanity's search for God, manifestations that are often marred by the evil that is in the world and in man. The Council acknowledged that there is much that is good and true in the various religions and also that many adherents of these religions sincerely seek God. Our infinite Lover does not refuse those who seek Him sincerely. The Catholic Church is God's chosen vessel of salvation, but those who are "invincibly ignorant" of the Church's role in God's salvific scheme can nevertheless be "baptized" by their "desire" for God and thus be saved. Like the Second Vatican Council and Pope John Paul II, Mary at Medjugorje reaches out to people of all religions with a message of God's unconditional love for them and of her own maternal love. Just as the Jews could not comprehend the love of God shown in Jesus Christ because they had certain preconceptions of God and the Messiah He would send, there are some Catholics who reject both Vatican II and Medjugorje because the Council's vision of God's love for all of humanity does not fit in with their preconceptions. While calling all men and women to her Son, however, Our Lady warns us at Medjugorje that "this world of our sorrows is without hope for those who do not know Jesus." [November, 25, 1991.]

- The most obvious connection between Medjugorje and current events can be located in the Blessed Mother's consistent call for peace. Right at the start she said, "Peace, Peace, Peace! Be reconciled! Only Peace. Make your peace with God and among yourselves." [26/6/81]. Describing herself as the Queen of Peace, she continued to beg for inter-ethnic and inter-religious harmony. The recurrent theme of peace was dismissed as banal by critics and even those responding to her call from Medjugorje did not take it very seriously. The horror of subsequent events in the former Yugoslavia is a terrifying and tragic testimony to the relevance of Medjugorje for the here-and-now. A poignant commentary on this theme comes from Fr. Jozo Zovko who was Medjugorje's pastor when the apparitions first began. "From the beginning of Medjugorje, the Blessed Mother has been speaking about the war; but we failed to understand. And from the very beginning, she has taught us precisely how to overcome this situation, indeed how to stop the war: With the power of prayer, with fasting." [*Mary's People*, October 25, 1992]. On June 25, 1992, he said, "Today, on this 11th anniversary, we have to remember these words: 'Protect Medjugorje, protect the grace which God through His mother sent here and gave to His Church.' Brothers and sisters, it would be a great tragedy if we did not live the message. When the Pope says,[5] 'Protect Medjugorje,' he mentions the messages first of all. Do we pray the rosary every day in our families? Do we live the message of prayer? Our Lady has been teaching us for 11 years: 'Pray, and through prayer you will achieve everything.' As much as we pray, that much we will win. We will enjoy as much freedom as we win with our weapons — prayer, fasting, Scripture, conversion, Mass, Confession. These are the steps along the way called Peace." [*Mary's People*, August 30, 1992].

• The climactic connection between Medjugorje and the temporal process is, of course, to be found in the Secrets [the notion of "secrets" is pre-figured in St. Paul's epistle to the Ephesians where he speaks of "God's secret plan" hidden in the past and unveiled only to those who have been selected to reveal it to the world]. As at some of her other apparitions, the Blessed Mother has promised to entrust the visionaries with a number of "secrets" that concern crucial forthcoming events in history — catastrophes and chastisements, in particular, that are caused by humanity's violation of fundamental laws of the spiritual world. These catastrophes are not to be thought of as "punishments": they should be understood in terms of cause and effect. If you jump off a skyscraper, the law of gravity will bring you crashing

---

[5] During his homily Fr. Jozo shared that when they had spoken together in Rome on June 17th, eight days earlier, the Holy Father had asked him to convey this message to the people of Medjugorje. We will present more of Fr. Jozo's homily later.

down. So it is in the spiritual world where the books have to be balanced sooner or later. The six visionaries have been told that they will receive ten secrets and that the apparitions will cease once all ten have been communicated. Two of the six have received all ten secrets, and the apparitions have stopped for them. The other four have received nine of the secrets, and the apparitions will stop for them too when they receive the tenth secret. The secrets will be unveiled to the world three days before the prophesied events begin. At Fatima, the first two Secrets concerned a vision of hell and the outbreak of the Second World War (the Third Secret has still not been revealed). Presumably, the Medjugorje Secrets have a similarly dramatic bearing on human history. Nonetheless, the public messages of Medjugorje are of greater importance than the Secrets, as pointed out by Fr. Slavko Barbaric, spiritual director of the visionaries. "If you knew something more about the secrets, would it make it easier to say 15 decades of the Rosary each day? I think not. Would it make it easier to fast two days a week? No. Well, these things — prayer, fasting, making peace, going to confession — this is the real message, the heart of Medjugorje." [*Mary's People*, October 25, 1992].

In the context of this last theme, we would do well to remember that Medjugorje cannot and should not be confused with several alleged apparitions that concern themselves simply with apocalyptic themes. John DeMers makes the appropriate distinctions: "Generally, critics who dismiss Medjugorje's messages as 'hysterical' are grouping them with the fruit of other alleged apparitions, locutions and private revelations around the world. There are reported supernatural exchanges that wallow in the apocalyptic, complete with Virgin weeping nonstop for a Church gone awry, a world irrevocably enamored of sin and a human race doomed to bloodshed. Articles disdainful of Medjugorje tend to quote its messages interchangeably with those of people like Sister Mary Elena Aiello ['All the world will soon be at war, and the streets will be stained with blood']...and Little Pebble of Australia ['The final act of World War III, with the atomic bombs and the missiles, will be followed by the ball of redemption which comprises the three days of darkness'].

"Interchanged, yes; interchangeable, no. Without drawing any final conclusions about these other reported visitations, we simply must realize their messages are not Medjugorje's. At no point in all these years of daily conversation has the Gospa reached such heights of frenzy or resignation. She has invited, encouraged, corrected and occasionally worried aloud — but she has never, for so much as a moment, written off humanity as a lost cause. She has never let the difficulties and temptations of our fragile existence overshadow the immeasurable light we carry within, our gift from her Creator and our own." [*Invited to Light*, New Orleans, LA, 1990, Trinakria Press, pp. 42-3]

Perhaps the most riveting proof of Medjugorje's authenticity is its focus on the Eternal and on the importance of seeing all the things of time in the light of eternity. Life on earth is a brief flight from womb to tomb, but it is our life here and now that determines the kind of life we will enjoy in the hereafter. Medjugorje is just as much at home with eternity as it is with time.

- About her reason for appearing in Medjugorje, the Blessed Mother said: "I am your Mother and therefore I want to lead all of you to perfect holiness. I want every one of you to be happy here on earth and every one of you to be with me in Heaven. This is, dear children, the reason of my coming here and my desire." [May 25, 1987]. Clearly, as we would expect, the Blessed Mother views our lives here in the perspective of our eternal destiny. Like the Incarnation and all the previous apparitions of Mary, the primary aim of Medjugorje is the salvation of souls. The path to Heaven is holiness and a passionate love of God: everything in Medjugorje is focused on putting us on this path.

- The sense of an eternal destiny and of a state of being outside space and time has never been as absent as it is in this modern age.[6] Perhaps to re-awaken our awareness of the "worlds" beyond death, Our Lady "took" the visionaries to Heaven, Hell and Purgatory. Such encounters with the dimensions beyond death have been experienced in previous ages by a number of reliable, rational individuals. In this century, the children at Fatima were given a glimpse of Hell. At Medjugorje, the children actually "went" there — and to Heaven and Purgatory. Obviously, the realities witnessed by the visionaries were presented in such a manner as to "make sense" to their mental topography: the literal descriptions are less important than the testimony that our choices in this life have eternal consequences. Medjugorje tells us all to live with the consciousness that we live on the brink of eternity: an eternity that was briefly unveiled by Our Lady. Whether or not the

---

[6] The Holy Father's words of August 1, 1989 (referred to later) come to mind: "Yes, today the world has lost the supernatural. Many people sought it and found it in Medjugorje."

Medjugorje secrets speak of the "end times" is less relevant than the fact that the public messages of Medjugorje speak of our own "end times". Every human being must die and death is truly the "end time" as far as he or she is concerned: Medjugorje tells us all to be prepared for this end time: only we can choose our own eternities. "The body, drawn from this earth," says Our Lady, "decomposes after death. It never comes back to life again. Man receives a transfigured body. Whoever has done very much evil during his life can go straight to Heaven if he confesses, is sorry for what he has done, and receives Communion at the end of his life." [July 24, 1982].

- While speaking of life in this world as a preparation for the life eternal, Our Lady also brings to our attention the existence and activity of pure spirits who play at least some part in the drama of salvation. Frequently she warns us about the Evil One and his ceaseless efforts to lead us away from God. "I call on everyone of you to consciously decide yourselves for God and against Satan. Dear children, you are ready to commit sins and to put yourselves in the hands of Satan without reflecting." [May 25, 1987]. Fr. Gabriele Amorth, the Chief Exorcist in the Rome Vicariate, writes "Generally it is the casting out of devils that is given first place among the Messianic signs when they are referred to in the Gospel. At Medjugorje, too, among the other extraordinary favours granted by the Virgin, there are already many reported cases of people freed from demonic possession." [*Medjugorje Messenger*, July/September 1989].

The meaning of Medjugorje, ultimately, lies in its meaning for every human being who has the opportunity to encounter it. Medjugorje is nothing less than the infinite love of God seeking the hearts of every one of us.

(iii) Medjugorje's Message for You

What is most breathtaking about Medjugorje is the picture of God we are given by Our Lady. At Medjugorje she confirms what we have always known in our hearts: God is our infinite Lover Who has loved us into being and Who woos us throughout our lives seeking only our love. All our fulfillment comes from loving Him. In her message of March 25, 1988, Our Blessed Mother tells us: "Dear children! Today also I am calling you to a complete surrender to God.

You, dear children, are not conscious of how God loves you with such a great love. Because of it He permits me to be with you so I can instruct you and help you to find the way of peace. That way, however, you cannot discover if you do not pray. Therefore, dear children, forsake everything and consecrate your time to God and then God will bestow gifts upon you and bless you. Little children, do not forget that your life is fleeting like the spring flower which today is wondrously beautiful, but tomorrow has vanished. Therefore, pray in such a way that your prayer, your surrender to God may become like a road sign. That way your witness will not only have value for yourselves, but for all of eternity. Thank you for having responded to my call."

About her own relationship to us, she says in her message of February 25, 1988: "You know that I love you and am coming here out of love, so I could show you the path of peace and salvation of your souls. I want you to obey me and not permit Satan to seduce you. Dear children, Satan is very strong; and, therefore, I ask you to dedicate your prayers to me so that those who are under his influence may be saved." On May 24, 1984, she says, "In any moment when it is difficult for you, don't be afraid. I love you even when you are far away from me and my Son." Again, "Give me all your feelings and all your problems. I want to console you in all your temptations. My wish is to fill you completely with God's peace, joy and love." [June 6, 1985]. And finally, "You don't know, dear children, how great is my love, and you don't know how to accept it. In many ways I wish to express it; but you, dear children, do not recognize it. You don't comprehend my words by your heart and so you are not able to comprehend my love." [May 22, 1986]. "Therefore, today I beg you to start with the burning love with which I love you." [May 29, 1986]

Medjugorje, then, is a message of love — of the infinite love of our Father in Heaven and of the tender maternal love of our Blessed Mother. It is this theme of love — heartbreaking, overwhelming, all-encompassing love — that draws the human heart to Medjugorje. Medjugorje is a love letter from God delivered by the Mother of us all — she who Scripture tells us is the Mother of God the Son, Daughter of God the Father and Spouse of God the Holy Spirit. Mother, Daughter, Spouse — through the intimacy of her union with the infinite-eternal Act of Love that is the Holy Trinity, Mary, a creature like us, shows all human beings how to be drawn into the Divine. At Medjugorje she invites us to sing the Magnificat to the Father, to kneel at the foot of the Cross before the Son, and to pray with her as at Pentecost for the Holy Spirit.

If we have learnt anything from Christianity, it is the fundamental truth that love in this world is accompanied by suffering. "God so loved the world" that His Son suffered and died at our hands, the same Son Who told us "Greater love hath no man than this, that a man lay down his life for his friends." "The Lamb slain from the foundation of the world," "the Lamb of God Which taketh away the sin of the world" continues to suffer in his Mystical Body ("Saul, Saul, why do you persecute Me?") At Medjugorje, the Blessed Mother tells us, "Consider how the Almighty is still suffering today on account of your sins." [March 29, 1984] and "Make reparation for the wound inflicted on the Heart of my Son. That Heart is offended by all kinds of sins." [April 5, 1984]. She herself weeps all the time for the souls lost in sin "Please, do not let my heart weep with tears of blood because of the souls who are lost in sin," [May 24, 1984] she pleads with us. The visionaries report that "Our Lady cries for people all over the world because they have not given their hearts to God and for this reason mankind is destroying itself." [Jakov, June 24, 1991].

Lost in sin and suffering, our souls crave for love — the kind of unconditional, unlimited love only God can give. Even one of the greatest crusaders against Christianity in this century, Bertrand Russell once said, "Nothing can penetrate the loneliness of the human heart except the highest intensity of the sort of love the religious teachers have preached. Whatever does not spring from this motive is harmful and at best useless." *[The Autobiography of Bertrand Russell* I]. It is to our scarred and lonely souls that Our Lady comes with her "burning love" taking us to our infinite Lover.

Medjugorje is not for the self-sufficient and the smug. Medjugorje is for people who are hurting, for people in despair, for the afflicted, for the lonely, for the helpless. We can truly understand Medjugorje only after God brings us to our knees and breaks open our hardened hearts. We can hear Our Lady's messages only if we listen with humility and compassion.

"I invite you to the greatest sacrifice," says Our Lady, "the sacrifice of love. Without love you are not able to accept either me or my Son. Without love, you cannot give an account of your experiences to others. Therefore, dear children, I call you to begin to live love within yourselves." [March 27, 1986]. The love we are called to is Divine not human love. "Dear children, God does not want you lukewarm and indecisive, but totally committed to Him. You know that I love you and that I am burning out of love for you. Therefore, dear children, commit yourself to love so that you will comprehend and burn with God's love from day to day. Decide for love, dear children, so that love may prevail in all of you, not human love, but God's love." [November 20, 1986]

From these considerations of Medjugorje as an outburst of Divine Love, we turn now to the concrete messages we receive there from Our Lady.

At Medjugorje, the Blessed Mother is offering us a program, a plan of action, which is nothing less than a formula for spiritual survival in the modern world and, in the final analysis, a path to holiness and to Heaven. Truly, this is a time of great grace when the Mother of God herself comes to us with a blueprint for our lives which takes us out of ourselves into her maternal heart so that she can present us to her Divine Father, to her Divine Son and to her Divine Spouse.

The Blessed Mother's blueprint for holiness and Heaven is detailed in the section LOVE LETTERS FROM GOD but we summarize below the essential structure of her invitation to us.

- **Start with complete conversion** to Jesus through Mary. "Today again I am calling you to complete conversion, which is difficult for those who have not chosen God. ...Put your life in God's hands." [January 25, 1988] "Today I want to call all of you to decide for Paradise." [October 25, 1987] "I am calling you to a complete surrender to God." [March 25, 1988] "These days I call you especially to open your hearts to the Holy Spirit." [May 23, 1985] "I am calling you today to the prayer of consecration to Jesus, my dear Son, so that each of your hearts may be His. And then I am calling you to Consecration to my Immaculate Heart." [October 25, 1988] "I want each one of you to open your heart to Jesus and I will give Him to you with love." [December 25, 1987] "Today I am calling you to reflect upon why I am with you this long. I am the Mediatrix between you and God." [July 17, 1986] "Today also I call each one of you to decide to surrender again everything completely to me. Only that way will I be able to present each of you to God." [November 25, 1987] Faith is a central element of conversion "Dear Madonna, what wish do you have for us here?" "That you have firm faith and confidence." [1981]

- **From conversion comes peace and reconciliation.** Peace and reconciliation are fundamental to the Medjugorje message. Everyone and everything that hurts or embitters us must be forgiven and forgotten; there are no exceptions. There is no conversion without peace and reconciliation. "Peace, peace, peace! Be reconciled! Only peace. Make your peace with God and among yourselves." [June 26, 1981] "Live peace in your heart and in your surroundings, so that all may recognize the peace, which does not come from you, but from God." [December 25, 1988]

- **Pray from the heart.** "Today I call you to prayer with the heart, and not just from habit." [May 2, 1985] This central theme is discussed in more detail below.

- **Go to confession at least once a month.** "Make your peace with God and among yourselves. For that, it is necessary to believe, to pray and fast, and to go to confession." [June 26, 1981] "One must invite people to go to confession each month, especially the first Saturday. I have invited people to frequent confession. Do what I have told you." [August 6, 1982] "Monthly confession will be a remedy for the Church in the West. Whole sections of the Church could be cured, if the believers would go to confession once a month." [December 1983]

- **Participate in Holy Mass as frequently as possible.** "Let Holy Mass be your life." [April 25, 1988] "Jesus gives His graces in the Mass. Therefore, consciously live the Holy Mass and let your coming to it be a joyful one. Come to it with love and make the Mass your own." [April 3, 1986] "What I want from you is to show me your love by coming to Mass, and the Lord will reward you abundantly." [November 21, 1985] "Unceasingly adore the Most Blessed Sacrament of the Altar. I am always present when the faithful are adoring. Special graces are then being received."

- **Fast on bread and water on Wednesdays and Fridays.** "Fast strictly on Wednesdays and Fridays." [August 14, 1984] "The best fast is on bread and water. Charity cannot replace fasting...everyone except the sick must fast." [June 21, 1982] The link between mortification and sanctification has been stressed by the Church from the earliest days. At Medjugorje, penance and fasting is linked to holiness.

- **Pray fifteen decades of the Rosary every day.** "Every day pray at least one Rosary: the joyful, sorrowful and glorious mysteries." [August 14, 1984] The Rosary is recommended by Our Lady as a powerful weapon against Satan. "Let the Rosary always be in your hands as a sign to Satan that you belong to me." [February 25, 1988]

- **Shun all sin and all occasions of sin.** "Dear children, I beseech you, surrender to the Lord your entire past, all the evil that has accumulated in your hearts. I want each one of you to be happy, but in sin nobody can be happy." [February 25, 1987] "I call each one of you to begin to live as of today that life which God wishes of you and to begin to perform good works of love and mercy. I do not want you, dear children, to live the message and be committing sin which is displeasing to me." [March 25, 1987] "Dear children, you are ready to commit sin, and to put yourselves in the hands of Satan without reflecting. I call on each one of you to consciously decide for God and against Satan" [May 25, 1987]

- **Read Sacred Scripture daily, sanctify the family** and practise daily family prayer. Pray for the souls in Purgatory, keep blessed objects on oneself, make reparation to the Sacred Heart of Jesus. The Blessed Mother also asks for faith in the apparitions at Medjugorje. In one of the first exchanges, the children ask, "Dear Blessed Virgin, why don't you appear in the church so that everybody can see you?" Her reply is "Blessed are those who have not seen and who believe." Again the children ask, "Dear Blessed Virgin, what do you want of these people gathered here?" "That they believe without seeing." Yet again, "Dear Blessed Virgin, what do you want of these people here?" "That those who do not see me believe like the six of you who see me."

- **Read the messages of Medjugorje and live them.** "I want you, dear children, to listen to me and to live my messages." [February 14, 1985] "Do not become arrogant living the messages and saying 'I am living the messages.' If you shall bear and live the messages in your heart, everyone will feel it so that words, which serve those who do not obey, will not be necessary." [September 26, 1985] "Dear children, if you live the messages, you are living the seed of holiness." [October 10, 1985] "Little children, I ask you to accept and live the messages with seriousness...Little children, each day, read the messages which I have given you and transform them into life." [December 25, 1989]

- **Only through love can we discern the signs of this time.** "Dear children! Today I call you to accept and live my messages with seriousness. These days are the days when you need to decide for God, for peace and for the good. May every hatred and jealousy disappear from your life and your thoughts, and may there only dwell love for God and for your neighbor! Only thus shall you discern the signs of this time. I am with you and I guide

you into a new time, a time which God gives you as grace...."
[January 25, 1993]

At first glance, Our Lady's program may seem nothing less than audacious to the global villagers of the twentieth century. But millions of our modern companions have shown that the program "works." "The good fruit of Medjugorje is unparalleled in the history of the Church!"[7] The "fruits" of Medjugorje of which we hear so often are actually a direct consequence of obedience to the messages of Medjugorje. There are some skeptics who acknowledge the undeniable reality of the conversions that took place in Medjugorje and the unprecedented levels of attendance at Mass and Confession while rejecting any connection between these events and the reality of the apparitions. The fruits of Medjugorje cannot be separated from the messages of Medjugorje. Once we understand the radical nature of the Medjugorje blueprint, we will easily recognize that implementation of this blueprint is what gives rise to the "fruits" of Medjugorje. Implementation is possible, of course, only because this is "a time of great grace."

Before closing, we must reflect for a moment on Medjugorje's message on prayer. Medjugorje, in one word, is prayer. Our Lady not only asks us to spend three hours a day in prayer but offers us fundamental insights on prayer so that we can comprehend its importance.

- On numerous occasions, Our Lady asks us to pray with the heart. "I am calling you, dear children, to pray with your hearts." [April 25, 1987] "If you pray from your heart, dear children, the ice cold hearts of your brothers will be melted and every barrier will disappear." [January 23, 1986]

- Prayer is our most direct route to God and to Our Lady. "Today I am calling you to prayer. Without prayer you cannot feel me, nor God, nor the graces I am giving you. Therefore I call you always to begin and end each day with prayer." [July 3, 1986]

- Prayer is joyful and precious. "Dear children, I beg you to open yourselves and begin to pray. Prayer will be joy. If you begin, it will not be boring because you will pray out of pure joy." [March 20, 1986] "You, dear children, do not realize the preciousness of

---

7 Fr. Michael O'Carroll, CSSp, author of five encyclopedias on the spirituality and doctrine of the Church, in a lecture at Notre Dame on March 28, 1991, said: "The good fruit of Medjugorje is unparalleled in the history of the Church!"

prayer. Now is the time of prayer. Now, nothing else is important. Now, nobody is important except God." [October 2, 1986]

- Our prayers play a definite role in Our Lady's participation in God's scheme of salvation. "I need your prayers." [August 30, 1984] "You have helped me along by your prayers to realize my plans. Keep on praying that my plans be fully realized." [September 27, 1984] "Dear children, I cannot help the world without you. I want you to cooperate with me in everything, even in the smallest things by your prayer from your heart and by surrendering to me completely." [August 28, 1986]

- Through prayer we can erase the evil of our past life. "Today also I invite you to prepare your hearts for these days when the Lord is about to purify you in a special way from all the sins of your past life. You, dear children, cannot do it by yourselves, and for that reason I am here to help you. Pray, dear children, only in that way will you be able to recognize all the evil that dwells in you, and abandon it to the Lord so that He may purify your hearts completely." [December 4, 1986]

- Prayer is a source of grace. "You, dear children, do not realize the preciousness of prayer. Now is the time of prayer. Now, nothing else is important. Now, nobody is important except God. Dear children, dedicate yourselves to prayer with special love. Only in that way can God give you graces." [October 2, 1986]

At Medjugorje, God is offering us a path to sanctification and holiness through Our Lady. "Therefore, little children," says Our Lady, "understand the greatness of the gift which God is giving you through me, so that I may protect you with my mantle and lead you to the joy of life." [March 25, 1990] This great gift of Our Lady is ours to accept — or ignore. It is her prayer and ours that you accept her call to conversion and bring her blueprint to bear on your life. Let us end with a reflection on her words on Medjugorje's meaning for us.

Dear children! I want you to comprehend that God has chosen each one of you, in order to use you in his great plan for the salvation of mankind. You are not able to comprehend how great your role is in God's designs. Therefore, dear children, pray so that in prayer you may be able to comprehend what God's plan is in your regard. I am with you in order that you may be able to bring it about in all its fullness. Thank you for having responded to my call. [January 25, 1987]

(iv) About this Book

Rarely, in the course of human history, has it fallen on ordinary men and women to behold the intersection of the supernatural and the natural. But such an intersection is indeed what Medjugorje is all about. **Medjugorje: A Time for Truth and A Time for Action** is a response to this majestic drama, the magnitude of which we can scarcely exaggerate. In this book, on the one hand, we seek to discern and affirm the truth about Medjugorje and, on the other, we endeavor to understand and assimilate the call to action proclaimed there. **A Time for Truth and A Time for Action** is necessarily a sort of anthology. Medjugorje is not merely an object of observation or speculation; it is a living reality that continues to spark powerful reactions from the world and the Church. To understand Medjugorje and to respond to its invitation we must hear first hand from some of the major thinkers and leaders who have been affected by it. In this book, therefore, we include the chronicles and testimonies of Bishops, theologians, spiritual leaders, scientists, journalists and the laity.

Medjugorje's primary importance derives from its role in salvation history. At the vanguard of salvation history is the Church. The Church's response to Medjugorje is clearly a "sign" for believers and an "Open Sesame" to the "Gospa's gold mine of grace." In the PROLOGUE to this book, we survey the different ways in which the highest authorities in the Catholic Church as well as prominent Catholics have welcomed Medjugorje.

The head of the Church, His Holiness Pope John Paul II, has made no secret of his positive appraisal of Medjugorje. So important, in the context of evaluating this phenomenon, are the perceptions and reflections of this most Marian of Popes that the next chapter is a study of his statements on Medjugorje.

To be sure, he will not make any official pronouncement on Medjugorje until the Church-designated machinery has completed its work. This is true even of causes he has personally espoused such as the canonizations of Padre Pio and Sister Faustina where he lets the officials responsible proceed with their investigations at their own pace. All apparitions authenticated by the Church, all canonizations conducted by the Church, all doctrines defined by the Church have had to go through the Church's apparatus of discernment before being given official approval. Of course, the doctrines of the Immaculate Conception and the Assumption were no less true before official definition by the Church than they were after. And Lourdes and Fatima were no less authentic before the Church deemed them worthy of belief than after. Neither these doctrines nor these apparitions would have been approved if the faithful had not pressed the case for them with rigor and vigor. In the case of Medjugorje too, devotees must help Holy Mother Church in its investigation by setting forth the case for approval to the best of their abilities. As is pointed out later in this book, one of the criteria that was deployed in reaching a favorable verdict on Lourdes was "the throng of people" it had affected.

In the same chapter we present also the testimony offered by that other famous Catholic: Mother Teresa of Calcutta. As she has said in numerous interviews and talks and letters, this living saint is deeply grateful to Our Lady of Medjugorje for the conversions she has brought about. Her response to Medjugorje is surely worthy of note for Catholics and non-Catholics. Even before the elaborate investigations of the Church were completed at Lourdes, the living saints of that era, Don Bosco and St. Catherine Labouré, had voiced their assent to the authenticity of the apparition. The same was true at La Salette where the holy Cure' of Ars, St. John Vianney, accepted authenticity while the investigative machinery was still in motion. Without a doubt, each one of these saints would have submitted to the final verdict of the Church even if that verdict contradicted their previous assessments. But it is safe to assume that holy people tend to have a deeper discernment of supernatural realities than specialists in the human sciences.

The third chapter in the **PROLOGUE** is a string of positive statements on Medjugorje from an extraordinary variety of Cardinals and Bishops from around the world. While some of the Bishops pay their personal compliments to the beneficial impact of Medjugorje (an implicit acknowledgement of authenticity because a tree is known by its fruits), others actually step on to the witness stand testifying to the authenticity of Medjugorje in the strongest terms. Particularly noteworthy in the latter category are the powerful testimonies of Cardinal Frantisek Tomasek, a patriarch of the Church in Eastern Europe, and Cardinal-designate Hans Urs Von Balthasar, one of the greatest authorities on mystical phenomena in the 20th century Church. This phenomenon of prominent leaders of the universal Church testifying to authenticity prior to an official verdict is simply unprecedented in the history of apparitions. Obviously such testimonies cannot anticipate the ruling of the Church, but they are clearly relevant data in the process of investigation.

Closely related to this favorable reception from the successors of the Apostles is the recent consecration of Croatia to the Queen of Peace by His Eminence Cardinal Franjo Kuharic, the Primate of Croatia. Cardinal Kuharic is President of the Yugoslavian Bishops' Conference, the body that is currently investigating the Medjugorje apparitions on behalf of the Church. The significance of Cardinal Kuharic's consecration cannot be exaggerated. In her apparitions in Medjugorje, Mary has asked us to designate her as the Queen of Peace.

In a speech preceding the consecration, Cardinal Kuharic calls us to "entrust, devote and consecrate ourselves to her, the QUEEN OF PEACE!" In an interview with *Medjugorje Gebetsaktion* [quoted in *Mary's People*, September 1992], Cardinal Kuharic even goes so far as to advise those who believe in Medjugorje that "People who believe and are convinced in conscience that with these messages they can stimulate people to the good — to conversion, to peace — **they should do it. This is a matter of conscience.**

Not just the hierarchy of the Church but some of the best Catholic theologians of our time have welcomed the Blessed Mother as she visits us in Medjugorje. We reproduce in the next chapter the testimonies of three of these great theologians. The first is the late Fr. Hans Urs Von Balthasar, often referred to as "the Pope's theologian" in the Vatican, who was made a Cardinal by Pope John Paul II shortly before his death. He has been described in Cambridge University as the greatest theologian since St. Thomas Aquinas. About Medjugorje, Von Balthasar said, "Medjugorje's theology rings true. I am convinced of its truth. And everything about Medjugorje is authentic, in a Catholic sense. What's happening there is so evident, so convincing." Also, "I have no doubt about the authenticity of the facts. The whole thing seems so consistent to me: the simplicity of the messages, the obedience to the messages which are in continuity with the messages given by the Blessed Virgin in previous apparitions."

Cardinal-designate Von Balthasar's insights on Medjugorje are followed by expositions from two of the greatest living Mariologists who have both pursued independent intensive investigations into Medjugorje and have both reached the conclusion that this is an authentic apparition. One is Fr. Rene Laurentin of France and the other Fr. Michael O'Carroll of Ireland. Fr. Laurentin is particularly well known for his expertise in the area of apparitions and has been described as the greatest living authority on apparitions in the Catholic Church. He spent over twenty years working on Lourdes, five years on Pontmain and nine years on the Miraculous Medal. He has now spent thousands of hours studying the apparitions at Medjugorje and has made at least twenty-five trips to the village. Fr. O'Carroll is the author of *Theotokos*, an encyclopedia of Mariology, and of four other encyclopedic volumes of theology and spirituality; he is also an authority on the apparition of Knock. He has written two books on Medjugorje, and in his latest *Is Medjugorje Approved?* argues that Medjugorje has been granted the same kind of de facto approval given to Knock.

The assessments of Medjugorje made by some other eminent Catholic thinkers will be of interest here.

- Dom Illtyd Trethowan of Downside Abbey in England. Dom Illtyd, author of such major works of philosophical theology as *Certainty:*

Philosophical and Theological, Absolute Value, The Absolute and the Atonement and *Process Theology and the Christian Tradition*, stated that he has been "much impressed" by the "effect of the 'apparitions' on these young people" and that "it is impossible to find any natural explanation of what has been happening."

- Professor Frederick Copleston, celebrated author of the nine-volume *History of Philosophy* analyzing every philosophy and philosopher from ancient Greece to the present day, remarked to his friend and fellow Jesuit Fr. Richard Foley, Director of the Medjugorje Center in London, that the reported apparitions in Medjugorje manifest a pattern that is consistent with the activity of the Divine in human history.

- Professor Elizabeth Anscombe of Cambridge University has made contributions to almost every field of philosophy and is regarded as one of the foremost contemporary moral philosophers. Professor Anscombe contrasted false and authentic apparitions in terms of message content and said that she finds the Medjugorje apparition to be credible and the messages there to be very good.[8]

In the mind of anyone who loves Our Lady, Medjugorje's significance will be seen in relation to Fatima, the other great Marian apparition of this century. In "Medjugorje, the Fulfillment of Fatima," three great authorities on Fatima show how Medjugorje continues and fulfills Fatima. Fatima, it has been said, told us what must be done to save the world; and Medjugorje shows us how to do it. Medjugorje is the Fatima peace plan in action.

In the second section, **WHO IS SHE THAT IS COMING FORTH?**, we study the phenomenon of Medjugorje itself and the evidence in support of its authenticity. It is pointed out first that even many of the non-religious media have begun to recognize that we are living in the Age of Mary in terms of the spread of Marian devotion. This attention from the secular world has reached its peak with Medjugorje. In previous ages the evidence for apparitions was carefully analyzed by Church-appointed theologians and experts who were sent on a fact-finding mission by the appropriate ecclesiastical authorities. Their studies were then subjected to the scrutiny of the Church, and a decision was handed down at some point on whether or not the apparition was "worthy of belief." Apparitions

---

8 These three references come from personal conversations and coorespondence with the above.

in the age of sophisicated communications technologies will necessarily be subjected to a level of intense scrutiny that was never possible in the past.

To its credit, Medjugorje has survived the kind of trial by fire that has brought down governments and heads of state. Moreover, the phenomenon itself is brought into the living rooms of millions so that the "raw data" is available to the general public. All these developments, of course, do not change the fact that it is the Church which makes the final decision.

We survey in this section the Church's criteria for authentic apparitions and apply them to Medjugorje. Medical studies done on the visionaries have confirmed that they are sincere and sane and that something scientifically inexplicable is taking place during the apparitions. It must be mentioned here that the kind of scientific and medical tests done on the visionaries during the apparitions are again unprecedented in the history of apparitions; but the visionaries have emerged unscathed from this scrutiny. In addition, there are over 1,000 documented cures and healings that have taken place at Medjugorje. In this section, we see also that the content of the Medjugorje messages is theologically orthodox. The evidence for authenticity is overwhelming. We conclude this section with Fr. O'Carroll's thesis that the Church has given the same kind of de facto approval to Medjugorje that it has given to Knock. Quite clearly, the Church will not give formal approval until it has completed its investigation. Whatever the nature of its final verdict, all those responding to Our Lady's call from Medjugorje are duty-bound to humbly submit to the Church's judgment.

In the third section, **"I THANK YOU THAT YOU WILL NOT BETRAY MY PRESENCE HERE,"** we study the major critics and critiques of Medjugorje. The evidence in favor of the honesty and mental balance of the Medjugorje visionaries is overwhelming. Almost all the critics of Medjugorje are motivated by ideological considerations. Their critiques tell us more about their theological biases than about issues relevant to the authenticity of Medjugorje.

Perhaps the clearest testimony to the truth of Medjugorje is the fact that it does not fit anyone's agenda. What enrages many about Medjugorje is the fact that it doesn't fit in with their pet peeves or their favorite theological perspectives. By the same token, we must admit that some have tried to "create" Medjugorje in their own image. Perhaps this charge could be made in regard to some involved in the Charismatic Renewal. We must stress that the visionaries are not charismatics, and the spirituality emerging from Medjugorje is modeled on classic Croatian Catholicism not on the Charismatic Movement. Medjugorje's main message to some branches of the Charismatic Renewal is to "Marianize" your movement. It is not "Charismatize" Marian devotion. Reflection on Mary's role as the Spouse of the Holy Spirit will be greatly beneficial in this context. Like it or not, the visionaries must be understood on their own terms.

Here are some of the agendas that Medjugorje does not fit:

The Charismatic Agenda: None of the messages of Medjugorje are endorsements of the Charismatic Renewal, and none of the visionaries are themselves charismatics. Some involved in the Charismatic Renewal may have a propensity to gravitate towards "signs and wonders" such as luminary phenomena and healings and may have been drawn to Medjugorje solely or mainly by such attractions. Such "signs and wonders," as in the Gospel, were, however, mainly intended to draw attention to the Medjugorje messages of prayer, fasting, confession, the Mass and peace. The signs and wonders were and are not ends in themselves.

The Anti-Charismatic Agenda: Neither does Medjugorje endorse the anti-Charismatic agenda. The touching spontaneity and affection with which the Charismatics responded to the call of Medjugorje has clearly been reciprocated by their Mother who calls all men and women to her. Like the Pharisees of old who sniffed at Jesus for consorting with publicans and prostitutes, the anti-Charismatics have denounced Our Lady of Medjugorje for daring to embrace these "emotionalists."

The Pre-Vatican II Agenda: Many of the worst critics of Medjugorje are the so-called traditionalists who see the Second Vatican Council as the root of all the evils in the Church today. With its invitation to all human beings (not just Catholics), Medjugorje seems to these traditionalists to be as wrong-headed as the Second Vatican Council.

The Post-Vatican II Agenda: Medjugorje seems just as alien to the Modernists who will not rest until there is a Third Vatican Council organized under their auspices. With its solemn affirmation of the truths of the Catholic Faith, of the reality of Heaven, Hell and Purgatory and of the importance of the sacraments and prayer, Medjugorje seems to be a throwback to pre-conciliar times to these Modernists. While some Modernists cannot help but be impressed by the Medjugorje phenomenon, they are just as repulsed by its orthodoxy. A good example is this statement by Tom Fox, the editor of the liberal *National Catholic Reporter*: " 'Our Lady,' Marija said, 'always tells the world to pray.' "Does she ever say anything at all about feeding the poor, visiting the sick, clothing the naked?" I asked. 'Just pray. And the rest will follow.' My reaction talking to Marija was one of frustration ... I left my interview feeling I had just gone back to a preconciliar time and had listened to religious imagery and theology I had not heard since the earliest days of my childhood. It was an unsatisfying interview, but Marija, in all her peasant simplicity, nevertheless appeared to be an honest person." [*National Catholic Reporter*, January 15, 1988, p.11]

The Static View of Marian Apparitions: Many critics of Medjugorje fault it for "contradicting" or "undermining" Fatima. That this charge is false is clearly shown in a chapter later in this section where we try to show that Medjugorje is the fulfillment of Fatima. What is revealing about this charge is the assumption of those who make it that the Blessed Mother stopped all activity after her apparition at Fatima. This attitude of mind is probably a Catholic counterpart to the static approach taken to the Bible by Protestant Fundamentalists. Like Scripture-alone Fundamentalists, Fatima-alone Catholics have no theological evidence to support their static views.

The Fluid View of Marian Apparitions: The charge could be made that some Marian devotees flock to every alleged apparition site in the world simply for the fun of it. They are, perhaps, less interested in Mary and her message for the world than they are in the phenomenon of apparitions. Medjugorje demands from its listeners a degree of discipline and application of doctrine in daily life that will leave mere enthusiasts aghast. Medjugorje is specific and concrete and makes definite demands of everyone. It will not tolerate browsers and invites us to a life-changing and lifelong commitment. Yes, there may be other authentic apparitions, but they are footnotes and pointers at best to the main text that is laid out for us at Fatima and Medjugorje.

The upshot of these distinctions is that Medjugorje cannot be pinned down or pigeon-holed as easily as its detractors and its devotees would desire. The message of Medjugorje is as universal as that of the Catholic Church. The fact that Medjugorje does not satisfy any sectarian agenda — and has therefore won the hostility of such sectarian groups — is an argument for its authenticity for reasons memorably explicated by G.K. Chesterton in his defense of Christianity.

It looked not so much as if Christianity was bad enough to include any vices, but rather as if any stick was good enough to beat Christianity with. What again could this astonishing thing be like which people were so anxious to contradict, that in doing so they did not mind contradicting themselves? I saw the same thing on every side. ... Thus, certain sceptics wrote that the great crime of Christianity had been its attack on the family; it had dragged women to the loneliness and contemplation of the cloister, away from their homes and their children. But, then, other sceptics (slightly more advanced) said that the great crime of Christianity was forcing the family and marriage upon us; that it doomed women to the drudgery of their homes and children, and forbade them loneliness and contemplation. The charge was actually reversed. Or, again, certain phrases in the Epistles or the marriage service, were said by the anti-Christians to show contempt for woman's intellect. But I found that the anti-Christians themselves had a contempt for woman's intellect; for it was their great sneer at the Church on the Continent that "only women" went to it. Or again, Christianity was reproached with its naked and hungry habits; with its sackcloth and dried peas. But the next minute Christianity was being reproached with its pomp and its ritualism; its shrines of porphyry and its robes of gold. It was abused for being too plain and for being too coloured. Again Christianity had always been accused of restraining sexuality too much, when Bradlaugh the Malthusian discovered that it restrained it too little. It is often accused in the same breath of prim respectability and of religious extravagance. Between the covers of the same atheistic pamphlet I have found the faith rebuked for its dis-union, "One thinks one thing, and one another," and rebuked also for its union, "It is difference of opinion that prevents the world from going to the dogs." In the same conversation a freethinker, a friend of mine, blamed Christianity for despising Jews, and then despised it himself for being Jewish.

I wished to be quite fair then, and I wish to be quite fair now; and I did not conclude that the attack on Christianity was all wrong. I only concluded that if Christianity was wrong, it was very wrong indeed. Such hostile horrors might be combined on one thing, but that thing must be very strange and solitary. There are men who are misers, and also spendthrifts; but they are rare. There are men sensual and also ascetic; but they are rare. But if this mass of mad contradictions really existed, quakerish and bloodthirsty, too gorgeous and thread-bare, austere, yet pandering preposterously to the lust of the eye, the enemy of women and their foolish refuge, a solemn pessimist and a silly optimist, if this evil existed, then there was in this evil something quite supreme and unique. For I found in my rationalist teachers no expla-nation of such exceptional corruption. Christianity (theoretically speak-ing) was in their eyes only one of the ordinary myths and errors of mortals. They gave me no key to this twisted and unnatural badness. Such a paradox of evil rose to the stature of the supernatural. It was, indeed, almost as supernatural as the infallibility of the Pope. An historic institution, which never went right, is really quite as much of a miracle as an institution that cannot go wrong. The only explanation which immediately occurred to my mind was that Christianity did not come from heaven, but from hell. Really, if Jesus of Nazareth was not Christ, He must have been Antichrist.

And then in a quiet hour a strange thought struck me like a still thunderbolt. There had suddenly come into my mind another explanation. Suppose we heard an unknown man spoken of by many men. Suppose we were puzzled to hear that some men said he was too tall and some too short; some objected to his fatness, some lamented his leanness; some thought him too dark, and some too fair. One explanation (as has been already admitted) would be that he might be an odd shape. But there is another explanation. He might be the right shape. Outrageously tall men might feel him to be short. Very short men might feel him to be tall. Old bucks who are growing stout might consider him insufficiently filled out; old beaux who were growing thin might feel that he expanded beyond the narrow lines of elegance. Perhaps Swedes (who have pale hair like tow) called him a dark man, while negroes considered him distinctly blonde. Perhaps (in short) this extraordinary thing is really the ordinary thing; at least the normal thing, the center. Perhaps, after all, it is Christianity that is sane and all its critics that are mad — in various ways. I tested this idea by asking myself whether there was about any of the accusers anything morbid that might explain the accusation. I was startled to find that this key fitted a lock. For instance, it was certainly odd that the modern world charged Christianity at once with bodily austerity and with artistic pomp. But then it was also odd, very odd, that the modern world itself combined extreme bodily luxury with an extreme absence of artistic pomp. The modern man thought Becket's robes too rich and his meals too poor. But then the modern man was really exceptional in history; no man before ever ate such elaborate dinners in such ugly clothes. The modern man found the church too simple exactly where modern life is too complex; he found the Church too gorgeous exactly where modern life is too dingy. The man who disliked the plain fasts and feasts was mad on entrees. The man who disliked vestments wore a pair of preposterous trousers. And surely if there was any insanity involved in the matter at all it was in the trousers, not in simply falling robe. If there was any insanity at all, it was in the extravagant entrees, not in the bread and wine.

I went over all the cases, and I found the key fitted so far. The fact that Swinburne was irritated at the unhappiness of Christians and yet more irritated at their happiness was easily explained. It was no longer a complication of diseases in Christianity, but a complication of diseases in Swinburne. The restraints of Christianity saddened him simply because he was more hedonist than a healthy man should be. The faith of Christians angered him because he was more pessimist than a healthy man should be. In the same way the Malthusians by instinct attacked Christianity; not because there is anything especially anti-Malthusian about Christianity, but because there is something a little anti-human about Malthusianism." [G.K. Chesterton, *Orthodoxy*, Garden City, New York: Image Books, 1990, pp. 104-105]

With Chestertonian common sense as our compass and the teachings of the Church as our signposts, we will now turn our minds and hearts to Medjugorje.

2. POPE JOHN PAUL II AND MOTHER TERESA ON MEDJUGORJE

The two most famous living Catholics are Pope John Paul II and Mother Teresa of Calcutta. Catholics and non-Catholics across the world look to them for spiritual and moral vision and leadership. Their powers of discernment have been manifested time and again as they have cried out as lonely but courageous voices in the wilderness against the evils of the modern age. Truly, they are witnesses to the truth who serve as exemplars of the Gospel message. For the Catholic seeking guidance on Medjugorje, the perspectives on the matter of these two champions of Our Lady should count for something.

As Fr. O'Carroll has memorably said, everyone in Rome knows how Pope John Paul II feels about Medjugorje. It is an open secret there that he has joyfully embraced this incredible phenomenon literally taking place in his backyard. Surely, it is no coincidence that such a great apparition of Our Lady should take place in the papacy of such a Marian Pope.

In the **Introduction** we have seen why the Holy Father will not make an official statement on Medjugorje until the Church-appointed commission completes its study. He shows the same restraint in the case of the canonization processes currently underway for Padre Pio and Sister Faustina: he will not make an official pronouncement in either case until the processes have been completed. And yet, as with Medjugorje, he has been emphatic in his support for these causes. All sons and daughters of Holy Mother Church who are convinced of the authenticity of Medjugorje should work within the structures of the Church to expedite official approval.

It must be remembered that Popes have generally not been outspoken even about approved apparitions because their primary duty is to preserve and teach the public revelation. Pope Paul VI [who was the recipient of a private revelation] was the first Pope to visit Fatima, and his visit came fifty years after the apparitions had taken place. Pope John Paul II has taken Marian apparitions with great seriousness and has made Fatima a major theme of his papacy. His pronouncements on Medjugorje ¡are the pronouncements not just of the Supreme Pontiff but of a Marian who is especially sensitive to Mary's role in human history. At Fatima, on May 13, 1991, he said Mary receives "everyone, all of us, the men and women of this century and of its difficult and dramatic history."

Even enemies of Medjugorje admit that Pope John Paul II looks favorably on Medjugorje. The *Catholic Counter Reformation*, one of the severest critics of Medjugorje, says in its July 1987 issue: "For some months now, the Pope has not ceased lavishing his encouragement on the seers and the propagandists of Medjugorje. I have in front of me an account of twenty or so of these favors, which serve to revive week by week the confidence of thousands of faithful who continue to go on pilgrimage."

Mgr. Angelo Kim, President of the Korean Episcopal Conference, reported in the Korean Catholic weekly, 11 November 1990: "During the recent synod in Rome, the Korean bishops were invited to lunch with the Pope. In particular Mgr Kim said to the Pope, 'Thanks to you Poland has now been freed from communism.' The Pope replied, 'No, not me, **but by the works of the Blessed Virgin, according to her affirmations at Fatima and Medjugorje.**'"

"The Archbishop of Kzangju remarked, 'In Korea, in the city of Nadju, there is a statue of Our Lady that weeps.' The Pope replied to him: '**And there are some bishops, as in Yugoslavia, who are against ...but you must consider the response of the people, the many conversions...All this is in line with the Gospel. All these facts must be studied seriously'**" (*L'Homme nouveau*, editor Marcel Clement, 3 February 1991).

To Bishop Hnilica, SJ, confidant of John Paul II, the Pope said: "**If I weren't Pope, I'd have been in Medjugorje already**" (Taped interview with the Bishop, 21 April 1989). This was confirmed by the late Cardinal Frantizek Tomasek, retired Archbishop of Prague, in an interview with *Medjugorje Gebetsaktion* (#21) "With his own ears on a visit to Rome he heard a comment by John Paul II that if he were not Pope, he would gladly go to Medjugorje to help at the work with the pilgrims."[9]

An abundance of other sources testify to the Holy Father's perspective on Medjugorje.

Bishop Murilo Krieger went with thirty-three priests from Brazil for a six day retreat in Medjugorje. During Mass at St. James Church in Medjugorje, Bishop Krieger revealed that during a general audience he told Pope John Paul

---

[9] The quotes not cited above are taken from *Is Medjugorje Approved?* by Michael O'Carroll, CSSp, Dublin, Ireland, Veritas, 1991, p.63

II about their plans to go to Medjugorje. On hearing this, the Holy Father invited him to concelebrate Mass with him in his private papal chapel. He then encouraged them, blessed them for their retreat in Medjugorje, and recommended himself to their prayers. "I spoke with the Holy Father on the 24th of February, 1990 ... I told him I had been to Medjugorje three times and that I was going to return the following week. He said, simply: **'Medjugorje is a great center of spirituality!'** Bishop Murilo Krieger of Florianopolis, Brazil, said he later asked if he could give the pope's blessing to the visionaries and the pope granted his request." [*National Catholic Register*, April 29, 1990].

Bishop Carl Fisher of Los Angeles was in Medjugorje in July, 1988. He testified that on July 7th, Pope John Paul II had responded to his statement "Holy Father, I'm going to Medjugorje" with "You go with my blessings."

In June 1986, twelve Italian bishops at a papal audience addressed this question to Pope John Paul II. "Holy Father, what should we advise about pilgrimages to Medjugorje? Many of our people are traveling to Medjugorje and returning to their parishes fasting, praying and doing penance." The Pope replied: **"Let the people go to Medjugorje if they convert, pray, confess, do penance and fast."** [*Medjugorje: Facts, Documentation, Theology*, (p.232), *La Vita Popolo*, February 1, 1987.]

Most Reverend Patrick J. Flores, Archbishop of San Antonio, Texas, accompanied by two auxiliary bishops, reported his dialogue with John Paul II in January 1989: "I said to him, 'Your Holiness, numerous persons from my diocese go to Medjugorje. I did not permit nor forbid them. What should I do?' The Pope answered me, **'Let the people go there.'** Encouraged by this response, I said to him, 'But they are inviting me to accompany them in the month of August.' The pope answered, **'Go and when you get there you pray for me!'** It is thus that I find myself here in Medjugorje with the blessing of the Pope." [*Message de paix*, Montreal, November-December, 1989]

Bishop Michael D. Pfeifer, O.M.I., Bishop of San Angelo, in his pastoral letter, *"The Gospel, Mary and Medjugorje"* published on August 5, 1988: "During my 'ad limina' visit to Rome with the Bishops of Texas this past April, in the private conversation I had with our Holy Father, I asked his opinion about Medjugorje. The Pope spoke very favorably about the happenings at Medjugorje, pointing out the good which it has done for people. During the luncheon the Texas Bishops enjoyed with our Holy Father, Medjugorje came up for further discussion. Again, His Holiness spoke of how Medjugorje has changed the lives of people who visit there, and that the messages, thus far, are not contrary to the Gospel."

Father Brendan Dalton of Miami, Florida, in a letter he wrote to me on July 1, 1990: "I did ask the Holy Father here in Miami after he had spoken to the priests, as he was on his way out, in English I said, 'Holy Father, when are you going to Medjugorje?' He looked at me, smiled, put up his hand and said, '**Not yet, but I'm praying!**' I know he is very favorable towards all the events in Medjugorje. I know from inside the Vatican that the Holy Father asked about traveling to Yugoslavia. Some priests and nuns from Cracow spent time in the village and then went on to Rome to meet with the Holy Father. He is given the monthly messages and has continually asked for an update on all the happenings."[10]

The Holy Father has met and blessed several of the Medjugorje visionaries. On January 10, 1993 the visionary, Mirjana Soldo (see: Dragicevic) told me that during her first trip to Rome she received a note from the Holy Father requesting that they meet privately. She said that they did so for about 20 minutes. (In response to my question, "Mirjana, were any pictures taken during that private meeting?" she answered, "No. That is something that should not happen. That wouldn't have been right. The only pictures of us together were the ones taken during the General Audience.")

A young Italian priest, Gianni Sgreva, while staying in the home of Marija Pavlovic during a pilgrimage in Medjugorje, was encouraged by the Blessed Mother (through an apparition to Marija) to begin a new religious community in the Church. Fr. Sgreva was concerned that it would be based on an apparition not yet approved. He quotes Cardinal Ratzinger's encouraging words to him on September 9, 1986: "Why are you worried about it? Medjugorje ... I'll take care of it ... go ahead." Thereupon Cardinal Ratzinger obtained for Fr. Gianni a private audience with the Holy Father for the next day, September 10th. Fr. Gianni quotes John Paul II's words to him: "**But, Father, what are you concerned about? This problem with Medjugorje? My services are concerned with it. The Madonna will open all the ways. Pray also for me.**" With emotion he then embraced Fr. Sgreva and gave him his rosary. The religious garb of Fr. Sgreva's community, Oasi della Pace, was designed by Marija Pavlovic, one of the visionaries of Medjugorje based on how Our Lady is dressed when she appears in Medjugorje! Oasi della Pace was given full recognition by the Catholic Church as a new religious community on December 25, 1990. Fr. Sgreva, along with six members of the Community traveled to the U.S. to give their testimony at the 1991 National Conference on Medjugorje at the University of Notre Dame. At the Conference Fr. Gianni shared that on July 31, 1985, three months after his

---

[10] Consider the following report from the *Eco di Medjugorje* (February, 1993, p 4): "'Do you know that the Pope reads the *Echo of Medjugorje?*' We replied: 'Yes, we know he reads the French version.' Marija [Pavlovic] responded: 'No, the Polish one — if not both, that is. On the 17th September, when Fr. Jozo gave a letter to the nun that works in the Pontifical apartment to hand over to the Pope, she said how she receives the *Echo* in Polish and how the Pope asks to read it too, so she always lets him read it first. I was present and heard her say it.'"

meeting with the Pope, the apostolic pronuncio in Yugoslavia, Msgr. Francesco Colasuono, in response to Fr. Gianni's question regarding the authenticity of Medjugorje, responded: "Father, Medjugorje represents the event of the century!" (12) [The October-December, 1990, issue of *Medjugorje Messenger* has a picture of Fr. Sgreva with Pope John Paul II and a detailed description of his new order.]

Fr. Jozo Zovko, O.F.M., pastor of St. James Church when the apparitions began, visited the Holy Father in the summer of 1992. During his homily in St. James on the 11th anniversary of the apparitions he announced that the Pope had told him during their meeting, "Tell Medjugorje that I am with you. I bless you. I beg you, protect Medjugorje, protect Our Lady's message."

It is clear, then, to all but the most desperate, clutch-at-any-straw foes of Medjugorje where the greatest champion of Our Lady of our generation stands on her apparition in Medjugorje. The standard refrain by Medjugorje critics that "the Church has not approved Medjugorje" has now turned to "I am not bound to believe what the Church has to say on private revelations." James G. Bruen says in *Fidelity*, If the Church says Medjugorje is worthy of belief, "I can't be required to believe it or to incorporate it into my spiritual life since it is private revelation." [*Fidelity*, January 1991, p.14]. To the diehards we say, do not worry, not only the Church, but the Blessed Mother herself respects your freewill. Our Lady calls everyone to her at Medjugorje but forces no one to come to her.

Let us turn now to the saint of Calcutta. Mother Teresa's love and reverence for Our Lady of Medjugorje is well known to anyone who has asked her about the apparition in Yugoslavia. The attitude of this living saint is encapsulated by this touching tribute: "I am grateful to Our Lady of Medjugorje. I know that many people go there and are converted. I thank God for leading us during these times this way." [*Mir Monthly*, 1989].

It is appropriate to mention here that on August 12, 1991 Mother Teresa granted me permission to quote from her letters in order to refute in this book attacks against Medjugorje. On April 23, 1991, I sent her a letter specifically mentioning Michael Jones' condemnation of Medjugorje in his *Untold Story* and my intention to publish a response. On August 12, 1991 she responded, "I give you permission to use my words for the glory of God and the good of souls."

In an interview with *Medjugorje Messenger* (July-September 1989), Mother Teresa responds to a number of questions on Medjugorje. She begins the interview stating, Mary "is my mother. She is the mother of Jesus. She is the source of our joy, especially in the communities of our Order. She is there to help. She is there to protect. She is there to guide us." When asked, "Could you say something about the Medjugorje message — confession, prayer, penance, fasting, peace?" she replied:

These are precisely the requirements for the present day. If we don't pray, we cannot fast. For what purpose does fasting serve if not that we might obtain pure hearts? A pure heart is a converted heart. To achieve conversion we need profound humility. If we are humble like Mary, we shall be capable of trying to be as holy as Jesus.

That is why our Mother is continually appealing to us to pray and fast. Prayer and fasting lead to a pure heart, and the pure of heart can see God. And when we see God in our neighbor we shall have peace, love, unity, joy and harmony.

I think that's the reason why Our Lady is asking us so much to lead a life of prayer and penance. For that gives us pure hearts, and without this we cannot see God. Our Lady was so pleasing to God, so close to Him, so full of grace, precisely because she had a pure heart. And having a pure heart is also a gift of God.

On the day of His resurrection, Jesus gave us the sacrament of penance. When we go to confession we go as sinners, full of sin. When we come away from confession we are sinners without sin, in other words, pure of heart. That is the greatness and joy of this gift God gave us on the day of the resurrection, the day of joy.

Question: Medjugorje's central message is peace. What are your thoughts about this?

Mother Teresa: "The world has never needed peace so much as now, for there is so much suffering. There is also so much evil, so much destruction, especially of life itself. I always come to the same conclusion: if even a mother can kill her own child, who, then, can prevent <u>others</u> from committing evil?

"God speaks about this very clearly in Holy Scripture: 'Can a woman forget her suckling child, that she should have no compassion on the son of her womb?' [Isaiah 49:15]

"Nowadays, many mothers, because of abortion, forget that they are mothers. And if a mother can do this, how easy it is for us to forget that each of us is a person created by God and in whom He lives! How can a mother who kills her child remember God's presence? If she destroys her child, she destroys the image of God, His very presence.

"Therefore the world and the Church have never needed holiness so much as today. I also believe that we have to bring holiness, this prayer and sacrifice, back to people. For what is holiness? It is prayer and sacrifice, being one with Jesus."

Mother Teresa made this emphatic appeal to pilgrims going to Medjugorje, "**Tell everyone who comes to Medjugorje: 'Pray to Our Lady of Medjugorje for a drug to cure AIDS!'** I believe that would be one of the finest gifts that Our Lady (who so loves our poor AIDS victims) could give us."

In concluding the interview, Mother Teresa specially recommended this prayer:

> *Mary, Mother of Jesus, give us your heart, so beautiful, so pure, so immaculate, so full of love and humility, that we may become worthy to receive Jesus in the Bread of Life, to love Him as you loved Him, and to serve Him in the poorest of the poor.*

3. WHAT CATHOLIC BISHOPS HAVE SAID ABOUT MEDJUGORJE

For Catholics, the reflections and testimonies in this chapter are second in importance only to the pronouncements of the Supreme Pontiff for we have here considered assessments of Medjugorje from the Successors of the Apostles. The true impact of Medjugorje can be gauged from this outpouring of affection and reverence for their Mother from the Princes and Shepherds of the Church. "We can only give astonished thanks for the awakening of faith," says Archbishop Johannes Joachim Degendhardt of Paderborn, Germany. Bishop Gabriel Diaz of Ecuador and Bishop Joseph Casale of Foggia, Italy, state, "Medjugorje is an extraordinary thing which invites us to change our lives. No one can remain indifferent about it."

Never before in the history of apparitions have we seen such a spontaneous and speedy response from the hierarchy of the Church to an apparition that is still under study. The witness of the Shepherds of the Church in itself now constitutes a significant datum in favor of the authenticity of the apparitions.

The testimonies and reflections reproduced here are not exhaustive or comprehensive. Numerous other bishops — over 100 — have visited Medjugorje and have commented favorably on it. Nonetheless, the statements made here by 40 Cardinals and Bishops provide a good flavor of the way in which the Universal Church has responded to the Blessed Mother's apparitions at Medjugorje.

(i) **Cardinal Joseph Ratzinger,** Prefect of the Sacred Congregation for the Doctrine of the Faith [Interview at the International Theological Summer Academy in Aigen, Austria on August 28, 1991; (Quoted in *Medjugorje Gebetsaktion*, #22, 1992 pp.4,5), *The Spring Must Be Understood so that It Can Flow Properly.*]

You know pretty well, I believe, the previous history, that is, that the bishop himself has taken a very critical stance towards it. We have not the right from Rome to withdraw the matter from him when there are no evident reasons to the contrary.

However, we have asked him, in the face of the significance that the Medjugorje phenomenon has attained, extending far beyond the diocese, on his own to turn over the process to the Bishops' Conference and by this to create a forum that is broader and — let us say — also less overburdened, less immediately exposed to the phenomena.

However, at the same time — and this is completely according to the sense of the viewpoint that I mentioned before — they said, 'We want to be concerned that this place, which has become a place of prayer and of faith, remain and come to be even more in the most interior unity with the entire Church.' That is to say, the Bishops' Conference offers its help towards an organization of this place of prayer that is genuinely effective pastorally and at the same time doctrinally pure. So this is, so to speak, the will of the bishops which now concerns the place and which is naturally an offer to the local authorities. At the moment everything is apparently blocked by the political events, but we hope nevertheless that this aim of the Yugoslavian Bishops' Conference which, in my opinion, holds good on this point and has been shown really as an instance being handled out of faith and great pastoral concern — that this then will also lead to a fruitful clarification of the whole matter.

(ii) Fr. Hans Urs Von Balthasar, Switzerland

Father Hans Urs Von Balthasar, the Swiss theologian, is widely regarded as one of the leading Catholic theologians of the twentieth century. His work *The Glory of the Lord* is viewed by many as the "Summa Christiana" of modern times. He was the director of Cardinal Ratzinger's doctoral thesis, his mentor and guide. Moreover, Father von Balthasar is the Pope's favorite theologian [Rooney-Faricy 3, page 22]. Fr. Henri de Lubac S.J. says "he is the greatest Christian thinker of our era" [*30 Days*, July 88]. He was awarded the Paul VI prize for theology, conferred in Rome by the Pope, for his many achievements over a long lifetime, in many branches of theology, anthropology, the theology of history and patristics as well as in aesthetics, especially musicology. Hans Urs von Balthasar died of a heart attack on the eve of the consistory [28 June 1988] in which he would have been created a cardinal of the Roman Catholic Church. He was 83.

"Medjugorje's theology rings true. I am convinced of its truth. Everything about Medjugorje is authentic, in a Catholic sense. What's happening there is so evident, so convincing."

(iii) Cardinal Joseph Bernardin,Chicago,Illinoiss, U.S.A [Article in Chicago's Archdiocesan paper, *The New World*, May 1, 1992]

Bosnia-Hercegovina, one of the newly independent nations which emerged from Yugoslavia, is now suffering through a barbarous civil war.

The violence is claiming more and more victims. Over 200,000 people have been driven from their homes. Houses of worship, public buildings and private dwellings lie in ruins. When you see the pictures of the people on television or in the newspapers, it is obvious that they know, in their own way, the tragic experience of Good Friday.

Bosnia-Hercegovina is the most recent republic to declare its independence on the Balkan peninsula. Like Slovenia and Croatia before it, Bosnia-Hercegovina voted in a free and fair national referendum to become an independent republic.

For more than 40 years, people of all faiths in that land have lived side-by-side in relative peace and harmony. Recently, in the capital of Sarajevo, Muslims, Orthodox and Catholics came together to demonstrate their desire for peace. It was a very concrete sign of the harmony of the different faiths and their desire for peaceful self-determination. Tragically, the forces of war confronted that peaceful demonstration with the bullets of snipers. Several of the demonstrators were wounded or killed.

The media has brought these terrible events to our attention, yet there is also another reason why this has such an immediate and personal impact on so many people here in the United States and, indeed, throughout the world.

Located in the Republic of Bosnia-Hercegovina is the small village of Medjugorje. It is a place of pilgrimage for millions of people who wish to honor the Blessed Mother under her title as Queen of Peace. All have been welcomed at Medjugorje: Orthodox, Muslim, Catholic, Protestant, Jew and any others who wish to pray there.

If we are to translate the hope of Easter into our world, we must do what we can to help the people of Bosnia-Hercegovina.

Medjugorje has been an oasis of peace in an increasingly stormy desert. There are no military installations there, no barracks, no communication centers, no industrial sites. Medjugorje has declared itself as "an Open City," a combat-free zone of peace. However, now the forces of war threaten Medjugorje itself. Such mindless violence must stop!

These days are critical for the people of Bosnia-Hercegovina. Indeed, what happens there touches all of us in some way. We face critical times. A new world order is taking shape. Its principles and values are ours to determine. Will it be an era that knows only the despair of Good Friday, or will we fuse it with the hope of Easter as well?

As we look at Bosnia-Hercegovina and other tragic situations that cry out for our attention, three firm principles point the way to their resolution.

"First, people have a right to self-determination. Those who seek to thwart this self-determination should be treated as moral lepers among the family of nations.

Second, the principle of solidarity impels us to share the pain of those who suffer. We cannot turn our backs on the people of Bosnia-Hercegovina. The United States has praised humanitarian assistance, and we must pay for United Nations peace-keeping forces as well.

Moreover, solidarity calls for us to live together in harmony and respect. It is the principle that brings together Orthodox, Muslims and Catholics to build a society that cherishes life and the rights of every individual who claims citizenship in that independent nation.

Third, we must make tragic situations like this one intensify our hunger for peace. In a world that has developed the technology to destroy itself, peace becomes an imperative. We cannot allow the forces of war to determine the future of Bosnia-Hercegovina, the home of the shrine of the Queen of Peace.

If we are to translate the hope of Easter into our world, we must do what we can to help the people of Bosnia-Hercegovina. If we are to move beyond that pain of Good Friday, we must rely on the grace of the risen Lord and the intercession of his Blessed Mother. If we are to build a new world order, then it must be based on self-determination, solidarity and peace.

(iv) Cardinal Franjo Kuharic, Primate of Croatia, Head of the Yugoslavian Bishops' Conference [Interview with *Medjugorje Gebetsaktion*, (#24, 1992, pp.4,5): Quoted in *Mary's People*, September 27, 1992]

People who believe and are convinced in conscience that with these messages [from Our Lady in Medjugorje] they can stimulate people to the good — to conversion, to peace — they should do it. This is a matter of conscience.

(v) Cardinal Augustine Mayer, President Pontificia Commissio *Ecclesia Dei*

Cardinal Mayer wrote to the author, on March 3, 1989:

I wish to thank you for sharing the results of the first National Conference on Medjugorje held at Notre Dame. I commend you for your zeal and I pray for the success of your efforts...
I will pray for you and your colleagues as you sincerely strive to spread the message of Mary.

(vi) Cardinal Jaime Sin, Manila, Phillipines [*National Catholic Register*, September 27, 1992]

Everything that was foreseen in Fatima is coming true. And there is a growing feeling that the justice of God might fall on humanity at any time. God is merciful, but God also wants justice. People are turning to Mary for help. The world has a beginning and so it will have an end. Maybe Mary has already seen the end and wants to save us. Our Lady has appeared on every continent to touch the lives of all people. God wants all of us to go to heaven, but some must go to hell. Perhaps God has sent Mary to save those she can.[11]

[Note: Fr. Rene Laurentin wrote his book, *The Apparitions of the Blessed Virgin Mary Today*, at the request of Cardinal Sin. Fr. Laurentin has informed us that Cardinal Sin believes in the authenticity of Medjugorje.]

---

[11] A front page article in the September 27, 1992, *National Catholic Register* reported these words from Cardinal Sin, the Archbishop of Manila. He spoke to the *Register* just before addressing the Baltimore International Marian Conference. Since the first Marian Conference of this kind — the 1989 National Conference on Medjugorje at the University of Notre Dame — conferences inspired by Our Lady's call from Medjugorje have spread throughout America. Forty took place in 1992 — more than 50 are planned for 1993! The article in the *Register* began, *"Mary, it seems, is on the mind of everyone these days. From Medjugorje to ...the message of Fatima to the words of Pope John Paul II, devotion to Mary is enjoying a tremendous, perhaps unprecedented, revival."*

(vii) Cardinal Giuseppe Siri, Genoa, Italy [R. del Car. 4 October, 1987]

The facts are facts and nobody can deny them. The Church will give a judgment. I can only say that I see many atheists leaving Genoa for Medjugorje who return with a rosary in their hands.

In an October 14, 1989 interview with *Medjugorje Gebetsaktion*, [#1, 1990, p.7] Bishop Paolo Hnilica added the following on Cardinal Siri:

Cardinal Siri too — he died just this year — told me this, when I was in Genoa (he was cardinal there at the time) for a Medjugorje meeting. At dinner he said to me 'I have noticed that the people who come from Medjugorje become apostles. They renew the parishes. They form groups in which they get together — prayer groups; they pray before the Blessed Sacrament. They hold lectures, lead discussions and bring others to Medjugorje. And these circles, these prayer groups spread out more and more. They renew the Church.' This was one of the greatest cardinals who gave this testimony about Medjugorje.

(viii) Cardinal Timothy Manning, Los Angeles, California, U.S.A.

I was deeply moved by my visit to Medjugorje.

The late Cardinal Timothy Manning, in a March 3, 1989 letter to the author regretting that he was not able to attend the 1989 National Conference at Notre Dame.

(ix) Cardinal Frantisek Tomasek, Czechoslovakia
[*Medjugorje Gebetsaktion*, #17, 1990, pp.26, 27]

The Czech Primate, Cardinal Frantisek Tomasek, then still Archbishop of Prague, explained face to face with visitors of Vienna Gebetsaktion that he is **personally most deeply convinced of the genuineness of the Blessed Mother's apparitions in the Hercegovinian village and has been able to make for himself a very clear picture of the true fruits of Medjugorje through numerous contacts with people who have received a decisive impulse for their religious life in Medjugorje.** With his own ears he heard, on a visit to Rome, a statement of John Paul II that if he were not Pope, he would like to go to Medjugorje to help at the work with the pilgrims.

Cardinal Frantisek Tomasek...was recently paid another visit by us.. There had been a first conversation together with Father Slavko Barbaric and two representatives of our Viennese "Gebetsaktion" on November 21, 1987. 'Priests and faithful are deeply grateful for each message, for each informative report, that we receive from Medjugorje', he said at that time. 'Step by step the Immaculate Heart of Mary will triumph. I am deeply convinced that Medjugorje is also a sign for this. This was his statement at that time. The situation at that point seemed to be yet fully hopeless.

This time at our visit in Prague on March 23, 1990, despite other pressing appointment obligations, the Cardinal received us again in audience visibly pleased and with a ready heart. We could also let the cassette recorder run freely and unhindered, which would not have been advisable in 1987 at our first visit, because of the political situation. To the question, whether he had expected so rapid a change, the Cardinal told us, **'Yes, we did expect that a bit, but not in such an extent as it has turned out. We have now a completely new hope for the future of the Church here. The Church here is now completely free; she can work in a completely free manner. This is something new. The future of the Church is something very, very important for us.'**

The Cardinal said that the heavenly Mother Mary is very deeply honored there and that the Catholics above all, precisely because they trust in her help, are optimistic about what concerns the future of the Church. Already for many centuries, the Blessed Mother has been deeply honored there by the people — now even more than ever. They are very deeply surrendered to the heavenly Mother Mary, and because of this they are so sure of the further good development of the Church. With the Blessed Mother everything is possible.

We then told Cardinal Tomasek of our plans. We in Vienna (Gebetsaktion Maria — Queen of Peace — Medjugorje) will print the messages now in the eastern languages as well. Something is already started, and we wanted to know what Cardinal Tomasek, as Primate of Czechoslovakia says about this. His answer in all simplicity **'We are very deeply grateful for this possibility to publish the messages in our languages, because with us this hope is very deeply rooted with respect to the future. The Blessed Mother Mary is always with us, with our people, because she has already been honored so long and so deeply.'**

We had not expected so uncomplicated a consent, and so we asked further whether the Cardinal would therefore take up no attitude of reserve, but rather accept that one takes in wholeheartedly what the Blessed Mother requires. **"Yes, this is completely clear to us. And therefore we are — I repeat — completely certain for the future of the Church here, because with us the faithful and also the priests are ready for every sacrifice for the kingdom of God, with the help of our heavenly Mother Mary. Our nation is very deeply surrendered to the Blessed Mother Mary. Medjugorje is therefore for us a great assurance for the future, and we are convinced that the way is completely open to us for a broader, completely new hope for the life of the Church among us. After such long times of trouble, we have now — I repeat and emphasize — all possibilities for life in the Church"**.

This was a conversation that had taken a completely different course than we, with our experience in the West, had expected. In this conversation with Cardinal Tomasek, everything came down to one thing: **'We are now free, and with the help of our heavenly Mother Mary, entirely new hopes will now be fulfilled.'**

(x) Cardinal Franjo Seper, Former Prefect for the Congregation of the Doctrine of the Faith [Jan '83, *Orthodoxy of the Catholic Doctrine*, by Father Milan Mikulich O.F.M.]

In one of our previous articles we had reported that Cardinal Franjo Seper, while still Prefect of the Sacred Congregation for the Doctrine of the Faith, after returning from Zagreb, Croatia, Yugoslavia, to Rome at the beginning of September, 1981, told this writer by telephone from Rome, that he was impressed by great happenings in Medjugorje, the main of them being a deep religious renewal of the people. According to the Cardinal, many were convinced about the genuine visits of Our Lady to the boys and girls. The only concern for him was the fact that their pastor, Fr. Jozo Zovko, O.F.M. was a charismatic. The question for the Cardinal was whether Our Lady did really appear to the children, or were the children under the influence of an enthusiastic charismatic priest's zeal and probably subjectively saw what was not objectively a reality!

Father Galic, O.F.M., who had read that statement of Cardinal Seper, told me recently, during my visit to West Allis, Wisc., that he personally had visited in 1981 Fr. Jozo Zovko, his classmate, and discovered from his own words that he, in spite of being a charismatic, did not influence in any way the children. In fact, the charismatic priest refused to believe at that time what the children were saying about the apparitions of Our Lady in Medjugorje.

(xi) Archbishop Frane Franic, Split, Croatia [Statement published in January, 1985]

It is unbelievable how often I have been asked by various Italian pilgrims and theological and medical experts to state my opinion about Medjugorje and the well known *'Statement of the Bishops conference of Yugoslavia'*. This statement was erroneously interpreted as *'forbidding all organized pilgrimages'*. To amplify the confusion *'L'Osservatore Romano'* published the Statement actually as an *'Announcement of the Secretariat of the Bishops' Conference of Yugoslavia'*, as well as the *'Announcement of the Commission for Medjugorje'* from the diocese of Mostar. This was interpreted to mean that the Holy See had *'forbidden'* all organized pilgrimages to Medjugorje, which is completely incorrect. *'L'Osservatore Romano'* published these 'announcements' which someone sent to them in the same way they receive other news, but the Holy See does not, and never did, have anything to do with them. Some people ask me: *'Why are you, a bishop in whose province Medjugorje is not situated, so interested in this case?'* I give the following answer:

1) The Archdiocese of Split, Makarska, is the nearest diocese to Medjugorje; therefore, in the beginning, the events in Medjugorje made a big impact on our archdiocese, especially after the first statement the Bishop of Mostar gave about Medjugorje. It forced me to become interested in the events because, as bishop of the nearest diocese, I have a duty to point out to my priests and parishioners the risks and benefits to the faith.

2) Many experts have approached me during the past year, among them have been famous theologians and mariologists, specialists, physicians and professors from the University of Milan. Many pilgrims have come to me, including a large number of young people, students, laborers, intellectuals and devout women and girls. They were unanimously enthusiastic about their pilgrimages to Medjugorje; they were deeply moved. I saw truly authentic conversions of nonbelievers in Jesus Christ and in God, the Creator and Redeemer of the world, and also witnesses who testified to unusual healings. An example is the recovery of Mrs.

43

Diana Basile, from Milan, from the incurable disease of multiple sclerosis. Her recovery was later documented by 142 medical documents and authenticated by the court of the Milan diocese. For several years the woman couldn't move, except in her wheelchair, and was blind in the right eye. She was half dead, but stood up from her wheelchair cured and able to see with her right eye again. This all happened in one moment.

3) I'd like to mention that I was again elected by the Bishops' Conference in Yugoslavia to be President of their *'Council for Religious Instruction.'* I've been President of that Council for several five-year terms and felt motivated to study the events in Medjugorje more closely. I had the help of many experts. For example, in the beginning there was Fr. Tomaso Beck, S.J.; and Fr. Faricy, American Jesuit, Professor of Spirituality at Greorian University; and later Fr. Laurentin, Fr. Scanlan, TOR, professor and president of the Franciscan University in the United States of America, articles by Hans Urs von Balthasar, and French and Italian theologians.

I was in Medjugorje once, at the beginning, before Christmas 1981, and again on December 16 and 17, 1984. Neither time did I lead any pilgrims but went as a simple pilgrim to see with my own eyes what I had read in the books, magazines and newspapers and heard in so many testimonials. In Medjugorje I celebrated Holy Mass, *simplicis sacerdotis*, without Bishop's symbols and ceremonies. In the church, no one greeted me as a bishop. I behaved like a simple priest, one of the faithful who came to pray and give thanks to God and the Mother of God for the 34th anniversary of consecration as a bishop [December 17, 1950-1984] and for my 72nd birthday [December 29, 1912-1984]. All this was as private and incognito as possible. I definitely didn't want to hinder the final judgment of the Church but to assist in an objective investigation. I subject myself in advance to that judgment.

When I returned from Medjugorje on December 18, 1984, I meditated on the meaning of the events there and compared Medjugorje, again and again, with Fatima. In Medjugorje I met a priest from Portugal and a Reverend Mother, the founder of the new Order of the Mother of God, who talked to me about the comparison between these two shrines. Then I understood the magnificent meaning of Medjugorje, a forlorn village in Southern Hercegovina, which is similar in many ways to the Neretva Valley near Split. They both have a scattered configuration of neighborhoods and similar languages. I was present twice at the *'visions'* of the children and had friendly conversations with them in their homes. It became even clearer to me that there are no deceptions here, no manipulations or hallucinations. There are serious religious experiences which attract masses of the faithful who feel the presence of the Spirit of God speaking not only to the Church in Hercegovina, but also to the universal Church, just as in Fatima.

1) In its time, Fatima was considered radically anti-communist and some rightist regimes used Fatima as a reference for their anti-communist politics. At that time it was popular to believe that Russia was the sole cause of the spreading of false beliefs, the cause of future war and danger to European Christian culture. However, it is clear today, merely through the messages of Medjugorje, that the origin of false beliefs lies also in *'Christian'* Western Europe in the fields of dogma and ethics with their secularism, materialism and dechristianization. Also, some Catholic theologians were the originators of fallacies. Thus, the danger of God's punishment, such as future war, comes not only from Russia, but also from the Western *'Christian'* states and from fallacies in the Church itself. Our Lady of Fatima looked much further into the future than we could see at that moment in history. We understand now that the danger of God's punishments comes from human errors and from sin in general and that the messages of Our Lady do not depend on politics but on conversion through prayer and penitence as the only way to the peace of Christ and Mary. The messages of Medjugorje preach love, in relation to the Cross, toward communists, Muslims, Eastern Orthodox, Catholics and especially toward those who intimate, with hostility, that the messages represent masks, conscious lies, selfishness and avarice. It's a real pleasure to listen to the children, Fr. Vlasic and the other Franciscans in Medjugorje, as they never complain about anyone, but talk about everyone with love. To me, that's a greater miracle than the extraordinary physical healings which occur in Medjugorje.

2) Medjugorje shines infinite new light on the prophecies of Fatima. The peace of Christ cannot be attained with weapons, money or cultural supremacy but only by prayer, penance and conversion.

3) The ecumenism of the Second Vatican Council is confirmed in Medjugorje. Even within the Church, some people oppose the teaching of ecumenism and consider it a misconception of Vatican II. However, the *'message of Medjugorje'* confirms the ecumenism

of Vatican II and puts it into practice where the Catholic and the Orthodox Churches meet with the Islam and the Marxist. These messages breathe life into Church doctrine. It is expressed by the simple messages of the children and the application of those messages in the everyday life of simple souls. It requires only a little good will to realize that, before our eyes, the Spirit of God is at work, forming a new Church of the Holy Spirit which relies on neither politics nor social systems, but on God alone. The Holy Spirit is renewing the world, renewing individuals and nations, renewing and saving individuals and social structures, but only by the help of love in the light of the Cross.

This phenomenon is so simple and yet so magnificent. We are witnessing the beginning of a new era in the history of the Church. The so-called *'Constantinian Church'* is disappearing and in its place emerges the true Church of the Holy Spirit whose invisible head is Christ, and whose visible head is the Pope. The authority of the Roman Pope is strongly affirmed in Medjugorje. If one should ask why the Franciscans don't obey the Pope and give the seven parishes to diocesan priests, Our Lady could answer as would Her own Son, *'Who gave me the power to distribute parishes between Franciscans and diocesan priests?'* No one said that the two Franciscans who were thrown out of the Order should disobey their superiors. They too have to subject themselves to the superiors, just as the whole province does. This simple conclusion can be drawn from the messages of Medjugorje. To lead the Church of love into conflict with the Church of law would be wasteful and antagonistic to the views of the Church.

(xii) Archbishop Aquila, [quoted in *Medjugorje Echo*, March 8, 1987]

I do not feel able to advise people against going to Medjugorje since, where I come from, people who had been absent from the Church for 10, 15, even 20 years went there and returned completely converted. I have now appointed a spiritual director for the Medjugorje prayer group; they come together to pray every Saturday and attend Mass together each Sunday.

(xiii) Monsignor J. Carboni, Bishop of Macerata, Italy, [quoted in
Medjugorje Echo, March 8, 1987]

When I go to any shrine, I do not go to admire the churches or
monuments; I sit in the confessional and from the confessions I hear
can evaluate just how good the shrine is. I have been to Medjugorje; I
did not seek out the visionaries nor the priests. I just heard confessions
for two whole days and this was enough to convince me that Our Lord
is present in Medjugorje — and so is Our Lady!

(xiv) Bishop Donat Chiasson, Archbishop of Moncton, Canada
[quoted from R. Laurentin, *Nine Years of Apparitions*,
The Riehle Foundation]

Journalist: "Bishop Chiasson, what is the reaction in your heart with
respect to the phenomenon of Medjugorje?"
Bishop Chiasson: "What delights me here is that the whole parish tries to
live the Gospel without compromise. I do not have an opinion to express on the
apparitions in Medjugorje. However, I believe in the message because it is
consistent with the Gospel."

(xv)Bishop Brendan Comiskey, Ireland [*Medjugorje Herald*, "Hunger
for God" November 1988]

Something strange is happening in Ireland in our time. In spite of
twenty-five years of liturgical reform and renewal, thousands of our
people flock to 'moving statues' and to 'unofficial' places of pilgrimage. Bus loads of Irish people pass hundreds of churches where Mass
is being celebrated, pass hundreds of tabernacles where Jesus is
present in the Blessed Sacrament, fly hundreds of miles from a country
where the Lord of the Universe graces thousands of places with His
sacramental presence, and journey to a Communist country...to see
several young people transfixed by some inexplicable experience. The
real question we should be asking in the Church today is not 'What
causes the statues to move?' but 'What is causing the people to move?'
Not for the first time God's people are 'saying' something with their
feet.

Many reasons have been advanced to explain why people, without
any encouragement from their pastors, and sometimes with their
explicit disapproval act in this way. It may be partly because of an
understandable curiosity and attraction to the sensational. Some would

explain it all away by calling such travelers theological and liturgical 'illiterates.' But one must then ask the question, 'Why are they so illiterate after a quarter of a century of preaching and teaching on the liturgical reforms of the Second Vatican Council?' And how does one explain the presence in Medjugorje of dozens of priests, more than a few bishops and archbishops? More importantly, how does one explain the reports of conversions, the quantity and quality of the reception of the Sacrament of Penance, the exemplary manner of Christian living of many of these pilgrims upon their return home? It is easy to be dismissive; it is much more difficult to explain it all.

I am growing more and more convinced that a better explanation is the hunger, the very real hunger in the hearts of many of our people today — a hunger for God. We must look at how this hunger is being addressed or ignored."

Bishop Comiskey then goes on to tease out and highlight what this hunger is (and in doing so is dealing with the basic need in our Christian lives). The Bishop says,

It is a hunger for more than doctrine however important and necessary doctrine is, and it is necessary and essential. Doctrine is a teaching; religion is a relationship. Doctrine is the grammar; religion is the story.

What people seek, the Bishop argues, is the experience of God, and he would say without this religious experience, doctrine, catechesis and liturgy are meaningless. The Bishop explains what he means by this experience of God and expresses the view that popular devotions in Ireland, and of the Irish people, have great potential in helping people to this experience. But our brief here really is not to present the Bishop's convictions and suggestions. Those one would have to read in full. Here we simply wish to present Bishop Comiskey's reference to Medjugorje, just as a reference. But one may add the comment that one cannot but be happy to see the reference set in the wider context of the great hunger of God that exists so palpably today. The Bishop may or may not go along with Medjugorje, but all people devoted to Medjugorje will certainly go along with the Bishop when he isolates today's fundamental need.

(xvi) **Bishop Joseph Casale**, Archbishop of Foggia, Italy, and **Bishop Gabriel Diaz Cueva,** Ecuador [quoted from *Eco*, No. 74].

Medjugorje is an extraordinary thing which invites us to change our lives. No one can remain indifferent about it. We will return."

(xvii) **Bishop Gabriel Diaz Cueva**, Guayaquil, Ecuador [quoted from *Medjugorje Gebetsaktion,* #16, 1990, pp.30,31]

After I was in an "Ad-Limina visit" in Rome, I had the opportunity to come to Medjugorje. This fulfilled a great desire. Since I had read several publications on the subject, I had had the wish for a long time to be able to come to this place of grace.

Certainly, the experiences which I have during these days here (in Medjugorje) were in a certain way predictable, since I had read some very impressive documentation by prominent theologians about the events here. I believe that I am able to say HERE THE HAND OF GOD IS AT WORK! And I pray for this, that the message of the most Blessed Virgin be accepted more and more. This message is not any different from the Good News (i.e., the Gospel), but they are still the words of a Mother who is concerned for the good of humanity and for the salvation of every single human being. I believe that what the Holy Virgin tells us is nothing other than an echo of the words of St. Paul: 'This is God's will — your salvation.' (1 Thes 4,3)

What also impressed me were the priests who concelebrated the Holy Mass here or visit the different places of apparition. The recollection, the faith and the devotion with which they do these are of themselves testimony of how very much the Holy Spirit is working in their hearts.

I hope that the messages which the Holy Virgin has communicated to us for so long will be of great use to the entire Church and to each one of us. I believe that we should give the gift of attention to her words, to her who tries to say through these simple and good young people (the visionaries) so much to us that will bring us to salvation.

It is something very important to try to be transmitters of this message of peace, of reconciliation, of love, of repentance and of dedication — for all which the Blessed Mother requires of us. Through prayer, namely the interior life with God, I believe we can really soften God's anger, which has been provoked by so many sins and misdeeds of humanity. The Blessed Virgin calls us repeatedly to prayer, fasting and dedication to God, through which we can attain everything from the mercy of God.

I believe that the messages of the Blessed Virgin have very much to do with the future of humanity and therefore also with the holy Church. In the entire course of Church history the Blessed Mother has again and again perceived her mission as that which the Lord gave her from the cross (when he said of her to John): "BEHOLD YOUR MOTHER!" She has really become the Mother of the Church and of the whole of humanity, and she continues to avail herself of this role that which the Lord gave her, as she stood at the foot of the cross.

(xviii) Bishop Nicholas D'Antonio, New Orleans, Louisiana, U.S.A. [quoted from *Mary's Message*, December, 1985]

I want to make Mary's message my Christmas message this year of the Lord 1985. Though not yet officially recognized by the Church, Mary's message is authentic. As at La Salette, Lourdes and Fatima, the Mother of God continues to appear.

This time She appeared in Medjugorje, Croatia, Yugoslavia, a communist state.

The apparitions to four girls and two boys began to take place on June 24, 1981, and continue to this day! At first, She appeared to the children on a hilltop on seven consecutive days. When the police barricaded the road which led to the hilltop, Our Lady began to appear to the "Six" in the fields, in their homes, and finally in the local Franciscan Church of St. James, where the apparitions still go on! With every appearance, She greets the children with 'PRAISED BE JESUS CHRIST!' Her principal role obviously is to draw all men and women to Her Divine Son! The children were prodded by their pastor to ask Her name. She responded, 'I AM THE BLESSED VIRGIN MARY!' She then recommended them to continue praying seven Our Fathers, and seven Hail Marys and seven Glory Be to the Fathers, together with the Creed, as they were doing on their own, for the sick and sinners! She also encouraged them to pray Her Rosary.

The purpose of the apparitions? She tells us in Her own words: 'I am the Blessed Virgin Mary. I came to convert the people of the world. I am the Queen of Peace. I came to bring peace to the world!' Now isn't that great Christmas news?

She later explained how this was to come about. She stressed the need of prayer, penance, fasting on bread and water on Fridays by those who are able to do it, conversion, reconciliation with one another and with God, and especially a firm faith as the preconditional means of avoiding catastrophic wars and thus assuring peace and the salvation of humankind. She recommended priests to keep their faith and to preserve the faith of the people. Does this message sound simplistic and trite? So does the Gospel to those who lack faith. The Holy Scriptures and tradition are full of examples how victories are won over seemingly insurmountable odds. If anyone knows the will of Her Son, She does! Let's step out in faith and do what She says. We want peace, not a nuclear holocaust! The diabolical and idolatrous lust for power and money in this age has brought about a crisis of faith and authority. There is almost total confusion in matters of faith and morals. The Evil One is enjoying a holiday!

Social justice, that is, the service of the common good, will not be realized until we stop trying to solve our world problems without the inspired teaching of the Church and the fulfillment of Our Lady's simple message. The best gift you can give Jesus on His birthday is to do what His Mother, the Queen of Peace, recommends you do. Merry Christmas and Happy New Year!"

Bishop D'Antonio again states in *Mary's Message* in December of 1986,

Last year my Christmas message concerned the apparitions of Our Lady, Queen of Peace, in Medjugorje, Yugoslavia, an event still under investigation by the Holy See.

On September 12, 1986, I was privileged to be present on two occasions while the visionaries Marija and Yakov conversed with the Mother of God. These apparitions have been taking place almost daily since June 24, 1981.

Once again, my message for the Christmas season is that of the Blessed Mother Mary. Her name means Beloved of God. She has made it clear that this will be Her last visions on earth. Scary, isn't it?

'Negotiations,' She declared, 'will not bring about world peace.' Only her Son's plan will work. And it couldn't be more simple. Briefly, what She requests is 'Prayer, prayer, prayer.' Any kind of prayer will do, provided it comes from the heart.

By praying, you and I will be enabled to 'do penance, go to monthly confession, fast on bread and water each Friday or on any other day of the week, or do without something else if we can't fast.' Let's do this and soon we'll discover what Mary means when She says, 'Convert yourself.' (Let this animate us: Mary does not want us to go hungry. Eat plenty of nourishing bread and drink plenty of water, on the day we decide to fast.)

The enclosed Miraculous Medal is a precious relic. I touched it to a medal first blessed by me, then by the Virgin Mary herself when She appeared to the seers. Mary explained that She would not bless religious articles unless first blessed by a priest. 'Whom you are not to criticize but pray for them,' She instructed.

The medal reminds us of what Mary's apparitions are all about; namely personal peace and world peace — a gift from Our Lord and Savior, Jesus Christ.

(xix) Most Rev. Johannes Joachim Degenhardt, Archbishop of Paderborn, Germany [quoted from *Medjugorje Gebetsaktion*, #23, 1992, p.33]

This statement is from the Archbishop's introduction to the celebration of the Eucharist at the Medjugorje Conference on November 7, 1991 in Paderborn.

MEDJUGORJE: We can only give astonished thanks for the awakening of faith.

On June 24 and 25 of this year the tenth anniversary of the first apparition of the Blessed Mother in Medjugorje could be celebrated. Around 180,000 people had come to this commemoration.

The celebration of this day has been called a minor miracle. That on this day believers from the entire world honored Jesus Christ and His Mother: that so many people come together in a political landscape threatened by civil war (generally in this year only relatively few pilgrims could come) that the four bishops celebrated together in the church in Medjugorje, among them the present bishop of Mostar — all this can be called miraculous.

Medjugorje lies in Bosnia-Hercegovina, near the border with Croatia which had and has to suffer the encroachments of the Serbians. In Bosnia different people have been living peacefully together as well as different religious communities: Catholic Croatians, Orthodox Serbs, Moslems from Montenegro and Albanians. Perhaps here too Mary's effectiveness for peace can be experienced.

Over ten years ago in Medjugorje Mary's first apparition took place before the children and young people who have since grown up. Then began an awakening of faith, first with the visionaries themselves. Their life from then on was monopolized by Mary. Their faith was challenged, strengthened and became completely alive and capable of bearing witness. Unbelief and doubt from church officials, ridicule and scorn from acquaintances, pressure and persecution by the communist community authorities — all this could not confound their faith conviction.

The awakening of faith began to spread in the village of Medjugorje. Whoever has been there and has experienced how most of the inhabitants have received Mary's call, how their lives in many ways has been stamped anew by faith, how by conversion, prayer, penance and celebration together of the Holy Mass, but also by a life of Christian love and readiness to serve in all areas of life, all give witness to their new life in faith. He can only give astonished thanks for the awakening of faith that he can come to know.

Continually, the effects of Mary's apparitions in Medjugorje spread farther abroad. Pilgrims came from the surrounding area, from all of Yugoslavia, from south and central Europe, from east, west and northern Europe, from overseas, indeed from the entire world. Finally there were almost 2 million in 1990, until, because of the political and military events of this year and interruption had to occur....We want...to ask Mary, the Queen of Peace, for her help, that peace in the world and peace in the Church be preserved in truth and love.

This second statement by the Rev. Johannes Joachim Degenhardt, Archbishop of Paderborn, comes from the diocesan newspaper of the Archdiocese of Paderborn, *"Der Dom"*, "MEDJUGORJE — Impulse of Renewal and of Christian Life", #9, of March 3, 1991.

In a remote corner of the world, in a tiny village in Herzegovina, something has moved, since which the entire Christian world has held its breath. For ten years now a stream of pilgrims and visitors has flowed towards Medjugorje, where several children — since then grown up — assert the Blessed Mother has appeared to them with messages for the entire world. A mountain of questions is piling up in the face of this "phenomenon of millions". The number of pilgrims has reached those of Fatima and Lourdes. Is there mass hysteria in progress here? What yearnings are at work here? Varying press reports produce more confusion. Helpful here is the response which Cardinal Ratzinger gives to the question concerning competent Church judgment: "One of our criteria here is to separate the viewpoint of the actual or presumed 'supernaturality' of the apparition from that of its spiritual fruit. The pilgrimages of old Christendom often concentrated on places about which our modern critical spirit would sometimes be dismayed, precisely with what concerns the 'scientific correctness" of the tradition linked to them. This does not hinder those pilgrimages from being fruitful, beneficial, salutary and important for the life of the Christian people.'

The fact in Medjugorje is that very many people have come, in some way, to this place — often half-curiously as a side trip from the Adriatic Sea; and there they have the surprising experience that deep springs of religious life break out in them. They see their own lives, the lives of their fellow men and of the Church in a whole new light. They come back to their home communities, share their experience there and would like to bring it in, which is often hard then, because they run up against misunderstanding and rejection. Can it be said in a few sentences what this awakening experienced there consists of?

The first is the experience of a living faith. Simple sentences of the Gospel, which perhaps have been heard for a long time, begin all of a sudden to radiate forth in a new light. Is it the simplicity of the countryside and its inhabitants which brings the sentences out of the Bible to light again and somehow makes them tangible?

Just as in the great classical pilgrim shrines, there is going on in Medjugorje the call to a renewal of life, to purification and conversion. The human being knows himself to be accepted, even in his guilt and sinful compulsion. In going around with the many pilgrims at the village, he experiences a lifestyle that is uncomplicated. He experiences that Christianity is attractive and can be lived. When he goes to confession — and most of them do this — this experience becomes intensified, completely as though he himself were being addressed and accepted and freed from old complexes, from guilt and failure. Medjugorje has since become the greatest confessional in the world. Priests who hear confessions there, experience movingly in their own bodies the workings of grace. A peculiar power of attraction goes out from the — usually overfilled — Eucharistic celebrations in the church or in the pilgrim place behind the choir room of the church. People assemble even long before and devote themselves to prayer. With this a great colorfulness and variety of the most different groups and people from all over the world becomes conspicuous. People move, they stand and walk and kneel, just as they are accustomed to at home. Americans come in odd attire, but still all know they are assembled and one in prayer. People who have not prayed any more for a long time experience how they can pray without difficulty for hours on end. Praying the rosary is not experienced as a burden, but rather as a give and take of call and response in deep community. The celebration of the Eucharist and adoration often draw on into the night. And finally one sees small groups praying around the church or everywhere in the area. Then, at home, in one's quarters with the Croatian hosts, it comes to long religious conversations. Everyone experiences that it is possible to speak openly about interior experiences otherwise so carefully guarded. The countryside invites one to long walks, ultimately even to the strenuous Way of the Cross up Krizevac and up the "Mount of the Apparitions." Everywhere are praying, talking and meditating people.

Among the most unforgettable impressions belong the fasting and the simplicity of the way of life. In Medjugorje nothing is organized and little is planned, and therefore everything goes so well. All of a sudden, one has an indescribable amount of time. Especially the fasting leads to an experience of newness of a spiritual strengthening and a clarity of knowledge. And somehow one knows himself to be accepted into the work of a world- encompassing spiritual renewal. Especially a part of this is peace, which holds its place at the center of the message of Medjugorje. Each of the pilgrims there experiences it vividly 'before the place' — from the people, from the surroundings, from the sense of lightness and the budding joy in his own heart. Does this new awakening that is being experienced at this place admit of being transferred? The many prayer groups being established all over in all the world confirm the 'invitation to freedom' as it is called in a filmed report by Hans Schotte on the events. This invitation seems to apply to the entire Church!"

(xx) **Bishop Joseph Devine**, Motherwell, England [quoted from a sermon at evening Mass in St. James, Spanish Place, in London on June 25]

Conversion, prayer and penance. They are the very stuff of the Gospel. That same trinity is also the core of the message of Our Lady in the apparitions which have been ascribed to Her in the modern era. There is nothing new in them. That is the guarantee of their authenticity. It is also the badge of their relevance for the Church today....

But looking around the world order, it is not the advance of peace which we see. Quite the reverse. So here we see a peace which has to be won for the world, a peace which has to be sought, a peace which has to be prayed for and paid for if a calamity is to be averted.

That is my understanding of Our Lady under the title of Queen of Peace, which title has been associated with recent happenings in Medjugorje. It is a peace which is yet to be, and only will be through a communal turning back to conversion, prayer and penance. But that turning back is nothing other than going to the very heart of the Gospel. It is the very stuff of the Christian life.

(xxi) **Bishop Wilhelm Egger**, Bolzano-Bressanone, Italy ("Pastoral Directions for Marian Devotion" released by his diocese on October 7, 1990 [quoted from *Medjugorje Gebetsaktion*, #21, 1991, p.26]

The message aims at the renewal of the individual, the Church and the world. It is a call to prayer and penance," writes the bishop and he states that Medjugorje "has become for many people a place of prayer and conversions.

(xxii) Bishop Carl A. Fisher, Los Angeles, California, U.S.A. [Interview with Fr. Richard Foley, *Medjugorje Messenger*]

Bishop Fisher is a handsome, alert looking man in his early 40's. We met over coffee in the Medjugorje parish house and had the pleasure of Fr. Slavko's company for part of the time. That was in August 1988. *The bishop began by telling us how delighted he had been to receive, only a day or two before, a special blessing on his pilgrimage from the Holy Father, accompanied by a warm hand-clasp.*

The Los Angeles prelate fully accepts Medjugorje by reason of the massive supporting evidence. Meanwhile, though, he submits his judgment in advance to whatever decision the Church arrives at in the matter. Accordingly, he came as a private pilgrim. Not until Medjugorje receives the stamp of public approval by the Church will bishops be authorized to lead official pilgrimages there.

For the record, Bishop Fisher has expressly asked me to assure our readers that he fully endorses all the positive impressions expressed about Medjugorje in our previous issue by his English episcopal colleague, Bishop Thomas McMahon of Brentwood.

Our Mother's Image
One of the particular things that struck the American prelate about Medjugorje is that it projects such a fresh and winning image of Our Lady herself. She comes across there, in St. Teresa's phrase, "more as Mother than as Queen." That is to say, she inspires us all the more effectively to draw closer to her Son precisely because she shows herself, through the visionaries, to be so tenderly maternal, human, sweet, gentle, understanding and approachable.

Accent on Youth

Another aspect of Medjugorje that particularly appealed to Bishop Fisher is its accent on youth. To begin with, Mary appears to young visionaries as a beautiful teenager herself. And Medjugorje's amazing appeal to youth finds eloquent expression in the instant magnetism it somehow exercises over young hearts, stirring their faith, inspiring them to pray, leading them to be Eucharist-minded, and, in not a few cases, raising them to the very heights of sacrifice and service.

Doubtless this wonderful Medjugorje quality promotes the zealous young Church leader to project exciting prospects of this kind on to the Los Angeles scene itself, where young people tend to be particularly exposed to hedonism and the subtle seductions of drugs and sensuality. It's just a matter of bringing Medjugorje's mighty charism to bear on them with its power to touch young lives and set them on fire with the love that burns in the hearts of Jesus and Mary.

Starlight for Priests

His Lordship was also very impressed by Medjugorje's remarkable influence over priests. For there the Mother of God is wont to give her priestly sons some really starlight gifts, inspiring and consoling them, giving them a fresh vision of holiness and apostolate, letting them see, as never before, what a privilege it is to share in her Divine Son's priesthood and bring His treasures of truth and sacramental grace to precious human souls.

As for the sacramental grace that flows through Confession, Bishop Fisher, like every other pilgrim, was amazed to see how copiously it does so in Medjugorje, where scores of priests sit in the open air and dispense the sacrament to long queues of penitents.

Healing and Signs

This practice, as we know, is but the local implementation of Our Lady's directive that everyone should go to Confession at least once a month — a practice which she has, as it were, prescribed as *medicine for the healing of the whole Western Church.*

Like every other pilgrim, too, His Lordship was amazed by reports of Medjugorje's so-called "secondary signs" — spinning sun, rosaries turning to gold, Our Lady's form replacing the stone cross, etc. — that are an ongoing and dramatic feature of this altogether extraordinary place. And he well sees their point — the point that has been made by Our Lady to the visionaries; these signs are meant to authenticate her apparitions and impress on us the burning urgency of her message to contemporary mankind.

(xxiii) Archbishop Patrick Flores, San Antonio, Texas [quoted from remarks made in Medjugorje in August, 1989, reported by *Message de paix*, Montreal, November-December 1989]

The Archbishop was accompanied by two auxiliary bishops, and reports his dialogue with John Paul II in January, 1989:

I said to him, "Your Holiness, numerous persons from my diocese go to Medjugorje. I did not permit nor forbid them. What should I do?"

The Pope answered me, 'Let the people go there. They pray there.'

Encouraged by this response, I said to him, "But they are inviting me to accompany them in the month of August.'

The Pope answered, 'Go, and pray for me.'

It is thus that I find myself here in Medjugorje with the blessing of the Pope.

(xxiv) Bishop Lawrence Graziano, O.F.M., San Miguel, El Salvador [*Medjugorje: An Affirmation and Defense* by Fr. Albert J. Hebert, p. 103]

Bishop Lawrence Graziano, O.F.M., former Ordinary of San Miguel, El Salvador, in November 1989 spent a week there. He has no doubts about the authenticity of the apparitions and would like to live in Medjugorje and minister to the pilgrims. However, he said it was more important to spread the message at home (which, for this bishop in exile, is currently Mt. Vernon, NY.) [*Poughkeepsie Journal*, April 1990]

(xxv) Archbishop Philip M. Hannan, New Orleans, Louisiana, [quoted from *Clarion Herald*, October 16, 1986, 'Fruits of Medjugorje Message Bring Good to World']

I cannot heal; only God can. I need your prayers and sacrifices to help me.

Please pray to Jesus. I am His Mother and I intercede for you with Him. But all prayer goes to Jesus. I will help. I will pray, but everything does not depend only on Me. It depends also on your strength, the strength of those who pray."

The only word I wish to say is 'conversion' to the whole world. I am saying this to you to tell everybody. I ask only for conversions. Be ready for everything and be converted. Give up everything that goes against conversion.

These are some of the messages given to a group of youths at Medjugorje, a very small village in Yugoslavia. The messages began on June 24, 1981, and have been occurring regularly ever since that date. They are extraordinary in their length of duration over such a span of years and their regularity in occurrence, almost daily.

The messages began as two young girls of the group (Mirjana and Ivanka) were taking their usual walk on that June 24.

The Blessed Mother spoke to them twice on that day, once when they were together and a second time when they were with a friend, Milka, as they went with her to chase home sheep in the fields near the village. Since then, the Blessed Mother has appeared and spoken to them on a regular basis in a room next to the parish church in Medjugorje.

The threshold questions about such apparitions are: Are these youths normal? Are the messages in conformity with Church doctrine and practice?

Everyone attests that the youths are normal, most of them average intelligence, one intellectually gifted (Mirjana Dragicivic). A sample of their conversations with priests indicates this normality.

Fr. Kraljevic asked Ivanka, a pretty girl now 21 years old, how she responded to the known 'wish of the Blessed Mother' that the girls enter a convent.

Ivanka replied, 'She told us it is Her wish that we entered a convent, but only those who have such a wish. She does not want anyone to disgrace the faith and the Church...To tell you the truth, as I feel right now, I do not want to enter the convent. I can live a Christian life, the same as a nun, raising children.'

Furthermore, the lives of the youths since the first apparitions have shown complete dedication to Christ — assisting at Mass every day, fasting on bread and water at least once a week, praying at length each day, performing their normal duties in school or at work, receiving regularly the Sacrament of Reconciliation.

As a priest remarked, 'What could induce them to act this way for five years, receiving no worldly compensation, unless the apparitions are authentic?'

In addition, the whole parish, has been revitalized. Almost every parishioner has become extraordinarily devout — attending daily

Mass, fasting, praying, standing in line to go to confession. Their devotion is Christ-centered.

Regarding the application of their devotion to bring peace to age-old antipathies among the Catholics, Orthodox and Moslems, Mirjana Dragicivic said, "The Madonna always stresses that there is but one God, and that people have enforced unnatural separation. One cannot truly believe, be a true Christian, if he does not respect other religions as well.'

Of course, the Church has not officially endorsed nor condemned the activities and claims of the youths in Medjugorje. But one can legitimately ask, if these be the fruits of the apparitions — peace, conversion, praying, fasting — can there be anything but good in it?

(xxvi) **Bishop Seamus Hegarty**, Raphoe, Ireland [quoted from *Medjugorje Messenger* in June, 1989, after a private pilgrimage to Medjugorje. There have been over 16,000 Catholic clergy who have been there to date.]

I had heard much about the Medjugorje phenomenon, and, as things turned out, managed to go there myself for five days in July, 1987. I went, of course, as a private pilgrim, a private person.

I couldn't help being enormously impressed by everyone, both local parishioners and those who visit Medjugorje from all over Europe and overseas. I also got a very clear impression that here in Medjugorje you are dealing with a center of prayer, of penance, and of reconciliation.

'By their fruits you shall know them.' Here the fruits are so manifest, so clear and impressive, both in Medjugorje itself and among those who return home after a pilgrimage, that they simply cannot be ignored.

Among many people from my own diocese that had been to Medjugorje I noticed the ongoing, positive results in relation both to their personal and family life. Thus I felt simply obliged to go to the place and find out for myself the source, the explanation, of this experience, this tremendous manifestation of faith, this high and exemplary Christian way of life.

Accord with Gospel Message
I have read the messages the Mother of God is said to be giving to the visionaries. And what I have seen and heard tells me that there is a strong accord, a parallel, between these messages and what the

Gospels say about the teaching of Christ. The emphasis lies very strongly on prayer, fasting, reconciliation and peace — themes that occur over and over again in Scripture. One thing is clear about the Medjugorje messages; they contain nothing that contradicts the Church's official teaching, which is based on Scripture as on a foundation. Here the emphasis is on prayer and on how to pray — that is, with more giving of ourselves and intensity, and new methods of prayer — prayer not only in words, but as something lived. But what is likewise emphasized in the messages is fasting. It has a long Church tradition behind it. Of recent years, however, it has fallen into disuse on a wide scale. Now it has been revived as a challenge that young people in particular, face up to in a dramatic way.

My most outstanding experiences in Medjugorje was that of hearing Confessions. One day I spent three hours doing so. And I am sure that during those three hours I heard more Confessions of the kind that are basic and come from the depths of the heart than during all the 21 years of my priesthood. I could not help being moved by the workings of grace — the clear workings of Grace, and also by the clear acceptance of the call to penance and reconciliation which expressed themselves so unmistakably in the quality of the Confessions I heard. So this experience will ever remain my most impressive and abiding Medjugorje memory.

Radiate Peace to the World

We recognize that in Medjugorje we are dealing with a genuine call to peace, and that peace is a divine gift for which we must pray. On the basis of what I myself observed in Medjugorje, and which everyone that has been there likewise observes, I believe that we are going to experience a radiation of this atmosphere of peace which has its origin, its center, in Medjugorje, thereupon extending itself over the entire world.

Prayer Groups and Rosary

Many prayer groups have been formed as a direct result of a pilgrimage to Medjugorje, an outcome of the religious experience people gain there and which they thereupon keep up and apply to their own life circumstances among their families and communities. Beyond doubt, the Medjugorje phenomenon has had a particular success in everything to do with fostering prayer. Not only do people pray more than is normal in parishes, but the quality of their prayer is particularly impressive.

The rosary, as we could expect, is one of the most important forms of prayer practiced by Medjugorje groups. What has strongly impressed me is that in its recitation the Biblical dimension of the mysteries is brought out so prominently.

Come and Join Us Father

As regards the Church — the official Church — it cannot afford to ignore this development. Bishops and priests must encourage these prayer groups, and, in my opinion, must also be present at them to give leadership and due advice and spiritual orientation. It must also be said that the laity who, with good intentions and devotion, come together to pray deserve every help and direction they can get from the clergy. While it is true the presence of a priest is not absolutely necessary at prayer meetings, it is nonetheless most desirable in order that exaggerations and unrealistic or mistaken ideas and explanations may be avoided.

It would be a great pity if Medjugorje's central message (prayer, fasting, reconciliation and peace) became obscured in any way or if excessive emphasis came to be placed on signs and wonders. Accordingly, the presence at these prayer meetings of the official Church in the person of the priest is very much to be desired."

(xxvii) Bishop Paolo Hnilica S.J., Titular Bishop of Rusado [*Madre di Dio*, 1986/4]

After my third visit in these places, I was able to arrange for a little more time to speak with the visionaries and also with the people who live close to them in everyday life. I wanted to examine and understand what reasons the one who talks against Medjugorje and is opposed to it had for doing so.

I am convinced that this is a case of slandering.

These children are not manipulated. They are simple and sincere. I see a supernatural aspect in these events. Morally, they force us to treat them very seriously. Upon my conscience, I must come to the conclusion that the voice of God is speaking with power at Medjugorje. Crowds of people go there to manifest by their piety their profound belief in those events.

Here at Medjugorje, something extraordinary is going on. Although these events are taking place in a country, small and not well known, they are happening within the Church and in the interest of all mankind.

We must not and we cannot take the gifts of God lightly.

(xxviii) Bishop Murilo Krieger, Auxiliary Bishop of Florianopolis, Santa Caterina, Brazil, (speech delivered in Medjugorje, January, 1988)

Dear friends, brothers and sisters. We three bishops and 33 priests will travel tomorrow (Friday, January 22, 1988) from Medjugorje to Rome. On Sunday we will be arriving in Brazil where our communities await us. We do not wish to leave this parish community without demonstrating in this way the gratitude and joy which is filling our hearts. We thank you for the friendly and family-like way in which we have been received by your prayers and fasts you have offered for us to complete this retreat well. Coming from Brazil we had only one desire: to come to Medjugorje and spend a week in 'Mary's School'. With Jesus, our teacher, we wanted to live his experience as Son and Disciple with His own Mother, the Virgin of Nazareth. We never dreamed that so many and such beautiful graces were awaiting us. Our retreat really began that day in Rome when we participated in General Audience on Wednesday (January 13) with the Holy Father. He told us particularly to affirm our faith and consecrate the duties we received by our priestly ordination, and indeed, to do it right at the tomb of St. Peter. The following day, because we wanted to live the spirit of the Marian Year, we went as pilgrims to St. Mary Major Basilica where we renewed our dedication to Jesus through Mary. On Friday, January 15 we had a second great joy. We concelebrated with Pope John Paul II in his private chapel. We shall never forget that wonderful and touching moment. After the mass the Pope greeted us and, thanking us for concelebrating, blessed our retreat.

Today, near the end of our visit in Medjugorje, we can announce with joy that we have indeed participated in a very blessed retreat. With joy and gratitude we recall our meetings with the priests who work here, their meditations and experiences, so profitable for us.

Equally grateful are we for the witness of faith, love and Marian devotion which your parishioners have given us here. Our meetings with your young people from the prayer groups was a true schooling in the gospel for us. Brotherly meetings with the pilgrims and the evening liturgy as well as our hikes to the Apparition Mountain and the Cross Mountain were unforgettable moments of prayer.

We have learned from our Mother and Teacher that in similar situations we must do as she did. 'treasure all these things and reflect on them in our hearts' (Lk 2:19). From the cross, Jesus, the Great and Eternal High Priest, gave us His Mother as our Mother. Imitating John the apostle and evangelist, we wish now to take her home with us to

Brazil, to our parish communities. We are all her children — parishioners, priests and pilgrims.

Let us continue together in the Eucharist and in prayer. The Saturday (January 23) when we shall visit the tomb of St. Peter again to end our retreat, we shall carry you in our hearts. At the same time while we continue our own 'Magnificat' — for the Lord has also done great things for us, we pray the Queen of Peace to bless you today and always. SHALOM! THANK YOU! HVALA!

Also from Bishop Krieger: "I spoke with the Holy Father on the 24th of February, 1990, ... I told him I had been to Medjugorje three times and that I was going to return the following week. He said simply, 'Medjugorje is a great center of spirituality!' Bishop Murilo Krieger of Santa Caterina, Brazil, said he later asked if he could give the Pope's blessing to the visionaries, and the Pope granted his request. [*National Catholic Register*, April 29, 1990]

(xxix) **Bishop John Magee**, Former Secretary to Pope John Paul II
[Fr. Bob Bedard, *Medjugorje Reflections*, p. 85]

Bishop John Magee, formerly the Holy Father's secretary, told David Little of Canada that, concerning the apparitions, "without question they are fully genuine."

(xxx) **Bishop Myles McKeon**, West Australia [quoted in *M. Messenger*, October, 1988, "From Australia With Love"]

An ever-increasing number of people in Australia, the USA, Hong Kong, Ireland and elsewhere kept asking me what I thought of Medjugorje. To which I would always reply; 'I don't know as I've read anything about it. How can I possibly speak about something of which I am ignorant?' Then the thought occurred, 'I'm going to Medjugorje to see, hear and experience it for myself.' Two priests belonging to my diocese had gone there earlier and were tremendously impressed.

Having now been myself, I can say by way of personal reaction, 'I love Medjugorje!'

What, then, were my impressions of Medjugorje? What do I tell people when asked about this new pilgrim-shrine? Naturally I must go along with the Church and declare that we await her official verdict, the conclusion reached by the commission that is investigating everything — as was the case at Lourdes, Fatima and Knock.

In the meantime, however, everybody is free to express his own opinion. Mine is as follows: I went to Medjugorje and observed the church jampacked and overflowing at every Mass.

We complain nowadays that people have stopped going to Mass and confession; also, that they do not pray any longer.

. But here in Medjugorje I saw the restoration of all those things whose neglect in many parts of the world has caused us sadness. I saw the wonderful crowds of people streaming in to the church — where they pray for three hours in the evening. Yes, the people remain there, for they want to pray. Indeed, even after three hours they stay on.

What I further observed in Medjugorje is that the whole ensemble is Eucharistic. And when anything is Eucharistic, it's bound to be good. When you see people coming back to the Sacrament of Reconciliation, it's terrific. And when you see young and old (and people belonging to every age group) saying the rosary, then you realize that Our Lady is clearly present. Indeed, one senses the presence here of Jesus and Mary.

God will bless everyone coming to Medjugorje and all who pray as is customary there. I say in conclusion, Thanks be to God and Mary for everything.

(xxxi) **Bishop Thomas McMahon**, Brentwood Diocese, London, England and Essex County, England, recently visited Medjugorje and said this about it in an interview with Fr. Richard Foley, S. J. and quoted in *Medjugorje Messenger*, October, 1988.

Bishop McMahon is surprisingly youthful in appearance and his manner in most gracious. So impressed was he by his visit to Medjugorje in mid-August that he now speaks with great enthusiasm about the place. This also explains why at very short notice, and notwithstanding a fearsome workload, he readily obliged me with this interview.

The Bishop is well aware, of course, that many other prelates from all over the world have been on private pilgrimage to Medjugorje. As for priests, they go there in their thousands; the present count is well over 13,000. And lay people go there literally in their millions, the total now being somewhere in the region of 13 million.

Bishop McMahon is also well aware that all private pilgrims must be prepared to accept whatever pronouncement the Church finally and officially makes about Medjugorje's supernatural claims. This could well be a matter of years, even decades. In the meantime, however, we

are perfectly entitled to believe privately in Medjugorje and, correspondingly, go there on private pilgrimage.

SIGNPOST TO CANA

What, then, were the Bishop of Brentwood's main impressions of
the sleepy little Yugoslav village that has already become a Mariopolis,
a City of Mary? The sincerity and genuineness about everyone and
everything struck him particularly, not least in the visionaries. On two
occasions he attended the apparitions (now held in the choir loft).
And he had a lengthy chat/interview with Marija in her home.

As for the general doctrine and messages coming to us from Our
Lady via the visionaries, they all square perfectly with Church teaching
and have deep Scriptural roots.

The bishop also spoke admiringly of the Franciscan staff and their
wonderful zeal and patience in coping with the pilgrim multitudes.
These throng the place day and night. And in the jampacked church,
where there's hardly even standing room and the summer heat is
oppressive, they display deep devotion during those rather lengthy
liturgies.

The 'Eucharistic dimension' was another thing that impressed
Bishop McMahon. It also indicates, he said, that Our Lady is here
directing us toward her Son — as she always does. 'Do whatever He
tells you.' The counsel she gave at Cana virtually encapsulates everything Medjugorje teaches us. Its message is simply an echo of her Son's
Gospel. For it urges us to make God paramount in our lives, to turn
away from sin, to cultivate deep faith, to pray more and better, to
practice penance (including fasting), and to promote divine peace not
only in our conscience but at every level of our social environment.

SPIRITUAL RICHES

Bishop McMahon told me that, like many other pilgrims, he has
received the quite special grace of desiring to pray more and be truly
prayerful, not merely content with 'saying prayers.' And he stressed the
value of this grace for priests in particular. As for the prayer groups
that Medjugorje has inspired all over, the bishop spoke warmly about
them. Besides encouraging people to pray in the way that best suits
them, they help them to love God more deeply and make themselves
open to His will.

Medjugorje's power to attract young people was another thing
that greatly impressed Bishop McMahon. So many of them, he said,
have grown disenchanted with the institutional Church and heavily

organized religion. 'Nevertheless,' he went on, 'they are hungry and thirsty for the things of the Spirit — and somehow, there in Medjugorje, they find an answer.'

OUR LADY'S URGENT BUSINESS

He also speaks about what he described as 'an amazing sight...one of the wonders of Medjugorje namely, the long lines of priests seated in the open air and the even longer queues of penitents awaiting their turn for confession.'

Like Cardinal Tomasek and other observers, the Bishop of Brentwood recognizes Medjugorje's potential as a dynamic source of renewal for the whole Church, all the way from its faith and prayer to its credal orthodoxy and sacramental life.

He further pointed out the profound significances of Our Lady's warning about fallen angels and the terrible reality of eternal damnation. Nor could anything be more timely. Our world has to a large extent lost its sense of sin and its consequences in the world to come. In this present world, too, large-scale sinfulness and abandonment of God do not go unpunished. Hence Our Lady of Medjugorje calls this 'the time of her admonitions.' Hence, too, the 'sense of urgency' that lies within her message. World peace is threatened as never before. And nobody is more concerned about this than the Medjugorje Madonna, who comes there under the express title of Queen of Peace.

(xxxii) Bishop Angelico Melotto

Here (in Medjugorje) I had experiences which greatly impressed me; I want to remain in Mary's school.

Comments made by Bishop Angelico Melotto at the conclusion of a November, 1988 retreat with Archbishop Franic, Bishop Chinole of Malawi (Central Africa) and 136 priests in Medjugorje *Queen of Peace Journal*, March 1989

(xxxiii) Bishop Gratian Mundadan, C.M.I., Bijnor Providence, India, visited Medjugorje in September, 1989, and related his experience there in his Christmas letter (*Mary's Mantle*, Winter 1990)

Still another visit I made — a visit to Medjugorje. That again was a great EXPERIENCE. I don't say anything about the apparitions of Our Lady to the children — The Church has not yet pronounced on it. What impressed me was the crowds attracted to this place. And they come to

PRAY and DO PENANCE. Hours and hours, without any fatigue or tiredness, they pray, day and night without any fatigue or tiredness; they pray, day and night without any difference; they climb the hills of apparition in prayer, meditation, on the passion of Our Lord. Their fervor left unforgettable impressions on me. I heard several stories of real conversion and spiritual awakening. Unwillingly, as from the Holy Land, I returned as my duty demanded me to come back to the diocese. But wanted to go again. All these confirming my conviction that Our Blessed Mother has taken in Her hands the task of converting the world to the Lord — The ERA of THE MOTHER!

We have just celebrated Christmas, the happy memory of the birth of Jesus who brought peace, love and joy for every human being. We must however reflect on the many millions of our brothers and sisters who have not experienced these blessings. We must pray that the world's systems be reorganized so that every single human being has a chance to enjoy these blessings. Many changes have occurred in the past year, events no one could have foretold or expected to happen so quickly. The Eastern block is cracking, the walls are crumbling. Generals resign, governments are brought down as people demand their freedom. This freedom will enable mankind to enjoy the blessings of the Incarnation. All these events began during the Marian Year. They are the result of the powerful intercession of Mary.

(xxxiv) Archbishop George H. Pearce S.M., Suva,Fiji [*Medjugorje: An Affirmation and Defense* by Fr. Albert J. Hebert, p. 105]

Archbishop George H. Pearce, S.M., retired archbishop of Suva Fiji, but currently very active in assisting the Bishop of Providence, RI, has been to Medjugorje twice. He firmly believes in the authenticity of the apparitions and message.

(xxxv) Bishop Ratko Peric, Mostar-Duvno, Bosnia [From the video *Medjugorje Oggi, La Voce Della Speranza*, filmed in November, 1992, — excerpt printed in *Echo of Medjugorje*, February, 1993, p.8]

Msgr. Peric, coadjutor of Mostar-Duvo (the diocese to which Medjugorje belongs) recently succeeded Msgr. Paovo Zanic who retired due to his age. In answer to the question, "Do you believe in Our Lady's apparitions in Medjugorje?", Bishop Peric replied, "I feel immense gratitude towards the Lord. He is always capable of communicating His messages to us men, in particular through His mother."

(xxxvi) Bishop Michael Pfeifer, San Angelo, Texas, U.S.A. [Excerpts from pastoral letter, *The Gospel, Mary and Medjugorje*, August 5, 1988]

The call of Medjugorje, as presently understood, is as old as the Gospel itself. There is no 'new way' to salvation being offered in the messages. There is rather a new reminder, a new call to be faithful to the Good News of Christ. If Mary is appearing at Medjugorje, then all must heed her message, because she, as the Mother of God, is the Mother of truth and goodness. If she is not appearing, then it would seem the messages still have a divine source and should receive our careful attention. In either case, Medjugorje cannot be disregarded. While it is easy to fall into a 'Medjugorje mania', which should be avoided, to say nothing is happening there is to deny the living, prayerful witness of hundreds of thousands who have gone there. There is something other-worldly taking place at Medjugorje. There seems to be a special Divine presence there, motivating and inspiring the millions who visit this village to have a new love of God, and to strengthen and renew their commitment to live out the Gospel of Christ.

(xxxvii) Bishop Francis A. Quinn of Sacramento, California [quoted in the February 16, 1989 *Catholic Standard Times*]

The spiritual energy among the townspeople and the pilgrims is indisputable. Something is happening in Medjugorje!...The visionaries appear to be genuinely convinced of the truth of what they report. And their account of Mary's conversations are well within the traditional teaching of the Catholic Church. Vicka, 24, possesses a very attractive, outgoing personality. What impressed me first was the naturalness of the situation and the casual manner and attire of the visionary. ...At approximately 5:40 p.m. during the glorious mysteries (of the rosary), Ivan turned toward the picture of Our Lady against the north wall, knelt and could be heard intermittently conversing quietly. There are as many as 1,500 people crowded in the church below, but during this four — or five minute interval, the recitation of the rosary stops and there is total silence. I filled those moments with petitions for the clergy and religious and laity of our diocese, for my family, for all the deceased who need our prayers, for all the needs of the Diocese of Sacramento.

(xxxviii) Archbishop Jan Sokol, Metropolitan Archbishop of Slovakia [Quoted from *Medjugorje Gebetsaktion,* #17, 1990, p.24]

At the official invitation of the archbishop and Slovakian Metropolitan, Jan Sokol, as well as the diocesan bishops of Kosice, Alojz Tkac and the Greek Catholic diocesan bishop Jan Hirka, the visionary, Ivan Dragicevic, of Medjugorje visited Slovakia; and this means that during his stay the apparitions of the Blessed Mother took place there daily.

Yesterday Ivan had the apparition in the presence of the Archbishop of Trnava, the Metropolitan Jan Sokol (who has already been in Medjugorje several times). It was a deeply moving experience.

(xxxix) Bishop Sylvester W. Treinen, Boise, Idaho, U.S.A. [Homily at the 1989 National Conference on Medjugorje, University of Notre Dame, May 14, 1989]

On the way to Rome, Bishop Thomas Connolly of Baker and I stopped to visit Medjugorje in Yugoslavia. Whether or not Mary is seen by the youths there, God is seen in the lives of all who live there and come as pilgrims. Conversion of lives to God is the wish of Mary for all of us. Conversions are visible in Medjugorje. I sat and knelt six feet away from Marija, one of the seers, though now 28 years old, a very normal looking and acting lady. It was an inspiring visit.

During our visit ad limina, I had 15 minutes of private conversation with the Pope. I told him then, 'I am just returning from Medjugorje. Some beautiful things are taking place there.' The Pope answered: 'Yes, it is good for the pilgrims to go to Medjugorje, to pray and to do penance. It is good.'

It is first hand; I heard it with my ears.

(xl) Archbishop Gregory Yong, on the occasion of the 7th anniversary of the Apparition at Medjugorje, in his homily in the "Cathedral of Singapore" says this about Medjugorje [*The Tablet,* July 30, 1988]

Halfway around the world from the site in Medjugorje, Yugoslavia, where the Virgin Mary is said to appear, the reports of Catholics who visited the scene has sparked renewed devotion in Singapore, say local church officials.

Churches are now packed at Sunday and daily Masses, including lunchtime Masses at the Cathedral of the Good Shepherd, according to Archbishop Gregory Yong of Singapore. The archbishop made the observation at a Mass June 25 — the anniversary of the alleged first apparition at Medjugorje seven years ago.

Never have we seen the Church packed with so many daily Masses as now. We are seeing the fruits of what is happening (i.e. in Medjugorje).

4. CARDINAL FRANJO KUHARIC'S CONSECRATION OF CROATIA TO THE QUEEN OF PEACE

As noted in the **Introduction,** on January 15, 1992, Cardinal Franjo Kuharic, Primate of Croatia and President of the Yugoslavian Bishops' Conference, in community with the members of the Croatian Bishops Conference, and 10,000 of the faithful, including a representative of the national president and members of the Croatian Parliament, consecrated Croatia to the Immaculate Heart of Mary, [*Glas Koncila*, #4 of January 26, 1992]. In his consecration, Cardinal Kuharic addresses Mary as the Queen of Peace. As we know, this is the title by which Mary has described herself in Medjugorje. In his speech prior to the consecration, Cardinal Kuharic draws attention to this fact.

> *Many in the world believe that the Mother of God has established herself also in the highlands of Hercegovina, and as Queen of Peace has called in Medjugorje for conversion and peace!... Precisely in our century [Christ] has set a great sign in the Church — the sign of the heart of a Mother! In the age of great physical power, in a society brutalized by a scorn for God reaching even to the destruction of human beings, in times of heartless violence God reveals the power of the motherly heart!* **HE IS SENDING THE MOST HOLY VIRGIN MARY RIGHT INTO SUCH A TIME AND INTO SUCH A WORLD** *to draw people anew to the only Redeemer, Jesus Christ, through the maternal Heart!...* **In her messages in the Church and in the world the Blessed Virgin Mary calls Jesus' call to awareness:** *'The time is fulfilled, and the kingdom of God is at hand; repent and believe in the gospel.' (Mk. 1:15)...*

With this introduction we reprint below the consecration that is an inspiration to all children of Mary.

Most Holy Virgin, QUEEN OF PEACE! On this solemn day on which our Croatian homeland was recognized as a sovereign and independent state — and with this a new era in the history of the Croatian people and all the residents of Croatia begins **— we bishops of the Church in Croatia consecrate our present and our future to YOUR IMMACULATE HEART.** Our faithful predecessors named you *Mother most faithful and Advocate of Croatia.* This you have been through our entire difficult history! With deep confidence we beg you, be an intercessor for us with your Divine Son and our Redeemer, Jesus Christ, that in our days peace may abide and our hopes for everything good for individuals and the people may be fulfilled!

In these troubles that befall our people and all the citizens, from our whole heart, we give ourselves over to Your motherly Heart, in our families, between individual men and peoples. **Humble Handmaid of the Lord and QUEEN OF PEACE, ask for peace for us of the Heart of Your divine Son and our Redeemer, as he gives it — peace in truth and in love, peace in freedom and justice, peace with God and peace with men.**

We want to show ourselves worthy of this peace and humbly regret our personal sins, the sins of our families, all the sins against God's commandments in our people!

Merciful Mother, Refuge of sinners, ask of God for us the gifts of the Holy Spirit, that with His power He may change the thoughts of men and their hearts to good, to justice and to peace!

Comforter of the afflicted, in the name of the innocent blood that was shed and in the name of the tears of the One who was wounded and driven out, and in the name of the suffering of the Innocent One, we beg you, through your intercession with our heavenly Father, to request for your human children a firm faith and an unshakable hope! MAY THE DAYS OF OUR DIFFICULT TESTING BE SHORTENED AND GOD'S PEACE RADIATE UPON OUR HOMELAND AND IN THE WHOLE WORLD.

Blest Mother, pray for us! Amen!

5. WHAT LEADING CATHOLIC THEOLOGIANS HAVE SAID ABOUT MEDJUGORJE

In the Introduction we gave a sketch of three great Catholic thinkers, Cardinal-designate Hans Urs von Balthasar and Mariologists Rene Laurentin and Michael O'Carroll, who carried out painstaking investigations of Medjugorje and reached the firm conclusion that it is an authentic apparition of the Mother of God. In this chapter, we study excerpts from their writings on Medjugorje.

(i) Fr. Hans Urs von Balthasar

Fr. Hans Urs von Balthasar interviewed by Fr. Richard Foley S.J. [quoted in *C. Herald*, February, 1988]

SWISS BOUQUETS FOR MEDJUGORJE, A GIANT FIGURE IN THE WORLD OF CATHOLIC THEOLOGY IS CONVINCED WHEN IT COMES TO VISIONS IN YUGOSLAVIA

Medjugorje's theology rings true. I am convinced of its truth. And everything about Medjugorje is authentic, in a Catholic sense. What's happening there is so evident, so convincing.

Bouquets seldom come more glowing than this one presented to the extraordinary little 'world village' behind the Iron Curtain by the distinguished Swiss theologian, Fr. Hans Urs von Balthasar. He did so in the course of an interview he gave me recently.

Balthasar is a tall, gaunt man who wears his 80 years extremely lightly. What has long established him as a giant figure in the world of Catholic theology and culture is his profound learning combined with wide vision. Also he has a unique gift for marrying up modernity with tradition. It came as no surprise when, last year, the Holy Father awarded him the Paul VI prize for theology.

Balthasar is on close terms with the likes of Cardinal Ratzinger and Laurentin. It was another theological giant — Karl Rahner — who referred to what he called 'the breathtaking versality' of Balthsar's writings. Anybody wishing to discover their key elements is recommended to consult the *Van Balthasar Reader* (T T Clarke, Edin.)

His views on Medjugorje have been expressed in sundry articles and private letters, as well as in the interview alluded to earlier. To begin with, he emphasizes our liberty and right to go there — or anywhere else we choose — as private pilgrims; solely those pilgrimages organized at an official diocesan level have been vetoed by the Yugoslav hierarchy.

Balthasar told me that he, too, has come across any number of people, including priests and even prelates, who dismiss Medjugorje as anything from irrelevant to impossible, yet have not taken a really hard look at the evidence. And he agreed with my verdict on theological liberals, they are liberal enough to question the Mother of God's freedom to appear where, when, and to whom she likes, and over as long a period of time as she likes. Yet the ordinary faithful, he pointed out, see divine realities instantly and uncomplicatedly. This is thanks to their instinct for Heaven-sent truths; we refer to this technically as sensus fidelium. Not for nothing did Our Lord tell us that the Father is wont to reveal things to plain, ordinary folk that blinkered wiseacres missed by a mile.

For Balthasar, the clinching proof of Medjugorje's genuineness is in the quantity and quality of its fruits. By going there on pilgrimage, or simply through such contacts as books, videos, et cetera, countless thousands have received rich graces. These graces pertain to things like peace of mind, a deepening of faith, the desire to pray more, courage to fast once or even twice a week on bread and water (or hot drinks), the resolution to frequent the sacraments regularly. Incidentally, Balthasar noted how pastorally wise and opportune is Our Lady of Medjugorje's recommendation of frequent confession as the very instrument to sanctify and renew the contemporary Church.

But it is not on spiritual things alone, he reminds us that Medjugorje has a direct bearing. It warns us that the very destiny of mankind is at stake. A catastrophe overhangs our world, almost certainly in the shape of nuclear war. And where Medjugorje differs in this respect from Fatima, the Swiss theologian points out, is that here we are invited by the Mother of God to help prevent this horror through prayer and fasting.

Given that "fullness of faith" is a recurrent Balthasarian theme, it is not difficult to see why he accepts Medjugorje so wholeheartedly. For its message is thoroughly uncompromisingly orthodox. And it nourishes within us respect for the Church's divine authority. Nor could this be otherwise, seeing that the message comes from her whom Balthasar has styled "the mother and model of the Church, the immaculate Church; the heart and center of the Communion of Saints."

Another Balthasarian concept finds in Medjugorje a fresh and exciting expression. It is what he terms Theodramatik — 'the drama of love being played out between God and the world'.

It is an ongoing drama, this. The God of love has transformed Medjugorje into a theater of holiness of which the leading lady in the divine drama is teaching and helping multitudes of people to make her message the very guiding star of the pilgrimage of faith and their lifelong adventure into the grace of God and the God of grace.

Closely linked in Balthasar's theology with divine drama is the communication of God's revealed truth. There is truth aplenty in what Medjugorje tells us. Its message coincides and dovetails with what the trumpet voice of John the Baptist proclaimed in the Judean desert. In fact, the message of Medjugorje could be described as the Gospel according to Gospa (the Croatian word for Our Lady).

Finally, the Medjugorje mystery is shot through with divine beauty — another central idea in Balthasar's theology. Beauty is manifold in that remote little corner of Yugoslavia. It is in the hills, the fields, the stars that look down, the soft winds that blow across the plain. It is in the faces and hearts of those wonderful people who live there. It is in the faith and prayer of the pilgrim throngs. Above all, it is in the glorified humanity and maternal love of Mary. Her presence it is that permeates Medjugorje with God's better beauty — grace."

(ii) Fr. Rene Laurentin

[From *The Apparitions of the Blessed Virgin Mary*, Veritas Publications, Dublin, 1990, pp. 82-85]

Medjugorje (Yugoslavia): ongoing since 24 June 1981

On 24 June 1981, six young Croatians saw a silhouette on the hill of Crnica near the Franciscan parish of Medjugorje in the Croatian region of Hercegovina. They were at the foot of the hill (Podbrdo), but they did not dare climb up. On the following day four of the original group returned — Mirjana, Ivanka, Ivan and Vicka. Ivan Ivankovic and Milka Pavlovic were absent, but they were replaced by Milka's sister, Maria Pavlovic and ten-year old Jakov. The others were aged between fifteen and sixteen. On the second day they climbed the hill, saw the Virgin close up and began to converse with her. Since then, the *Gospa* (Croatian for Our Lady) appears to them every day. She is young, clothed in a bright, silver-grey garment, and has wavy black hair beneath a white veil. Around her head there is a circle of twelve stars. Her eyes are blue. She looks at them with extraordinary affection.

From 25 to 29 June the apparitions took place on the hill of Crnica which overlooks the hamlet where the visionaries live (Biakovici). However, the police soon made the hill out of bounds.

From 30 June the apparitions took place secretly in order to avoid the police, and gradually the church became the location. They occurred between the rosary and Mass in the presence of huge crowds of parishioners and pilgrims. To shield them from the curious, the visionaries were moved to a small adjoining changing-room cum sacristy which thus became the 'chapel of the apparitions'.

Initially the local bishop was favorably disposed. However, for reasons of local politics and, in particular, an ongoing row between himself and the Franciscans, he forbade the visionaries to use any premises adjoining the church. For this reason they transferred to the local presbytery. The move was somewhat to the detriment of the liturgical coherence of the event. In August 1987 the presbytery was also forbidden as a location by the bishop. Again a solution was difficult to find. Since then the apparitions take place in a more discreet fashion — in the home of each visionary or, if the visionaries are in the church for Mass, behind locked doors on the gallery with no witnesses.

Two of the first group of visionaries no longer see the apparition, having received the tenth and final secret from Our Lady — Mirjana at Christmas 1982 and Ivanka on 7 May 1985. The Virgin promised them an apparition once a year — on her birthday [18 March] for Mirjana and on the anniversary of the first apparition [25 June] for Ivanka.

The substance of the message was given on the first five days. It recalls the essence and urgency of the gospel — return to God through conversion, faith, prayer and fasting. Through these practices a divided world will gain peace and reconciliation.

This message is followed closely in the parish. There is no other parish in the world where so much prayer takes place. It is marked by crowded daily masses, personal prayer, recitations of the rosary and bread and water fasts every Wednesday and Friday. Many prayer groups have emerged which contribute to the building up of the faith.

Some of the reconciliations have been spectacular. The parish had been divided and in the 1940's violent quarrels between the hamlets of Biakovici and Medjugorje had led to armed fighting and deaths. 'Now we are all brothers,' say these former enemies.

There are ten well-kept secrets regarding the destiny of the world. They will be revealed in due course, three days before each of them is fulfilled. The visionaries would have us understand that many of the secrets have to do with the threats hanging over the world abandoned to sin and preparing its own destruction.

The 'secret' messages are somewhat problematic. They may well prove a disappointment because even the saints were mistaken in matters of prediction. It would be imprudent to accept these 'secrets' as gospel.

As regards the essence of the events, after seven years I, as an expert, am convinced. The fruits of holiness are admirable among the visionaries whose growth in spirituality is astounding and has not diminished their natural simplicity, in the parish and surrounding area where so many prayer groups and vocation circles have sprung up, among pilgrims where conversions multiply, and in the dozens of confessors who are in attendance every day (on 25 June 1988 there were 150).

Added to this is the evidence of medical tests which excludes all traces of the pathological. Then there are cures. In all some 330 have been recorded since 1981, some of which have been remarkable. Two have been confirmed after investigations that would have done more than justice to similar tests carried out at Lourdes.

Damir Coric' (born 23 July 1960) had contracted internal hydrocephalus with subdural hematoma. He had been operated on five times since 1980; meanwhile he had become bedridden, was unable to walk, speak or eat and had lost control of his bowel movements. In July 1981, after Vicka had prayed for him, he regained his speech, was again able to walk and regained perfect health. In October 1983 he went back to work in a compressor factory in Mostar. The medical examination which he underwent on that occasion found that he was perfectly fit for work. However, tests made in 1980 still bear witness to noticeable deterioration of part of the brain.

The other cure was that of Diana Basile. She had been suffering from multiple sclerosis since 1972. She was blind in her right eye, had difficulty in moving her arms and legs and suffered from urinary incontinence. She felt a great sense of interior warmth as she entered the little chapel of the apparitions for the visionaries' ecstasy. Her whole life passed before her as in a film. She was cured. The next day she walked the ten kilometers from her hotel to Medjugorje and, barefoot, climbed the steep hill of the apparitions.

Finally, in April 1987 the bishop came to Rome to present the draft of his negative judgment. However, Cardinal Ratzinger requested him to dissolve his commission of inquiry. The Cardinal took the matter out of his hands and handed over responsibility to the Yugoslav episcopal conference. I have no intention of anticipating the outcome; in any case a definite judgment cannot be made until the apparitions have ceased.

One thing, however, did impress me deeply. When opposition was at its greatest, coming as it did from the police, the government and the bishop simultaneously, when the place was thronged with crowds and there were no facilities for their reception, I believed that all was lost and that in those impossible conditions the only outcome could have been illuminism, disillusionment, revolt or despair. But when the situation was at its worse (during the years 1984 to 1986) the difficulties served only to increase priests', visionaries' and parishioners' devotion to prayer in which they found solutions. This is one of the pillars of my conviction as an expert.

(iii) Fr. Michael O'Carroll
[From: *Medjugorje: Facts, Documents, Theology*, Veritas Publications, Dublin, 1986, pp. 197-199]

Reference to God must be the absolute criterion. With that norm in mind I have no hesitation, at the end of this review of different, disparate, complex and complicated evidence, in asserting that the apparitions at Medjugorje are authentic divine signs. I have weighed the arguments against, admirably stated by Fr. Laurentin. I do not find that they prevail.

Are there too many apparitions? Who is to decide on number but the Almighty? In what way could repetition undermine reality? The apparitions do not last long. Their frequency could be a concession to the repetitive age in which we live. It could, as Laurentin suggests, be specially designed to offset the incessant, prolonged repetition of Marxist propaganda.

Such considerations too may be apposite to the multiplicity of words. One cannot expect total verbal consistency here. It does not exist in the Gospels. And we must not forget that God in such communications leaves a margin for error. It would be angelic to receive and transmit everything heard in moments of ecstasy with total accuracy.

The objection based on politics is scarcely pressed any longer. There may be moments of sporadic change; but the regime seems to have come to terms with things beyond its mental categories, in which it can discern no threat to its institutions.

Catholics, on their side, seem to have come to terms with certain rules of conduct which seemed a threat to the post-consiliar ethos and mores. If the directives are radical, traditional, far-reaching, it is because they are consonant with the Gospel — a demanding code of conduct, if ever there was one. It must be remembered also that certain demands made by Our Lady are addressed to the privileged ones who are already living in an exalted spiritual world, not a world that makes its inhabitants abnormal, but one which fosters heroism.

The thirst for heroism is unquenchable in the human spirit. There will always be those who choose the heroic way. More readily if they have every reason to rely on exceptional help.

We have had to deal at length with the tension between Medjugorje and the local bishop. It has been fully illustrated in the foregoing chapters. The question of the diary which almost induced paranoia in the bishop is thus explained: a) there is a pocket notebook of July 1981; b) there is a diary kept from 12 October to 13 December 1981 (a half page each day); c) there is a notebook given by Fr.

Yanko Bubalo to Vicka during his questioning of her so that she could note each apparition; d) there are three large notebooks in which Vicka writes down the life of Our Lady as she reveals it each day since the end of 1982. In none of these writing materials is there anything about the Bishop.

Against these objections one must align so many reasons for accepting authenticity. Some are mentioned and developed at length by Laurentin, others by Dr. Franic. In summary it may be urged that

a) the visionaries have survived a systematic drive to nullify their testimony, to subvert their so edifying way of life, to pervert their witness; their tenacity is awe-inspiring;

b) they have, day after day, during five years, spoken of spiritual realities with entire orthodoxy;

c) thrown suddenly into an existence so different from what they knew and lived with, they show no signs of abnormality. They have, on the contrary, impressed experts by their normal behavior and sincerity;

d) they live exemplary lives of prayer, fasting, detachment from the evils of their age and peers, materialism, pleasure-seeking, waste of time in entertainment — pop music and so on, not to mention the terrible addictions which plague their contemporaries;

e) they manifest respect and obedience, true love towards the Church at a time when so many, even Catholics, adopt a critical, irreverent attitude towards it — with which goes their love for the Pope and their fidelity to him. He in turn (and it is noteworthy) has sent them tokens of his favour, autographed photographs with the message *Pax Vobis*.

In *fine* let us adopt the biblical advice: *Judge the tree by its fruits*. The fruits here have been so overwhelmingly good, in the parish which is transformed, in the lives of countless people who admit that they have been brought back to the practice of their religion or to more serious commitment through contact with this holy place and the prayer movement which is daily in it. The fruits have been miraculous in some cases. These alleged miracles I have not described or discussed in detail, as it would take too much space. I accept the records in a number of cases as reliable.

There are, finally, the luminous signs. The photograph of a women's figure near where the cross should be, but without the cross, has been widely circulated. Photographers cannot explain how a woman should appear where none was visible at the time of the photograph.

The sun dance has been seen by many. Probably the most striking instance was on 29 May 1985, when it was witnessed by Fr. Rupcic and others. The Franciscan included an account of the phenomenon in a report which he sent to Rome for the attention of the Holy Father.

6. POPE JOHN PAUL II: "MEDJUGORJE IS THE FULFILLMENT OF FATIMA"

[Commentaries by Cardinal Frantisek Tomasek, Fr. Milan Mikulich, Fr. Luigi Bianchi, Fr. Rene Laurentin, Fr Robert Fox, and Bishop Paolo Hnilica.]

We have already alluded to the intimate relationship between Medjugorje and Fatima. This connection was most clearly discerned by the sons of Our Lady who served her in the countries where Russia "had spread its errors." We think here especially of Pope John Paul II of Poland, Cardinal Frantizek Tomasek of Czechoslovakia and Bishop Paolo Hnilica, a concentration camp inmate under Stalin. The Holy Father first introduced Medjugorje to Bishop Hnilica, a great devotee of Fatima, with the words "Medjugorje is the fulfillment of Fatima." And Cardinal Tomasek, "the Iron Cardinal," said in 1988 [*Medjugorje Gebetsaktion,* 1988] "Personally, I am convinced that Medjugorje is the continuation of Lourdes and Fatima. Step by step, the Immaculate Heart of Mary will triumph. And I am also deeply convinced that Medjugorje is a sign for this." Bishop Hnilica, a close confidant of both Sister Lucia of Fatima and of His Holiness, Pope John Paul II, has said that "Precisely in Medjugorje, Our Lady of Fatima — the Madonna of Medjugorje — on the 25th of August, called for everyone, for all those who live out the spirit of Medjugorje, to help Her to be able to bring about Her victory which She predicted at Fatima." Bishop Hnilica's commentary on the relationship between Fatima and Medjugorje is of such critical importance that it will be included in great detail at the conclusion of this chapter.

The seeming "coincidences" that characterize the histories of both Fatima and Medjugorje have been studied earlier in A CHRONOLOGY OF COINCI-DENCES and do not require repetition here. It is the intersection of these coincidences that enables us to call Medjugorje "the fulfillment of Fatima." Neither Fatima nor Medjugorje, however, is important simply because of the supernatural phenomena associated with them or because of their Secrets. Their primary importance lies in their messages for the world at large. In this respect, both Fatima and Medjugorje reiterate the same urgent appeal for prayer, penance, and conversion. Medjugorje in a special way is also the synthesis of the central themes of the other two great apparitions, Guadalupe and Lourdes. Whereas the primary theme at Guadalupe is evangelization, Lourdes is associated primarily with healing. At Medjugorje we have cures and healings as in Lourdes, a concern for evangelization as at Guadalupe and a focus on prayer, penance, and conversion as at Fatima.

We will begin the commentaries on the relationship between Fatima and Medjugorje by reprinting the text of an interview on this theme with Cardinal Frantisek Tomasek. Cardinal Tomasek, the late Archbishop of Prague, was described thus by Pope John Paul II on June 26, 1991: "To me that man of God signified the faith and heroism of a devastated but living Church." His Eminence Cardinal Tomasek died in Prague on August 4, 1992.

Upon his death Pope John Paul II sent the following telegram to the Archbishop of Prague, Most Rev. Miloslav Vlk, [*L'Osservatore Romano*, August 12, 1992]:

> With great emotion I learned the news of the pious death of the esteemed Cardinal Frantisek Tomasek, Archbishop emeritus of Prague. I express my great sadness at the death of an intrepid pastor who, in his long ecclesial ministry, showed himself to be an authentic pillar of the Church, an undaunted witness to the Gospel and a strenuous defender of the Christian faith and the rights of the human person. Although confined and for years prevented from freely exercising his episcopal mission, like a solid oak, he never let himself be intimidated and always gave a shining example of strength and trust in divine Providence as well as of fidelity to the See of Peter. I thank the Lord for having given His Church this eminent figure of a priest and Bishop; I fervently pray that after such great suffering He may welcome this good and faithful servant into His eternal joy. I send to Your Excellency, to the whole Archdiocese, and to all those who share in your sorrow at his death the comfort of my Apostolic Blessing, a sign of my intense sharing in the general mourning.

Pope John Paul II

"THE IMMACULATE HEART OF MARY WILL TRIUMPH"

An interview with Cardinal Frantisek Tomasek

The late Cardinal Frantizek Tomasek, Archbishop emeritus of Prague, Czechoslovakia, was interviewed by Fr. Slavko Barbaric, O.F.M. of Medjugorje and two representatives of *Gebetsaktion Medjugorje* in his Episcopal Palace on November 21, 1987. (Source: *Medjugorje: Gebetsaktion* 1988, #1 -Postfach 18, A-1153 Vienna, Austria)

Your Eminence, what do the apparitions at Medjugorje mean for you?
The Marian apparitions at Medjugorje mean a great deal for us, especially because for us in Czechoslovakia, devotion to the Blessed Mother is deep and lively. With us there is a great interest in Medjugorje. Priests and faithful are deeply grateful for every message, every report that we receive from Medjugorje.

POPE JOHN PAUL II: "MEDJUGORJE IS THE FULFILLMENT OF FATIMA"

Personally I am deeply convinced of the apparitions in Medjugorje and am deeply grateful, especially because of the emphasis on prayer, the rosary and fasting. Many who have been in Medjugorje have told me how precisely that love which the Blessed Mother emphasizes is really practiced there. The people are very kind; in Medjugorje one can experience what the love of God and the love of neighbor are.

What significance do you think Medjugorje has?
Personally, I am deeply convinced that Medjugorje is the continuation of Lourdes and Fatima. Certainly the ecclesiastical commission has the final word, but we must even now joyfully accept and live the messages.

Could you tell us about the most beautiful, happiest experience of your own life?
The happiest experience of my life is certainly the consciousness of living with Christ. My worst and saddest experience is to see that there are believers who give no witness. I am thinking first of all priests here.

What would you say to priests in relation to the apparitions in Medjugorje and to visiting this place of pilgrimage?
I would say to priests who want to go to Medjugorje: Most important is your own personal experience; this experience will require then no further words. The experience of nearness to God is decisive. Then the consequence of this experience is to carry that which was experienced, the message, further and to spread it.

When you hear in the messages "Peace!" — do you believe that peace is possible today?
Yes, peace in our hearts! For what is most important is that peace begins in the heart, and this is surely the salvation for all human beings.

What thoughts or experiences do you connect with this, when you hear of the apparitions of the Blessed Mother in Medjugorje?
On that I'd like to say that I had a very happy youth. My mother prayed often, especially that I would become a priest. I grew up in an atmosphere of devotion to the Blessed Mother. From my youth I was with the Marian Congregation. Every day I attended Holy Mass. We prayed the rosary daily. I see in the message of Medjugorje also a message for mothers.... My youth was always happily joined to God.

Could you tell us anything else from your rich experiences?

Although I have three years of forced hard labor behind me, I was interiorly always full of peace. (Smiling, the Cardinal added in English, 'Keep smiling!') It is lovely to live in the consciousness that one is near to God. This also gives us the strength for the most profound Christian optimism, which — despite all tests — has never left me.

How do you see the future of the faith in your country?

I am deeply convinced, step by step, the Immaculate Heart of Mary will triumph. And I am also deeply convinced that Medjugorje is a sign for this. I am very grateful to you for having come to me and reported on this great place of grace. This all fills me with a great inner joy, and it strengthens me on my own way. It fills me with a great inner power.

(With a gleam in his eye, he added to a young doctor in the group of visitors: "For this old man, this visit today is better than any medicine.")

Fr. Milan Mikulich, a Croatian priest based in the U.S. who is editor of *Orthodoxy of the Catholic Doctrine*, has followed Medjugorje from the very beginning. Fr. Mikulich's comparison of Medjugorje to Fatima and Lourdes is given below [an excerpt from the Fall 1985 issue of *Orthodoxy of the Catholic Doctrine*: "The apparitions and visions at Medjugorje follow the same pattern of those in Lourdes in 1858 and Fatima in 1917."]

Considering the facts that the apparition and visions at Lourdes and Fatima occurred 123 years and 64 years, respectively, before the apparitions and visions at Medjugorje and that the young seers of Medjugorje, in their circumstances, did not have any previous knowledge, as Vicka personally confirmed, of the events at Lourdes and Fatima, it would be impossible to say that they fraudulently copied the behavior of the seers at Lourdes and Fatima. It would be more correct to conclude that the same heavenly Agent — Our Lady — directed in all three places, Lourdes, Fatima and Medjugorje, these actions the way She chose.

CIRCUMSTANCES OF APPARITIONS VERY SIMILAR AT LOURDES, FATIMA AND MEDJUGORJE.

The similarities found in all three cases make us believe that the Lourdes and Fatima apparitions are indeed the blueprints of the Medjugorje apparitions.

The message of Our Lady in all three places is the same: conversion of the world to God.

The response of the seers to Our Lady in all three places is the same: a filial obedience to the Heavenly Mother in delivering Her message to the world.

The reaction of those in charge of the Church and civil society in all three places is the same: at first it is mixed with unbelief, ridicule and total rejection.

The reaction of the public, however, is rather positive: the faithful believe the seers, accept the message of Our Lady and follow it.

The seers of Medjugorje used to say: All people believe us except the police and the priests!

THE WAY OUR LADY APPROACHED THE SEERS AT LOURDES, FATIMA AND MEDJUGORJE

Our Lady appears in all three places to innocent youngsters of the peasant families.

She appears to them in a deserted and remote place — Massabille, Cova di Iria and Podbrdo.

She appeared suddenly, preceded and surrounded by a bright light.

She invites them to come again according the time prescribed by Her.

She tells them not to be afraid of Her; she would do no harm to them.

She tests them and their loyalty by not appearing on some occasions when they expected to see Her.

She appears with Her Rosary and prays with them and tells them that they should pray the Rosary daily.

She tells them She wants them to be Her messengers to the world.

She asks them to pray for sinners.

After several visits, She tells them her name: at Lourdes, She is the Immaculate Conception; at Fatima, She is the Our Lady of the Rosary and the Immaculate Heart; at Medjugorje, She is the Blessed Virgin Mary and the Queen of Peace.

She gives them heavenly messages for the benefit of the world — to quit sin and to return to God!

She also gives them some secrets, which are not to be revealed until She tells them.

THE WAY THE SEERS ACTED WITH OUR LADY AT LOURDES, FATIMA AND MEDJUGORJE

The seers, on the other hand, in seeing Our Lady for the first time, were frightened and doubtful She was a Heavenly Vision. Therefore, they test Her by sprinkling Holy Water on Her, and She proves their action by Her heavenly smile and thus confirms that She is not the devil.

The seers ask Our Lady whether some of their friends are in Heaven and She answers them that some are , and some are not yet.

They accept gladly all that She asks of them to do or not to do.

In all three cases, they describe in the same way Our Lady's features and Her dress.

In all three cases, the seers, without any fear, deliver Her messages of conversion and penance to the world, but they keep jealously the secrets She confided to them.

The seers see Heaven, Hell, Angels, Saints and Jesus.

THE WAY THE CHURCH AND CIVIL AUTHORITIES TREATED THE SEERS

In all three cases, the least sympathetic to the seers are the Church and civil authorities. The seers are mistreated when interrogated by the ecclesiastics; they are arrested by the police as those who disturb the order and peace. Even the Bishops make fun of them, laughing at and ignoring them.

THE WAY THE FAITHFUL REACTED TO THE SEERS AT LOURDES, FATIMA AND MEDJUGORJE

However, the general masses of the faithful are more and more joining the seers, accept the messages of Our Lady and practice them; they follow the seers to the place of the apparitions where they kneel and pray.

This takes place at Lourdes and Fatima even after the apparitions were ended. At Medjugorje, where the apparitions and visions are still occurring, there is a constant flow of devout pilgrims who come to seek heavenly help through the Mother of God.

THE NUMBER OF PILGRIMS AT LOURDES, FATIMA AND MEDJUGORJE

No doubt, there must have been a large number of pilgrims at Lourdes and Fatima from their first apparitions. On the occasion of the

50th anniversary of the Lourdes apparitions, which was celebrated in 1908, it was estimated that during the course of 50 years over 5 million pilgrims came there to kneel and pray.

At Medjugorje, however, on the occasion of the 4th anniversary of the apparitions there, which was celebrated in 1985, it was estimated that over 4 million pilgrims visited that place for the same purpose.

One has to admit that in our times there are better and faster transportation means which may account for the larger overflow to Medjugorje, even from distant lands and continents, but, on the other hand, there is nothing there for human comfort to attract people — no hotels, no motels, no restaurants, no public facilities.

What brings them there? Nothing but the desire to experience the heavenly atmosphere in the presence of the Mother of God who is at work there distributing, even in miraculous ways, the temporal and spiritual favors and graces.

THE CHURCH'S POSITION TOWARD THE APPARITIONS AT LOURDES AND FATIMA

It is known that the apparitions of Our Lady at Lourdes and Fatima are officially approved by the Church as authentic.

However, it is to be remembered that it took four years for those at Lourdes, and thirteen and half years for those in Fatima to be approved.

The Commission appointed by the Bishop of Lourdes, after pursuing its investigation for more than two years, communicated to Bishop Laurence the results of its patient and thorough work.

'Yes,' the Commission said, 'the voice of the people hear the voice of God. Those thousands of pilgrims who had come, since February 1858, and knelt at Masabielle, had not been deluding themselves; the Lady of the Grotto was indeed Our Lady.'

On the basis of this report of the Commission, Bishop Laurence, who at the beginning was laughing with others, at Bernadette's visions of Our Lady, signing the decree of approbation of the apparitions at Lourdes said: 'We are convinced that the Apparition is supernatural and from God... Our conviction is based on the testimony of Bernadette, and above all on the events which have occurred since, and which can only be explained by divine intervention...The testimony of Bernadette is of great importance in itself, but it derives entirely new force...from the marvelous deeds which have been performed since the first event. If the tree is to be judged by its fruit, we can say that the Apparition described by the young girl is supernatural and divine, for the effects it has proceeded are supernatural and divine.'

The people undoubtedly were grateful to Bishop Laurence for issuing such a statement, but he did not make the apparition more authentic than they were on the first day!

The symbiotic relationship between Medjugorje and other Marian apparitions, Fatima in particular, is also considered here by three other leading Mariologists. In his book *Fatima and Medjugorje*, Fr. Luigi Bianchi, a well known authority on Fatima, writes:

The message of Medjugorje is a continuation and a complement of the message of Fatima. It is the extraordinary verification of it in substance. It is the same message of peace for this century of the most dreadful wars in history and of the menace of a fiery deluge of an atomic apocalypse. Fatima happened in 1917 towards the end of the First World War. Medjugorje is happening between the Second World War and the dawning of the third millennium. The Mother of God guides us toward the door of peace.

The first words of Fatima and of Medjugorje are those of the Annunciation: 'Do not be afraid' (Luke 1:30).

The messages are illustrated, attested to and confirmed by signs in the sky, which have happened at both Fatima and Medjugorje."

Why this new message at Medjugorje? Because those of the Cova de Iria had not been listened to and remain not understood.

Here is the commentary of Mariologist Rene Laurentin:

Our Lady at both Fatima and Medjugorje has chosen little ones, the young, the unsophisticated. They have the wisdom of the pure and the innocent. In both apparitions the children met with severe opposition — Free Masons, anti-clerics, and the leaders of Portugal in 1917; Communists governing Yugoslavia in the 1980's. In both cases there has been interrogation by police, who menaced and jailed them (for a long time for Fr. Jozo Zovko in Medjugorje).

The messages of Fatima and Medjugorje are identical. To surmount the menaces which weigh on the world you need prayer, penance, conversion, for mankind to return to God, and the invitation to pray the Rosary.

The objective is the same — peace in spite of all the things that divide us socially and continue to destroy man. And the ways are the same, a return to God through Mary.

The progression is complementary. Fatima told us what we had to do; Medjugorje is showing how to do it."

Fr. Laurentin also notes, "The hours of the apparitions follow a progression. At Lourdes, they took place in the morning. At Fatima, at noon. At Medjugorje, in the evening. Is it the end of a long day?"

The best known apostle of Fatima in the U.S.A. — "the Fatima priest" — is Fr. Robert Fox. Fr. Fox spoke recently at the 1992 Medjugorje National Conference at Notre Dame University. In a subsequent interview he commented thus on the relationship of Fatima and Medjugorje:

Although Medjugorje has not been authenticated by the Vatican, the fruits of the transformation of souls and the conversions are great. This cannot be the work of the Devil... What we have at Medjugorje are not new prophecies, but Our Lady in a motherly way reaching out to her children. The messages are so simple that the youngest child could understand it... Medjugorje is fulfilling what Fatima promised." [*South Bend Tribune*, May 10, 1992]

We will conclude this chapter with Bishop Hnilica's analysis of the real and profound relationship between the two greatest apparitions of this century. [Note also *God Renews The World Through Mary*, in the second section of the appendices.]

Msgr. Hnilica, the Titular Bishop of Rusado, is a member of the Jesuit Society. He is the founder of the Association, *Pro Deo Fratribus*, a charitable body of members involved in assisting the Church and peoples of the East, particularly those peoples who are being oppressed by militaristic atheism. He speaks frequently regarding the Messages of Our Lady of Fatima and their relevance to Russia today. He has spoken several times with the only surviving visionary of Fatima, Sister Lucy as well as several Holy Fathers regarding the situation of the persecuted Church in Eastern Europe.

The Bishop was born in Slovakia, March 30, 1921. During the Stalinist persecution which took the Bishop's country by veritable storm, the Bishop was a young seminarian. He read in that time the book of St. Louis de Montfort's

Consecration to Jesus through the Immaculate Heart of Mary. This was an important step in the spiritual development of Padre Paolo, as he is known to his people. Our Lady was the way given by God for him to become a priest.

He was ordained on the 29th of September, 1950 in secret. Scarcely three months after his ordination, Padre Paolo was consecrated a bishop, following instruction which he received from his provincial, the only Jesuit who was not caught by the police. The circumstances were just as dramatic as those of his priestly ordination. He was likewise consecrated a bishop in secret. The mission field given to him by his consecrating bishop was as he was told, "Peking, Moscow and Berlin." Such a diocese, of course, did not exist. However, the mission of the new bishop was to help those brothers and sisters persecuted under communism.

After having consecrated a new bishop (the present Cardinal Korec), to guarantee the survival of the underground Church, Bishop Hnilica flew to Rome to bring this and other very important information to Pope Pius XII. Pope Pius XII subsequently asked Bishop Hnilica to remain in Rome.

Under the inspiration of Pope Paul VI, Bishop Hnilica founded his Association, at present, *Pro Deo et Fratribus*. In all the following years, the Bishop traveled throughout the world to give witness to the needs of the Eastern European Church. Simultaneously, he promoted the consecration to the Immaculate Heart of Mary according to the requests of Our Lady of Fatima. This request of Our Lady particularly involved Russia.

On March 24, 1984, Bishop Hnilica carried out a significant act that reflects the scope of the Fatima message and may perhaps be considered a sign foretelling the events that were to awaken the countries of Eastern Europe. John Paul II during the same days, March 24 and 25 consecrated the world and Russia to the Immaculate Heart of Mary.

Bishop Hnilica, guided by the prayers of Mother Teresa of Calcutta, whom he was visiting at the time, returned to Rome via Moscow. He received the visa rather miraculously since he was considered one of the number one enemies of Communism.

Padre Paolo recited the prayer of Consecration in the Church of St. Michael which is located in the center of the Kremlin, the offices of the communist government. After reciting these prayers united with the Holy Father in Rome and all the bishops in the world, he then secretly celebrated a Holy Mass in the adjoining Church of the Assumption.

In these blessed hours, the Bishop said, "I felt during the Consecration that communism would be overcome because now Russia was placed into the Heart of Mary from the Vicar of Christ himself and all the bishops in union with him."

Upon his return to Rome, Bishop Hnilica met with John Paul II, who was touched by the Bishop's actions and viewed them as a providential sign that God desired this Consecration.[12]

The Bishop is also convinced that under the present Holy Father, guided so closely by Our Lady, the Triumph of Her Immaculate Heart shall take place. In this sense, Bishop Hnilica invites everyone to participate in this heavenly plan of God the Father initiated in Fatima. Prayers, sacrifices, as well as material support are needed to assist in the conversion of Russia and thus of the world.

Another point of import which the Bishop continues to assert is that during this age, Our Lady is manifesting herself as Co-redemptrix, as may be discerned from the Message of Fatima.

Bishop Hnilica follows quite closely as well, the events and spiritual movements of Medjugorje seeing in these events the continuation of all that was begun in Fatima. Two years passed, he was able to travel to Russia with one of the visionaries of Medjugorje as well as the parish pastor. He is convinced that all these Marian movements will come together in a united manner to help the Church of the East and Russia as Our Lady has continually requested. Today, we may see these Marian movements which the Bishop refers to as gaining world-wide momentum and unity.

Our Lady comes in our time in such a strong presence to lead us to the fulfillment of Her Triumph promised in Fatima. I believe that every authentic apparition of this century will lead to the right and full understanding of the message of Fatima: 'in the end my Heart will triumph... Russia will be converted.' These are the times in which the Lord through the Co-Redemptrix and Mediatrix of all the graces wants to conquer the entire world beginning in Russia. In this land of martyrs will begin very strong the Triumph of Our Lady, that I believe means first of all the reconciliation between the Orthodox and the Catholics through prayer and charity. This sign of unity will be the biggest sign of the glory of God in the world so that all people will believe that Jesus is coming from the Father! (Jn. 17:21)

---

[12] It was during this meeting that the Holy Father said to Bishop Hnilica: "You should go to Medjugorje. Medjugorje is the fulfillment of Fatima!"

Bishop Hnilica's address to the
1992 National Conference on Medjugorje
at the University of Notre Dame

...This is — more than ever — a crucial and decisive hour of history; the messages of the Madonna of Medjugorje are being received continually concerning the extraordinary character of the moment in which we live.

This century of ours, loaded in this way with events, began under the sign of the Virgin of Fatima, who — with maternal solicitude — turned her glance particularly to Eastern Europe and to Russia.

History itself shows us here how much it would lie in the heart of the "Lord of History" to show to the entire world what role His Mother would have in the conversion of the people who have suffered the cruelest of religious persecutions and whom we see in our day as the ultimate dramatic moment, particularly in the region of Bosnia-Hercegovina.

Pius XII said that "the message of Fatima" — which is one of the greatest interventions of God in the history of humanity since the death of the Apostles — can be understood only if the reality of communism is recognized.

Lenin, the founder of the Communist Party which incarnates the Marxist doctrine, was to say, "God is my only personal enemy. I would prefer a millionaire exploiter and atheist to a believing proletarian." And then "It is necessary to root atheism in such a way as to exclude once and for all any possible restoration of religious sentiment. Three-fourths of humanity can die so long as the remainder become Communist."

As Leo XIII predicted "Woe to us! If this Marxist doctrine, which is the greatest plague that ever existed, would ever become a social and political system; it will destroy human relations and society right to their roots!"

This is why Pius XI said, "We are seeing today what history has never before seen. There are unfurled to the wind the satanic banners of war against God and against religion, in the midst of all of the peoples and in every part of the world."

At Fatima the Madonna had predicted from Russia would be born an atheistic movement that would be spread into all the world, that it would be the cause of persecutions and that the Holy Father would have much to suffer. We Christians of the East have truly understood this message only in the concentration camp. There indeed we could touch with our hands what this thing, Communism, is and what is the only remedy to be saved — to consecrate yourself to the Madonna engaged as the leading person in this greatest battle of all centuries against Satan. For this reason I would say to you that this was not our struggle but Hers.

This apocalyptic struggle — as Paul VI inspiringly disclosed to us in the "Signum Magnum" — has been declared overbearingly by the perpetual enemy, by the "father of lies," Satan, who throws up his most terrible challenge to God. It was the greatest attack against the Truth of the man who is Christ. If the Truth is gone, the human being is annihilated in his very being.

The field of this apocalyptic battle chosen by the Evil One is Russia and successively her satellite states. The weapon to subdue them is the gaudiest of lies — militant atheism.In a very few years, a terrible poison has been spread about in numerous nations, which — as the Madonna had predicted at Fatima — lost their natural, civil and religious identity. They came to be annihilated, because the roots of human existence were demolished.

Therefore look at the absurd reason for the war in the former Yugoslavia. The poison of the Communist doctrine still continues to run through the veins of the heads of government like Serbia, which is hurling itself against innocent and defenseless populations like that of Croatia.

Our indignation is not towards the Serbia populace but towards those who are guiding their destiny, blinded by satanic hatred.

Just in the year in which the devil hurled his battle cry against God, through the communist ideology that considers Him as its first and greatest enemy, the Madonna at Fatima sounded the alarm and Her sorrowful appeal to the universal Church. She requested the consecration of Russia and of the world to Her Immaculate Heart and the devotion by them on the first Saturdays of every month, promising that in this way "Russia will be converted and the world will be granted a time of peace." The motive was simple and was declared by this same Virgin of Fatima — because "God wants it."

In virtue of the consecration to Her Immaculate Heart, Russia would have rediscovered God. It is, in fact, to Her maternal care that the Lord has confided this immense people. The Lord himself has revealed to Sister Lucia of Fatima that "He wants that all His Church recognize this consecration as a triumph of the Immaculate Heart of Mary, in order then to extend Her cult and to place the devotion to this Immaculate Heart alongside the devotion to His Divine Heart."

The Redeemer and the Co-Redemptrix, the Mediator and the Mediatrix, the Advocate and the Maternal Advocate — here is the inseparable union of two Hearts, which the Holy Trinity has wonderfully worked. On the level of divine Providence, the inscrutable decree of God's love has established that precisely in our days, in this twentieth century — illumined by a multiplicity of Marian apparitions — the vocation of Mary most holy would be revealed more profoundly to the entire Church and to humanity.

The message of Medjugorje comes to bring to completion that which the Madonna had begun, announced and promised at Fatima.

Precisely in one of her messages [that of August 25, 1991], the Madonna placed the message of Fatima into relation with that of Medjugorje, the prelude to Her definitive Triumph.

Saint Louis Marie de Montfort has prophesied this extraordinary Marian epoch, which the Madonna announced at Fatima for this century. The Saint speaks of the Reign of Mary which will come through the action of the Holy Spirit, in which the Madonna will be truly Queen of all hearts, exercising Her maternal sovereignty in all the life of the Church and of humanity. Such a maternal dominion will be the prelude to a splendid new Christian blossoming in the Church and in the world.

St. Maximilian Kolbe, another great prophet from just in our century, has echoed St. Louis de Montfort, announcing — on the strength of his extraordinary Marian charism — that in not a little time the statue of the Immaculata would be enthroned on the Kremlin in Moscow.

Mother Teresa of Calcutta, with whom I have worked for many years and who has opened seven religious houses in Russia, told me that the entire secret of her success consists in "always letting herself be guided by the hand of the Madonna". This is the profound meaning of the consecration: in everything let yourself be guided by the Madonna like children at the hand of their own mother!

God the Father sends His Son's Mother, today as then at Nazareth, to manifest to a dehumanized world His maternal Face, full of inexpressible solicitude for each of His children. It is in this light that we ought to look at Fatima (John Paul ll has called it "the spiritual capital of Europe") and at Medjugorje.

The Communism spread by Russia into all the world was the greatest force that had ever been marshalled against God, against the Church and against humanity. This has collapsed not by means of physical force or by diplomatic skill, but through the mercy of God united with the blood of millions of martyrs and to the unceasing prayers of so many faithful in the West as well — above all, the prayer of the Rosary, the most effective, the most powerful.

It is this same prayer, your own included, which will also bring the victory to this last communist fortress, that of the former Yugoslavia. It is certainly not by chance that the last wall to collapse is found precisely in the land chosen by the Madonna to bring to completion the message of Fatima. A land of the East!

Humanity has an extreme need of a "supplement for the soul", which only charity and prayer can give it. The Madonna, like then at Bethlehem, even more than the "star" of the Magi, is the One who leads to Jesus, who offers us Jesus.

She who is prayer incarnate — our most lively, most immediate contact with Jesus — has been called "Star of the New Evangelization" by John Paul ll. It is she who teaches us truly to pray, because without true prayer we cannot develop any work of evangelization.

Dearest young people, in these moments of prayer and of adoration I want to invite you to consecrate all your life to the One who is continually giving birth to new life. At her disposal put your energies for this work of evangelization that is so urgent and vital.

In this moment of dramatic sufferings for the Croatian people but also for the other neighboring peoples immersed in the darkness of a satanic war, we have confidence that the victory is already ours because the Madonna has promised it, but not without us!

To you I also recommend Russia, which remains close to my heart and which is coming to be invaded more and more by such a religious thirst. It is only we Catholics who are lacking in that land. Mother Teresa of Calcutta very much laments this Catholic absence in that land. Would that God will raise in the midst of you such apostles for Russia!

I want to thank you and to encourage you anew to become apostles of the Madonna for the Triumph of Her Immaculate Heart, which I am convinced will be accomplished under the Pontificate of John Paul ll, "lux ex oriente." He has fully accomplished the request of the Virgin of Fatima, in union with all the bishops of the world consecrating the world and "the peoples of whom You yourself have requested their consecration"!

Together with him, today and always we want to repeat to the Madonna, "Totus tuus ego sum et omnia mea tua sunt, oh Virgo gloriosa et benedicta!..."

I began speaking about the triumph of the Immaculate Heart of Mary. But we could ask here, after what we have heard about Bosnia-Hercegovina and Medjugorje, how can we still speak of Mary's triumph?

But take courage! Have no fear! Even if Medjugorje should be destroyed so that there remains not one stone upon another, Medjugorje will not be destroyed. Because Medjugorje is already in the 30-million hearts; the spirit of Medjugorje lives in the 30-million souls — those who have been pilgrims in Medjugorje — and tens of millions others that there are around the world.

I travel a great deal in the world. I can say that the Medjugorje movement today is the strongest, most vibrant one in the Church around the world. But one characteristic of the Medjugorje movement that is not found in the Lourdes movement or Fatima movement is the familial aspect, the solidarity of all those who live the spirit of Medjugorje. Wherever I go, into whatever country in the world, when I encounter any Medjugorje group, I find myself suddenly as if at home, within my own family. So I truly find myself as if with my own family and at home among you, too. It is this spirit of unity, of family, of solidarity that will bring victory to the Immaculate Heart of Mary, victory of the Church, the victory of Christ.

Precisely in Medjugorje, Our Lady of Fatima — the Madonna of Medjugorje — on the 25th of August called for everyone, for all those who live out the spirit of Medjugorje, to help her to be able to bring about her victory which she predicted at Fatima. The first time she spoke of the triumph of her Heart, the

Madonna — the same Madonna who appears in Medjugorje — appeared in Fatima in 1917. And she spoke of a system that was being born as the greatest enemy of God, that was being born in Russia, which would raise up wars, persecutions against the Church. Many millions would be martyred. I believe what we are seeing today in the Serbian part of Yugoslavia is the residue of this militantly atheistic communist system.

Pius XI, twenty years after the apparitions in Fatima, spoke of this enemy in these words: "We see today something which history has never before seen, a system organized against everything that is divine and religious in every part of the world. And truly," he went on to say, "this persecution, this struggle surpasses all the persecutions under Nero or Diocletian or any other persecution in the history of the Church." And truly in those seventy years hundreds of bishops have been imprisoned and have died in prison, as well as tens of thousands of priests, tens of thousands of sisters, and tens of thousands of lay Christians — millions.

Still, about ten years ago, a newspaper in Moscow wrote these words: "We do not fight with Believers nor their priests. We fight God, to tear him from the hearts of the believers." At the same time an atheist newspaper wrote about the celebration year of the millennium of the baptism of Russia to be held in Russia: "We know that there will have been 1,000 years since the baptism of Russia in 1988." And this atheistic newspaper, wrote ten years ago: "On that date of the millennium there should not remain even a trace of God nor of Christ nor of the Madonna nor of Christianity in the Russian people."

In the face of this system seventy-five years ago, the Madonna had the courage to predict the triumph of her heart and the collapse of this system. And what is the condition that the Madonna has asked of us for this victory? I have spoken several times with Sister Lucia of Fatima. And she said the first favor the Madonna has asked of us, her children — making us all her children, all the faithful — will be to accept readily all the crosses which the Lord should send us for the salvation of sinners. The other thing, which she asked at Medjugorje too, is prayer and faith to believe and to love the Lord for those who do not love, who no longer believe. In the concentration camp, when we meditated on this message, we said we ought to pray, make sacrifices also for the police who mistreated us there. We saw many who converted. They came secretly to go to confession and receive communion.

The second condition that the Madonna has asked, as the most important power, is the consecration of Russia on the part of the Holy Father and all the bishops of the world. We could say that the central and principal key in the message of Fatima and of the victory of her Heart over Satan will be Peter, the Holy Father.

Therefore we can understand why a persecution exploded against the Pope — a moral, defamatory persecution. Practically all of us were imprisoned for fidelity to the Holy Father. After a certain amount of time that we were in the concentration camp, political commissars came to discourage us, saying, "If you separate from the Pope, if instead of the Pope in Rome, you recognize the Patriarch of Moscow, you can be freed immediately." We grasped this, that today Satan understands where the foundation of the Church is, who his principal enemy is. It is Peter.

We meditated just exactly on this, because Jesus said to Peter: "On you Peter (Rock) I will build my Church, and Satan will not be able to do anything against her." And what's more, in the Last Supper Jesus said, "Simon! Simon! Satan has requested to sift you, to tempt you, to persecute you. But I have prayed for you that your faith may never become less, and that you will confirm your brothers." And we felt that our fidelity to Peter strengthened us to remain faithful to Christ as well. We said that only He can strengthen our faith, that any bishop — even if there are about 4,000 bishops in the Church — any of them can be sifted. The only one who cannot be sifted is the Bishop of Rome, as Christ has guaranteed to him.

We also felt this concerning the assassination attempt on this Holy Father, because Providence had foreseen it was he who was to consecrate Russia. "And precisely this attack," the Holy Father told me, "had brought me to understand most of all the importance, the seriousness of this message from Fatima." And when, after he left the hospital, I brought him this statue of Fatima, he said these words to me: "In the hospital, in suffering, I understood that the only solution for the gravest problems in this world, to save the world from war (it was ten years ago, when there was great danger), to save the world from the greatest danger, from apostasy from God, from militant atheism, the only solution is the conversion of Russia according to the message of Fatima." There he confided this statue to Russia. In Poland he had constructed a chapel where the Madonna looks toward Russia. In ten years, the walls that have cut off Russia have practically collapsed.

On that occasion, the Holy Father told me, "Russia is the hardest, most urgent, most dangerous mission field; and it is necessary to look for the best strengths of the Catholic Church." So! that is why I am here among you today.

And on August 25 the Blessed Virgin herself said to everyone from Medjugorje that she needs our help, the whole Medjugorje movement, for her triumph in Russia. In what does the full triumph of the Immaculate Heart of Mary consist? It is not only in the collapse of the enemy, Communism, but in the reconciliation of the two sister Churches, the Orthodox and the Catholic. For 900 years the Mystical Body of Christ — if I may say so, the Heart of Christ — has been bleeding because of this schism. For the two Churches — Orthodox and

Catholic — are like twin sisters who have the same faith in God, the same love for Our Lady.

Perhaps the Orthodox have a more sincere, simpler love for Our Lady than we Catholics. Sometimes our theologians have scruples. "If I have too much love for the Mother of Jesus, then perhaps there will be too little left for Jesus." The Orthodox don't have these scruples. They love the Mother, because she is the Mother of Jesus.

What can we do towards this reconciliation? I am sure that today, after 900 years, we have our greatest chance, an occasion, that God wants at last that this reconciliation come about. The Orthodox Church and the Russian people have never found themselves in a situation so difficult as today. When I was in Moscow last year at the patriarchate, I met the priest in charge of charities. And he asked me if I knew that in Russia there is famine. They need everything. And he asked me in the name of what Catholic situation I was coming to help Russia and the Orthodox Church. And I said, "In the name of the Marian institutions and movements — those of Fatima and of Medjugorje." Then he embraced me. We once again became neighbors. He said three times, "Don't forget, even if perhaps others forget us."

We must not fear anything that God may give us today for this reunion of the two Churches, Catholic and Orthodox. And we ought to pray much and do much, for this reunion, this union, may come about under this pontificate.

Because truly, when this Pope was elected, it was a bombshell all around the world, and it fell just exactly right. When I met him for the first time after the election, I said these words to him, "Holy Father, I am certain that the principal mission task of your pontificate should be the consecration of Russia with all the bishops, and consequently the conversion of Russia." And he told me, "Paolo, I am ready for the consecration, even tomorrow, if you are — with these bishops.". We know that he has done that consecration now.

I began by speaking about the Triumph of Our Lady's Immaculate Heart and I will speak now about this Triumph that Our Lady has predicted and promised and what we can do for this triumph.

We know that when Europe was in great danger from the Turks, before the battle of Lepanto, Pius V, after inviting the Christian armies to defend Europe, invited all Christians to do penance — to fast and to pray. And Sulieman, the Turkish Sultan who was the leader of the enemies against Christianity, said, "I'm not afraid of the Christian armies. But I am afraid of that old man — his prayer." He was afraid of the prayer of the pope. And we know that this battle was won with the special intervention of Our Lady. She helped the Christians to win. And on another occasion in Vienna, when Sobieski came from Poland with thousands of soldiers to defend Europe, they began their battle with the prayer, "Jesus and Mary, help us!" And they won!

POPE JOHN PAUL II: "MEDJUGORJE IS THE FULFILLMENT OF FATIMA"

But today Our Lady is not looking for weapons used by soldiers, she is looking for our hearts! Therefore, Our Lady asked in Fatima for the consecration of the world and Russia to her Immaculate Heart, because she wanted conversion and not destruction. And we know that the Holy Father did do this consecration. After the consecration in 1984 the Holy Father said to me, "It is not enough to do this liturgical act — this official act of the consecration — because every Christian, everyone has to be consecrated to Our Lady. Every bishop has to consecrate his diocese to Our Lady. Every head of a family, the family's father, the family's mother, has to consecrate to Our Lady his/her own family. Everyone of us has to consecrate himself/herself, to Our Lady."

I would like to underline that the Holy Father did the consecration completely — in the perfect way — as it was requested. I asked Sr. Lucia of Fatima about this. After the consecration Sr. Lucia of Fatima told me, "Yes! The Holy Father has done the consecration! There is nothing more for him to do." The Holy Father has done what he was to do. Now we must do what we have to do — what Our Lady is asking from us! First of all, Our Lady wants us to accept all the sufferings, all the crosses that the Lord sends to us, and to accept these sacrifices for the salvation of sinners (and for our own salvation).

Our Lady in Fatima requested that we believe in God more, we hope in God more, we love the Lord more for those who do not believe, who do not hope, who do not love the Lord — that we offer our supernatural fruits (merits) for others. This is the weapon , the means by which Our Lady will win today — the means through which Our Lady will triumph today.

Once Pope Pius XII said, "Yes, we have to fight against Communism, but with the weapon of Jesus with the Cross! Because it was through His death on the Cross that Jesus won and Jesus overcame sin. And Jesus, also today, wants to redeem this world — but through us! We are His co-workers, co-redeemers. Our Lady was the first co-worker of God, of Jesus. Even more she wa sthe co-redemptrix. And today the Queen of Peace, the co-redemptrix is inviting each one of us to become like her — co-redeemer!

When we were in the concentration camps we didn't understand what we could do now in prison for the Lord. We, as priests, understood that we couldn't celebrate the Holy Mass on the altar. We couldn't make any pastoral service. Then we understood that in that time (and today) what we had to do, and what the Lord wants is to have us as co-redeemers. We have to celebrate the Holy Mass with our own body and blood.

I'll give you another example. The nuns, who were also in prison at that time in Czechoslovakia, wrote me, that at 1:00 a.m. in the morning they would come to the factory realizing, "We come today to our work, to our altars. The machines are our altars on which we celebrate the Holy Mass with Jesus Crucified. All night long we celebrate our Holy Mass. And such a Holy Mass! Our crucifixion is in our hearts!" And so today, Jesus is seeking co-redeemers for the salvation of the world.

St. Paul, when he was in prison, understood this mystery of co-redemption. He said, "I complete in my flesh, in my body, what is lacking in the passion (in the suffering) of Jesus." Of course Jesus could have saved us only with His blood. But for the salvation of the world He wanted that it has to be fulfilled through us, through also our own spiritual or physical blood, through our hearts. Jesus, with this call, showed us the greatest work that He has entrusted to us! This gives us our greatest dignity, and *is our greatest mission.* And so all the people in that time who suffered (and today suffer) rejoiced; they had such great joy in their hearts. They were not frustrated, but they understood that *the greatest mission is to suffer with Jesus Christ!* Many of those priests, sisters and lay people in prison, said, "We thank God for this persecution from Communism, because it is through this persecution that the Lord has given us the possibility to know and deepen the greatest mystery of our faith — the Cross.

Each one of us is called to become co-redeemer with Jesus and Mary for the salvation of the world *through our own consecration to Our Lady!* And Pope Paul VI, when he went to Fatima, explained what it means to consecrate ourselves to the Immaculate Heart of Mary. He said, "Through the consecration to Our Lady, our hearts will become like the heart of Mary." And Paul VI, repeating the words of a Church Father, said "May our hearts become like Mary's heart. In our hearts may we have the same attitude, the same joy, the same love and need to glorify the Lord as Our Lady had (and has)." I hope that everyone of us has already consecrated himself/herself to the Immaculate Heart of Mary. The best example today, the model of this consecration to Our Lady, is our Holy Father: "TOTUS TUUS!" It means that I belong only to Jesus through Mary. I can't use myself for me, but I have to give my heart, my life — my entire life — to Jesus through Mary!

And so this attitude to be really only for the Lord through Our Lady has to penetrate, has to form all our daily work, our daily prayer, our daily life. Beginning from today, all my time, all my doing: *only to Jesus through Mary.* Mary has to guide me — has to lead me — that all my life will be a gift for Jesus.

In so many messages Our Lady in Medjugorje is asking us to give our life, to give our prayer for this work, for the redemption of the world. Today Our Lady needs each one of us for her Triumph. It is not the Triumph for Our Lady only. It is first of all the Triumph of the Lord! And this Triumph, as she said in Fatima, has to begin in Russia so that all the world will have peace. Not everybody can go today or tomorrow to Russia but everybody, each one of us, can become a missionary for Russia, an apostle for Russia. We can become apostles of her heart through our lives *in living the messages that she gave in Fatima and that she is giving in Medjugorje.*

POPE JOHN PAUL II: "MEDJUGORJE IS THE FULFILLMENT OF FATIMA"

Every Marian Movement, every Marian Christian is invited to become an apostle for this Triumph of Our Lady. Because we have to change not only Russia, but also the entire world through our own conversion and through our own donation to the Lord through Mary. And *in a special way this mission, this call, is given to the Marian Movement of Medjugorje.*

Once I presented to the Holy Father a group of doctors who analyzed and studied the events of the apparitions in Medjugorje. And the Holy Father, on this occasion, said these wonderful words: "Today the world has lost the sense of the supernatural. The world has lost the sense of God, of religion." And the Holy Father said, "Today many, many people are finding the supernatural in Medjugorje — in praying, in fasting, in doing penance." I said that the Marian Movement of Medjugorje is one of the most important and wonderful movements of Our Lady today. And so I and you, everybody who went to Medjugorje and returned, are called to save this world, to renew this world because we are in a deep crisis of secularism and we have to bring back to the Lord our society, our humanity. We have to feel ourselves responsible also for all the happenings in the world today. We don't do enough to transform and renew the world today.

Once a very close friend of the Holy Father told me — this person knew that in America there are thousands of Medjugorje groups (this friend of the Holy Father's knew also how many people and priests are coming to Medjugorje from America) — this person said, "These people from America who are going to Medjugorje, who are building prayer groups, these people are our hope to renew Catholic Christianity in America! These people are our hope for the future to renew America!"

I would like to thank you also in the name (in the intention) of the Holy Father. And I would like to thank you with the "Thank You" expression in the Russian language. "Thank you very much," in the Russian language is "spasibo." But the meaning of "spasibo" is much more than only "Thank you." It means, "God save you." "Spasibo," "thank you," was said by Lenin, Stalin, Brezhnev, Gorbachev — everybody in Russia. And for this reason I say to you also, God save you, God save you all, and through you may the Lord and Our Lady save the whole world!

God bless you!

7. URGENT MESSAGES FROM MEDJUGORJE

The preceding chapters serve as a prelude to the main body of arguments in favor of the authenticity of Medjugorje developed in the next two sections. Before proceeding to these arguments, however, we should like here to give you, dear reader, a reality test.

An argument about an abstraction is not the raison d'etre of this book. Rather, we seek here to open your mind and your heart to the message of your beloved Mother inviting you to her Son. At Medjugorje, she is concerned not simply with reminding us yet again of the Gospel forgotten and forsaken by a world that has reached the end of its tether. In Medjugorje, she also calls out for conversion, for total surrender to God, for a life of holiness and love. She wants you to come to the truth and also to put the truth into action in your life.

It is in this context that we invite you to prayerfully meditate on these two poignant messages from Medjugorje, one concerned with the need to disseminate the messages and the other with the urgency of applying these messages in one's personal life. Let us strip ourselves of all our pretensions and our self-importance as we contemplate these deadly serious missives from the Mother of God. We are talking here not just about the intellectual but about the spiritual and the moral, and one's over-riding obligation to one's conscience.

Dear Children! You are responsible for the messages. The source of grace is here, but you, dear children, are the vehicles transmitting the gifts. Therefore, dear children, I am calling you to work responsibly. Everyone will be responsible according to his own measure. Dear children, I am calling you to give the gift to others with love and not to keep it for yourselves. Thank you for having responded to my call. [May 8, 1986]

Dear Children! Today as never before I invite you to live my messages and to put them into practice in your life. I have come to help you and therefore I invite you to change your life because you have taken a path of misery, a path of ruin. When I told you convert, pray, fast, be reconciled, you took these messages superficially. You started to live them and then you stopped because it was difficult for you. Now, dear children, when something is good you have to persevere in the good and not think that God does not see me, He is not listening, He is not helping and so you have gone away from God and from me because of your miserable interest. I wanted to create of you an oasis of peace, love and goodness. God wanted you with your love and with His help to do miracles and thus to give that as an example. Therefore, here is what I say to you. Satan is playing with you and with your soul and I cannot help you because you are far from my heart. Therefore pray, live my messages and then you will see the miracle of God's love in your everyday life. Thank you for having responded to my call. [March 25, 1992]

II. WHO IS SHE THAT IS COMING FORTH?

1. MARY: HER "TIME" HAS COME

In this section, we will see Medjugorje the way the world has seen it, through the paintbrushes and cameras of the mass media, and we will ponder the phenomenon both on its own terms and in the context of the Church. Essentially, we are trying here to assess the case for Medjugorje.

For all Christians this is an exciting time to be alive. The worldwide proliferation of reported apparitions of the Mother of Jesus have convinced many that we have entered the *Age of Mary* prophesied by St. Louis de Montfort: "It was through Mary that the salvation of the world was begun, and it is through Mary that it must be consummated...." (*True Devotion*, Article lll, #49). Bishop Paolo Hnilica, at the 1992 National Conference on Medjugorje, said, "St. Louis Marie de Montfort has prophesied this extraordinary Marian epoch, which the Madonna announced at Fatima for this century. The Saint speaks of the Reign of Mary which will come through the action of the Holy Spirit, in which the Madonna will be truly Queen of all hearts, exercising her maternal sovereignty in all the life of the Church and of humanity. Such a maternal dominion will be the prelude to a splendid new Christian blossoming in the Church and in the world." Three months later the front page of the *National Catholic Register* proclaimed, "Mary, it seems, is on the mind of everyone these days. From Medjugorje to ...the message of Fatima to the words of Pope John Paul ll, devotion to Mary is enjoying a tremendous, perhaps unprecedented, revival," [*NCR*, September 27, 1992].

The sudden collapse of Soviet Communism is perceived by some to be a fulfillment of the Fatima prophecy. The global impact of Pope John Paul II has drawn special attention to his fervent Marian theology and spirituality. In acknowledgment of these stupendous phenomena all centered on her, Time

---

[1] In response to Our Lady's call, on the same weekend as the 1991 National Conference on Medjugorje at Notre Dame, June 14 - 16, an underground Marian Apostolate held a public conference in Leningrad (soon to be renamed St. Petersburg) — reportedly the first of its kind in Russian history — consecrating all of Russia and the Soviet Union to the Immaculate Heart of Mary and publicly renouncing all ties with Satan. Just a few minutes before midnight on December 31, 1991, the Pilgrim Virgin Statue of Our Lady of Fatima was carried in procession through Red Square as the communist flag was being lowered from over the Kremlin for the last time! Coincidence? St. Maximilian Kolbe had prophesied communism would end and Our Lady would be manifest in Red Square before 1992!

magazine, the most popular newsmagazine in the U.S. and perhaps the world, devoted its December 30, 1991, cover story to the Blessed Virgin Mary.[1] Despite the sensationalism and the superficiality characteristic of the popular press, the Time story on Mary is remarkable for the sense of awe that it seeks to evoke in its readers. Here are a few highlights from the article:

> When her womb was touched by eternity 2,000 years ago, the Virgin Mary of Nazareth uttered a prediction: 'All generations will call me blessed.' Among all the women who have ever lived, the mother of Jesus Christ is the most celebrated, the most venerated, the most portrayed, the most honored in the naming of girl babies and churches. Even the Koran praises her chastity and faith....
>
> Yet even though the Madonna's presence has permeated the West for hundreds of years, there is still room for wonder — now perhaps more than ever. ...A grass-roots revival of faith in the Virgin is taking place worldwide. Millions of worshippers are flocking to her shrines, many of them young people. Even more remarkable are the number of claimed sightings of the Virgin, from Yugoslavia to Colorado, in the past few years....
>
> Some Protestants are softening aspects of their hostility. Church of England theologian John Macquarrie has proposed revisions of such dogmas as the Assumption of Mary into heaven, which could then be seen as a symbol of the redemption that awaits all believers. Theologian Donald Bloesch of the University of Dubuque says fellow conservative Protestants 'need to see Mary as the pre-eminent saint' and 'the mother of the church.'...
>
> No one can take more satisfaction in the growth of faith in the Virgin... than John Paul II. Devotion to Mary was ingrained in the Pope in his Polish homeland, where over the centuries the Madonna has been hailed for turning back troops of the Muslim Turks, Swedish Lutherans and, in 1920, Soviet Bolsheviks. The precious Black Madonna icon was a mobilizing symbol for the country's efforts to throw off communism, and is still a unifying image for the entire nation.
>
> When he was made a bishop in 1958, John Paul emblazoned a golden M on his coat of arms and chose as his Latin motto "Totus tuus" (All Yours)-referring to Mary, not Christ.[2] Once he put on St.Peter's ring, John Paul made Mary's unifying power a centerpiece of his papal

---

[2] The Holy Father's motto is taken from the first two words "Totus tuus" of St. Louis de Montfort's short formula of Marian Consecration: "I am all yours and all that I have is yours, most loving Jesus, through Mary, your Holy Mother." Time's statement needs clarification.

arsenal. He has visited countless Marian shrines during his globe trotting, and invokes the Madonna's aid in nearly every discourse and prayer that he delivers. He firmly believes that her personal interces- sion spared his life when he was shot at St.Peter's Square in Rome in 1981; the assassination attempt occurred on May 13, the exact anni- versary of the first Fatima apparition.

Moreover, John Paul is firmly convinced, as are many others, that Mary brought an end to communism throughout Europe. His faith is rooted in the famed prophecies of Mary at Fatima in 1917. According to Sister Lucia, one of the children who claimed to see her, the Virgin predicted the rise of Soviet totalitarianism before it happened. In a subsequent vision, she directed the Pope and his bishops to conse- crate Russia to her Immaculate Heart in order to bring communism to an end."

The Time article is by no means an exposition of orthodox Marian doctrine. On the contrary, it devotes inordinate space to the aberrations that abound in the menagerie of modern liberal theology. Radical reductionists, feminists and liberation theologians are all granted a shot at Mariology in the article. Readers who lack a sense of history often forget that there are no new heresies; the most far-fetched theologies of today's fringe theologians have appeared and disap- peared time and again in the past. When the smoke of sensation clears away and the dust of fashion settles down, only the Church and its constant, universal Tradition remain in the running. Equally important, the Mother of God is not a mere object of idle abstract speculation but is directly active in history.

Laudably the Time article ends with an appreciation of this dynamic nature of Mary's interaction with the world: Mary "remains one of the most compelling and evocative icons of Western civilization. Renewed expressions of her vitality and relevance are signs that millions of people are still moved by her mystery and comforted by the notion of her caring. Whatever aspect of Mary they choose to emphasize and embrace, those who seek her out surely find something only a holy mother can provide."

The growing awareness of Mary's activity in the world has been most powerfully symbolized and concretized at Medjugorje. So much so, Time's sister publication Life devoted its cover to Medjugorje under the caption "Do You Believe in Miracles?" in July 1991. Medjugorje has received similar attention from a large part of the secular media, from television networks in Europe and the U.S. as well from the major print publications. A front page article in the November 9, 1992 *Wall Street Journal* featured Medjugorje with particular reference to the peace it emanates in the midst of the bloody conflict in Bosnia. The article quotes visionary Marija Pavlovic, "The Virgin is wiser than us. For her, there is no Serbia or Croatia. She says Satan is present on all sides in this war." The paper comments, "In blood-spattered Bosnia, such even-handedness is astonishing. In other ways, too, the war has enhanced Medjugorje's fame as an oasis of peace and mystery."

Not just the non-religious media but even world leaders like Ronald Reagan and Mikhail Gorbachev have been intrigued by the phenomenon of Medjugorje. It is clear even to non-believers that something is going on that requires an explanation. Is it indeed the case, we wonder, that the Medjugorje visionaries are actually witnessing an apparition of the Blessed Virgin Mary?

Our objective in this section is to study the evidence for the authenticity of the Medjugorje apparition, and we will begin this process with a survey of the ways in which the global media have both investigated and portrayed Medjugorje.

2. THE WORLD AS WITNESS: MEDJUGORJE IN THE MEDIA

One of the distinctive features of the modern world is the enormous impact and influence of the mass media, the print publications and the television networks in particular. Media journalists do not simply report the "news"; they investigate the alleged facts behind the news, they provide their own commentary on the news (commentaries that are often passed off as a part of the news), and sometimes they even "create" the news.

So severe is the scrutiny of the media that it can dictate the rise and fall of political careers — even of governments and heads of state. Claims of any kind made to the public are swiftly torn to shreds by investigative reporters who are trained to pick up the scent for a kill.

Modern apparitions, of course, have to confront the challenge of the media, not simply because they are public events but also because they involve the most extraordinary claims imaginable. Medjugorje has become the highest profile apparition of the modern age. As such it has been subjected to intense and relentless scrutiny by the media. In many respects, the media has performed the function of an investigative body — a body through which viewers and readers themselves can participate in the investigative process.

Amazingly, Medjugorje has emerged unscathed from the media's trial by fire. Some sophisticated media veterans have even confessed their bewilderment in the face of this phenomenon. In this chapter, we study the reports on Medjugorje that have appeared in leading publications in the English-speaking world.

Many of the media reports on Medjugorje have been written in the flippant style unfortunately favored by certain journalists. Flippancy in itself is no aid to investigation; it simply irritates the serious reader. Nevertheless, we will find much that is insightful and thought-provoking.

There is one question we must ask ourselves after we reflect on the reports quoted below: If the mass media, the prime investigative arm of the modern world, could not bury Medjugorje as a fraud, we must be prepared at least to study the claims of this apparition on its own terms.

(i) *The Wall Street Journal* [November 9, 1992]

FORWARD INTO BATTLE? NOT HERE,
WHERE THE VIRGIN REIGNS

The artillery duel begins midway through Mass, just before the Virgin appears.

Kneeling in the choir loft of a Catholic church, a young man and woman suddenly stop praying. Eyes open, lips moving silently, they speak to a figure visible only to them. Cannons thump in the distance. After a moment, the two resume praying, joined by pilgrims who have come here to witness the apparition of Mary.

...In war-torn Bosnia, faith has proved stronger than fear. A few pilgrims still visit Medjugorje — to watch and speak with its visionaries and to hear from them a divine message that is strikingly at odds with the slaughter and strife all around.

..."The Virgin is wiser than us," she [visionary Marija Pavlovic] says. "For her, there is no Serbia or Croatia. She says Satan is present on all sides in this war."

In blood-spattered Bosnia, such even-handedness is astonishing. In other ways too, the war has enhanced Medjugorje's fame as an oasis of peace and mystery. At one point, the war front was only three miles away — so close that Easter Mass was held in a sandbagged cellar. Planes and artillery ravaged nearby towns. But only six shells hit Medjugorje. The casualties: one cow, one chicken, one dog.

The sole air raid on the town ended with a few bombs exploding harmlessly. ....Dragan Kozina, the town's mayor and military commander, ... is struck by another seeming miracle. "Of 150 local men who have gone off to war, two have been injured slightly and none have been killed. You have to believe that either we are very lucky," he says, "or that someone is protecting us."

(ii) *Time* [7 July, 1986]

The visionaries say that the gray-robed Virgin, revealing Herself as the Queen of Peace, appears each evening between 6:00 and 6:45,[3] emerging from a cloud of light. Speaking Serbo-Croatian, the youths say, She utters spiritual admonitions, and has revealed ten secret oracles of coming events that they are to disclose later. According to the youngsters, the Virgin advocates bread-and-water fasting on Fridays and confession at least once a month.

For some, the frequency of the visions is reason enough to doubt the youths' story. Not for Lee Lawrence, a freelance writer who works in the U.S. consulate at Zagreb. He says, "People don't keep up a hoax for five years."

(iii) *Life* [July 1991]

It was at the spot of the iron cross that the visionaries — as they are called now — say they first say the Virgin. Two girls were on a path, talking and in the

---

[3] The discrepency in time, according to different accounts is due to the fact that during the Summer schedule, Our Lady appears at 6:40pm; durring the Winter schedule, 5:40pm.

distance, as the story goes, they saw a woman bathed in light, hovering above the ground. "The *Gospa*," one said, and they scurried away to find their friends. They came back, six this time, and saw her again, although she remained in the distance, silent, with babe in arms. The next day five teenagers and one child — Ivanka Ivankovic, 15; Mirjana Dragicevic, 16; Ivan Dragicevic, 16 (no relation to Mirjana; none of the visionaries is related); Vicka Ivankovic, 16; Marija Pavlovic, 16; and Jakov Colo, 10 — returned and upon seeing the Virgin ran to her feet, dropped to their knees and prayed. Since then they have been condemned and celebrated, prodded and poked, monitored by machines, interrogated by priests, police, psychologists, reporters and pilgrims. And yet 10 years after their first walk up Apparition Hill, only one fact remains beyond dispute: every evening, no matter where they are, whether in Medjugorje or in another country, the visionaries fall to their knees, gaze toward heaven and move their lips in mute appeal to an image no one else can see.

(iv) *Newsweek* [20 July 1987]

VISITATIONS OF THE VIRGIN, VISIONS IN YUGOSLAVIA ROIL THE CATHOLIC CHURCH

Six years ago, on a rocky hill overlooking the farming village of Medjugorje in southwestern Yugoslavia, six youngsters reported seeing a vision of a beautiful woman with a shining face, black curly hair, blue eyes and a gray coat. When they asked for Her name, She smiled and answered: '*The Blessed Virgin Mary.*'

Since then the Virgin has appeared daily to the four girls and two boys in private, at church and, for the last five years, at 6:40 every evening at the local parish rectory. Only the youths, all but one of whom are now in their 20's, see and hear the Virgin. Each reports seeing the same three-dimensional figure and receiving the same message of world peace. All say they have had a promise from the Virgin of a spectacular physical '*sign*' on the mountain of Medjugorje that will convince even atheists that the messages are from God. And all downplay their personal roles; says one, '*I am not a star, I don't have a desire to be a star.*'

Despite the unassuming airs, and the remoteness of Medjugorje, the news has excited true believers throughout the Roman Catholic world. Millions have treked to the isolated village. Thousands claim to have witnessed miraculous lights and sights. Hundreds report cures of everything from cancer to strokes. In short, Medjugorje would seem destined to join Lourdes and Fatima as centers of Pilgrimage, healing and devotion to the Virgin Mary.

Vatican officials prefer to be cautious; they have instructed the Yugoslav hierarchy to impanel a second commission, which could take many years to determine whether the visions are worthy of belief.

Medjugorje's true believers aren't waiting, and they have tradition on their side. They know from the histories of Joan of Arc, Saint Bernadette of Lourdes and the visionary children of Fatima that local officials have routinely opposed visionaries, only to be overruled by the faith of the people. And the people are coming — by tourist bus, car and bike and on foot, sometimes more than 50,000 on holy days. Already 290 miracle healings are under study by Catholic physicians. Crowds of faithful have claimed to have seen mysterious fires, columns of light and 'MIR' — the Serbo-Croatian word for peace — etched in the heavens. Just last month Jan Thomas, a young travel agent from New Orleans, climbed the hill of the original vision where she insists she saw a crude wooden cross suddenly light up. '*It wasn't flash photography,*' she says. '*I saw the vision of Jesus' face on the cross.*'

(v) *U.S.News and World Report* [March 12, 1990]

WHAT'S IN A VISION?

Holy apparitions can inspire faith. Frauds can test it.

By midafternoon, St. James Catholic Church in the remote Yugoslav village of Medjugorje is filled with pilgrims — many of them from the United States, Canada and Australia. At precisely 5:40 p.m., silence falls over the sanctuary, broken only by the clicking and whirring of flash cameras aimed at the choir loft where two young women kneel, their eyes transfixed on a blank wall, their lips moving in silent prayer. In a few moments, the women emerge from the loft, bearing a new message from Our Lady of Medjugorje urging a deeper devotion to her Son and closer attention to peace, prayers and penance.

It is a scene that has been repeated daily — with some variation — since June 24, 1981, when six village children, including the two young women, reported that the Virgin Mary appeared to them on a nearby hillside.

Yet church officials say they must be sensitive to avoid trampling the tender faith of new converts or those whose belief has been renewed because of an apparition. They follow a careful regimen in deciding whether an apparition is authentic. When an event occurs, the local bishop usually names a commission of theologians, psychologists and others to interview those involved and to weigh other evidence, including what effects the phenomenon is having on the public. Positive effects might include more conversions or simply greater prayerfulness. The commission reports to the bishop, who pronounces a verdict.

If the church finds an apparition authentic, members are not required to believe. The church, for example, only "warmly recommends" acceptance of the Marian apparitions at Lourdes, Fatima and Guadalupe, says the Rev. Eamon Carroll, a theologian at Loyola University in Chicago. But when it comes to the healings and penance linked with those shrines, says Carroll; *"These, the church feels competent to say, are God's work."*

At Medjugorje, the daily apparition has been accompanied over the years by other unusual occurrences. Thousands of pilgrims have reported watching the sun spin and dance in the sky. At night, mysterious lights are said to engulf a stone cross atop a rugged mountain, and images of Jesus and Mary are sometimes seen in the clouds. There are accounts of rosary beads turning from silver to gold and of sudden and miraculous healings.

But many believers say the *"real miracle"* of Medjugorje is not what happens in the church loft or in the Yugoslav sky. It is the change they see in the lives of the pilgrims, many of whom come to this remote village out of curiosity, some as little more than nominal Christians, but who leave with a deepened spirituality and a resolve to live more closely attuned to God and the church. *'People come looking for themselves and looking for God,'* says Father Leonardo Orec, a Franciscan monk and parish priest at Medjugorje. *'They find both here.'*

Even if the church rules negatively on Medjugorje, it is unlikely to change many minds among the growing millions of true believers. *'Medjugorje has brought me closer to my faith, and that can't change,'* says Joy Conti, a lawyer from Gibsonia, Pa., who says she was a *'Sunday Catholic'* before her 1987 pilgrimage. Many, like Father Jozo Zovko, who was the parish priest at Medjugorje when the apparition was first reported, are convinced that the effects of Medjugorje will speak louder than anything the church might say. *'One only needs to recognize the fruits,'* says Zovko, *'and they will tell you what kind of tree bore them.'"*

(vi) *The New York Times* [18 November, 1985]

YUGOSLAVS ARE ABASHED: MONEY FROM A MIRACLE

Medjugorje, Yugoslavia — About three million pilgrims have come to this village in the last four years, in what has been a mixed blessing for both the Communist government and the Roman Catholic Church.

Since June 1981, a vision of the Virgin Mary has been said to be appearing every evening at precisely the same time to a group of young villagers — six at the outset, four now. A series of tests and examinations by teams of Yugoslav and foreign medical and theological specialists has not shaken the visionaries' insistence on the reality of the apparitions. It has also left some of the examiners convinced that the phenomenon cannot be explained by normal criteria.

(vii) *The Times of London* [27 July, 1987]

INCREASING DEVOTION TO MARY

Spectacular 'appearances' by the Virgin Mary continue to be reported round the world at the rate of about one a year, most of them too spurious to warrant further interest. But international attention has been seized by the now famous apparitions in Medjugorje in Yugoslavia, which are still continuing seven years after they started and which have become a major attraction for tourists and pilgrims.

To sober post-Enlightenment secularists there is something both fascinating and slightly shocking about such phenomena, no doubt partly because of the affront contained in the implication that the Virgin Mary always prefers ignorant peasants for Her self-disclosure — perhaps as She was one Herself.

It is a feature of such cases, however, that the less one knows about them the easier they are to dismiss. And the same principle applies to the whole issue of devotion to the Virgin Mary. It refuses to go away.

Originally regarded in the other churches as an ignorant or superstitious taste peculiar to Roman Catholics and the Eastern Orthodox, the last two decades have seen an expanding interest in the Marian cult elsewhere, mainly in the Church of England but also among some of the Free Churches.

The Reformation brought a reaction against medieval abuses in this area largely because the Reformers saw the cult of Mary as one of the ways in which the church's practices were obscuring the truths of the Gospel. This, like much else, was hardened into doctrinal opposition: but nevertheless some pious regard for Mary survived in parts of the Protestant tradition.

The mariology — or mariolatry — rejected by the Reformers in the sixteenth century was rather different from the form it later took, and Protestant criticisms were implicitly acknowledged in the way the Second Vatican Council treated the subject in the early sixties.

The usual theological treatment nowadays emphasizes that Mary's significance derives wholly from Her Son. The Second Vatican Council said 'it did not hesitate to profess this subordinate role of Mary' and declared that nothing in Marian devotion could 'take away or add anything to the dignity and efficacy of Christ, the one Mediator.'

It seems logical that the elimination of the role of Mary from within certain areas of Christian practice and belief is likely to lead to the gradual weakening of some important Christological doctrines. For She has traditionally been honored under the title '*Mother of God*' on the grounds that She conceived Jesus the incarnate Second Person of the Christian Trinity, through supernatural intervention.

Stress is also placed on Her free consent to this divine conception, implying that the Incarnation itself only happened because of Her consent. In terms of what the Incarnation means to Christians, this is a remarkable thing to say about one human act of will, and explains why the person who made it has always been regarded as special.

(viii) *The International Herald Tribun* [July 21 1987]

YUGOSLAV TOWN FLOURISHING ON VISION OF THE VIRGIN
by Jackson Diehl (Washington Post Service):

Medjugorje, Yugoslavia — Ivan Dragicevic and Marija Pavlovic, two well dressed, clean-cut young people from this tiny village, stood in the stifling heat of a priest's cluttered office one recent evening and recited a prayer to the Virgin Mary in their native Serbo-Croatian.

Around them pressed a tight semicircle of Roman Catholic priests from the United States, Italy, Ireland, Switzerland and South America, clutching rosaries and sweating heavily in their white collars. On their flanks, members of four American package tours focused home video cameras, making tapes for hand-to-hand circulation around the U.S. heartland.

Mr. Dragicevic and Miss Pavlovic suddenly broke off their prayer and dropped to their knees. Pressing their palms together and staring intently upward, toward the top shelf of an ordinary bookcase, at the plaster statuette of Mary on it and at a crucifix attached to the wall.

For four minutes they held that gaze, occasionally mouthing indistinguishable words, while the witnesses and cameras looked on.

For the 2,212th consecutive evening, by these youths' account, a miraculous vision had occurred. Beginning at 6:40, they had seen and conversed with Mary, who they say reveals Herself to them. The Virgin, by their account, has singled out Medjugorje, a poor, isolated mountain hamlet near the Adriatic coast in central Yugoslavia, and six of its youths to receive Her message for the rest of the world.

(ix) *The Reader's Digest* [February 1986]

The children described to the crowd what the Gospa looked like. Having identified herself as the "*Blessed Virgin Mary*," the apparition added, 'I come as the Queen of Peace.' Soon there occurred the first of many strange phenomena

115

described by eyewitnesses: the word mir, 'peace' in Serbo-Croatian, appeared in huge flame-colored letters across the night sky, ending above the parish church in Medjugorje.

Marija and Ivan, both now 20, pray softly, their heads bowed, eyes closed. Jakov, 14, fidgets, looks around and is likely to smile at visitors. It is precisely because of this that the change — from childlike impatience to pure joy once the vision of 'ecstasy' begins — is more apparent in him. Just after 5:40, they stand side by side facing a wall on which hang a crucifix and a rosary. Suddenly, as if with one movement, they cross themselves, fall to their knees and simultaneously gaze up at the same point. They then listen, smile, or nod their heads. They speak — their lips and throat muscles move — but without making a sound. These movements occur individually, at different moments: they are apparently having different conversations at the same time. Sometimes they nod together — She seems to be saying the same thing to them all.

Then, simultaneously and unexpectedly, their eyes and heads shoot up; one or another might sigh "Ode" ('She's gone'), and the expression of enchantment leaves their faces. They make the sign of the cross, stand up, smile and talk, then separate to make notes describing what they saw. Their impressions of the Gospa's mood sometimes differ, but the visual details always tally.

A NUMBER OF INVESTIGATIONS have tested the validity of the visions. In 1983, a Yugoslav psychiatrist and paraphychologist, Dr. Ludvik Stopar, hypnotized Marija shortly after a vision and found that her account under hypnosis was identical to that in full consciousness. After neuropsychiatric and physical examinations on all the youngsters, he concluded that they were 'absolutely normal adolescents with no psychopathological symptoms.' Twelve Italian physicians also found no evidence of hypnosis, manipulation or drugs.

In 1984 a team of French doctors under Prof. Henri Joyeux of the University of Montpelier conducted electrocardiograms, electroence-phalograms, tests on ocular movements and reflexes, and tests on auditory nerves and larynx muscle movement. The doctors documented the simultaneous fixing of the gaze on an identical point, with eye movement beginning and ending at the same moment and the cessation of the blinking reflex to sudden light.

The team concluded that the phenomenon was scientifically inexplicable. They defined it as *'a state of intense, active prayer, partially disconnected from the exterior world, a state of contemplation and of healthy communications with a definite person whom only they can see, hear and touch.'*

(x) *The Guardian* [17 September 1984]

Thousands attend Mass very reverently each evening in the parish church of St. James, and people walk about the country lanes praying. Lapsed Catholics of all ages have returned to the church. The local clergy have been overwhelmed by the demand for their services. Extra priests come in relays to hear confessions and to minister to the people. It is said that family and community life has changed completely, with families that used to quarrel now praying together and fasting one day a week on bread and water, and farmers who previously feuded now helping each other in their fields. But the changes are most remarkable amongst the young people. They are the most committed of all, many of them living their lives around their new-found faith, and with an increasing number wishing to enter the religious life as priests and nuns.

While I report here what I saw myself, this tallies exactly with what many other have told me, and with what can be seen on photographs and videotapes. Each evening, while the rosary is being prayed by larger numbers of people in the church, the young visionaries enter a chapel off the main altar. They stand in front of a small altar and crucifix, and begin to say the Lord's Prayer. Suddenly, and simultaneously, they drop to their knees and their prayer ceases. Their eyes appear to focus on the upper area of the wall in front of them, but their faces take on a strikingly absorbed expression which remains absolutely undisturbed throughout the vision, and regardless of the somewhat irreverent activities of photographers and curious pilgrims.

At times, the young people's lips move silently, as they appear to take their turns in a conversation. They may smile and nod their heads, but they never look at each other or acknowledge any visible event going on around them. After a few minutes they all gasp, as with one voice, signalling the disappearance of the — vision. Then they make the sign of the cross and stand up. They are immediately once more aware of their surroundings and of the other people in the room, and they begin to respond in a friendly way to people's greetings.

The six visionaries are now aged between 13 and 20. One of them, Mirjana, 19, who is a student at Sarajevo University, has apparently received the visions intended for her, but the other five, Jakov, 13, Ivanka, 18, Ivan, 19, Vicka and Marija, 20, have all been present in the chapel nearly every day for the three years. Naturally, there has been considerable suspicion about the visions, not least from the local Catholic Bishop of Mostar. However, the visionaries have given every appearance of being normal teenagers, open and friendly to all who approach them, serious but not intense in attitude, and popular amongst their contemporaries. They have also survived persistent and close questioning, not only by the local police and by psychiatrists appointed by the authorities. All have pronounced them normal, and this over a period of three years of daily exposure to public interest and scrutiny.

It seems inconceivable that the young people could either be the perpetrators of a deliberate hoax, or that they could have been manipulated into such an elaborate hoax by their clergy, as has been alleged by the authorities.

WHO IS SHE THAT IS COMING FORTH?

There is no commercialization of the events. Money is refused by the young people if ever it is offered. Personally, I have not met anyone who has experienced these events who did not conclude that the supernatural explanation was more plausible than any other so far proposed.

(xi) *Libre Belgiue* [January 9, 1984]

AT MEDJUGORJE, THE INHABITANTS BELIEVE, PRAY AND FAST.
DID THE VIRGIN APPEAR IN YUGOSLAVIA?

The biggest miracle which needs no proof nor confirmation is the real explosion of faith we have witnessed in this village of old Hercegovina.

Who says this? The Archbishop of Split, a large Yugoslavian town to the North East of Dubrovnik. The village about which he speaks is Medjugorje, diocese of Mostar.

It all began on June 24, 1981 on the mountain Crnica which dominates the village. Around 6:30 p.m. five young people saw a *'Lady in* bright light. Shocked, they fled...to return, however, the next day at the same time with a sixth child. They are Ivan (15), Vicka, Marija, Marijana (all 15), Ivanka (15) and Jacov (10). The Lady appears again and introduces Herself: it is the Virgin Mary, as the seers suspected. Since then She returns almost every night, at the same time in the summer, an hour earlier in the winter. Her message is a faithful echo of the very first exhortation of Her Son: Convert and believe the Good News. (Mark 1, 15) The insistence of the Mother of God on conversion is especially urgent here: *'I will ask My Son, but convert!...I only ask for conversion..... Renounce everything, be prepared...'* To carry out this 'metanoia' (conversion). This return to God She recommends prayer, especially communal prayer and penitence, especially fasting with bread and water on every Friday. The other great theme of Her message is peace. She introduces Herself in these words: I am the Queen of Peace. And while several parts of this planet are gripped in war (Afghanistan, Iraq, Lebanon) while we talk about warheads, SS 20 and Pershing and while the threat of a third world war is again haunting our minds, Mary assures us that peace is still possible if we want it. On what condition? Only one, but imperative: Ask the Lord.

By prayer and fasting we can still prevent this war which threatens us and also the other social cataclysms and even natural disasters. Because nothing is impossible for God!

To underline this conditional promise of peace, the word MIR (Peace in Croatian) appeared in large luminous letters in the sky of Medjugorje, on a July

1981 evening, above Mount Krivezac, which is dominated by a 4 meter high cement cross elevated for the Holy Year 1933. All the inhabitants of the village, including the pastor, have seen it. They have also witnessed several other unexplainable phenomena, the most spectacular occurring in October of 1982 when a large light appeared resembling a forest fire, but on a mountain which is made up of rock, where no trees grow, only a few prickly bushes or shrubs and when they were examined, there was no trace of any fire. The fire brigade which rushed to the scene found no fire, no burned material.

(xii) ABC [*20/20*, June 17, 1988]

JOURNEY TO FAITH

WALTERS: In a small village in Yugoslavia, six youngsters claimed to have seen the Virgin Mary again. Millions of people from all over the world believed in their visions enough to make pilgrimage there. Stone Phillips followed one group of pilgrims from the United States and, whether or not you are a believer, we think you'll be moved by the experience of this 'Journey to Faith.'

STONE PHILLIPS: (voice-over) It is early evening at Saint James Church in Medjugorje, an isolated village in the mountains of Yugoslavia. The weekday mass is filled to capacity, as always. As the service continues below, a few people in the choir loft kneel near a young man named Ivan Dragicevic. It is 5:40 p.m. and Ivan is speaking to someone only he sees. The people around him watch as he mouths words soundlessly. They fervently believe that they are witnessing a miracle, a divine revelation that will have great impact on the world. They believe that Ivan and several other young visionaries in Medjugorje converse each day with the Blessed Virgin Mary the mother of Jesus Christ.

PHILLIPS: The apparitions here in Medjugorje are said to have begun June 24, 1981. It was about four o'clock in the afternoon, and two young girls were walking along this road. 15-year old Ivanka and her friend, Mirjana, 16 years old. Ivanka, who was mourning the death of her mother at the time, happened to look up at the hillside and she says she saw in the distance, about 200 yards away where that cross now stands today, the shining figure of a woman. She turned to her friend and said, 'Look, Mirjana, the Madonna,' (voice-over) Within a day, the two girls had shared the secret with four of their friends, who also saw the vision. Understandably, Ivan was startled by the experience.

IVAN DRAGICEVIC: Although I was distant from Her, meeting Her frightened me but the shock of this experience awakened me to a new life.

PHILLIPS: (voice-over) On the second day, 17-year old Vicka Ivankovic says the visionaries were drawn to the Madonna.

WHO IS SHE THAT IS COMING FORTH?

VICKA IVANKOVIC: And we went up the hill. We did not walk. It felt as if we were flying through the air. We crossed so many rocks and thorns, but nothing scratched us, not a scratch, and we found ourself beside Our Lady. We were with Her on the hill and those of us who are more courageous talked to Her. I did not say anything.

PHILLIPS: (voice-over) The children were not outwardly exceptional in any way. Ten year old Jakov Colo was the youngest.

JAKOV COLO: At the beginning, we asked ourselves why we were chosen, because we are not different from others. Once we asked Our Lady and She said She is not after the best.

PHILLIPS: (voice-over) The difficult climb to the site of the first apparition is filled with symbolism. Ascending the steep rocky path is a way of doing penance, atonement for past sins. Some of the pilgrims are beginning to be emotionally affected. For them, this inhospitable, rock-strewn hillside is a holy place. But seven years ago, the crowds who believed the story told by the children and who gathered here with them risked persecutions, even imprisonment, by the authorities. In the summer of 1981, the Yugoslav police, convinced that they were confronted with a case of mass hysteria, banned the gatherings and attempted to arrest the children. The visionaries fled through the vineyards towards Saint James Church. The pastor hid them in the church and, from then on, the apparitions would take place there.

Despite the crackdown, huge numbers of pilgrims, desperate for a sign which would confirm their faith, assembled every day at 5:30 outside the rectory where the visionaries were now said to be receiving the apparitions. Every day, the children praying together, then falling to their knees at the same moment, their voices becoming inaudible.

IVAN: We see Our Lady in three dimensions. We talk with Her. We see Her as I see you now. She is wearing a gold dress, light veil, black hair.

VICKA: And She is supported in a cloud and, for Christmas, She comes with little Jesus, little Baby Jesus in Her arms.

PHILLIPS: (voice-over) Understandably, many people remained suspicious. They thought the youngsters could be lying or deluding themselves. The children were subjected to a battery of psychological and physical tests, measuring brain waves, heartbeat and involuntary eye movements during the apparitions. The head scientist was Professor Henri Joyeux from the prestigious Montpellier University in France. He'd arrived prepared to discredit the apparitions. He left convinced that the visionaries were not lying or having hallucinations.

HENRI JOYEUX, Professor of Medicine: The clinical observations made on these visionaries permit us to affirm that these children are perfectly normal and of sound mind and body. The phenomenon reveals itself as being scientifically inexplicable.

(xiii) NBC [*Inside Edition*, September 1990]

IS IT A MIRACLE OR A FRAUD

BILL O'REILLY: Why are millions of Americans spending thousands of dollars to go to a small town in the middle of nowhere? The answer to that question is extremely controversial. For nine years six young people have said that Mary, the Mother of Christ, is appearing to them. For nine years, nobody has been able to disprove that, including the U.S. State Department. Inside Edition traveled to Medjugorje, Yugoslavia, to investigate and what we found may surprise you!

They come every day, thousands from all over the world. They come because Mary, the Mother of Jesus Christ, is said to be appearing here in Medjugorje, Yugoslavia. For the American pilgrim the trip costs thousands of dollars, still they continue to come.

Some believe the visionaries are fabricating their story, but Father Phillip Pavich, an American priest who heads the team protecting the visionaries, believes the young people are telling the truth.

FATHER PAVICH: They had plenty of chances to cut out, plenty, they didn't cut out at all, so when they've been grilled like that and they've been tested, they've been wired-up, and they've been questioned by pilgrims from around the world, human relationships demand I accept their testimony until I can prove otherwise, and I can't prove otherwise.

BILL O"REILLY: Neither can anyone else. The visionaries have passed a battery of lie detector tests and psychiatric examinations.

This all began in June of 1981, when six children shocked their parents, when they had said they had seen and talked with Mary, the Mother of Jesus Christ. Now, this kind of thing usually goes away quickly and quietly, but it has been nine years, the children are now adults, they have not yet been discredited, and they say they are still in touch with Mary. For visionary Maria Pavlovic, now 25, life is a constant challenge, as she is sought out by pilgrims from all over the world. We spoke to Maria through an interpreter at her modest home. Did Our Lady ever tell Maria why She appeared to her?

MARIA PAVLOVIC: We asked Her once and She said She chose us; we told Her we were not the best of people, and She said God allowed Her to choose, and it was us She chose, we don't know why.

BILL O'REILLY: Because of the tremendous numbers of Americans visiting Medjugorje, Inside Edition has learned that the U.S. State Department launched its own investigation, the results of which have been kept quiet until now. The former U.S. Ambassador to Yugoslavia, David Anderson was in charge of the investigation.

DAVID ANDERSON: I sent two of my political officers to Medjugorje; one a failed priest, one an Irishman, to take a very hard look at what we thought we were seeing and they came back and reported.

BILL O'REILLY: What did they tell you when they came back?

DAVID ANDERSON: They came back and said: 'Mr. Ambassador, you won't believe this, but there's something there!'

BILL O'REILLY: For many, only visual proof will convince, but for millions of others, the apparitions of Mary at Medjugorje is a reality, this small hamlet in the middle of nowhere is now one of the holiest places on Earth, and perhaps, that is the Miracle of Medjugorje. We could find no evidence that the Church, or the young people involved, are benefitting financially from any of this, the only people making money are in the travel industry.

(xiv) TV Talk Shows

The Oprah Winfrey Show [November 23, 1988]

THE POWER OF PRAYER

OPRAY WINFREY: If you think religious miracles only happened in the days of Jesus or back when people wore sandals, think again because today we have almost an entire audience filled with people who have come to share a secret about what they have learned after visiting a small town in Yugoslavia known as Medjugorje. Several youths there claim to have daily visits with the Virgin Mary. And as you just witnessed in the video tape, millions of people have visited the town and come back either physically or spiritually transformed, they say.

OPRAH (voice-over) The video tape you're watching right now was taken in 1985 in Medjugorje, Yugoslavia. These six youths you see right now are captured in the state where they claim to be able to see, hear and speak with the Virgin Mary. Each day since June of 1981, they would enter the apparition room where you now see them and after reciting several prayers would fall to their knees and at 5:45 p.m. the exact time, they would meet with Mary each day. Now, although you may see others in the room, only these young people are able to see Mary in three-dimensional form. If this does sound a little strange to you, you should know that all six of these young people have been subjected to a battery of every test imaginable, testing their physical and mental states. All six were found to be psychologically sound, and no trace of the visions that were reported were lies or hallucinations.

3. THE AUTHENTICITY OF THE MEDJUGORJE APPARITIONS

(i) Overview

Let's face it. Prima facie, the Medjugorje apparitions appear to be "for real" beyond the shadow of a doubt. As the television cameras peered into the apparition room and zoomed in on the visionaries conversing with the Gospa, we knew in the pit of our stomachs that something extraordinary was taking place here. The accompanying commentaries by "experts" and "authorities" somehow lacked "the power and the glory" of the phenomenon itself. When the entire picture — the totality of visionaries witnessing an apparition, healings, luminary phenomena, Masses and confessions and on and on — is held up to view, the observer is left with an overpowering sense of the supernatural breaking through the ordinary.

Obvious as all this may seem, however, in this skeptical age we have to storm a whole host of barricades and battlements before we can give our assent even to the obvious. Inevitably, the process of analyzing an event such as an apparition is an artificial, stilted process that will leave out the freshness and the simplicity of what is taking place. To appreciate the beauty of the Mona Lisa is an instinctive, immediate experience. To analyze one's experience of the beauty of this painting is not similarly simple and swift and pleasurable. Much as we would prefer to let Medjugorje be Medjugorje, we must perforce engage in the torturous process of analysis and clarification because the clear waters of this phenomenon have been muddied by deceit-driven doubt and malicious attack; a little filtration and chlorination, we hope, will keep at least some of the pollutants at bay.

Although our primary concern is with the authenticity of the reported apparitions at Medjugorje, we must begin our inquiry with the question of how it is possible to determine whether any apparition is authentic. This question must be analyzed on several levels.

On one level, the question is whether the apparent witness to an apparition is telling the truth when he or she claims to experience some kind of contact with another reality. If this question can be answered affirmatively, then the next question that should be asked is whether or not the visionary is hallucinating or suffering from some sort of psychological disorder. Understandably, any claim of close encounters with the supernatural is not likely to be universally accepted. No amount of evidence would have convinced a dogmatic skeptic like Emile Zola who actually saw a lady cured of a terminal disease in the healing waters of Lourdes but refused to believe that anything supernatural was involved. Nevertheless, there are certain principles of rationality that may be applied in evaluating the link between the subjective experience of the visionary and objective reality.

Finally, if application of these principles leads to the conclusion that the visionary is not a victim of self-deception, the question must then be "who" or "what" is being experienced. If the source of the experience is not a fertile imagination or a fevered brain, we must decide between two further options — the divine and the diabolic. "Signs and wonders," after all, can come from either side. On this last question, the Church, after centuries of experience in these areas, has established a series of litmus tests that have been supplemented by the lessons learnt in each authenticated apparition.

All three phases of the process of confirming the authenticity of an apparition are entirely dependent on subjective judgments which every person must make individually in the light of the evidence and of personal experience.The Church *as Church* teaches on matters of faith and morals, claiming infallibility in pronouncements made through the exercise of the ordinary and the extraordinary magisterium with regard to the public revelation (the Old and New Testaments and the Tradition handed down from the earliest days); infallibility is not claimed in the arena of private revelation. The Church *as Mother* provides pastoral guidance to its children when confronted with claims of private revelation, phenomena that appear to have a supernatural origin but which are not, strictly speaking, a part of the deposit of faith of which it is the guardian. The Church as Church speaks authoritatively on the theological soundness of the messages received at an apparition, but it will not make any pronouncement as to whether or not any given apparition actually took place because it does not claim infallibility in determining the validity of claims involving empirical data.

"Empirical" is here understood to include such acts of sense perception as physical observation which are characteristic both of the scientific enterprise and of apparitions. Although certain ecclesiastical authorities tried to suppress Galileo's works, at no point did the Church *as Church* make an *ex cathedra* statement on the soundness of his theories. God gave us our senses and our minds to use in exploring and understanding His universe. The mysteries of faith, such as the doctrine of the Trinity, are in principle beyond the range of unaided human reason, and it is here that public divine revelation is indispensable. The frame of reference of the sciences, on the other hand, is within the reach of the human mind (despite its many limitations). Apparitions, by their very nature, are quasi-empirical phenomena. But they are not entirely empirical affairs, and they have a theological dimension that has to be analyzed in terms of the frame of reference set by the Church.

In this chapter we are concerned with the Church's criteria for authentic apparitions, and we will focus on these criteria and their application. How do you examine an apparition on "its own merits?" As we have noted, the Church has set up a litmus test of sorts for discerning the authenticity of an apparition.

The first apparitions of the Blessed Virgin were reported as far back as the first century, and claims of Marian apparitions and messages have surfaced in almost every century. While some of these claims are clearly legendary, other apparitions were reported by saints and holy men and women. The thorough empirical and theological investigation that is now characteristic of the Church's approach to influential claims of apparitions began with the modern apparitions. Well known apparitions in the last two centuries include the Miraculous Medal in 1830, La Salette in 1846, Lourdes in 1858, Pontmain in 1871, Knock in 1879, Fatima in 1917, Beauraing in 1932 and Banneux in 1933.[4] Hundreds of other claims of apparitions have been made in this century, and many of these have been knocked out of court by ecclesiastical authorities on legitimate grounds of obvious fraud or heresy. More often than not, the Church plays the role of a skeptic because it is a defender of the truth and has a pastoral responsibility for safeguarding its children from error and superstition. Additionally, the Church is charged with protecting the public revelation, and it has an obligation to prevent an obsession with private revelations from subverting the absolute priority of the public deposit of faith.

In its investigation of an apparition, the Church first utilizes the services of scientific methods and personnel. In the course of such an investigation, writes Fr. Michael O'Carroll, "The norms of critical history must be strictly applied; the resources of normal and paranormal psychology, fully used. Error can enter at any stage of the alleged communication. If error is clearly discovered, through deceitful testimony, psychiatric disease, mistaken observation, or defect in a spoken or written narrative, an adverse judgment may be pronounced to avert further harm." (1) Local bishops and commissions set up by the bishops play an important role in this phase. Fr. O'Carroll also points out that the reliability of a

---

[4] It is not widely known that apparitions of Our Lady beginning on March 25, 1976 in Betania, Venezuala, were recognized as authentic by Bishop Pio Bello Ricardo on November 21, 1987. Her messages in Betania parallel her messages in Medjugorje, and the apparitions there continue! In San Nicolas, Argentina, Bishop Castagna leads tens of thousands of the faithful in procession on the 25th of each month in celebration of her coming to San Nicholas. He has given his imprimatur for the book of messages which has been published and he approved the new Basilica (laying the cornerstone himself) requested by Our Lady. The Bishops Conference of Argentina is very favorable towards the events in San Nicholas. In one of her messages in San Nicolas it is reported that Our Lady said that this was how she had expected to be received in Medjugorje! (A reported message from from Our Lord to the visionary on June 6, 1986: "If this generation does not listen to the message of my mother, it will perish. I ask everyone to listen to her. Man's conversion is necessary...My Heart wishes the salvation of all souls and loves them, even those who are in sin." [*An Appeal From Mary In Argentina*, Fr. Rene Laurentin, Riehle Foundation, 1991].

visionary's testimony is dependent on his or her credibility as a witness. Three criteria are relevant here: "Is the witness (a) a competent observer, (b) an accurate reporter, (c) truthful?" (2)

In 1974, the Congregation for the Doctrine of the Faith issued a document listing the positive and negative criteria relevant in assessing the authenticity of a private revelation and these are listed below.

Positive Criteria

1. Moral certitude or a high probability that the facts are consistent with what has been claimed.

2. The persons involved are psychologically balanced, honest, living a good moral life, sincere, respectful toward church authority.

3. Immunity from error in theological and spiritual doctrine.

4. That there be sound devotion and spiritual fruits, such as the spirit of prayer, testimony of charity and true conversion.

Negative Criteria

1. That there be no manifest error regarding the facts of the event.

2. That there be no doctrinal errors attributed to God, Mary or a saint.

3. That there be no evidence of material or financial motives connected with the event.

4. That there be no gravely immoral acts by the person on the occasion of the revelations or apparitions.

5. That there be no psychopathic tendency in the person which might enter into the alleged supernatural event; no psychosis or collective hysteria of some type.

Theological analysis of an apparition must, of course, center on the doctrinal soundness of the messages received and transmitted by the visionaries. This focus on doctrinal soundness must be supplemented by discernment of a certain degree of conformity with precedents set by authentic apparitions. These precedents include the following: apparitions with public consequences are generally witnessed by children (Lourdes, La Salette, Pontmain, Fatima, Beauraing and Banneux); the visionaries are given some secrets of a significant nature that may or may not be revealed in the future (Lourdes, La Salette, Fatima); official approval of the apparitions comes only after the persistent and prayerful efforts of the faithful themselves often in the teeth of opposition (Lourdes, La Salette, Fatima); and some kind of public sign is given at the end of the apparitions as a mark of authentication for those who would not believe until then (the cloak with the image of the Virgin in Guadalupe, the Miraculous Medal, the grotto with healing waters at Lourdes, the dancing sun at Fatima). None of these precedents apply in all authenticated apparitions, but they are helpful guidelines. In addition to these precedents, apparitions are also to be judged by the fruits they bear, principally their spiritual fruits although physiological healing and other such "signs" must not be discounted.

Two other factors are sometimes **inaccurately** cited as precedents. One is the need for conspicuous sanctity in the visionaries and the other is the limited duration of an apparition.

In the first case, an apparition is not granted as a reward for a saintly life but is a free gift bestowed lovingly (as apparent in the content of the messages themselves). Only two visionaries have been canonized: St. Catherine Labouré and St. Bernadette.[5] The La Salette visionaries did not distinguish themselves in their later lives. Though they were criticized for certain unfortunate situations, no one questioned the authenticity of the apparitions on the grounds of the visionaries' shortcomings. It must be remembered too that every utterance of a visionary has never been seriously regarded as authoritative — even after authentication of the apparition witnessed by the visionary. Fr. O'Carroll notes that "Mental development over a period of time may also colour a story once told barely. All authorities admit that the recipient of a genuine apparition may still be mistaken in particulars." (3) It must be remembered that the document on criteria for judging alleged private revelations issued by the Congregation for the Doctrine of the Faith states that "there be no gravely immoral acts by the person" but only "*on the occasion* of the revelations or apparitions." Visionaries are

---

[5] Considering the treatment of the visionaries in Medjugorje by Church authorities let us bear in mind that, according to Fr. Rene Laurentin, at one point St. Bernadette recanted and said she had invented the apparitions at Lourdes — as a result of her treatment by church officials during interrogations following the apparitions. Furthermore, Fr. Laurentin has observed, "This critical (unhealthy) situation of our times...led me to say (without being contradicted) that Lourdes would not have been recognized if its same apparitions had happened a century later," (*The Church And Apparitions — Their Status and Function: Criteria and Reception*, Report given at the 1989 National Conference on Medjugorje.)

neither infallible nor impeccable — and friends and foes of a reported apparition err alike if they expect the recipients of the apparition to fulfill such conditions.

The second factor cited as an authoritative precedent — the limited duration of an apparition — cannot be taken too seriously. Authentic apparitions in the past have ranged from days to months. In the case of Fatima, it can be persuasively argued that the duration of the apparitions must be measured in years because the initial apparition in 1917 was followed by later apparitions witnessed by Sister Lucia in 1925 and 1929.[6] In any event, it is not for us to judge how and when an apparition would have accomplished its intended aims.

In the context of this discussion on precedents, it must be remembered that normally the Church yields its judgment on an influential apparition only after the phenomena under review have ceased. This is the case partially because all the data required for such a judgment will be available only when the apparition has ceased. While official approval can only be given after an official pronouncement on the apparition, the faithful do not necessarily have to withhold assent to the authenticity of a given apparition if they have reasonable grounds for accepting it as authentic. Neither Lourdes nor Fatima would have been officially approved if the faithful had withheld assent to the authenticity of those apparitions before they were approved. The Church launched an investigation of the apparitions, on the basis of which they were approved, only because of the fervent and persistent conviction of the faithful. As has already been mentioned both St. Catherine Labouré and Don Bosco gave their hearty assent to the apparition at Lourdes before it was officially recognized. In fact, the final verdict on Lourdes cited "the throng of people" it had attracted as one of the criteria in favor of its authenticity. Fatima, it must be remembered, was approved by the Church only after thirteen years of investigation.

Since the authorities investigating reported apparitions do not have personal experience of the apparitions themselves, it is not surprising that they often choose to be cautious before they pass judgment. Delay is almost inevitable in such contexts. Only in the case of two approved apparitions — Guadalupe and Akita — did the investigating Bishops themselves personally witness extraordinary events. Official approval in the case of both these apparitions was (not surprisingly) all but instantaneous. But in the case of most other reports of apparitions, the general pattern of the subtlety and "invisibility" of the object of faith is preserved.

The Church *as Church,* it cannot be stressed enough, is concerned primarily with the data of public revelation and with the interpretation and application

---

[6] On May 13, 1917, Our Lady told Lucia, "I came to ask you to come here for six consecutive months, on the thirteenth day, at this same hour. ...And I shall return here again a seventh time." We still await the seventh apparition of Our Lady of Fatima in the Cova da Iria!

of this revelation. The assessment of claims of private revelation and other phenomena that involve an empirical dimension is important but secondary to the primary mission of the Church, and the majority of claims of apparitions have not been investigated by the Church. Often enough, when claims are made of an apparition or of an experience of mystical union with God and when these claims are not accompanied by doctrinal deviation, the Church has simply allowed the test of time to be the ultimate determinant. If the devotional momentum of the faithful, the *sensus fidelium*, persists, the Church, in many cases, has either officially conveyed its approval or has implicitly recognized the credibility of the witnesses (this was the case at Knock which has not been formally approved but which received a papal blessing from His Holiness John Paul II).

Even when the Church has thoroughly investigated an apparition, or any other claim of private revelation, and yields a positive judgment, this judgment is not presented as an infallible judgment. In 1877, the Congregation of Rites affirmed that "The Apostolic See has neither approved nor condemned such apparitions or revelations but merely permits Catholics to believe in them — where they have the support of credible witness and documents — with a purely human faith." (4)

It should be noted here that infallibility does not extend to judgments made by bishops in their individual capacity. The Second Vatican Council explicitly taught that "bishops, taken individually, do not enjoy the privilege of infallibility". [*Lumen Gentium*, chapter III, section 25.] Nevertheless, the Council stresses that the laity should show proper submission and respect to bishops in their governance of the Church, keeping in mind their immense dignity as successors of the apostles. "Like all Christians, the laity should promptly accept in Christian obedience what is decided by the pastors who, as teachers and rulers of the Church, represent Christ." [*Lumen Gentium*, chapter IV, section 37.]

The Council lays down the procedures for settlement of disagreements between the laity and their bishops. "By reason of the knowledge, competence or pre-eminence which they have, the laity are empowered — indeed sometimes obliged — to manifest their opinions on those things which pertain to the good of the Church. If the occasion should arise, this should be done through the institutions established by the Church for that purpose and always with truth, courage and prudence and with reverence and charity towards those who, by reason of their office, represent the person of Christ." [*Lumen Gentium*, chapter IV, section 37.] Once the Church has completed its investigation, a negative judgment on a purported apparition must in every case be received with humility and obedience. Although such a judgment is not infallible in itself, the paramount principle here should be obedience to proper authority. The martyr

St. Maximilian Kolbe rightly said, "My superiors can make mistakes; I make no mistake in obeying them." The only antidote to the Satanic drive of disobedience that stains the human will is obedience to rightful authority.

(ii) Medjugorje and the Criteria for Authentic Apparitions

In the light of all of the above, we can turn our attention finally to the question of the authenticity of the apparition in Medjugorje. We begin by noting again that two of the greatest Mariologists of our time, Fr. Rene Laurentin and Fr. Michael O'Carroll, initiated their own painstaking investigations into the apparition and are now entirely convinced of the authenticity of this apparition. Fr. Laurentin, we have seen, is particularly well known for his expertise in the area of apparitions and has been described as the greatest living authority on apparitions in the Catholic Church. As was to be expected, his labors on behalf of the Blessed Mother, particularly at Medjugorje, have won him many enemies. For the most part, critics of the apparition either lack specific expertise in Mariological matters and in the history of apparitions or did not make a serious effort to gather detailed empirical data on the spot [one hurried trip to Medjugorje does not count as a serious effort]. Although their arguments are flawed by these deficiencies (and are sometimes just frivolous), we will examine their critiques in the next section.

When we are dealing with claims of the supernatural, the basis of any judgment will to a great extent depend on the available facts. Now the "facts" of history and especially of salvation history are accounts of events or experiences narrated by witnesses. When we are dealing with such eye-witness accounts of an event or an experience given by an individual, the background of the individual may help us to decide with some degree of certitude whether or not he or she is telling us the truth. When children or unlettered peasants tell us of some extraordinary experience they had, we are predisposed to give them a fair hearing, other factors being equal (such as their mental stability). We can reasonably assume that there is a high degree of probability that such witnesses would not concoct such stories. We will not, of course, believe them blindly, but this initial factor in their favor will serve as a green light for our taking the time to pursue further investigation. While it is possible that a child or a peasant with a vivid imagination could concoct a plausible but false story, we would have a better chance of seeing through their story than of seeing through a story fabricated by a writer, a lawyer or a philosopher. The Christian Faith was spread around the world through the witness to the extraordinary event of the Resurrection given by a group of unlettered peasants and fishermen. Their very background served as a powerful support in favor of the veracity of their accounts at that time and does so even today. In this context, it must be noted that almost every approved Marian apparition was reported by peasants or children. In Medjugorje too, the six visionaries are peasant children: Ivanka Ivankovic, Mirjana Dragicevic, Vicka Ivankovic, Marija Pavlovic, Ivan Dragicevic and Jakov Colo. When they first witnessed the apparition of the Blessed Mother, Ivanka was 15 years of age, Mirjana 16, Vicka 17, Ivan 16 and Jakov 9.

The credibility of the visionaries as witnesses comes first in any analysis of authenticity. In this age of instant mass communication and globe-spanning rapid transit systems, the recipients of the reported apparition in Medjugorje became the objects of unprecedented personal scrutiny. With millions of strangers literally stomping through their front yards and with their every move under constant observation, it was all but a miracle that the Medjugorje visionaries kept their sanity. When one was not friendly enough for the crowd's satisfaction, he was accused of being dour and short-tempered. When another was friendly to all the milling mobs who dropped in on her, she was accused of having an artificial smile. For some the visionaries in person were disappointing because they were so ordinary — halos apparently would be in order. For others the visionaries were too other-worldly — all this business of glimpsing Heaven and Hell and Purgatory was simply preposterous in the reckoning of this breed of critic.

(iii) Scientific and Medical Studies

Dispensing with these and like trivialities, we must consider the credibility of the visionaries as witnesses not just in terms of the accidents of personality but with reference to their mental soundness and the depth of their sincerity. This is where the psychiatrists, psychologists, doctors and other scientists play an important role. Never in the history of apparitions has as much scientific scrutiny been directed at a reported apparition and its apparent recipients than at Medjugorje. Various teams of scientists have subjected the visionaries to a barrage of tests. Some of these analyses are described in detail in *Scientific and Medical Studies on the Apparitions at Medjugorje*, a book co-authored by Professor Henri Joyeux of the University of Montpelier who headed one of the medical teams that examined the visionaries (his co-author was the indefatigable Fr. Laurentin who continues to seek expert scientific analysis).

Two aspects of the Medjugorje apparition were susceptible to scientific analysis. First, it was important to ascertain the mental health of the visionaries. Secondly, the physiological processes of the visionaries during the apparition had to be analyzed. Both aspects are obviously related, for a study of the visionaries during the apparitions could give a good snapshot of their mental makeup. On both counts, the tests provided remarkable results. Brain, vision, hearing, voice and cardiac functions were monitored during the apparitions with electro-encephalographs, electro-oculographs, eye reflex tests and the study of evoked auditory responses. Professor Joyeux's team concluded from their studies that there were no clinical signs of individual or collective hallucination, no individual or collective hysteria, no neurosis, no catalepsy, and no pathological ecstasy. Electroencephalograms and clinical observation made it clear that the visionaries were not sleeping, dreaming or hallucinating during the apparition. Studies were carried out by other teams of scientists including an Italian group of doctors who could find no evidence of hypnosis, manipulation or drugs.

Tests also confirmed the visionaries' insensitivity to pain during the apparition. Some of the tests were rather questionable. For instance, a long needle was forced into Vicka during an apparition (she showed no response at the time and was surprised to find blood on her shoulder after the apparition). On another occasion, 90 decibel sounds were suddenly directed at a visionary's ear with no reaction; similarly, a visionary remained unaffected when a 100-watt bulb was flashed at his eyes during an apparition. Heated silver discs applied during an apparition did not evoke a reaction. Again, nylon threads applied against the cornea did not even cause a blink. When an apparition begins, the eyes of all the visionaries present converge on one spot and stay there for the duration of the apparition.

During the apparition, the visionaries converse soundlessly with their visitor: although their lips move and it is obvious they are involved in a conversation with someone, no voices are heard. At the beginning of most apparitions, the visionaries enter into a state of ecstasy and simultaneously start their soundless conversation.

It must be noted that in the Medjugorje apparitions, as in previous apparitions like Lourdes and Fatima, the visionaries experienced different levels of ecstasy and correspondingly different levels of dissociation from the material world. There was a definite evolution in the level of the ecstasy as the apparitions progressed. Professor Margnelli, a neuro-physiologist who studied the visionaries, holds the view that in the beginning the visionaries had "one foot in both worlds" and remained "partially earth-bound while acting as an intermediary between the people present and the apparition. But they had undeniably matured since then, evolving into a state of consciousness — not at all morbid — in which all their attention was concentrated on the apparition, to the exclusion of everything else." (5)

Professor Joyeux notes: "In summarizing the results of all the tests, we are inclined towards the following hypothesis: there is real communication, from person to person and of a voluntary nature, which does not use the ordinary sensory channels (which have been suspended, disconnected, immobilized) but is achieved in a more immediate fashion at a spiritual level. However, this communication is perfectly integrated and in direct continuity with the psychic life of the visionaries; it takes a shape just as knowledge of an ordinary, three-dimensional, concrete object does. The nerve centers of the brain are involved in this act of knowing with the difference that instead of decoding from vibrations, the visionaries' impressions are received in a more immediate fashion, the nature of which we do not know. The perception by the visionaries of the person who appears, the Virgin, is not strange for them. It provokes in them normal, coherent reactions, analogous to those aroused in us when we converse with our neighbors: expression, dialogue, surprise, smiles, answers, etc." (6)

It must, of course, be understood that no apparition can be captured by a microscope, a telescope or any kind of scientific apparatus however sophisticated it may be. When you are dealing with a phenomenon which apparently transcends normal sensory channels, it would be imprudent to expect verification or disconfirmation by using instruments designed to deal with normal sense data. Scientific methods and instruments are nevertheless of benefit in studying the visionaries themselves — particularly when they are actually witnessing the apparition.

The tests used in monitoring the visionaries have by and large yielded positive results. By the nature of the case, these tests cannot be cited as "proof" of the apparitions. Their role is simply that of ruling out fraud or mental disorder — and that is about as far as science can go in shedding light on Medjugorje. As with any other investigation into this sort of phenomenon, the results of these inquiries will always be disputed and criticized. The tests have served a valuable purpose in demonstrating beyond reasonable doubt that the visionaries are sincere and sane and that something inexplicable is taking place during the purported apparition. While sincerity and sanity are not sufficient conditions for proving the authenticity of an apparition, they are necessary pre-conditions.

At this point it will be helpful to quote some of the scientists who have examined the visionaries. The conclusions of these scientists are significant for two reasons, on the one hand they are distinguished authorities in their respective fields of inquiry, and, on the other, they have dedicated their time and sophisticated resources to investigate the Medjugorje apparitions.

By far the best known investigator, we have noted, is Professor Henri Joyeux, a neurologist and cancer specialist from the University of Montpelier Faculty of Medicine. Professor Joyeux led an interdisciplinary team of investigators that carried out a rigorous study of the visionaries. Professor Joyeux's interview with the magazine *Paris Match* is quoted here.

Another well known Medjugorje investigator is Dr. Marco Margnelli, a neurophysiologist from Italy, who is one of the foremost authorities in the area of ecstasy and altered states of consciousness. Dr. Margnelli came to Medjugorje as an agnostic who sought to discredit the Medjugorje phenomenon. After his visit to Medjugorje he became a practicing Catholic. His interview with the *Medjugorje Messenger* is reprinted here.

Also cited here is the work of Dr. Luigi Frigerio of the Mangiagalli Clinic in Milan, Italy, who led a team of ten medical doctors and one electronic engineer in investigating Medjugorje. The interview with Dr. Frigerio cited here originally appeared in the Italian *Il Tempo* and was later translated.

Finally we cite here the work of Dr. Phillipe Loron, the former head of the prestigious Neurology Clinic at La Salpetriere Hospital. In the following article in *Medjugorje Messenger*, Dr. Loron "shows how all the medical evidence fully supports the Medjugorje apparitions."

We turn now to the scientists.

Professor Henri Joyeux Interview with *Paris Match* [Summer 1985]

The magazine *Paris Match* interviewed Professor Henri Joyeux, a cancer specialist at the Faculty of Medicine in Montpelier, France, in the summer of 1985. Ghislaine Raby of London furnished a translated copy to MIRecorder which published the following edited version of the interview (*MIRecorder,* St. Joseph, pg 86):

Q: Paris Match: How did you, as a professor of medicine, come to be interested in the apparitions in Medjugorje?

A: It was providential. A friend of mine asked me to read Fr. Laurentin's book so that he could obtain a scientific view on these supernatural events. During the first week of the apparitions, in June 1981, the visionaries had been examined by two Yugoslav doctors to see whether they needed psychiatric treatment. The doctors honestly testified to their psychological and psychiatric fitness. Apart from my being a neurologist or neuro-psychiatrist, I am interested in all phenomena which science finds inexplicable.

The main purpose of our first medical expedition was to take observations only. In March 1984, four of us drove there from Montpelier. I was the only doctor in the group; a friend, who is an electronic engineer, Mr. R. Dubois-Chabert, accompanied us. On the 24th June, 1984, I had expected to see the young people in a particular state of ecstasy, rigid and tense. But the five of them — one doesn't receive any more visions — Ivanka, 17 years old, Ivan, 18, Jakov, 13, Vicka, 19, and Marija, 18, seemed very natural and normal. They certainly did not fall into ecstasy as one would from a ladder. They enter slowly into an ecstasy. No violence nor abnormality could be seen in their behavior. The first two ecstasies I witnessed lasted for less than two minutes. During this time they appeared to be talking to someone we did not see: they articulated words we could not hear. Only towards the end we heard them again praying the 'Our

Father': the Virgin Mary, they explained, usually starts the first words of the 'Our Father...' At the end of the ecstasy, their gaze followed upwards and one or more said 'ode' which means 'She is going.s'

We studied very carefully video tapes made during 35 ecstasies. In slow motion we noticed that it was not always the same one who pronounced the word 'ode'. Often two or three pronounced it at exactly the same time. We were able to meet the young people outside these meetings...I played football with Ivan and had a chat with each of them about what is happening everyday in their spiritual encounter and their daily lives. The interpreters were various persons, religious and non-religious speaking French or English. This first expedition in Medjugorje was of a great importance to me for I must admit that before I left for Yugoslavia, I was rather skeptical.

Q: And then you went back?

A: On coming back to Montpelier, I immediately contacted some of my colleagues, specialists in neurology, neuro-psychiatry, sleeping disturbances, neuro-physiology, ophthalmology, otorhino-laryngology and cardiology. We decided to conduct a full investigation of these supernatural phenomena. Not all of my colleagues agreed to it, some being reluctant to deal with sacred events, others worried of getting into trouble. We decided, considering the difficult circumstances of the situation of Medjugorje, (Communist country, 1200 miles from Montpelier, language) to make several expeditions taking plenty of time. They took place on the 9th-10th June, the 6th-7th of October, the 28th-29th December, 1984.

Q: Did the children agree readily to being examined?

A: When we first arrived in June, we could not get them to agree straight away. Firstly, they could not see the purpose of it but most of all they felt guilty of disobeying Our Lady since after Doctor Botta, from Milan, did some investigations, they asked Her what She thought about these experiments and She had stated: 'It is not necessary.' But young Jakov, because of our insistence, ended the discussion by suggesting, 'We'll ask Our Lady as we are going to see Her anyway' At the end of the ecstasy on the 28th of June 1984, the young people all agreed that Our Lady's answer was: 'It is good you thought of asking me. You may have it done.' For us who do not see the Virgin, we had the impression that it was the wall in front of which they knelt that had changed their minds completely. They had been against it, but now they had become like lambs, ready to accept whatever we asked.

Q: Which experiments did you perform?

A: None of them gave scientific proof that the Virgin is appearing to the visionaries and this is impossible to achieve. These many experiments (polygraphy) can be repeated or multiplied, but I consider that the results we have obtained up to now allow us to draw some important scientific conclusions. With Pr. Jean Cadihac we did, before, during and after the ecstasy an electroencephalogram (brain-waves recording) and an electro-oculograme (movement of the eyes). With Doctor J. Philipott we proceeded to study the visual function experimenting with ordinary reflexes in the eyes (reflexes of contraction of the pupil reacting to light, reflex in blinking when the eye is exposed, screen test consisting in setting a cardboard screen in front of their eyes during the ecstasy).

We have also studied with Doctor F. Rouquerol their hearing faculty by recording the effect of a measured sound injected into the ear of one of the visionaries (70 decibels before the ecstasy and 90 during it, which corresponds to the noise of an internal combustion engine at high speed). Ivan did not hear this noise though he reacted to a feeble noise before the ecstasy. This proves that during the ecstasy Ivan is as if disconnected from the outside world, though his hearing faculties function normally. We have also recorded their blood pressure and heart beats. As I said, the main video-recordings have been examined with the greatest accuracy, especially by Pr. J. Cadihac.

On returning in October 1984, the young people objected in being treated again. They again asked Our Lady if they should submit themselves to it. The answer was clear 'You are free.' So after some explanations of the experiments, they agreed to them.

Q: What questions did you pose, and what results did you get?

A: We needed to know if the cerebral function, the sight function, the hearing and phonation were subject to modifications during the ecstasy in comparison to the period before or after. It was strictly necessary to answer the following questions: Is the ecstasy a state of sleep, a dream-state, an illusion, an illness such as epilepsy, hysteria, a cataleptic state, a nervous disorder, or a pathological ecstasy? The main purpose of our work was to obtain very accurate scientific data by observing how the main organs were functioning. In addition we considered that clinical observations were important though not so technically orientated. In this case you need to rely on ordinary common sense and medical common sense. As a matter of fact, there is no need to be a doctor to recognize that the young people are normal and sane in body and mind."

Q: In the end, what results did you get and what are your conclusions?

A: The phenomena of the apparitions at Medjugorje cannot be explained scientifically. According to experiments carefully conducted, we can affirm that there has been no pathological modification in the parameters which have been investigated. In one word, these young people are healthy and there is no sign of epilepsy nor is it a sleep or dream state. It is neither a case of pathological hallucinations nor hallucinations in the hearing or sight faculties connected with an abnormality in the functioning of the peripherical sensorial receivers, the hearing faculty or sight. Neither are there any paroxystical hallucinations as testified by the electroencephalogram nor delirious hallucinations nor acute mental confusion. It is neither hysterical nor a nervous disorder nor a pathological ecstasy because the visionaries show no signs of these conditions in any of the clinical examinations. It cannot be a cataleptic state for during the ecstasy, the facial muscles are operating in a normal way. We can also ascertain that the intentness of the movements in the orb of the eyes of all the visionaries is in perfect timing with each other at the beginning and the end of the ecstasy. During the ecstasy there is a perfect convergence of their eyes and there is a strong feeling of a face to face encounter between the visionaries and a person we cannot see.

Their behavior presents no pathological signs. During the ecstasy they are in a state of prayer and inter-personal communication. They are not drop-outs, dreamers or people who are tired or distressed. They appear to be free and happy, well-rooted in their country and the modern world. At Medjugorje, the ecstasies are not pathological nor a trick. They do not belong to any scientific denominations. It is more like a state of deep, active prayer in which they are partially disconnected from the physical world, in a state of contemplation and coherent sane encounter with a person whom they alone see, hear and can touch. We cannot reach the transmitter but we can ascertain that the receivers are in a state of sane and good working order.

Q: So you really believe that the Virgin Mary is appearing there?

A: As scientists we can make no conclusion in such a matter. This can be answered only by competent people such as the local Bishop and the theological commission who are advising him. In Lourdes, the Catholic Church did recognize the 18 apparitions of the Virgin Mary to Bernadette. At Medjugorje, if the Virgin Mary is appearing, She will have appeared more than 1500 times...it would not surprise me if one day the Church does recognize these apparitions.

Q: If the Virgin Mary was not appearing, could it be a trick?

A: Through the many experiments we have made, we can exclude this. Crowds of people have been there from all over Europe, the States and even from Japan...Most of the many French people I have met there, or even those who have been there back here, have been transformed; they feel peaceful and happy and keen to return there. I would not state that the Virgin Mary is appearing in Medjugorje; but if God exists, why should this not be possible? *And so say all of us!*

Dr. Phillipe Loron interview with *Medjugorje Messenger* [October - December, 1989]

Dr. Philippe Loron is former head of the prestigious Neurology Clinic in La Salpetriere hospital, Paris. He shows how medical science has been involved to such an extent in evaluating the phenomenon of ecstasy. And, in the process, what was confirmed in several ways was the moral and psychological integrity of the visionaries. These young people are healthy in body and mind, balanced and well-attuned to the modern world. By no means are they "fringe" types — dreamers, distressed or hysterical.

We can classify the results of the medical investigations under three headings — reaction to pain; heart and circulation parameters; and various neurophysiological tests.

REACTION TO PAIN

Ever since medieval times, certain tests have been applied to alleged ecstasies: pricking, pinching and burning. These naturally provoke a reaction in normal subjects. A characteristic feature of ecstatics, however, is that they are insensitive to pain. Vicka conformed to this rule. When suddenly pricked with a needle, her face did not register the slightest reaction.

Italian doctors confirmed this absence of sensitivity by using an algometer; it registers resistance to skin-burns of up to 50°C. Three visionaries had reacted normally before ecstasy. During it, however, pain disappeared and they showed no reaction. This test was halted after seven seconds as a cutaneous lesion occurs after that.

CORNEA SENSITIVITY

Similarly, the visionaries' cornea sensitivity was tested by using a nylon hair, the length of which could be adjusted according to the intensity of pressure to be applied. Normally the slightest touch on the cornea makes the eyelid blink and results in a contraction. During ecstasy this sensitivity of the cornea was totally absent. When confronted by an intensely bright light (a 1000-watt bulb placed in front of the eyes) there was no blinking movement of the eyelids. We may note that with two of the visionaries, the normal blinking movement was absent throughout the ecstasy, while in the others it was reduced by one-half.

HEART ACTIVITY

Measurements of pulse, arterial pressure and ECG (electrocardiogram) recordings were made before, during and after ecstasy. In all phases the heart rhythm was rapid — over 90 beats per minute. Of four visionaries studied, two showed a reduction in cardiac frequency during ecstasy, the two others an acceleration. These results are not significant, doubtless reflecting merely a difference in emotional behavior.

A state of exaltation was ruled out anyhow by arterial pressure, which tends to fall whatever the pattern of heartbeat frequency happens to be. The ECG findings were normal.

BRAIN TESTS

By the application of electrodes to the scalp, these ECG tests make it possible to record the continuous electrical activity of the underlying cerebral cortex. We are dealing here with a regular electrical activity of very low amplitude (less than 100 microvolts).

In the case of a resting subject — that is, someone who is awake but has their eyes closed — it is in the posterior part of the brain that the alpha rhythm frequency (8-13 hertz) is found. When the eyes are opened, however, this rhythm usually disappears. Corresponding to a state of sleep or of epilepsy are certain recognizable waves or rhythms. And the same applies to organic brain lesions.

EEG recordings were made of three visionaries before, during and after ecstasy. Besides establishing the absence of any kind of cerebral anomaly, they registered, during the state of ecstasy, an alpha rhythm over the entire cranium — and this while the eyes remained open!

EYE TESTS

The photomotor reflexes were normal during ecstasy, the pupils contracting in the usual way to light. However, as we have seen, there was no blinking when the cornea was stimulated or when the eyes were confronted by light. When we juxtapose this data with the EEG recordings that show a diffuse alpha rhythm, we are faced with a scientific enigma. Indeed, in neurological terms it is altogether inexplicable.

The recording of eye movements produced remarkable results. Two electrodes were placed in position, one at the side of the eye and the other above it. These continually registered the motor activity of the eye muscles during eye movements associated with vision.

A simultaneous recording of all this was made with regard to two visionaries. Before ecstasy, both recordings showed normal spontaneous eye movement. As soon as the ecstasy started, however — that is, when the visionaries began

WHO IS SHE THAT IS COMING FORTH?

seeing the apparition — their eye movements ceased simultaneously (to within one-fifth of a second of each other). And they also resumed simultaneously (again to within one-fifth of a second of each other) when the ecstasy ended.

Such synchronizations can only be explained by the intervention of some external "object" holding their gaze — but which those around them could not see.

It was further noted that the video-recordings of the visionaries, made that same day, showed the convergence of their gaze. It also made it possible to estimate that the apparition was at a distance of between 50 cm and one meter on a horizontal plane.

VOICE AND HEARING

When the visionaries spoke to the apparition without making any sound, the laryngeal function corresponding to sound ceased. However, the movement of the mimic musculature corresponding to the articulation of words remained normal. This fact cannot be explained scientifically.

The recordings of Ivan's hearing function before and during ecstasy showed a perfectly normal result. But, during ecstasy, he did not hear an input of 90 decibels (equivalent to a loud explosion) and showed not the least reaction of surprise.

SOMEONE IS THERE

Professor Joyeux declares that the phenomenon of the Medjugorje apparitions is scientifically inexplicable. "No category of science," he says, "appears capable of defining the phenomenon. We would be prepared to define it as a state of active prayer which is intense and partially disconnected from the external world. We could define ecstasy as a state of contemplation and of coherent, healthy communication with a distinct person whom only the visionaries can see, hear and touch."

There are several arguments to support the view that we are dealing with a person who is distinct and external to the visionaries themselves:

- Their convergence of gaze;
- The simultaneous timing, without any signals, of their kneeling and the cessation of eye movements when the ecstasy starts — all confirmed by the video-recordings;
- The simultaneous timing of the disappearance of the visionaries' voices and their subsequent reappearance when they say "who art in heaven" (the first two words, "Our Father," the visionaries tell us, are intoned by the Blessed Virgin herself);
- The simultaneous timing of their raising of heads and gazing upwards when the ecstasy is over.

Thus the visionaries have an extraordinary perception of a person who is "supernatural" to them. Such perception goes beyond the ordinary modes that function by normal neurological routes. This "supernatural" experience enables them to enter God's mode of duration, which is eternity — an experience quite beyond our ken.

Actually, the visionaries have no idea of the time that elapses during the apparitions. Whether these be short or extended (from 54 seconds to 45 minutes), they are filled with feelings of love and joy.

Dr. Marco Margnelli interview with *Medjugorje Messenger* [Summer 1988]

I am a non-believer and therefore went to Medjugorje with a critical spirit, ready to welcome any evidence that would contradict it or expose it as a fake. But, from the studies I have done on change in states of consciousness in children, I have to addmit that here in Medjugorje I have verified and documented, with the help of instruments, *a genuine state of ecstasy.*

In my opinion, there is certainly no lying. The Medjujorje visionaries enter a different state of consciousness — that which is scientifically termed the 'alpha state.' Whether they then actually see the Madonna or it be a case of 'suggestion phenomenon' inexplicable to us — that is a matter for theological competence on which I am unable to pronounce.

But we were certainly in the presence of an extraordinary phenomenon. Since returning from Yugoslavia I have been thinking about it continually; and I confess, I also ask myself non-scientific questions as well, such as what the meaning of the whole thing can be.

Dr. Margnelli explained that he had not done an electroencephalogram as the French investigating team had already seen to this. But he made several other checks and investigations. He concluded: 'As a scientist I can only declare that the children really pass into another state of consciousness — a condition that one can also reach through meditation techniques, such as auto-training, though not as profoundly. Nor are the children lying, otherwise they would react to tests of a sensory and painful kind.'

SOME AMAZING FACTS

Speaking about his personal reaction, Dr. Margnelli added: "The events surrounding the phenomenon also surprise me. There is a video done by a colleague; it records our work. In it one can see the absolutely synchronous movements with which the visionaries act...Also there are films taken by people I know, such as of the cross which dominates the hill nearby — and which 'disappears'. There is absolute silence of the birds that gather before sunset in the square. They suddenly and simultaneously all go silent as soon as the apparition begins every evening at 18:45.

The doctor went on to speak about a perfectly normal and responsible woman from Milan who told him the following amazing narrative. In his own words: 'She was gravely ill with leukemia and had gone to Medjugorje wishing to be embraced by the Madonna. After the apparition one of the visionaries, singling her out from among the hundreds of people present, ran up and embraced her, saying, 'That's the embrace you wished to receive from the Madonna.' She is now cured of her illness.'

Dr. Margnelli also related a story about a medical colleague of his from the same Mangiagalli Hospital in Milan: 'He told me that he was singled out in the same way by one of the visionaries who, speaking Croatian, asked in a loud voice; 'Where is the doctor from the Mangiagalli in Milan? The Madonna has asked me to tell him that She is pleased with the work he is doing.'

Dr. Margnelli concluded: "If anyone had told me these things before my journey here, I would have laughed at it. We are certainly in the presence of an extremely interesting phenomenon. Whether we are dealing with an authentic apparition or something else we cannot explain, I cannot say. It is a question I prefer not to put to myself."

There is a happy postscript to all this. From being a non-believer the good Dr. Margnelli has since become a practicing Catholic.

Dr. Luigi Frigerio interview with "Il Tempo" translated in Orthodoxy of the Catholic Doctrine [October 9, 1985]

The Medjugorje phenomenon appears to be authentic and scientifically unexplainable.

The four young people, since June 24, 1981, claim to see Our Lady every day. For two other girls the apparitions ceased. These two have received all ten secrets! The girls and the boys are not sick nor do they deceive. This is a unanimous response of two medical teams which used different methods in subjecting the 'seers' to various scientific tests.

Our team of French specialists, under the supervision of Professor Henri Joyeux of Montpelier University, has made four missions to Medjugorje during the year of 1984 and published the results of its inquiry in a volume entitled "Etudes Medicales et Scientifiques sur les Apparitions de Medjugorje" — Medical and scientific studies of the apparitions of Medjugorje — which will soon come out in Italy and be published by Queriniana.

Another group, led by Dr. Luigi Frigerio of the Mangiagalli Clinic in Milano, Italy and composed of ten medical doctors and of one electronic engineer, conducted investigations on the 'seers' on 7,8 and 9 of September, 1985.

It is necessary to point out that these inquiries completed on the young people — Vicka Ivankovic, 21 years old, Ivan Dragicevic, 20 years old, Maria Pavlovic, 20 years old, Jakov Colo, 14 years old (Joyeux performed tests also on Ivanka Ivankovic, who is not a daily 'seer' any longer since May 7, 1985) cannot clearly provide a direct answer to the question, whether the girls and the boys see or not Our Lady, neither do they intend to violate the authority of the local bishop Pavao Zanic of Mostar, who with the assistance of a Commission, composed of theologians and doctors, is to issue the official judgment on the events of Medjugorje.

Meanwhile, the inquiries of Joyeux and Frigerio can provide and have provided serious signs of the authenticity, excluding, that is, deceit or pathological explanation. In the medical field, and obviously only in this field, the clinical tests belie Bishop Zanic of Mostar, who in his *'non-official position'* of October 30, 1984, spoke of the Medjugorje events as the fruit of a 'collective hallucination.'

Medical doctors have cleared only one aspect of the complicated phenomenon, on which the authoritative judgment of the Church is expected.

However, the fact stands that, either because of the scientific progress which took place, or because of the extended apparitions, which until now occurred 1500 times, each lasting on the average between 2 to 3 minutes, never a similar event has been studied more in depth from the medical and scientific point of view.

Although the results of the various examinations are still under study, Frigerio has already given us three results.

One of the members of his team, Professor Santini, neuro-psycho-pharmacologist, who for many years has studied the problem of pain at the Columbia University of New York, has conducted the exams with algometer (a device for measuring the intensity of pain caused by pressure) to control the sensitiveness of the girls and boys during the apparitions. These results confirm those obtained by the Joyeux team.

It has been scientifically proven that the girls and the boys do not fake and do not deceive.

In fact, the results clearly show that there is a modification on the threshold of pain: during the ecstasy the 'seers' are in a complete analgesias (a state of not being able to feel pain), which is not the case before or after the ecstasy.

For the neuro-physiologist, Professor Margnelli, the principal Italian medical scholar of the ecstatic phenomena, from the analysis of the principal vital functions (respiratory, cardiac functions, pressure, pulse, etc.) compared before, during and after the ecstasy, it comes out that the girls and the boys live an authentic mystical ecstasy.

Also Joyeux has expressed the same results with these terms: 'I expected to see the youngsters in a state of ecstasy very special, with a certain rigidity and tension. On the contrary, they looked to me natural and simple. It cannot be said that they fall into ecstasy as if one falls from a ladder. They entered into ecstasy.'

The more engaging study that the Frigerio team proposed to itself, regard the evoked acoustical, visual and somato-sensorial potentials, or the response of the cerebral trunk and the cerebral bark to the visual, acoustical and peripheral stimuli studied before, during and after the ecstasy.

Without pretending to give the definite result, because the final result is still under study, Frigerio reports that medical doctors have recorded the response of the brain to the existence of the stimuli which the girls and the boys perceive during the ecstasy: the stimuli of the acoustical type when they hear a voice, or the stimuli of the visual type when they see a figure. However, the nervous routes remain perfectly open.

But since the girls and the boys, in spite of being awake, are in a general anaesthesia, the exams are in contradiction among themselves in the sense that it is not possible that there is absence of pain when the nervous routes are open. This fact cannot be explained naturally.

The phenomenon, argues Frigerio, can be only preternatural or supernatural. If it were preternatural, it would not leave the girls and the boys free, but they are perfectly free!"

Polemicists will either dismiss the results of the tests as being unworthy of acceptance or give their own critical interpretation of the test data. Even the most skeptical, however, cannot but admit that there has been no detection of clearcut fraud or psychological disorder. Such detection could not possibly remain an "untold story" in view of the fact that the drama of the apparitions is now being played on a global stage before an audience which includes sensationalists who would like nothing better than an opportunity to debunk the whole thing. The skeptics we will always have with us. Even Lourdes and Fatima did not convince all and sundry.

Those who know the visionaries personally testify to their normalcy and transparent honesty — and to the fairly marked differences in their personalities. They have no airs and are puzzled by their celebrity status. Two of them are happily married and two have considered the religious life. Fr. Milan Mikulich, an American priest of Croatian origin who first introduced Medjugorje to the American public and who conducted Mirjana's wedding, recounts how impressed he was with them from the very beginning. In the early days of the apparitions, Fr. Mikulich interviewed the visionaries repeatedly and intensively

— so intensively, in fact, that they were concerned. He says that the interviews revealed to him a group of children who were simple and honest and who were never inconsistent or self- contradictory. This was true then and it remains true today.

So much for the questions of deception and self-deception. Other relevant considerations in studying the authenticity of the apparitions are accompanying miracles, the kind of messages received through the apparitions, and finally the judgment of the Church.

The miracles that are said to have accompanied the Medjugorje apparitions have attracted almost as much attention as the apparitions themselves. Numerous healings and cures have been associated with the apparitions. The best known are the cases of Daniel Setko, a boy who had never talked before but gained his voice after the visionaries asked for the Virgin's intercession and of Diana Basile, a cripple who had suffered from multiple sclerosis for 12 years but was suddenly healed in the apparition room.

Over one thousand cures and healings in Medjugorje have been documented. Claims of miracles, however, are not very likely to convince those who say that miracles are intrinsically impossible. But a dogmatic refusal to examine the evidence for a scientifically inexplicable phenomenon is as wrong-headed as a superstitious tendency to accept any claim of a miracle at face value. More information on cures and healings is given in Appendix 1.

"Signs and wonders" kinds of miracles are also part and parcel of the Medjugorje story. Villagers and pilgrims at different times claim to have seen Mary standing beside or in front of the cross on top of Mount Krizevac. The letters MIR, Croatian for "peace," have been brilliantly displayed across the sky. Various luminous phenomena have apparently been observed at various times. A huge host has sometimes been seen hiding the sun. Also, the sun itself has often been observed spinning in circles. On one July night in 1981, a group of villagers who had climbed Mount Krizevac with the visionaries claimed to have witnessed a golden globe of light descending from the heavens that split into thousands of pieces over them. It has often been reported that rosaries have changed color — usually taking on a golden hue. Often photographs taken at Medjugorje, when developed, have images of Jesus or the Virgin Mary. To be sure, these phenomena can be explained away or ignored. At the very least, however, they call out for some kind of explanation.

Signs and wonders are apt to make some people suspicious because of the Scriptural warnings about deception by false angels of light. But the existence of counterfeit notes does not mean that genuine currency does not exist. Our Lord often performed signs and wonders in order to draw attention to His authority and to His message (and His enemies often attributed these miracles to diabolic sources). Traditionally, all human encounters with the supernatural have involved some kind of naturally inexplicable phenomena — ranging from the burning bush in the Old Testament to the sun miracle witnessed by over 70,000 people in Fatima. These accompanying phenomena are clearly of secondary importance but they help reinforce the pilgrim's premonition that "something is going on."

Diabolic phenomena, it must be observed, tend to be displays of raw power that are anarchic, meaningless and frightening. Divinely directed miracles, on the other hand, serve a supernatural purpose, form a definite pattern and lead witnesses to faith and holy lives. The Medjugorje phenomena clearly seem to belong to the latter category. The miracles have helped confirm the credibility of the apparition and the importance of applying the main apparition messages in our daily lives. Moreover, Medjugorje has re-awakened faith in many who lost it and has brought thousands of others to the Faith.

As significant as externally observable miracles are the miracles that are purely spiritual. Hundreds and thousands of pilgrims have undergone spiritually transformational experiences at Medjugorje. Those who have struggled with drug addictions have been cured of their slavery (a remarkable phenomenon considering the odds against recovery from a chemical addiction). Those who were filled with hatred and bitterness — feelings often submerged in the subconscious — or driven by unholy obsessions have been liberated from their slaveries at Medjugorje. Peace and reconciliation are not just the central message of Medjugorje but are living realities that can be experienced there. The "inner" miracles cannot easily be quantified or articulated. But they are personally relevant for those who experience them. "Personally relevant data" may only have evidential value for oneself but they are significant at least for that reason: the blind man who received his sight from our Lord could not be made to deny the reality of the miracle he experienced despite all the efforts of the Scribes and the Pharisees.

Spiritual fruits of Medjugorje such as the numerous confessions and Masses have been obvious even to skeptics and cynics.

(iv) Obedience to Authority

Another compelling factor in favor of the authenticity of the Medjugorje apparitions is the attitude of the visionaries to their Bishop. His Excellency, Bishop Zanic has become the best known foe of the apparitions and has called the visionaries "liars" and "trained robots," among other things. The visionaries have borne these diatribes with patience and charity. Nothing reflects Lucifer more clearly than the normal human tendencies to rebel against all authority. These tendencies have become very prominent in the Catholic Church in the second half of this century among both conservatives and liberals. Many would-be visionaries who claimed to have witnessed apparitions showed the true source of their experiences by their virulent attacks on the Pope and on bishops.

All this stands in stark contrast to the reverent attitude taken by the Medjugorje visionaries to their chief persecutor (unfortunately this is sometimes not the case with their defenders). Although bishops do not enjoy the privilege of infallibility, they do have disciplinary authority over their dioceses. If such authority is misused, then there are definite channels available to seek rectification. Public disobedience and criticism, however, are spiritually dangerous. Although Bishop Zanic does not now have any authority over the investigation of the apparition, the visionaries continue to obey his order forbidding the apparition in the church. In fact, when Mirjana visited Fr Mikulich in Oregon, she expressly stated that the apparition of the Blessed Virgin would have to take place in a chapel and not in the church — despite the fact that the chapel was too small to accommodate the huge crowds that had gathered there. Fr Mikulich explained to her that the church in Oregon was his church and not Bishop Zanic's but Mirjana responded that wherever she went, Bishop Zanic continued to be her bishop and therefore she was bound to submit to his authority in disciplinary matters.

Here is what the various visionaries have to say about their Bishop: Marija: "The Gospa tells us that we must love him and that we must pray for him. I do it." Ivan: "I pray. I pray especially when I hear that he says something which does not correspond to the truth." Vicka: "I recommend him every day in my prayers." Jakov: "The Gospa has recommended to us to pray for the bishop; that is what I do every day." Mirjana: "In my daily prayer, I devote five to six Our Father's for him." Ivanka: "I pray." (7)

Doctrinal deviation is a clear mark of fraud or diabolic influence and it is this aspect of the Medjugorje apparitions that we will study next.

(v) The Message of Medjugorje

Most Marian apparitions have dwelt on the themes of penance and reparation and the need to turn to God through conversion and prayer. Medjugorje is no different in this respect. There are some (like the retired Bishop of Mostar) who complain that the lack of something original makes the purported apparitions banal at best. But Christianity reflects what St. Augustine called the Beauty which is ancient and ever new. The public revelation granted to the Church at the beginning remains the same throughout history. The development of doctrine is an unfolding of deeper mysteries already present in embryo. Claims of theologies and messages that break with the past must be looked at with suspicion (such claims are legitimate in the sciences which deal with ever more refined analyses of empirical data but questionable in revealed theology which takes a certain body of primordial revelation as the given). Accordingly, claims of private revelation have been measured by their theological consistency with the deposit of faith. The Bishop of Mostar's criticism on the score of banality ("everything else is as in the other apparitions, prayers, penance, conversion"), then, is actually a point in favor of Medjugorje.

To be sure, the major apparitions have laid emphasis on one theme or another. In Medjugorje, the main emphasis has been on peace and reconciliation, but the five essential messages of Medjugorje are:

- Peace
- Reconciliation
- Conversion
- Prayer
- Fasting

Despite the longevity of the apparitions and the numerous meetings between the visionaries and the Lady, these simple, succinct messages have remained at the heart of the apparitions.

This being said, we should note that a number of other theological pronouncements are associated with Medjugorje. Certain distinctions must be made in studying this body of data.

- There are the public messages given to the visionaries for transmission to the world at large.
- There are the ten secrets that are being or have been given to the visionaries.
- There are private communications between the visionaries and the Gospa.
- There are the question and answer sessions where the visionaries ask the Gospa questions of their own or which they were given by others.
- There are the journeys taken by some of the visionaries to Heaven, Hell and Purgatory.

It should be clearly understood that the messages of Medjugorje are the messages in the first category that have been expressly issued for public dissemination. In his study of 700 Medjugorje messages, Bill Reck of the Riehle Foundation quantified the number of messages on specific themes: 198 messages were on prayer, 62 on conversion and reconciliation, 45 on fasting, 45 on peace and love, 40 on the existence of Satan, 22 on the value of the Mass, 14 on holiness, and 11 on reading Sacred Scripture. Apocalyptic messages are not dominant themes.

The most comprehensive and authoritative work on the theological content of the Medjugorje messages is Professor Mark Miravalle's *The Message of Medjugorje*. Professor Miravalle, in fact, did his doctoral dissertation on the theology embodied in these messages. In his judgment, "The message contents which constitute the Public Messages from Medjugorje are in full doctrinal conformity with the Gospels, Apostolic Fathers, Vatican II, Postconciliar documents of the Magisterium, and the Marian messages of Lourdes and Fatima. This is the premise of a doctoral thesis successfully defended at the Pontifical University of St. Thomas Aquinas in Rome, and which premise is accepted by two of the world's foremost orthodox mariologists, Father Michael O'Carroll of Ireland and Father Rene Laurentin of France." (8)

The secrets given to the children have been relatively uncontroversial because they have remained secret. This much is known about them: some concern catastrophic events in the future. Each of the visionaries are being given ten secrets concerning these future events. Two (Mirjana and Ivanka) have received all ten secrets, and the regular apparitions have ceased for them. The other visionaries have received nine of the secrets, and the apparitions will cease for them once they have received all ten. The first secret will be revealed to the world three days before the event it speaks of takes place. The third secret apparently concerns a lasting sign that will be left in Medjugorje itself on the hill where the apparition first began. This sign will be a testimony to unbelievers that the apparition was authentic. Secrets of this kind were given to the visionaries of La Salette, Lourdes and Fatima. Guadalupe, Lourdes and Fatima also had a public sign that came at the end of the apparition.

The most serious controversies over the messages of Medjugorje have risen over some of the questions and answers between the visionaries and the Blessed Virgin. Among these a major charge is the claim that Medjugorje promotes a false ecumenism that borders on syncretism and universalism. It is said that Medjugorje tends to encourage the view that all religions are equal and that it really does not matter which religion you belong to. It must be said that this charge is based on total misunderstandings and even miscommunications of the actual messages.[7]

To begin with, let us see how Christianity views not just other religions but humanity in general. In Timothy we read that God is a Savior "who will have all men to be saved and to come unto the knowledge of truth" (I Timothy 2:4)

---

[7] For example, in answer to Fr. Robert Fox's question (during an interview in the October/ December, 1992 issue of the *Fatima Family Messenger*) "The children (now young adults) reportedly have our Blessed Mother making statements which seem to say one religion is as good as another," Bishop Paolo Hnilica responded, "Such reporting is incorrect as attributed to Medjugorje. Our Lady never told the children one religion is as good as another."

Romans tells us "For when the Gentiles, which have not the law, do by nature the things contained in the law, these having not the law, are a law unto themselves: Which show the work of the law written in their hearts, their conscience also bearing witness, and their thoughts the meanwhile accusing or else excusing one another." (Romans, 2:14-15). This vision of a God Who desires the salvation of all men is related to the Christian revelation by St. Augustine's famous doctrine of the baptism of desire in which unbelievers who implicitly desire God and desire to follow His will are also saved — a doctrine implicitly taught by the Church for centuries. This does not, of course, mean that all men and women will necessarily be saved: only that everyone will be given enough grace to choose God with the possibility always that this grace could be rejected.

While claiming to preserve the "deposit of faith" revealed by God Incarnate in a final and definitive act of revelation, the Catholic Church has consistently recognized much that is good and true in various religions. It has recognized too that many adherents of these religions are sincerely seeking God within the constraints of their cultural and religious environments and that Christ died for every one of them. These teachings have been powerfully set forth in one of the classic documents of the Second Vatican Council:

> All men form but one community. This is so because all stem from the one stock which God created to people the entire earth (cf. Acts 17:26), and also because all share a common destiny, namely God. His providence, evident goodness, and saving designs extend to all men (cf.Wis. 8:1; Acts 14:17; Rom. 2:6-7; Tim. 2:4) against the day when the elect are gathered together in the holy city which is illumined by the glory of God, and in whose splendor all peoples will walk (cf. Apoc. 21:23 ff.).
>
> Men look to their different religions for an answer to the unsolved riddles of human existence....
>
> The Catholic Church rejects nothing of what is true and holy in these religions. She has a high regard for the manner of life and conduct, the precepts and doctrines which, although differing in many ways from her own teaching, nevertheless often reflect a ray of that truth which enlightens all men. Yet she proclaims and is in duty bound to proclaim without fail, Christ who is the way, the truth and the life (Jn. 1:6). In him, in whom God reconciled all things to himself (2 Cor. 5:18-19),men find the fullness of their religious life.
>
> The Church, therefore, urges her sons to enter with prudence and charity into discussion and collaboration with members of other religions. Let Christians, while witnessing to their own faith and way of

life, acknowledge, preserve and encourage the spiritual and moral truths found among non-Christians, also their social life and culture. The Church has also a high regard for the Muslims. They worship God, who is one, living and subsistent, merciful and almighty, the Creator of heaven and earth, who has also spoken to men. They strive to submit themselves without reserve to the hidden decrees of God, just as Abraham submitted himself to God's plan, to whose faith Muslims eagerly link their own. Although not acknowledging him as God, they venerate Jesus as a prophet, his Virgin Mother they also honor, and even at times devoutly invoke. Further, they await the day of judgment and the reward of God following the resurrection of the dead. For this reason they highly esteem an upright life and worship God, especially by way of prayer, alms-deeds and fasting. (9)

It is in the context of these teachings of the Church that we should examine the messages on the adherents of different religions that have been given at Medjugorje. It is important too that we clearly distinguish between the religion itself and the adherent of the religion. The first is a human construct and the second is an eternal human soul made in the image of God.

Here are the specific messages on the question delivered at Medjugorje:

- Pray, pray! How many persons have followed other beliefs or sects and have abandoned Jesus Christ. They create their own gods; they adore idols. How that hurts me! If they could be converted. That will change only if you help me with your prayers. [9/2/84].

- In God differences do not exist among his people; religion need not separate people. Every person must be respected, despite his or her particular profession of faith. God presides over all religions as a king controls his subjects, through his priests and ministers. The sole mediator of salvation is Jesus Christ. It is not equally efficacious to belong to or pray in any church or community, because the Holy Spirit grants his power differently among the churches and ministers. All believers do not pray the same way. It is intentional that all apparitions are under the auspices of the Catholic Church. [1983].

- It is you who is divided on earth. The Muslims and the Orthodox, for the same reasons as Catholics, are equal before my Son and me. You are all my children. Certainly all religions are not equal, but all men are equal before God as St. Paul says: It does not suffice to belong to the Catholic Church to be saved, but it is necessary to respect the commandments of God in following

one's conscience. Those who are not Catholics are no less creatures made in the image of God, and destined to rejoin someday,
the House of the Father. Salvation is available to everyone, without
exception. Only those who refuse God deliberately, are condemned. To him who has been given little, little will be asked for.
To whomever has been given much (to Catholics), very much will
be required. It is God alone, in His infinite justice, Who determines the degree of responsibility and pronounces judgment.
[1984-1985].

About these pronouncements, Fr. Laurentin comments: "The message of
Medjugorje has been faulted for its ecumenism. *In Messages and Teachings*
(Appendix 2), I have published all the texts relative to this affair. From them we
reach the following conclusions:

-The seers are not at all indifferentists. It would be easier to
reproach them with the fundamentalism which often characterizes the
faith of simple folk.
-The objectors did not understand the messages according to the
language and local culture, in which "religions" refers to persons (the
people of a religion) and not doctrines. — You are not Christians if
you do not respect the other religions: Moslem and Serbian, the Virgin
is supposed to have said to Mirjana, according to her.
The confusion is obvious: to be Serbian is a question of *nationality*, not *religion*. And if the predominant religion of the Serbs is
Orthodoxy, the Serbs who are in power in Belgrade are no longer
orthodox but atheistic Marxists, officially without a religion.
The improper wording is the result of Mirjana reporting, in
keeping with everyday language, something that the Gospa said weeks
earlier. This is the main key to the ambiguities exploited by the
opponents.
What is the meaning of these incriminated messages? They invite
us to respect *persons*. And that is no small matter in this country
characterized by the 'Balkan' tensions and violence, which are more
serious, although better accepted, than those which are destroying
Lebanon. Whence this message from the Virgin: 'Love your Moslem
brothers (Croats converted to that religion at the time of the persecution). Love your orthodox Serbian brothers. Love those who govern
you (atheistic Marxists). (10)

There is no hint of syncretism in these statements if they are understood in the context of Church teaching. In addition, we should note that some of the apparitions of the Blessed Virgin emphasized doctrines that had just been defined by the Church — but only after they had been defined. An example is the emphasis on the Immaculate Conception at Lourdes. Similarly, it does not seem to be a coincidence that her messages at Medjugorje concerning adherents of different religions fits in so coherently with the teaching that had been crystallized in the Second Vatican Council.

The other controversial message at Medjugorge concerns Hell. Coupled with the spoken messages come messages of a visual nature: the visions of Heaven, Purgatory and Hell. Here is Vicka's vivid description of Hell:

> She described the people in Hell going naked into a great fire. 'When they come out,' she said, 'you couldn't tell whether they were men or women, for they had blackened skin like animals.'

Although similar visions of Hell have been seen by saints and mystics through the centuries, it should be clear that the visions are not necessarily literal representations of the realities they symbolize. Fr. Slavko Barbaric, the spiritual advisor to the visionaries, explained that he does not take these representations literally because the function of the vision and the visionary is not to describe Heaven or Hell but to bear witness to the reality of another world. Heaven, Purgatory and Hell are presented to the children in the manner in which their senses and conceptual frameworks can best comprehend them.

The depictions of the world to come are intended to act as vivid reminders of the fact that all our choices ultimately are choices for Heaven or Hell — and Our Lady's objective in Medjugorje is to draw us to Heaven. We are asked to pray and to fast, to mortify ourselves and to do penance, to confess our sins and to receive the Eucharist so that we can we can make the right choices and overcome the World, the Flesh and the Devil. In Medjugorje, the Blessed Virgin tells us, "I invite each one of you to consciously decide yourself to be for God and against Satan. I am your Mother and I want to lead you all to perfect holiness. I want every one of you to be happy here on earth and for every one of you to be with me in Heaven. This is my desire and my mission here."

In Marian apparitions of previous centuries, the Blessed Virgin would ask for penance and reparation. It is significant indeed that in the two most famous apparitions of this century (Fatima and Medjugorje), she was forced to draw back the veil of space and time and reveal the ultimate consequences of evil. And while at Fatima Our Lady gave the visionaries a glimpse of Hell, in Medjugorje she actually took them to Hell.

(vi) Testimonies[8]

The National Conference on Medjugorje held each year at the University of Notre Dame has drawn thousands of participants from as far away as Australia, Italy, Poland, Norway, Africa, Japan, Yugoslavia, France, England, Ireland, Bermuda, Puerto Rico, Russia, Canada, and all of the 50 United States. Bishop Nicholas D'Antonio, Vicar General of the Archdiocese of New Orleans, opened the 1991 National Conference by declaring, "We have more conversions from Medjugorje than any place in the world! ... I don't recall in history anything comparable to the Medjugorje events. Could it be as has happened in the past, God wants to exalt the humble and put down the proud with the rallying cry "Vox populi, vox Dei" ("The voice of the people: the voice of God")? To give an example of the voices that rang out clearly at that conference...

* Lylan Mitchell, a Buddhist from Vietnam, was suffering from cancer in 1989 when a friend gave her the book, *Medjugorje: The Message*. Finding it difficult to read, she contented herself with looking at the pictures. '...After I looked at the pictures, and the outside cover with the picture of the Virgin Mary, it struck me, She's so humble, so holy, I need you, Mother!' After her doctors said that there was nothing more that they could do for her, she responded, 'No, doctor, I'd like to go to Medjugorje and ask Mother Mary to make intercession for me... If I die I rather die in Medjugorje where Mary will receive my soul. ...My body is nothing. Too many problems! So I offered that to God. If I come home without healing, that's O.K., as long as the Blessed Mother and Jesus will help to save my soul.' *(Lylan experienced many graces in Medjugorje. After giving her testimony at the Conference she was baptized and received into the Catholic Church.)*

* Becky Moody, a sixteen year old teenager from South Bend: "I heard about Medjugorje at the first conference here at the JACC.[9] At the time I really didn't know how to say the 'Hail Mary'. I was sitting with my brother. We had come to the conference not knowing anything about what Medjugorje was like or what it was

---

8   These are just several testimonies given in 1991 at the National Conference on Medjugorje (held each year at the University of Notre Dame). More than 50 conferences throughout America, inspired by Our Lady's call from Medjugorje, have already been scheduled for 1993! (Audio tapes of the National Conference on Medjugorje are available through *Resurrection Tapes*, 1203 E. Lake St., Minn., MN. 55407).

9   The major conference facility at Notre Dame

about. ...I decided that day that I wanted to go to Medjugorje. That night I went home and I said the first words to Mary I ever said. I was kind of nervous because this was odd to me speaking to somebody who wasn't God and who wasn't in the room: 'Mary, will you please take my brother Joe and me to Medjugorje?' I didn't know when. I didn't know how. We didn't know any people involved with Medjugorje hardly, but I just said it. And lo and behold, three months later and a billion rosaries later we ended up in Medjugorje. When we got to Medjugorje we just started praying and praying over and over. Prayer is what we lived for. When we were there it felt so easy to pray. It came so easily and it felt so strong. ...In Medjugorje we saw many, many miracles and we saw many signs in the sun and moon and stars, but when we came home, it wasn't the miracles that we wanted to talk about. It was the change that had come over us inside. What happened to me in Medjugorje was what happened in my heart and my soul..."

- "My name is John Simons. I'm 26 years old and I'm from Ireland. I won't particularly go into my sordid past. I used to manage a transvestite punk band in Dublin and I was everything that goes along with that — sex, drugs and rock and roll. In 1988 I went to Medjugorje. My distraught Irish mother decided that there was nothing else that might recover me. Our Lady did great things for me there. I'm definitely not a saint. But I was invited to be one by Jesus through Mary in Medjugorje and so far it's the best invite I've had in the last 26 years..."

- Luthern Pastor, Dr. Jeff Dire, a clinical psychologist: "Medjugorje changed my heart like nothing else. It has made a radical difference in the person that I am. ...This afternoon as I stand before you, I'm still a Lutheran Pastor. But I know I can't much longer live in both worlds. I know that I'm going, very soon, to do all that's necessary to renounce my ministry in the Lutheran Church and officially align with Roman Catholicism. Some people have asked me 'Why not remain a Lutheran Pastor and continue to pray the rosary and continue to go to Mass and continue to serve the Lord in that capacity?' And the answer is really simple. I'm dead serious. Because I've got this sneaky suspicion that Our Lady is Roman Catholic. Our Lady comes to this world in response to a question her Son asked almost 2,000 years ago: 'When the Son of man comes, will He find faith on earth?' Will He? Yes, because of Medjugorje!"

- Wayne Weible, a Protestant journalist whose newspaper report on Medjugorje has over 25 million issues in print: "For five years I've carried a cross — that I have remained Protestant. And I'm still Protestant. And technically I will be a Protestant for a few more months. But I must say to you today, now, here in Our Lady's University, I am not Protestant. I am Catholic. This message [of Medjugorje] is a message for every faith, for every person of every faith. But we are in the 10th anniversary of Medjugorje: the 10th year of grace and it is an urgent time now because we have had 10 years to prepare our hearts. We've had 10 years to find the truth. And now we must face what it is Our Lady is asking of us in 1991. She is asking that we be family. And that family must be one! One family. Not a many myriad of families, but one family under God. One! ...I'm to speak on the good fruits of Medjugorje in the lives of Protestants. Well, the good fruit is that we know the truth. And as we know, 'the truth sets us free.' Therefore the truth leads us back to the true family, back to the historical church, back to where we should be as family, as one: that's the Roman Catholic Church! ...[Medjugorje] has led me to the Holy Eucharist! It has led me to realize that that's the flesh and blood of Jesus and it has led me to believe that that is the heart of this Church!" *(At Mass during the New Orleans Conference on Medjugorje the following December, Archbishop Philip Hannan received Mr Weible and his wife into the Catholic Church.)*

- Joe Bertels, a successful businessman who had lost his Catholic faith during his college years, went on vacation to Yugoslavia, inadvertently ending up in Medjugorje. Although he regretted being in a place of religious pilgrimage he decided to join the crowd entering St. James for the evening Mass, since there was nothing else happening in the village: "After that Mass I was in profound shock. Everything that I knew had been turned upside down. The material world that I thought I was living in I found out did not really exist. I found out that the first thing in life is God and everything else revolves around Him." It was at the moment the priest elevated the Eucharist that he found his life completely change. "I surrendered myself to Jesus. I am testifying concerning the Eucharist and the real presence of Christ. I am telling you as I stand here Jesus Christ is present in the Eucharist. The real presence of God exists in the Eucharist!"

- Rock star Michael O'Brien, (whose video "It's Cool to Convert" has been released on MTV), former marathon world record holder, Alberto Salazar, and professional football player, Mark Bavaro, all shared how Our Lady's call from Medjugorje has changed their lives and filled them with love for God and gratitude for their Catholic faith.

These are just several of the voices that rang out at that Conference. A remark by the Apostolic ProNuncio in Yugoslavia (at the time also the representative of the Holy See in Russia) quoted by Fr. Gianni Sgreva during his address at the Conference comes to mind: "Father, Medjugorje represents the event of the Century!"

Address by Fr. Gianni Sgreva at National Medjujorje Conference, 1991

Dearest Brothers and Sisters and dear Friends! "You will recognize them by their fruits." I see this word of Jesus being fulfilled today in you, in all of us...

Be on your guard against false prophets, who come to you in sheep's clothing but underneath are wolves on the prowl. You will know them by their deeds. Do you ever pick grapes from thorn bushes, or figs from prickly plants? Never! Any sound tree bears good fruit, while a decayed tree bears bad fruit. A sound tree cannot bear bad fruit any more than a decayed tree can bear good fruit. Every tree that does not bear good fruit is cut down and thrown into the fire. You can tell a tree by its fruit. (Mt. 7:15-20)

I found that it was very important to begin with the reading of this text from the Gospel, because with these words of his, Jesus here points to the plan of this conference itself. "You will recognize them by their fruits." In this text of Matthew's Gospel, chapter 7:15-20, we find the plan that Jesus wants to give to this conference. The text from the Gospel begins with these words: "Be on your guard against false prophets, who come to you in sheep's clothing but underneath are wolves on the prowl."

Now the title of this conference starts off from this important saying of Jesus, which has to do with prophecy itself. The fruits of true prophecy will be recognized. Therefore, prophecy — according to Jesus — is the tree, the true tree from which are born the fruits. It is important, then, in this moment to establish what might be the prophecy that is confronted in Medjugorje. I have been asked to present a testimony on the new Marian Community, "Oasi della Pace" ("Oasis of Peace"). And you understand well that this raises a theological problem — not just a theological problem alone, but a juridical problem as well, connected with the theological one. And the theological and juridical response derive from the fact that we succeed in understanding what the true prophecy of Medjugorje consists in.

We all know quite well how the events in Medjugorje are still under the judgment of the Church, and the Church is now examining the facts of Medjugorje with great responsibility, with great conscientiousness. I myself spoke with the Holy Father, John Paul II. It was April 14, 1985. The Pope said to me, "Father, I pray every day for a good outcome from the events of Medjugorje." And July 31, 1985, finding myself in Mostar, I met there the Apostolic Pro-Nuncio in Yugoslavia, Msgr. Francesco Colasuono, the representative at the time of the Holy See in Russia. And he said to me, "Father, Medjugorje represents the event of the century. And we need to study it very well from the theological and scientific points of view." You know that currently the commission of the Yugoslavian Bishops' Conference is studying with great competency the problem of Medjugorje. But the work of the Commission is not yet finished, not only because the apparitions are not yet ended, but precisely because the amount of theological work that this examination requires is truly great.

But you all know well about the document that the Yugoslav bishops released April 11 of this year, which documents reads thus: "On the basis of the investigation accomplished until now, it is not possible to affirm that we have to do with supernatural apparitions and revelations." And after having affirmed this, the Yugoslavian bishops admit the presence of a great fruit, which is Medjugorje itself. When the bishops of a country speak, it is all the particular (local) churches of that country that are speaking. Now, the Church of Yugoslavia, the communion of particular (local) churches of Yugoslavia, have recognized on their own soil the presence of this great fruit. But not only this: from this text it is evident that the bishops have opened the eyes to the entire worldwide movement that surrounds Medjugorje.

What was it then that happened on April 11, 1991? The Yugoslavian bishops, without anticipating the conclusions concerning the events of Medjugorje, have set forth a document with which they have declared that there truly is this presence, both national and worldwide, of the fruit which is Medjugorje. If we are present here during these days for this conference, it is precisely because we put into act for the bishops of Yugoslavia that Medjugorje is a worldwide fruit, in itself.

But pay attention to the language that I used! The bishops admit the presence of a fruit, of a fruit nationally and of a worldwide fruit. But they have not yet spoken of the tree that produces this fruit. And it is from here that the theological and juridical problem is situated. I think that all of you understand that it would be very important to me to clarify the question of the theological and juridical basis of the prophecy that Medjugorje is. A new consecrated family could not be born or recognized in the Church, if the tree from which this new reality comes is not understood. Then, how is it possible that a new community exists of consecrated life within the Church, if the tree is not recognized from which this ecclesial family derives?

On March 10, 1991, the Pope went to Portugal. And before arriving in Fatima, he pronounced these prophetic words. Now there follows a literal translation of these very important words of Pope John Paul II:

Confronted by the upheavals that shake the different continents here and there, confronted by the insistent rhythm of the subversion of things and of values which undermines the security and even the life of nations, I make my hope that of St. Augustine, when confronted by the attack from the Vandals of the City of Hippo, in response to an alarmed group of Christians from his church who had sought him out. The Holy Bishop reassured them saying, 'Don't be afraid, dear children. This is not an old world that is ending. It is a new world that begins. A new dawn seems to be rising in the sky of history, inviting Christians to be light and soul to the world that has enormous need for Christ, Redeemer of man.'

Brothers and Sisters, this is the tree. This is the prophecy. The tree is identified with this prophecy of our Pope John Paul II. "Don't be afraid, dear children! This is not an old world that is ending. It is a new world that begins."

Brothers and Sisters, this is the solution, the theological and juridical solution of the problem of Medjugorje. We stand not before apocalyptical evils! We stand before a new world whose dawn is arriving! "A new dawn," says the Pope, "seems to be rising in the sky of history, inviting Christians to be light and soul of a world that has enormous need of Christ, Redeemer of man."

Brothers and Sisters, we must understand the profound significance of these words! We have two great workers in the history of man today. The first worker is the Holy Spirit. The second worker is called "Mary." However, both — the Spirit and Mary — do not work without the great prophet of the new times, Pope John Paul II. This is the reason, because the Pope is completely connected with the events of Medjugorje.

You may know well, I found myself in the Piazza of St. Peter's when this Pope began his pontificate. On that day the Pope said to the whole world, to all the social systems, to all political systems: "Open the doors to Christ!" Within a few days it will be ten years since the time when the Madonna in Medjugorje said exactly these words: "Open the doors to Christ! Open your hearts!"

Already in his first encyclical, *Redemptor Hominis,* John Paul II spoke of the year 2000, of the Jubilee Year 2000. He said that all the years in preparation for the year 2000 are years of an Advent. Therefore we are in the years of Advent. We are in the years of the great dawning. We are in the years that are preparing for the coming of the great Sun of Justice — Christ the Lord.

Brothers and Sisters, they asked me to speak to you of the Marian Community, "Oasis of Peace." But you must understand well that one can't speak of this community if he has not within him the story of this Advent. In the encyclical dedicated to the Holy Spirit, *Dominum et Vivificantem,* the Pope about twenty times invites the entire Church and the entire world to look toward the year 2000, the Jubilee year of the Incarnation of Jesus Christ. In one passage of the encyclical, the Pope says, "I see all the Church in a Cenacle." This means that the Church is preparing to be born. And you here during these days are the Church that is being born.

The Pope underwent the attack on May 13, 1981. One month after this assassination attempt on the Pope, you know that these events in Medjugorje began. There have been ten years of profound collaboration among the Pope, Our Lady and the Holy Spirit. There is an important word in the prophet Isaiah.

> Lo, I am about to create new heavens and a new earth;
> The things of the past shall not be remembered or come to mind.
> Instead, there shall always be rejoicing and happiness in what I create;
> For I create Jerusalem to be a joy and its people to be a delight.
> (Is. 65:17-19)

This is the time, Brothers and Sisters. We are preparing that New Pentecost that Pope John XXIII spoke of already in 1959, the prophecy of the prophet Joel: "Men and women, young and old, from every social condition will prophesy," said the prophet Joel. These are the words that the apostle Peter took up in his first sermon in Jerusalem. But the Pope has given the prophecy of a new world, of the dawning of the new Church. The Pope represents the *Magisterium* of the Church. And therefore in the Pope this prophecy already receives its discernment, its authenticity.

Brothers and Sisters, let us be sure; we are in the presence of good fruits, because these fruits are caused by this good tree, which is the prophecy already subjected to the discernment of Pope John Paul II. And this is how the problem of Medjugorje is resolved. Medjugorje itself is not a tree. You know that Our Lady is appearing in many parts of the world, in so many parts that we know and in so many parts that we don't know of yet. Then Medjugorje itself is a great fruit of a tree already approved in itself by the Church. This tree is the prophecy of the new heavens and the new earth, of a world that will not end, of a world that is beginning in these days of the Advent of the year 2000. Then the trees from which springs forth the great fruit of Medjugorje is the New Pentecost.

The evening of December 4, 1985, I was taking off my priestly vestments in the sacristy of Medjugorje. Marija Pavlovic approached me and she said, "Father Gianni, the Madonna spoke of you this evening." Immediately I answered, "What did she tell you?" "No, I won't tell you right away. You have to put yourself in prayer and recollection." I was left a little upset in the face of Marija's words. But I agreed to go with her together in prayer the following day. Then Marija gave me the message of the Madonna. Our Lady said: "Tell Gianni that I want to speak to him personally." I did not believe it. I told her, "If you see Our Lady again this evening, say to Our Lady that Fr. Gianni wants only facts and signs, and few words." But there was one thing that I liked right away. It came to my mind immediately that Our Lady said my name then.

Both fruits and signs began right away. On June 6, 1986, Our Lady spoke for the second time, because I asked Marija Pavlovic to ask Our Lady if all these signs that I was meeting were coming from her. In fact, Our Lady answered affirmatively. She said now active prayer is necessary, and in the future her Lord would think of everything. And thus in friendship with Marija Pavlovic, that which she desired to make more and more clear, her eventual calling with the coming together of various brothers and sisters from various nationalities, after going on for about two years, in 1987 the experience of the Marian community "Oasis of Peace" began physically.

Now the community is recognized by the Church. On December 25, 1990, you know that Canon Law requires that when a community is begun, the members sign a private contract among themselves. This private agreement was signed March 25, 1987. We all know that this is the Feast of the Annunciation to Our Lady. The community was supposed to be recognized by the Church on December 8, 1990. Instead, the bishop decided all of a sudden to place it as dated December 25, 1990. You know very well that there are nine months from March 25 until December 25, from the Annunciation to Christmas, between conception and birth. This too is a sign, wanted by Our Lady.

Why is this community too a new Pentecost? Or why is it situated in the great prophecy of a new Pentecost? A first response: Because it represents a model of the new Church. The consecrated life is offered to all the components of the Church. The community itself is a model, a small model of the entire Church —

men and women, celibates and married couples, lay people, deacons and priests — all the Church, united and traversed with the consecration of their vows, and in its turn, offered to God through Mary: a new community that represents a new Church.

When the Lord made me understand this inspiration, I didn't know of any similar experience in the Church. I remember that September 9, 1986, I had a long conversation with Cardinal Ratzinger. I submitted this inspiration to him. And he encouraged me to follow it, pointing out to me the Church's juridical formula. And it is exactly at that occasion with Cardinal Ratzinger that he told me there must be no fear of a community whose vocations are born from Medjugorje. For it is always necessary to distinguish the fruits from the tree that the fruits eventually come from.

A second reason for the newness of this community: It represents a new humanity. Number 12 from the Rule approved by the church says that in the community the purity of communion is lived — man and woman, celibate and married, together to realize the true image, of that which is the image of God represented both by man and by woman. With respect to the integration of the charisms of celibacy and marriage, two vocations, two charisms stirred up simultaneously by the Holy Spirit, two charisms that ought to be consecrated by the radicality of baptism. Imagine the married couples who live the vows of poverty, chastity and obedience to live out the intercession for peace. Truly it is a new way to live out the Christian sexuality in the maximum respect for God's original design. The new image of the woman herself, who lives the originality of her spirituality at the side of the man without losing her psychological identity, which is different from that of the man. A new humanity, exactly because the specific aim of this new mixed and contemplative community is the same preoccupation of the Virgin for the peace of the world, for peace in our hearts. How we lived out this petition in the months of the Gulf War this year! How the brothers and sisters of this community intensified their prayer, so that the peace plan of John Paul II could be followed! And thanks be to God, it came about. After two months there is no more suffering.

In fact the community lives this intention for a new humanity through a peace founded on God, on the primacy of prayer, against spreading atheism and materialism. In all the ideologies, as the Holy Father has called to mind in his most recent encyclical, *Centesimus Annus,* whether in ideologies of Marxist origin or the ideologies of the liberal stamp, God is God before everything, as the absolute point of the new life of man.

The third reason — there is represented a new Church and a new humanity. This new community inspired by the message of Our Lady at Medjugorje not to be an enclosed (cloistered) community, but open to receiving, is a cardiac clinic for those who are sick for peace. The parable of the Good Samaritan:

When Jesus alone bent down to him on the road to receive with him all those who had been marginalized. See! Jesus takes the brother or sister wounded in his heart. He takes him to the community where there are brothers and sisters, already for their parts, were just as wounded, in a community where precisely with those who have been wounded and who have lived as much experience of distance from God, precisely by a special grace from the Lord and from Mary, which is the true guide of this community, they can become true good Samaritans for their own brothers and sisters who are seeking peace. In fact, if the specific aim of the community is with the intercession for peace and to live the experience of peace, the first method of receiving is exactly that of living expiation for everything that impedes peace in the human heart.

On December 25, 1990, this little child, which is the Marian Community, "Oasis of Peace," fruit of the fruit of Medjugorje — Medjugorje for its part is a fruit of the tree of the great prophecy — was recognized and inscribed in the Church's registry as a newborn babe.

Brothers and Sisters, we are living in a New Pentecost, giving thanks to God — all of us who are here this evening. Each one of you present in this arena this evening is a member of this New Pentecost, that is arriving in the world and in the Church. Every one of us come from this fruit that is Medjugorje.

So we receive this evening our task. The Marian Community, "Oasis of Peace," has started its path, its road, its life. But each one of us must follow the life Our Lady wishes of him in order to be a collaborator of this New Pentecost that is arriving... God bless you!

(vii) Medjugorje and the Church: Bishop Michael Pfeifer and Mariologist Michael O'Carroll

All the factors that we have seen thus far provide good grounds for affirming the authenticity of the Medjugorje apparitions. The verdict of the Church on an apparition must be seen in the context of historical precedents and the phenomenon itself. The major apparitions went through three phases of "confirmation" before the Church issued its verdict. The first phase of confirmation involves the actual experience of the visionary or the visionaries and their certainty on the matter. The second phase involves the shared experience of the masses who are, so to speak, affected by the "force fields" generated by the apparition. The third phase of confirmation is the public "lasting sign" left after the apparition: the cloak with the image at Guadalupe, the healing spring at Lourdes, the miracle of the sun at Fatima. The third phase is intended for those who could not participate in the first two [in fact, at Medjugorje Our Lady specifically says that this sign is strictly for unbelievers]. But the lasting sign is available only after the apparitions themselves are over and this has not yet happened at Medjugorje. Note that each phase of confirmation is sufficient evidence for those who receive it: for the visionaries the first phase is sufficient, for the masses who believe initially the second phase is sufficient. The third phase has been promised at Medjugorje but those who have participated in the first two phases do not need to wait for the third before they make up their minds. The Church itself reaches a judgment only after all three phases have passed muster. This is as it should be in view of the Church's need to be cautious and prudent when it comes to matters that are near and dear to her children.

John DeMers provides an insightful overview of the issues we must consider in reflecting on the Church's position on Medjugorje:

> The first group of 'reasons' [why people reject Medjugorje] would seem the simplest to clear away, requiring only accurate information about the church's teaching on apparitions, about science's growing body of apparition knowledge and about the ecclesiastical tangle that has, sadly, produced so many untruths about Medjugorje. Unfortunately, it is difficult to convince the average human being he needs any information he doesn't already have — and even more difficult to break through with information that threatens any part of the conclusions he has drawn so conveniently and so soon.
>
> This is the problem we perceive in the battery of statements phrased as questions that often turn discussions of Medjugorje into pseudo-theological gridlock. Here are just a few of them: 'Why should I believe anything's happening there before the Church tells me I have to?' 'How do I know the whole thing isn't a hoax, or some kind of hallucination? How do I know these people aren't crazy? Why should I believe in Medjugorje when even the Bishop in charge doesn't believe?' And finally, 'Why should I go there when the Vatican has said Catholics shouldn't? The Pope has told priests not to go — told everybody that it's not real like Fatima or Lourdes. So why do people keep going?'
>
> As with a marriage counselor facing a troubled young couple for the first time, there is so much anger, distrust and mangled information on these questions it is tempting to give up and move onto the next appointment. Yet we who believe cannot give up, cannot surrender these people who question — precisely because, as we've seen in our own lives, they have so much to gain.
>
> The Church's teaching on apparitions is complex enough to hold at arm's length anyone who feels he doesn't need to know. Yet there is a need to understand these teachings in light of Medjugorje — and at

least a few principles that are both dramatic and accessible. For instance, those waiting for the Church to mandate belief in Medjugorje should know that it never will. Those waiting for the Church to set infallibility behind the authenticity of apparitions should know that it never does. And those believing that the Church accorded some absolute benediction to Lourdes, Fatima or any other private revelation should know that it never has.

Absolutes, it turns out, are few and far between when the Church is dealing with apparitions. In a Church founded on the absolute truth of God's Revelation in scripture and the absolute teaching authority given by God, apparitions have drawn an extremely limited endorsement. 'Even if,' St. Paul said for his time and ours, 'an angel from heaven should preach a gospel other than the one we preached to you, let him be eternally condemned' (Galatians 1:8). The Church has always distinguished between Revelation (those teachings in Scripture or tradition that are essential to faith) and revelation (those private insights into salvation that can never be considered essential). To deem apparitions necessary would be to portray Scripture and sacred tradition as incomplete, something we as Christians cannot do.

In addition, there are problems with even the most accepted apparitions that prevent them from attaining a higher level of authority. They are — as we see so clearly after scientific experiments in Medjugorje — "senses facts," subject to both ambiguity and subjectivity. They also can undermine the Church's authority as an institution, considering the tendency of some believers to give them more credence than teachings of the Church. And finally, they tend to exist in contradiction to the most basic definition of faith: 'being certain of what we do not see' (Hebrews 11:1). Christ Himself said nothing less, to the doubting Thomas in us all: "Blessed are those who have not seen and yet have believed. (John 20:29) [John De Mers, *Invited to Light,* Trinakria Press, 1990, pp.96-97]

As we have seen earlier, the Church does not claim infallibility in ruling on the authenticity of an apparition. Nonetheless, the faithful must submit in obedience and humility to the ruling of the Church even in such a matter as this which involves disciplinary authority and not the infallibility of the magisterium. Nothing decisive for salvation hangs on one's view of a private revelation. Everything hangs on one's view of the public revelation. The Church's primary concern, understandably, is with the latter.

The responsibility for the investigation of the Medjugorje apparition has been transferred by the Vatican from the Bishop of Mostar (Medjugorje is in the diocese of Mostar) to the Catholic Bishops Conference of Yugoslavia. The following statement from the Bishops Conference is a preliminary report on the study of the Medjugorje phenomenon carried out by the Conference: "From the very beginning, the bishops have been following the events of Medjugorje through the local bishop, the bishop's commission and the commission of the bishops' conference of Yugoslavia for Medjugorje. On the basis of studies that have been made to this moment, it cannot be confirmed that supernatural apparitions and revelations are occurring there. Yet the gathering of faithful from various parts of the world to Medjugorje, motivated by reasons of faith, requires the pastoral attention and care of the bishops. Therefore, in the spirit of Church communion, our bishop's conference is willing to assist the diocesan bishop in organizing the pastoral activity in Medjugorje, so that a proper liturgical and sacramental life may be promoted, and so that manifestations and contents that are not in accord with the spirit of the Church may be prevented and hindered."

This succinct statement stands in obvious need of clarification and commentary. To this end, we quote below commentaries on the import of this statement from three of the leading authorities on Medjugorje.

Father Michael O'Carroll [This statement was made before the publication of his *Is Medjugorje Approved?*]: "On October 21, Bishop Franjo Komarica was principal celebrant at the Croatian Mass and he announced that henceforth there would be Yugoslav bishops regularly celebrating there — to date six, I believe, have come. He is the president of the investigating commission set up by the National Episcopal Conference in January 1987 on orders from Rome after the diocesan commission had been dissolved. As Rene Laurentin has said, there can be no definitive statement on the apparitions while they continue and especially while the part of the communications entrusted as secrets to the visionaries have not been divulged. Nonetheless, by the participation of the bishops in Mass and ceremonies at Medjugorje, a milestone has been passed; there can now be no going back. The bishops could not so act if they had fundamental doubts [about the apparitions' authenticity]." (12)

Professor Mark Miravalle: "The brief communique by the Yugoslav Bishops is in no sense a final and definitive judgment on the supernatural nature of the Medjugorje apparitions. The intent of the communique was primarily to address the need for proper pastoral care to the many pilgrims coming to Medjugorje from all over the world, and the Bishops' Conference is establishing a liturgical and pastoral program so that the happenings amidst the pilgrim faithful will remain 'in conformity with the spirit of the Church." It is this pastoral concern for the pilgrims that the communique fundamentally addresses. The statement in the communique that at this point in time 'one cannot affirm that we are dealing here with supernatural apparitions or revelations' in no way represents a definitive pronouncement on the authenticity of the Medjugorje apparitions. That the supernatural origins of the apparitions at this time cannot be 'affirmed' does not indicate a negative final decision and completely leaves open the possibility of a final positive judgment as to its supernatural nature. A definitive statement regarding the authenticity of the apparitions was simply not the intent of this two paragraph communique, which did not come directly from the Commission of Inquiry investigating Medjugorje, but from the general Conference of Yugoslav Bishops." (13)

Fr. Rene Laurentin: The first conclusion arrived at by the bishops is seen to be all the more solid when we reflect that an official recognition of Medjugorje's supernatural character was, in actual fact, impossible. Part of the message remains secret and the apparitions are still continuing. So the definitive conclusion remains suspended — open to the judgment of those who are examining the matter. With this in mind, the growing number of pilgrims who come to Medjugorje 'in the spirit of faith, require the bishops' attention.' (14)

We must also consider the bishops' statement in the light of what the Yugoslavian bishops themselves have said about it. The Archbishop of Belgrade, His Excellency Franc Perko, who is a member of the Pontifical Theology Commission, stated categorically that "It is not true that the bishops' document leaked at the end of November states there is nothing supernatural about Medjugorje. The prelates wrote: 'non constat de supernaturalitate.' There is an enormous difference: the first cannot be interpreted definitively but is left open to new developments." [30 Days, March 1991, p.55].

Perhaps the most insightful commentary on the bishops' statement comes from Rupert Ederer, a member of the Advisory Board of *Fidelity* magazine. *Fidelity* is edited by Michael Jones, one of the most vociferous critics of Medjugorje.

> But let us get back to E. Michael Jones and *Fidelity*, on this, their 10th anniversary as editor and magazine to see if there is a prudential chink in the editor's armour.
>
> In this advisor's judgement, based on my own experience at the site, E. Michael Jones erred in taking such a prominent (several issue long), negative position on the Medjugorje episode.
>
> No one has to accept private revelation, even approved private revelation, to remain a Catholic in good standing. The requirements for such standing are mercifully minimal. However, it is rash to anticipate the Church's own decision on such matters, since one could substantially be out on the proverbial limb if it is financially sawed off. The journalist is tempted to exposés. The scholar, and you are one, Michael, steers clear of sensation and from preemptive strikes (scoops?)

especially where Rome is concerned. Ultimately though, the Apostle Thomas became St. Thomas notwithstanding his skepticism and the mild reprimand which the risen Christ administered.

Incidentally, I do not feel that the April 10, 1991, declaration by the Yugoslavian bishops vindicates what has become the *Fidelity* position.

The characteristically ambivalent statement by the Commission of the Yugoslavian Bishops' Conference for Medjugorje must be as frustrating for Rome as are some other statements by national Bishops' conferences in these times. One would think that after long study and disputation they could have come out with something more forthright than: "...it cannot be affirmed that supernatural apparitions and revelations are taking place..." One is tempted toward the conclusion: it also cannot be affirmed that supernatural apparitions and revelations are not taking place.

In the next sentence, the bishops express their assurance of continuing pastoral care of the many faithful who come to Medjugorje from various parts of the world. The fact is that neither the bitterly opposed local bishop, nor the Commission of Bishops has dared to interdict the entire operation — or perhaps Rome will not let them do so!

Cardinal Ratzinger expressed what seemed like thinly veiled frustration with the bishops' approach. Recently [August 28, 1991, as reported in *Der Fels*, October 1991], before the 3rd International Theological Summer Academy in Aigen, Austria, in reply to a question about Medjugorje he indicated precisely this point.

While the Bishops did not say 'Constat de supernaturalitate' (there is something supernatural going on), they also did not say 'Constat de non supernaturalitate,' (there is clearly nothing supernatural going on). Instead, the Cardinal pointed out, they chose the formula: 'Non constat de supernaturalitate,' which he translated in German as: 'es steht nicht fest, dass da Ubernaturliches ist.'

This translates in English as: 'It is not clear that something supernatural is going on here.' Ratzinger added that the supernatural was hereby not absolutely ruled out. Thus, it appears that the principle of subsidiarity, if not collegiality itself, may have to be overridden once again by Rome, because so many bishops' conferences seem constitutionally unable to come to grips with their responsibility to deal with matters in a forthright, unequivocal, unambivalent manner.

And so, dear Michael, based on my own experience in Medjugorje, I am inclined to believe: Constat de supernaturalitate; and you will quite probably stick by your: Constat de non supernaturalitate! Meanwhile, the tragic, ongoing, tribal warfare in Yugoslavia will perhaps also relieve the Yugoslavian bishops of their responsibility to provide the necessary 'pastoral care' for the millions of pilgrims who would continue to come to the little mountain village." [*Fidelity*, December 1991, p.17].

As we will see, it is Fr. O'Carroll's contention today that the statement of the Yugoslavian bishops taken in conjunction with certain subsequent events leads to the conclusion that Medjugorje has now been "approved" in the same manner that Knock has been approved — although he distinguishes "approval" from a statement declaring authenticity. He holds that what the Yugoslav Bishops Conference has said and done amounts to such approval of Medjugorje.

The statements and actions of the Yugoslavian Bishop's Conference on which Fr. O'Carroll based his analysis and his conclusions were further amplified and confirmed, as earlier mentioned, in the following statement issued by Cardinal Joseph Ratzinger, Prefect of the Congregation for the Doctrine of the Faith [published by *Medjugorje Gebetsaktion Maria #22, Spring 1992*]: "We want to be concerned that this place [Medjugorje], which has become a place of prayer and of faith, continue to be and become even more perfectly one with the entire Church; that is, the Bishop's Conference offers its help towards an organization of this place of prayer that is genuinely effective pastorally and, at the same time, doctrinally pure. So this is, so to speak, the will of the bishops which now concerns the place and which is naturally an offer to the local authorities. At the moment everything is apparently blocked by the political events, but we hope, nevertheless, that this aim of the Yugoslavian Bishops' Conference — which, in my opinion, holds good on this point and has been shown really as an instance being handled out of faith and great pastoral concern — that this then will also lead to a fruitful clarification of the whole thing."

On the question of whether a Catholic can accept the authenticity of Medjugorje, we quote relevant excerpts from the pastoral letter of Bishop Michael Pfeifer of San Angelo on this issue.[10]

The question may arise: "Can a Catholic accept the contents of private revelations and integrate them into one's life before the Church makes an official pronouncement regarding the apparitions?" The

---

[10] It is worth noting that on August 5, 1988 Bishop Pfeifer made public his Diocesan Pastoral Letter *The Gospel, Mary and Medjugorje* -the month before Mike Jones came out with his **Untold Story**.

answer, by the Church's own teaching and experience, is "yes," provided that, after prudent and cautious examination of the reported revelations, nothing is found in the content of the revelations that is in any way contrary to Church teaching on faith and morals.

I believe here it might be good to reflect a little deeper on how the Church views apparitions. When we give our assent to an apparition, we are not assenting to any new truth of the faith. It seems to me that it is primarily the virtue of Hope which we directly engage in our acceptance of the Church's decision about the authenticity of an apparition. It is an act of childlike confidence, the motive of which is our trust in the Church's mission of leading us to salvation. We can say that we are then assenting to and leaning upon the gracious mercy of God, by which He has willed to intervene and direct us toward our ultimate destiny, the Kingdom. We are responding to His loving stimulus, to His gentle, and at times, not so gentle reminder that we are on a pilgrimage which is filled with perils, and yet always destined to lead us into His loving presence. Our response is one of childlike trust, confident in His power and mercy.

To pursue this a little further, in the case of an apparition of Mary, we are responding not only to the fact of her appearance, and thus recognizing and accepting God's fatherly intervention, but we are also assenting to the great things God has done in her and for her. We are honoring her presence in our midst as a sign of eschatological hope. This means that like Mary, we are called to willingly and totally surrender ourselves to our God. If so, then our kind and faithful Lord will lovingly guide us on life's journey to a new, future life of glory and peace which far exceeds our dreams. We are saying 'Yes, we trust in you, Lord, and we shall heed your exhortations,' and the basis for our confidence is the solid conviction that the Lord shall do the same good things for us that he has done for her.

It is for these reasons that we should look upon apparitions as a charism, that is, a gift of God's Spirit for the building up of the Church, literally the edification and sanctification of the Christian people. In fact, we can view them as prophetic gifts, not in the sense that they foretell the future (even when that aspect of prophecy is part of the message, it is secondary in importance), but in the more profound sense that apparitions mediate and interpret God's mind and will for us at this particular time. Prophecy has been described as the conquest of hope in each generation.

Father Rene Laurentin, a renowned theologian and historian of apparitions, comments on the apparitions in his book, *The Appari-*

tions at Medjugorje Prolonged: "The abstract principle that is often stated in these cases; i.e., to wait for the judgment of the Church before becoming interested in these apparitions or making pilgrimages, is erroneous. If no one went to these places where the Heavenly seems to manifest itself, then the authority of the Church would have no reason to preoccupy itself with it, and especially not to have to put forth a judgment about it. It was necessary to make a judgment on Guadalupe, La Salette, Fatima, Beauraing, and Banneaux, because of the crowds assembling there and creating a lot of attention. The "sense of the faithful" had recognized an authentic message and had gone there. The authority of the Church had only to verify this spontaneous discernment, and to extract errors that mankind may have claimed as a gift of God.

In the past, the faithful began to act upon the contents of private revelations before the Church's approval was given. For example, the Church only approved the apparition at Fatima thirteen years after the events. Medjugorje, therefore, remains open for acceptance and integration by any individual as the Church continues her official investigation.

What has been the position of our Holy Father as regards the claimed apparitions of Medjugorje? In a public papal audience in June of 1986, when he was questioned by 12 Italian bishops about Medjugorje, the pope had this to say, "Let the people go to Medjugorje, if they convert, pray, confess, do penance and fast."

During my "ad limina" visit to Rome with the Bishops of Texas this past April, in the private conversation I had with our Holy Father, I asked his opinion about Medjugorje. The pope spoke very favorably about the happenings at Medjugorje, pointing out the good which it has done for people. During the luncheon the Texas Bishops enjoyed with our Holy Father, Medjugorje came up for further discussion. Again, His Holiness spoke of how Medjugorje has changed the lives of people who visit there, and that the messages, thus far, are not contrary to the Gospel. (15)

The central strands of Fr. O'Carroll's thesis are presented below:

Change of Authority

The Yugoslavian National Episcopal Conference has an unenviable task. When Bishop Zanic was ordered by the Roman authorities in May 1986 to dissolve his enlarged commission, authority in regard to Medjugorje was transferred to the Episcopal Conference. They were to nominate a commission which would investigate the whole matter anew. In January of the following year a communique issued on behalf of the Conference and signed by the Archbishop of Zagreb, Cardinal Kuharic, and Bishop Zanic, announced that this commission had been constituted. Neither the membership of the commission, nor that of the scientific commission, which they are thought to have called on, has been published. We do know the name of the president of the commission, Bishop Frano Komarica. Ultimately, the higher body composed of the hierarchy has to assume responsibility, which, as we shall see, it has done eventually.

'Eventually' may imply dissatisfaction, if not criticism. True, we have heard nothing for almost four years by way of a decision, while things were taking their well-known course: pilgrimages increasing in number and participants, continuity of the apparitions, seminars and large congresses in different countries, especially in the United States, an incessant production of books, articles, reviews, videotapes and cassettes, flourishing Medjugorje centers and prayer groups.

Vatican II encouraged us to think that this is the age of the people of God. Not altogether dissimilar is the upsurge of people power in countries where a tyrannical regime had seemed unshakeably entrenched, the Philippines in February, 1986, the countries of eastern Europe in 1990, 1991. There is an obvious difference between natural and supernatural forces. But there may be grounds of analogy.

The Voice of God's People

A question which Vatican II solved, one which Cardinal Newman had made particularly his own, is the relationship between the people of God and doctrine; this is the vindication of 'the sentiment of the faithful', for expounding which Newman was denounced to Rome as a heretic by an English bishop. Thus speaks the Council: 'The body of the faithful as a whole, anointed as they are by the Holy One (cf. Jn 2:20,27) cannot err in matters of belief. Thanks to a supernatural sense of the faith which characterizes the people as a whole, it manifests this unerring quality when "from the bishops down to the last member of the laity" it shows universal agreement in matters of faith and morals.' (16)

Newman maintained that, at the time of the Arian crisis in the fourth century, i.e. the worst heresy of the Church's history, the laity saved the day. May we compare the worldwide faith in the apparitions of Medjugorje with this unshakeable faith of the fourth century laity in the divinity of Christ? Many bishops then, as Newman makes clear, did not believe in the divinity of Jesus Christ. Athanasius of Alexandria has passed into history with the caption "Athanasius contra mundum," because he was alone among very many Arian, that is heretical, bishops. We are prone to think that the errors and mistakes of the past will never happen again. Is the sentiment of the faithful always active, always needed?

The members of the Yugoslav Episcopal Conference have to ask themselves this question. They may consult Vatican II for guidance. There they will read: 'For, by this sense of a faith which is aroused and sustained by the Spirit of truth, God's people accepts not the Word of men but the very Word of God (cf. 1 Th 2:13). It clings without fail to the faith once delivered to the saints (cf. Jude 3), penetrates it more deeply by accurate insights, and applies it more thoroughly to life. All this it does under the lead of a sacred teaching authority to which it loyally defers.' (17)

To mention figures is not to advocate theology by opinion poll or public survey, to substitute popular plebiscite for the Teaching Authority. But one way in which the Teaching Authority may see its way to identify with the sentiment of the faithful is to study accurate records of lay profession of faith.

To date, that is within a period of ten years, an estimated ten million people from across the world have come to Medjugorje. These included some twenty thousand priests, and one hundred bishops. Those who come are animated, as the bishops themselves admit, by faith; they manifest an intense Catholic life; they join in communal prayer with fervor and may be seen in private recollection in and around the parish church. Above all, they approach the sacraments, the Eucharist, and, in vast numbers, Penance, something which may well be unique at the present time. At times upwards of 150 priests are needed to administer the Sacrament of Penance in Medjugorje, so great is the demand. Pastoral experience in many places registers a serious decline in the numbers of those seeking sacramental absolution.

This is how the faith of the people of God expresses itself in this place. The investigating commission must take note of the fact. They have a responsibility to the whole Church in the matter, for if the message has been delivered by the Mother of God and if its impact on so many lives has been so marked, it is taken out of the domain of the optional and carries an imperative. It can no longer be said that bishops are responsible only for their own part of the Lord's vineyard. If collegiality means anything it means solidarity throughout the whole episcopal order. Pius XII, appealing in his Fidei Donum for volunteer priests from European dioceses for missionary lands, especially Africa, was, as he made clear, applying this principle. There is a similar call to the Yugoslav hierarchy to interpret rightly the sentiment of the worldwide faithful on a question that originated within their jurisdiction, but which very soon had repercussions far beyond it.

It is not lacking in respect to ask what they are waiting for. The phenomena of Medjugorje have been, with the exception of one significant element (the secrets), exposed to investigation and inquiry in a way unparalleled in such cases. The visionaries have been questioned, reported and photographed, in everyday life and in the moments of ecstasy. What they have to say that they can say is very well known. It is, again let it be said respectfully, difficult to see what the investigating commission could discover. But they have been given authority in the matter and deference must be shown them. No theologian would claim infallibility for them, but they have an important role.

Theological Consensus

Besides the testimony of the believing faithful, there have been other significant contributions to their subject on which to draw. The final judgement here calls for a knowledge of theology, specialized theology. A number of theologians with the required competence have studied the phenomena at Medjugorje and rendered judgement. They include Hans Urs Von Balthasar, one of the greatest theologians of modern times, and one particularly well versed in the domain of special mystical graces; Rene Laurentin, whose utterly unique expertise has been described; Robert Faricy SJ, Professor of Spirituality at the Gregorian University in Rome, and Lucy Rooney SND, who lectures in the same university department; Heribert Muhlen, a theologian of the Holy Spirit and representative of the German hierarchy to the Renewal Movement; Sr Briege McKenna, an exceptionally gifted spiritual director and preacher of retreats to priests, herself richly endowed with charisms; Michael Scanlan OFM, president of Steubenville Franciscan University, a graduate of Harvard Law School; Dr Richard Foley, SJ, and, especially, Archbishop Franic, already mentioned.

Not only theologians, but scientists of repute have carried out research on the visionaries, in moments of ecstasy and in their everyday life. They include Mario Margnelli, a specialist in parapsychology, in particular the phenomenon of induced 'ecstasy' (a non-practising Catholic when he went to Medjugorje he is now practising), and Giorgio Sanguinetti, a psychiatrist attached to Sacred Heart University, Milan. But the immense achievement of Rene Laurentin was to persuade Professor Henri Joyeux, of Montpelier University Medical School, to come to Medjugorje and carry out encephalograms on the visionaries in ecstasy.

All these scientists have given favorable judgement on the visionaries. Their findings have been made public and are available to the commission. It has been said again and again in recent times that the Church respects scientists and values scientific competence. Why should the Yugoslav hierarchy not encourage its commission to use the findings of all this research which is strictly relevant to their investigation? Does one reject a treasure?

We have not been informed on the attitude of the commission to those who have unofficially gone over the ground which they have to cover officially. Questions were being asked as to why they delayed their decision for almost four years. They have an easy answer: the apparitions are still continuing. It is difficult to give a final judgement on something of this nature which is not complete. I am not their apologist and I do not feel bound to defend them in the length of time they have taken. With respect, I suggest that they were hoping that time would provide a way out of their dilemma. That dilemma arises from the massive evidence that favours approval on the one hand and, on the other, the utterly unyielding opposition of the Bishop of Mostar to Medjugorje. Understandably they wished to avoid confrontation. They had the proof of the Bishop's refusal to change in the pamphlet which he issued in March 1990. The note of defiance which it sounded was a challenge to them.

But there was for them another factor not to be overlooked. It is common knowledge that John Paul II believes in the authenticity of the apparitions, but will not take an official position out of respect for the bishops of the country. The Pope has sent his blessing to the visionaries — I have personally seen the autographed portrait he sent to Jacov. He has encouraged pilgrims to go to Medjugorje and has admitted to Bishop Hnilica that if he were not Pope he would have gone there himself.

The First Declaration

The silence was broken in November 1990. After a meeting of the hierarchy on 27 and 28 November the following communique' was sent to Rome: 'Ever since their beginning the bishops have been following the events in Medjugorje as seen through the local bishop, his local diocesan commission and that of the Yugoslav Episcopal Conference. On the basis of inquiries conducted up till the present time, one cannot affirm that we are dealing here with supernatural apparitions or revelations. However, the constant concourse in Medjugorje of faithful coming from different parts of the world and animated by motives of faith calls for the bishops' attention and care. Accordingly, our episcopal conference, moved by the spirit of ecclesial communion, is ready to assist the local bishop in organizing pastoral matters in order to promote a solid liturgical and pastoral programme, thus forestalling and preventing phenomena and happenings not in conformity with the Church's spirit.'

This statement deserves and needs close study. Many people interested in Medjugorje were happy with it. It was, by its terms of reference, interim, 'on the basis of inquiries conducted up till the present time'. The bishops could not make a blanket assertion on authenticity for two plausible reasons; a part, an important part, of public interest, of the message received by the visionaries, is secret. They have not divulged it yet. Secondly, the apparitions are continuing, and common sense in this particular case may demand that a final verdict await completion but, as we have seen, there is here no binding obligation.

But there have been 'secrets' in many previous apparitions of Our Lady. The two children at La Salette were given secrets, which they sent to the Pope. St Bernadette was given three secrets for herself; she said that she would not tell them even to the Pope. Long after Fatima was approved, the surviving seer, Lucia, revealed that she had received three secrets, two of which she disclosed. St Catherine Laboure,' the saint of the Miraculous Medal, kept her personal identity secret — though we now know that the secrecy was not as cast-iron as was generally believed, merely because, despite the saint's absolute discretion, people guessed. The special characteristic of the Medjugorje phenomenon, in comparison with all of these, is that though the secrets have been preserved, there is no secret about the fact that they exist and that they will be made public one day.

So things could and would have continued as heretofore. But this was not to be. Suddenly a world-wide campaign of disinformation erupted around the bishops' communiqué. Papers, even Catholic papers, carried headlines proclaiming that the supernatural origin of the apparitions had been rejected outright; Medjugorje was finished. Some commentators stretched their luck a bit too far, even asserting that it was well known that within the Vatican the general response was doubt. These people scarcely knew of John Paul's opinion, nor of the support given to Medjugorje by the exiled east European bishop, Mgr. Hnilica, resident in Rome, with many Russian contacts and enjoying the confidence of the Pope.

Perhaps the Yugoslav bishops could have made things clearer (18) It is known that the meeting which preceded the communiqué was stormy. It is in no way derogatory to Bishop Zanic to suggest that he would have been at the heart of the storm; he has strong views and expresses them in season and out of season. It would have saved much discussion if the communique' stated very explicitly that the bishops were not giving a definitive judgement. This was made clear afterwards by the secretariat, which was approached by the editor of one of the best Medjugorje reviews circulating presently, *Gebetsaktion*, appearing in Vienna, issued in several languages. I quote from this excellent review:

Official Rejection of Disinformation
The following emerges from information received from the secretariat of the Yugoslav bishops' conference and from several members of the investigating commission that is responsible for the events in Medjugorje:

1. As of this date, the investigating commission has offered no definitive judgement concerning the supernatural character of the events of Medjugorje.
2. The investigating commission is charged by the bishops' conference to continue further with its work, too.
3. The secretariat of the bishops' conference has taken no position on the events of Medjugorje. It is astonished that the Italian news agency "ASCA" could have come by such information.

It appears that certain circles are in very much of a hurry to distribute incorrect reports concerning Medjugorje within the public mind, and by this to create a pre-judgement before the official report of the Yugoslav bishops' conference becomes known. Through this, apparently, confusion is supposed to be brought about, so as to render more difficult a possible positive decision.

From an interview with Cardinal Kuharic on Croatian TV on 23 December 1990, one can conclude that the Yugoslav bishops' conference — including the cardinal personally — is taking a positive stance toward the events in Medjugorje.

We meet here the perennial problem of communication and what can be done by those resolved to exploit highly nuanced language maliciously. However, there is a very important point in the second paragraph of the bishops' declaration which must be considered. The general tenor of the paragraph is a recognition of the 'sentiment of the faithful'. The bishops use this phrase as particularly justifying their interest and their pastoral duty as they see it, 'animated by motives of faith' (another translation gives 'motivated by reasons of faith').

Faith in what? It is essential to ask this question for it is the faith of the pilgrims which prompts the bishops' concern. It is not faith in the general truths of the Catholic religion; if it were so, people would not travel across the world to Medjugorje to express it; they would stay at home. If they go to this Yugoslav village it is because their faith has as its object the apparitions taking place there. Anyone with the slightest acquaintance with the entire movement knows well that this is the essential motivation.

People go in large numbers to Medjugorje because they believe that Our Lady is appearing there. The hierarchy of the country is publicly committed to supporting them.

A Milestone

Not only in word or promises, but in very deed. Something of immense consequence happened in the village church last October which passed unnoticed by media workers either indifferent or opposed to Medjugorje. On Sunday, 21 October, Bishop Frano Komarica, president of the episcopal commission, came to celebrate the Mass. He announced that from now on members of the Yugoslav hierarchy would come to do as he was doing.

If Bishop Komarica or his episcopal colleagues had any serious reservation about the sequence of events to date they could not contemplate any such course of action. They do not merely come to pray in a private capacity. They have come, nine of them to date, to lead the people of God in the great central act of Christian worship, the Eucharist.

Lex orandi lex credendi

Public worship has always been a sure indicator of the Church's belief. Is it so today at Medjugorje? We are instructed in the Roman document on apparitions that approval of a particular devotion which has originated from an apparition does not mean approval of the apparition. So we need to remain circumspect while noting encouraging features of the development.

One is the direct commitment of the Yugoslav hierarchy. Over a hundred bishops from different countries have come as pilgrims to Medjugorje. They have come privately; they do not have jurisdiction in the country. The Yugoslav bishops have pastoral responsibility, as they make clear in their statement of 27 and 28 November.

Secondly, they have decided within ten years to take this decision, which is public, explicit and meaningful. Consider the case of Knock shrine, one of the best known sanctuaries of Our Lady, the goal of the Pope's pilgrimage to Ireland (his words) in 1979. There never has been a formal declaration by a pope or bishop that Our Lady appeared in the Mayo village on 21 August 1879, though two commissions, at an interval of some sixty years, investigated the matter, and on each occasion had the assistance of one of the most remarkable witnesses in the entire chain of apparitions and private revelations, Mary O'Connell.

Not only that, but for fifty years no bishop, Irish or foreign, put in an appearance at Knock. But for many decades Knock has been considered an approved shrine; it was the scene in 1990 of a spectacular miracle, the instantaneous cure of a young married woman suffering from multiple sclerosis whose husband, at home at the time, had a vision of the miracle taking place. In passing, it should be said that the latest miracle reported from Medjugorje, which took place on 8 December 1990, was of a person suffering from the same disease.

Conclusion

No bishop so far in the history of the Church has been able to state categorically: From personal observation of this apparition I certify that the witness to it is speaking the truth. Church representatives deny direct certainty but can seek maximum converging probability. How they must proceed has been made clear in the preceding pages.

As I said in the first page of this booklet, Medjugorje presents unusual features. In the light of the first ten years' history and the official statement and consequent practice, can one answer affirmatively the question which is the title of this short work?

One must bear in mind the massive expression of the 'sentiment of the faithful', the remarkable theological consensus, the elimination of every kind of psychic disorder and disturbance in the diagnoses of the visionaries made by scientists of the highest competence, and the chain of the miraculous which is unending.[11]

---

[11] While I was present in St. James Church in Medjugorje on November 12, 1988, it was announced that the five medical experts on the Bishop's Conference of Yugoslavia's Commission investigating the apparitions were also present in Medjugorje. They stated that they had concluded their findings: "the children are healthy in every way. There is no pathological condition that could be said to be influencing them." It was reported that the Bishop's Conference now awaited only the judgement from the theological experts on the Commission.

With such very determining factors one must especially give place to the entirely spiritual dimension of the whole phenomenon, the conversions, the fervor in prayer, the intense sacramental practice, the worldwide bond of fraternity at a time when human kind is desperately seeking to overcome division and dissension, and the overruling programme of peace.

Let the thoughtful reader weigh, with these things in mind, the action of the Yugoslav bishops, which I have characterized as a milestone. What else can it mean but approval of Medjugorje? How else could the mighty spiritual adventure now end but with formal approval of the apparitions 'when the fullness of time has come'?

Michael O'Carroll, CSSp, *Is Medjugorje Approved?* [Dublin, Ireland, Veritas, 1991, pp. 30-41, pp.61-2]

III. I THANK YOU THAT YOU WILL NOT BETRAY MY PRESENCE HERE

1. CRITICS AND SKEPTICS

The critics and the skeptics we will always have with us. Catholics in particular and Christians and theists in general have never been able to convince everyone of the truth of their convictions — it's so much easier to deny or dispute fundamental insights than to understand and expound them. This is particularly true when we are dealing with insights and revelations that require a definite sensitivity to the deeper dimensions of reality and a certain level of sophistication in making correlations between available data and relevant interpretations. The foregoing considerations apply with equal force to affirmations and analyses concerning apparitions. Consequently, it would be foolish to expect unanimous acceptance of the mystery of Medjugorje.

Of Medjugorje we might well say what Archbishop Fulton Sheen famously said about the perception of the Catholic Church in the U.S: "There are not over a hundred people in the United States who hate the Catholic Church. There are millions, however, who hate what they wrongly believe to be the Catholic Church, which is, of course, quite a different thing." The Medjugorje that is thrust aside by the skeptics is not the Medjugorje of the apparitions and the visionaries but the Medjugorje of tourist traps [although the tragic war in Bosnia has eliminated this particular feature], the Bishop of Mostar versus the Franciscans, etc.

Before proceeding to representative critics and critiques, we must unload some of the excess baggage referred to above. It is unfortunate but true that perhaps the worst enemies of Medjugorje are sometimes proponents of the apparition themselves. Some have, for instance, wanted to co-opt the Medjugorje phenomena into the Charismatic movement. The Charismatic Renewal as a whole is undoubtedly a great gift to the Church. But at least a few in this movement have reason to beware of defying authority or denying the Tradition and teaching of the Church and it is of these few we speak here. Rather than appreciating the visionaries and the apparitions on their own terms, certain enthusiasts — as mentioned earlier — have sought to explain the phenomena solely in Charismatic categories.

Other excesses abound. Some "friends" of Medjugorje try to exalt the apparitions there by making disparaging comments about Fatima and Lourdes. They forget that Medjugorje is a continuation of Fatima — Fatima in action today — and not an isolated episode. (The director of the apostolate sponsoring the National Conference on Medjugorje at the University of Notre Dame opened the 1991 conference by saying, "In my personal opinion the great apparition of the

I THANK YOU THAT YOU WILL NOT BETRAY MY PRESENCE HERE.

20th century is Fatima. Our Lady is not in competition with herself.") To downplay one in favor of the other is to rob Peter to pay Paul.

Secondly, it may be true that some have gone to Medjugorje seeking some kind of supernatural titillation. There may be pilgrims who seek signs and wonders and who are disappointed if they do not end up with gold rosaries and a private apparition. Since we "all have sinned and fallen short of the glory of God", and "Faith is the assurance of things hoped for, the conviction of things not seen" (Heb.11:1), few of us are probably completely free of at least a little bit of this craving. But the Church has wisely warned against a faith that is based on private revelations. Although a faith based on "signs and wonders" is fragile and should be warned against, we must not thereby conclude that "signs and wonders" do not take place and that people should not acknowledge such "signs and wonders" if they do take place. Certain Catholic experts commenting on Medjugorje [see *Our Sunday Visitor*, February 2, 1992] are so nervous about what they perceive as a thirst for signs and wonders that they concern themselves simply with this thirst and not with the evidence for a specific supernatural phenomenon itself. No one denies that for some a thirst for signs and wonders exists. And we can reasonably assume that the occurrence of actual signs and wonders would trigger a response from those who have the thirst for them. But it would be foolish to conclude (as some of these experts do) that apparitions and supernatural phenomena exist merely because this thirst exists. That would be putting the cart before the horse. If we accept all the assumptions and pronouncements of these experts, we would have to deny the Gospel miracles as well as Lourdes and Fatima.

Thirdly, the various money-making enterprises that sprang up in Medjugorje before the war turned off many visiting pilgrims. But materialism in a holy place is no worse or better than materialism anywhere else — only more conspicuous. And such materialism is on display in holy places like Lourdes as well.

Fourthly, it is unwise to hang onto every word uttered by the visionaries as if one were dealing with individuals who are infallible and impeccable. Visionaries at authenticated apparitions have made mistakes in their everyday judgments and opinions. So have saints. If its guidance on doctrine that we seek then we should turn to the public revelation preached by the Church. Private revelations are primarily intended to turn our minds and hearts toward the public revelation and to help us grow in interior devotion and in the practice of our faith. One point must be mentioned in this context which will be taken up in greater detail presently. The Medjugorje visionaries have transmitted two kinds of data. On the one hand they have given the messages which the Blessed Virgin has entrusted to them specifically for transmission to the world. These are the messages of Medjugorje. On the other hand, the visionaries have asked their supernatural visitor a whole host of questions, some of them their own and some from other sources. These questions range from matters of local interest to matters of greater significance such as the question of when the apparitions would end. On such issues, the possibility of misunderstanding and misrepresentation is particularly acute as we shall see. Discussions on issues of this kind are clearly peripheral in relation to the messages that were specifically and categorically given by the Blessed Virgin but we shall study them anyway since the critics have gleefully displayed some of these exchanges as evidence for their contentions.

Finally, we must condemn in the strongest terms any effort to publicly and personally attack or denigrate the retired Bishop of Mostar. We can legitimately dispute his conclusions on Medjugorje (as we could his conclusions in economics or physics) but we cannot forget his dignity as a successor of the Apostles. We cannot forget either that the drama of Medjugorje takes place in the context of a bitter historical feud between the Franciscans and the secular clergy and the messages of peace and reconciliation are particularly relevant in this context for both parties. The Franciscans who have the privilege of being the knights of the Queen of Peace can best serve their supernatural Sovereign by showing due reverence to their natural lord.[12]

It may be well to add here that allegations of sexual immorality have been hurled at one of the Franciscans involved with Medjugorje in the early days. Fr. Tomislav Vlasic, it is alleged, is the father of a son born to Manda, an ex-Franciscan nun, in 1977. The controversy was triggered off by a letter allegedly received by the Bishop of Mostar at the height of the conflict between him and the Franciscans. The letter (which had no return address) concerned Vlasic's paternity and was purportedly written by Manda, who was now living in Germany. The bishop tracked down the ex-nun but she denied writing the letter and all allegations regarding Fr. Vlasic. Manda had been staying at the house of Herr Ott, a 94-year-old German gentleman, but left after the Bishop's visit. Herr Ott is said to have later uncovered copies of some of the correspondence between Manda and the father of her son (why Manda would have made copies of her letters is a mystery but convenient for the critics). The hard facts of the matter are these: we have a series of letters the authorship of which is in dispute; we have as Fr. Vlasic's chief accuser someone who is also his chief antagonist; we have Manda denying that Fr. Vlasic is the father of her son; and we have testimonies to Fr. Vlasic's innocence from those who know him best. It is more than likely that the truth of the whole matter will be known some time in the future [readers should pay particular attention to the data brought to light in this volume by Dr. Adrian Reimers and Dr. Nicholas Bartulica]. Until then it would be

---

[12] As a personal footnote my conscience impells me to state that in twelve pilgrimages to Medjugorje I have never heard anyone in the village — priest or lay person — utter an unkind word about the bishop. This was even the case when I once relayed to the priests some uncharitable remarks about them the bishop had shared with me earlier that day. I remember being struck by the response: silence. They made no attempt to defend themselves.

sheer slander to point a finger at a man who has patiently borne every manner of vilification for his prayerful efforts to live out the messages of Medjugorje.

For some critics the Vlasic controversy is the crux of the case against the authenticity of Medjugorje. This attitude of mind is puzzling at best. Fr. Vlasic came to Medjugorje well after the apparitions had begun and was relieved of his position as pastor by the Bishop of Mostar in 1984. The genesis and continuing dynamic of the Medjugorje phenomenon can hardly be attributed to someone who joined the audience after the first act of the play had come to a close and who left in medias res in tragic disgrace. Bishop Zanic summoned the visionaries to Mostar on November 29, 1985, to present his case against Fr. Vlasic.[13] While they were deeply saddened by the accusations, they could not see what bearing it had on the authenticity of the apparitions. But, as we shall see later, any stick is good enough to please some critics if it can be used against the apparitions.

The Vlasic controversy is valuable in highlighting a factor that is not often noticed. One of the favorite tacks taken by the critics in warning against the "perils" of Medjugorje is to point out that the Devil could be using it to discredit Marian devotion in particular and orthodoxy in general. The "devil" factor, however, is relevant in more ways than the critics comprehend. If the apparitions in Medjugorje are genuine, it is unlikely that they have gone unnoticed by the Evil One particularly in view of the spectacular conversions and piety engendered by them. Where the woman with her heel on the head of the serpent is present, the serpent too is present. And it is only to be expected that the empire of evil will strike back when it perceives any threat to its dominion. The visionaries themselves have reported direct temptations from the Devil — temptations they were only able to resist with the aid of the Blessed Virgin and her Son. But the forces of evil are not likely to strike only at the source of their affliction. What better way to discredit the apparition than to discredit anyone associated with it in the public mind — this includes not just the visionaries but their defenders. Even if the horrific accusations against Fr. Vlasic were true, then they illustrate something that has always been known: the enticements of the flesh are the tools in trade of the Evil One, tools which have trapped some of his worst enemies. The visionaries themselves, it is reasonable to assume, enjoy special protection but their defenders and their critics presumably only have the normal means of grace by which they can resist the temptations of the world, the flesh and the Devil. It would be prudent for all concerned to bear this in mind.

---

[13] Earlier the bishop had given Fr. Vlassic an ultimatum: either he swear on the crucifix handed to him by the bishop that he had invented the Medjugorje apparitions, or the bishop would make public these scandalous charges. Needless to say, Fr. Vlassic refused. Instead the priest embraced the crucifix swearing that he had not invented the apparitions. The bishop followed through on his threat.

As with most of the great debates of history, both sides in the discussion on the authenticity of Medjugorje have more or less the same set of facts — although there are definite disputes on some of the purported facts that are of great significance in making a fair judgment. The different perspectives on the phenomenon basically derive from different ways of interpreting the same data. The bones of contention stem from principles and applications of these principles in drawing inferences from data. In addition, the role of bias, ideology, emotion, and other extraneous factors cannot be ignored in view of the fact that these factors are clearly reflected both in the content and tone of the writings of at least some of the partisans and critics. The disputes on some crucial pieces of data are relevant in making a final judgment but are not serious enough to preclude meaningful discussion both on the facts themselves and on the interpretation of these facts.

The critics of Medjugorje face the same problem as the first critics of Christianity: they confront a phenomenon that demands explanation, a phenomenon that has a very real impact on vast numbers of people. Those who experience a phenomenon of this nature develop an explanatory framework that makes sense of their experience. The experiencing and the understanding of the experience in terms of an explanatory framework are two distinct processes. Although distinct, the two processes are as closely related to each other as a caterpillar is to the butterfly it becomes.

Critics of claims of this kind either deny the phenomenon altogether or try to explain the phenomenon in entirely different terms, in explanatory frameworks that are foreign to those who experience the phenomenon. To be sure, critical analysis in itself can be extremely positive. Not all claims to experiencing a phenomenon can be taken seriously without further ado. In some cases, critical study of the claims can help in better understanding the phenomenon and its implications. In other cases, serious, thorough and painstaking investigation of a given claim may show that the claim was not warranted or credible. These constructive applications of critical analysis presuppose some degree of objectivity. When an analysis tends to ignore or distort facts and to be driven by emotional or ideological considerations, then it becomes destructive and illegitimate. Instead of seeking truth, such an inquiry seeks to suppress truth.

The classic tack taken by destructive criticism is to formulate some variety of conspiracy theory that purports to explain a phenomenon in a new light, a light which discredits the commonly accepted understanding of the phenomenon. Conspiracy theories usually involve the operation of obscure factors and principles that are hidden from the uninitiated. A framework is built around these hidden variables to "explain" a given phenomenon. All the facts relating to the phenomenon are forced into the framework proposed by the new theory. Facts which don't fit into this framework are either ignored or explained away. The history of science, of course, is littered with corpses of theories which were based on distorted or incomplete evidence. The history of conspiracy theories, however, is not quite as clean and clear - cut. The hidden variables in these theories are so well hidden that it is all but impossible to prove or disprove their existence.

Although their creators would like to believe otherwise, conspiracy theories with their vacuum cleaner view of events and individuals are neither invulnerable nor irresistible. The Achilles' heel of the conspiracy theorist is the awkward fact. If there is an accretion of awkward facts, then these must be firmly and continuously brought to the forefront of discussion. In the face of such data, the implausibility of the theory becomes self- evident. The framework of hidden variables soon begins to look like a dike of desperate inventions designed to hold back the flood of facts.

The question before us is whether or not the flood of facts unleashed by the Medjugorje phenomenon has an inner dynamic that cannot be "captured" by the theories of critics and skeptics. To answer this question we must examine the skeptical theories themselves and pay particular attention to the hidden variables to which they are anchored.

One thing we know. There is one variable in most of the theories of the critics and skeptics that is not hidden (or at least cannot easily be hidden). The variable in question is a person, His Excellency Pavao Zanic, the retired Bishop of Mostar.

Curiously enough the strongest critiques of Medjugorje have emanated from conservative Catholic circles. Almost invariably, these critiques and the theories that seek to sustain them derive from or are inspired by the Bishop of Mostar. For the most part, the "facts" and "inferences" that energize the various critiques are supplied by Bishop Zanic. To that extent, the critiques are parasitic: they would hardly get off the ground on their own steam. In fact the credibility of the critiques as they are presented and perceived stems mainly from their link with Bishop Zanic. On the other hand, the well known critiques of the Medjugorje apparitions have refined and "cosmeticized" the Bishop's arguments so as to make them more plausible and attractive than they were in their original form. Some would even say that the critics have brought these arguments back to life. As such these critiques merit the careful attention we will give them in these pages.

Bishop Zanic's feelings about the Medjugorje phenomenon are almost as famous as the apparitions themselves. What may not be as commonly known is the historical context of the conflict between the secular clergy of the region, represented pre-eminently by the Bishop, and the Franciscans. Tragically, the apparitions and the visionaries were dragged into the middle of this unfortunate and entirely unrelated conflict. The historical background must be briefly outlined. The Franciscans have been serving the Catholics in Bosnia and Hercegovina (the province in which Medjugorje is located) since the time of the

Crusades in the thirteenth century. Their proudest moments came when the Catholics came under the reign of the Ottoman Turks in the fifteenth century. In the religious persecution that followed, the secular clergy fled the country and the Franciscans alone remained to serve the faithful. Many of them became martyrs who were slain in the most savage fashion — they were disemboweled, skinned alive and the like. Their sufferings gave rise to the popular (though inaccurate) saying of the region: "The only real priest is a Franciscan." Things did not improve when Bosnia-Hercegovina came under the Austro-Hungarian Empire in the nineteenth century. In some respects, they got worse. The Austrians sought to depose the Franciscans from the region and to bring in secular clergy who were ready to do their bidding. They had limited success in this respect and the Franciscans had to give up many of their parishes to the secular clergy. In 1942, for the first time a secular priest was appointed bishop of Mostar, a traditional stronghold of the Franciscans. From that time, the intrigues intensified and the conflicts became more bitter — and it must be said that there were dark spots on both sides. Bishop Zanic, who was the auxiliary bishop until then, became full Bishop of Mostar in 1980. Bishop Zanic turned out to be a master strategist and managed to outmaneuver the Franciscans on almost every front. When the apparitions began in 1981, the Bishop's primary concern was its relevance for the conflict between the Franciscans and the secular clergy which he called "the Hercegovina affair." The visionaries, understandably, tried to stay away from the whole matter. But this proved to be impossible.

Bishop Zanic's dramatic emergence as the chief critic of the apparition is especially ironic in view of the fact that he was the principal champion of its authenticity at the outset. Even before the parish priests in Medjugorje accepted it as genuine, the Bishop publicly committed himself to the authenticity of the apparition. In a sermon July 25, 1981, Bishop Zanic said, "Six simple children like these would have told all in half an hour if anybody had been manipulating them. I assure you that none of the priests has done any such thing. The accusation is insulting and must be firmly rejected. Furthermore, I am convinced the children are not lying."

In the August 16, 1981 edition of *Glas Koncila* (The Voice of the Council), a Croatian Catholic paper, Bishop Zanic made his first official statement on the apparitions: "The public awaits a statement from us about the events at Medjugorje. ...What can we say about what is happening at Bijakovici? One thing is certain: the children are not being urged by anyone, least of all by the Church, to make untruthful statements."[14]

Unhappily, this idyllic state of affairs was not to last. The ghosts of troubled history returned to haunt the setting of this supernatural drama. From being a witness for the defense, Bishop Zanic became Prosecutor while laying claims to being Judge and Jury. From the view that "It's certain, the boys and girls are not lying," the Bishop moved to the position that "I am entirely, one hundred percent, sure that all these stories of apparitions are a pure lie, a swindle, a falsehood" and "I will destroy Medjugorje". It may well be asked: what caused this radical reversal, this sudden and total change in the Bishop's attitude to the visionaries and the apparition? Three explanations have been advanced by observers. Fellow critics hold, of course, that subsequent events and analysis forced the Bishop to reach the conclusion that the apparition was a fraud. The plausibility of this explanation depends for the most part on the cogency of the Bishop's critical arguments — particularly in view of the fact that no significantly new fact came to light after the Bishop delivered his initial seal of approval on the apparitions. Other observers, some of them neutral and some in favor of the apparitions, attribute the Bishop's change of heart to the visionaries' failure to back him up in his ongoing confrontation with the Franciscans. A third, more disturbing, explanation has been advanced by some who have been close to the events. According to Fr. Ldjudevit Rupcic, a Professor of New Testament at the Franciscan School of Theology in Sarajevo who served on the Theological Commission of the Yugoslav Bishops' Conference from 1969 to 1980, Bishop Zanic was intimidated into a reversal of his initial stance by the Communist authorities of the region.

Fr. Rupcic is no stranger to the coercive methods of the erstwhile Communist regime in Yugoslavia having spent five years (in 1948 and from 1952 to 1956) in prison for "hostile propaganda" against the state. It is his contention in his *The Truth About Medjugorje* that Bishop Zanic evolved from staunch defender to determined foe of the apparitions under pressure from a ruthless regime [a regime, incidentally, that subsequently attempted to crush Catholic Croatia and then Bosnia Hercegovina]:

Immediately after the apparitions, "one can rightly say that the bishop was the leader of those who were accepting Medjugorje." His attitude encouraged those who, for whatever reasons, did not, as yet, take a positive attitude towards the apparitions.

Shortly after this, however [summer of 1981], the bishop began to change his mind about the events, although there was no important

---

[14] It was only with difficulty that Fr. Jozo Zovko, O.F.M., was able to convince Bishop Zanic not to declare the apparitions authentic at their very beginning. On the occasion of the 11th anniversary, June 25, 1992, Fr. Jozo shared during his homily in the parish church in Medjugorje, *"Brothers and sisters: I was closed to Medjugorje in the beginning because I was afraid that the communists were manipulating the children. But the children persevered and were not angry with me. Many priests came here to convince me. Bishop Zanic came five times to Medjugorje before I was taken to prison [August 17, 1981]. Once the bishop was so angry with me. "What do you want?" he asked me. "I believe in this more than in Lourdes."*

change in Medjugorje itself to account for it. The explanation for the bishop's change of attitude is to be found outside Medjugorje.

The Communist and (officially) atheist state management in Yugoslavia soon began to take note of the fact that the Bishop of Mostar's positive stance toward the apparitions — expressed clearly in his oral and written statements, as well as in his public appearances — stood in contrast to the official state attitude toward the events, namely, that the apparitions were counter-revolutionary. This had been publicly announced on July 4, 1981 in Sutjeska by the then-President of the Communist Republic of Bosnia-Herzegovina, Branko Mikulic. Officials of the State Security Police, through the Executive Committee, summoned Zanic to Sarajevo and there threatened to imprison him unless he stopped speaking in favor of the apparitions. Their threats worked impressively on the bishop, who returned to Mostar another man. It is difficult to say, at this juncture, just how much the bishop really had to fear. People react differently to situations like these.

During this same period, Fr. Jozo Zovko was also summoned to see the U.D.B.A. [State Security]. They threatened Fr. Jozo with imprisonment if he didn't change his (favorable) stance towards the Medjugorje apparitions. No doubt, the threats leveled at the bishop and at Fr. Jozo were similar, since they were both "guilty" of the same "crime." But Fr. Jozo continued to act according to his convictions while, at the same time, trying not to provoke the U.D.B.A. into carrying out its threats. Fr. Jozo, as pastor of the parish, wished to continue to influence the course of events in Medjugorje — events he was now convinced were coming from God through the Gospa.

(Shortly before this, Fr. Jozo's original dilemma about the apparitions had been dramatically resolved. While reciting the rosary with the people in the church, the Gospa appeared to him in a vision. After that, he applied himself to the service of the apparitions with his whole heart.)

Faced with the threat of imprisonment, Fr. Jozo continued to support Medjugorje, knowing full well the risks to which he exposed himself in doing so. The bishop, however, in the same situation, and confronted with the same threat, reacted differently. Unfortunately, for some men, humiliation is to be preferred to suffering.

Immediately after his face-to-face meeting with the U.D.B.A., the bishop called Fr. Jozo and related to him how he had been interrogated by the Executive Committee in Sarajevo and how, on his arrival back in Mostar, 12 of his priests had met him and upbraided him for his positive stand on Medjugorje." At that time, the bishop did not indicate that he no longer believed in the apparitions, even less that he had found some evidence against them. On August 17, 1981, Fr. Jozo was arrested and, in the end, sentenced to three and a half years of hard labor because of his stand on Medjugorje. Imprisoned with him were Fr. Ferdo Vlasic and, later on, Fr. Jozo Krizic.

The situation grew more and more tense. In those days it was very dangerous to utter even a word in favor of Medjugorje. For example, when a hardly noticeable comment appeared in "Nasa Ognjista," which is published in Duvno, the Secretary of the Religious commission of the Republic, Filip Simic, angrily attacked the editorial staff of the paper, saying that both state and religious authorities (here having in mind Bishop Zanic and the Franciscan "provincial" Pejic) had agreed that nothing should be written about Medjugorje. With that, "Nasa Ognjista" was suppressed.

Immediately after he was released from prison (February 18 1983), Fr. Jozo paid a visit to the bishop. In the conversation, among other things, they touched on Medjugorje. The bishop tried on this occasion to justify his actions, stating that, under the circumstances, it was not "possible" for him to have acted differently than he did, threatened as he was by the U.D.B.A. with imprisonment. Besides this, he mentioned once again the pressure brought to bear on him from diocesan priests and from some Franciscans not to intervene on Medjugorje's behalf. He said that priests had written, reproaching him for his support of the apparitions. These [diocesan] priests were against Medjugorje and feared that the Franciscans would gain prestige if the apparitions were approved. He also referred to a small circle of Franciscans around Pejic which, through Nikola Radic, the temporary delegate general of the Franciscan Province of Herzegovina, had asked the U.D.B.A.for a favor and, therefore, were in no mood to offend it for the sake of Medjugorje.

In such a situation, the bishop had 'had' to think of his own interests, he told Fr. Jozo. 'How could I have acted differently?' the bishop asked. 'I could not have gone to prison for Medjugorje,' he said, thinking of the U.D.B.A. threat, 'nor did I wish to go from being bishop to assistant pastor of a village,' referring to pressure from his diocesan priests. He feared the U.D.B.A. because they could imprison him, and his priests because he was a newcomer in the diocese and the clergy had threatened him with some sort of boycott [if he had continued to support Medjugorje].

Because of his fears, and because he saw the possibility of being attacked on all sides, he realized he faced the choice of either abdicating [his authority] or completely rejecting Medjugorje.

So, in the case of Medjugorje, he decided to adopt a strategy of complete silence, so that, for some time, he said nothing at all publicly. But this tactic brought him neither peace nor security; for, suddenly, Medjugorje began flourishing. Both the friends and adversaries of Medjugorje expected the bishop to issue a clear statement. His silence satisfied no one.

And because he was not ready to contradict his previous statements, he had to discover some means by which he could keep the powers at bay and still present himself in public as an honest person. (The imprisonment of Fr. Jozo had convinced him that the threat coming from the U.D.B.A. was serious.)

Therefore he began to invent 'arguments' against Medjugorje from which one could 'see' that cowardice had not caused him to change his attitude, but his new-found 'reasons'. In order to assuage the guilt of his cowardice — which tormented him greatly, knowing as he did, that there were witnesses to it — he looked for a cure in 'energetic' words and 'courageous' deeds. This, of course, accomplished nothing, for his life was not in danger, but they did please his blackmailers — those who had forced him to turn against Medjugorje in the first place.

Such actions not only brought the bishop the assurance that he would not find himself in prison or his leadership rejected, but gave him a chance to demonstrate how "courageous "and 'resolute' he was toward those who were incapable of doing anything against him. He contrived the story that he had known, from the very beginning, that the children were lying. And, as time went on, his contradictions bothered him less and less. When Fr. Jozo reminded him of these things when he appeared before the "commission," the bishop declared: 'It is not important what I believed [then], but what I do not believe [now]!'

In the beginning of the apparitions, Zanic declared, 'the children are not lying,' and 'the children are speaking exactly what they feel in their hearts' (July 25,1981). Those statements were based on the many hours of interviews the bishop had with the visionaries. "If there were just one child, one could say: 'this kid is so hard-headed that not even the police can make him speak.' But six innocent simple children like these would have told all in half an hour if anybody had been manipulating them."

Notwithstanding all this, the bishop started, first, to suppress facts, then invent them, and, finally, to transform them, never forgetting to attach his monstrous explanations to them, so that out of all this, anyone could "see" that the Medjugorje events were not true.

As for the bishop's defense of the Franciscans, Milan Vukovic, Fr. Jozo's attorney, wrote to Zanic on April 23, 1990 about his [Zanic's] intervention on behalf of the Franciscans with the federal president of the SFRJ dated November 1,1981: 'It is needless to speak about your intervention, for you intervened in order to prevent newspapers from writing in such a [negative] tone [about the Church.] But you forgot to intervene for Fr. Jozo who was already at that time in prison (since August 17,1981). You must admit that using such an intervention as proof of your case with regard to Fr. Jozo is misguided.'

'The same is true about your intervention [with the Commissioner of Religious Affairs], Mohammad Besic, for you intervened on March 9, 1982. Not only this, but your intervention to Mr. Besic has this sentence: 'I beg you to read the enclosed materials so that you can appraise whether this important paragraph of the law has been re-spected, and whether the sentence of the district court has been lawful or not. If you appraise that the sentence has been lawful and that the pronounced sentences correspond to the gravity of the crime, then please do not undertake anything.'

'Consequently,' continues Vukovic, 'you wrote to me how you interceded for Fr. Jozo. But you did not include in your intervention this man [Fr. Jozo] who was imprisoned precisely as a result of the words of welcome he addressed to you [in Medjugorje]. Forgive me, but your intervention was one intended for the public.' The attorney, disgusted, goes further: 'If you, to whom Fr. Jozo's words were di-rected, still prefer the police prosecution's tales, then everything is clear. How grotesque it is when the police prosecutor's case and the plot against Fr. Jozo, based on the meaning of Fr. Jozo's words in his greeting to you, succeeded because you would not appear as a witness on his behalf in the court to clarify what Fr. Jozo actually said to you.' (16)

If Fr. Rupcic's account of the sequence of events is true (and it must be admitted that his evidence is impressive)[15] then the rationale for the Bishop's change of heart can be traced to the power of the Marxist-Leninist state. Repression and intimidation of the religious leadership is a familiar feature of totalitarian rule. Few religious leaders have consistently and forcefully resisted this kind of treatment. Even those of us who all too easily assume that we would

---

[15] After sending Fr. Rupcic's book Fidelity contributor requesting a review for the magazine Jones received the reply that in the reviewer's opinion "it was a masterful piece and raised some legitimate questions that could be true." Needless to say he choose someone else to write the review.

go to the Gulag or to the guillotine in defense of our Faith must not dare to pass judgment on those who crack under pressure. Whether Bishop Zanic's reversal on the apparitions was motivated by fear of the authorities is something that is known only to Bishop Zanic and to God, and we should leave the matter there. Our only obligation is to examine the evidence adduced by the Bishop in defense of his changed position. We must, however, deplore the undertone of acrimony that is a recurrent feature in Fr. Rupcic's work.

Another explanation for the Bishop's transformation into a critic is the seemingly inevitable intersection of the apparition and "the Hercegovina case" and the fact that the pronouncements of the Blessed Virgin on the matter did not go in the direction desired by the Bishop. On several occasions he asked the visionaries to find out what the Blessed Virgin had to say about the conflict between the Franciscans and the secular clergy. The visionaries were reluctant to bring this issue before their Visitor but even more reluctant to ignore the Bishop's request. As BBC correspondent Mary Craig puts it in *Spark from Heaven*, "The Madonna was not allowed to remain outside the dispute. Even on his first visit to Medjugorje, the bishop had asked if she had commented on the Hercegovina problem. The children, more or less ignorant of the facts, said she had promised that with prayer and patience it would soon be sorted out. All succeeding requests for information met with the same vague reply." (17)

These difficulties were compounded by a public confrontation between Bishop Zanic and two Franciscans, Fr. Ivica Vego and Fr. Ivan Prusina. The two friars had vigorously resisted Bishop Zanic's attempts to gain control of his diocese and in retaliation he suspended them from the priesthood and had them expelled from their order. Questions remain as to whether all of this was done in accordance with canon law but passion seemed to have taken precedence over procedure in the whole affair. The two friars sought the Blessed Virgin's advice through the visionaries. One of them, Vicka, empathized strongly and vocally with them and their plight. Unfortunately, the entire episode became inextricably involved with the apparition in the Bishop's mind and appear to have led to his disenchantment with the visionaries.

We quote two accounts of the events, one from Mary Craig and the other from Fr. Rene Laurentin:

> Vicka, Marija and Jakov came to see the bishop in Mostar. Without preamble, Vicka, never noted for her tact, passed on the Lady's criticism that he had been over-hasty in suspending the two friars. She did not enlarge on the theme, since Father Vlasic had already advised her to be careful how she answered questions. So, after delivering herself of her brief message, Vicka became evasive. 'I hear the Madonna gave you a message for those two priests,' pressed the bishop. 'Which two priests?' asked Vicka wide-eyed. ....Vicka returned on 3rd

April saying that the Lady had scolded her for telling the bishop less than the whole truth. 'She told us all about these friars... and says they are completely innocent. She said it three times.' Zanic was furious. 'Go away,' he shouted at Vicka, reportedly adding, 'And when your Lady finally reveals her true colours and curses God, be sure and let me know.' (18)

Fr. Laurentin attributes the Bishop's change to this incident in particular: "A Roman Cardinal told me of the enthusiasm of Bishop Zanic for Medjugorje during the summer of 1981. In August and September of that same year, he made public statements on two occasions: in the press and to the President of the Republic. What then could have turned him against the apparitions and when? It is a long story, the details of which I spell out elsewhere. In short, his quarrel with the Franciscans, which has nothing to do with Medjugorje, interfered with the apparitions which were taking place in the Franciscan parish. This interference was fictitious and it has done incredible damage, on which I shall not dwell. ...Devastated by the sanctions imposed on them and believing to be within their right, they [the two friars] went to pray in Medjugorje and asked the opinion of Our Lady. It was certainly a mistake to question her on this emotion-charged affair, since Jesus Himself refused to sit in judgment on personal family disputes (Luke 12:14). The answers of the seers, who were filled with compassion for the two Friars, included some differences in respect to the bishop: deference on the part of Marija, severity on the part of Vicka (who was still young and impetuous, quick to flare up for justice, as a righter of wrongs). She now admits that she went too far, out of compassion for the two Franciscans. ...In short, the opposition of Bishop Zanic stems simply from an emotion-charged and unfortunate local quarrel, which has interfered with the pure phenomenon of the apparitions." (19).

He concludes thus. "The principal argument of Bishop Zanic is reduced to the following: The apparition criticized the bishop. Therefore, it is not the Virgin. ...It was certainly an error to question the apparition about this local quarrel. 'The Virgin is not an employee standing at the gate of Heaven,' as Bishop Zanic so rightly says, and the answers transmitted by certain seers are colored by the emotion aroused by their pity for the two young Franciscans who are being punished. Vicka has admitted this deforming factor. At any rate, she kept these 'messages', with the most complete discretion and it is the bishop himself who published them all over as proof that statements so contrary to the bishop could not come from the Virgin." (20).

For Bishop Zanic, the Blessed Virgin's apparent reprimands were not only unacceptable but clear evidence of the fraudulence of the apparitions. Theologically, the idea that the Blessed Virgin is constrained from reviewing the actions of bishops is simply not sound.[16] Those who have followed the pronouncements of Sister Lucia of Fatima will note that these often concern actions popes and bishops have failed to take or should take and the like. Fr. Laurentin notes that "Dialogue between the visionary Lucia and the last six Popes has been difficult. Ever since the 1930s she has requested them to consecrate Russia to the Immaculate Heart of Mary. Pius XI and John XXIII did not accede to this request. Pius XII, Paul VI and John Paul II have renewed the act of consecration on eight different occasions, each time adding further precisions at the request of Lucia. But Russia remains unconverted and Lucia feels that the often repeated act of consecration has not been done 'as the Virgin wished it.' No doubt, we are only at the beginning of the discussions on these matters. A certain amount of tension remains between Lucia (the details of whose requests have varied from time to time) and the Pope who is not infallible in this matter. Outspoken commentators haven't helped the matter."[17] Popes are not infallible when it comes to decisions and actions of this kind, which do not involve dogma, and neither are the bishops.

Another potential explanation for the change in the Bishop's perspective on the apparitions and the visionaries is the possibility that he came to his negative conclusion purely on the basis of the evidence. As we have said, the plausibility of this explanation varies in direct proportion to the cogency of his arguments. Such an emphasis on sound arguments is not an unreasonable one in this context as can be illustrated through an example. Imagine a scenario in which a man strongly affirms his belief in the existence of God and presents powerful arguments supporting his position. Suppose now that on a subsequent date he affirms his disbelief in the existence of God with equal vigor and attempts to lay

---

[16] Later on in this section we will see that Archbishop Franic willing accepted the reprimands he reportedly received from Our Lady through the visionaries in Medjugorje.

[17] The evidence, as we saw earlier, has since come in. Bishop Hnilica testified at the 1992 National Conference on Medjugorje that Sr. Lucia, the sole surviving visionary of Fatima, had told him that the Consecration has now been accomplished *as the Blessed Mother requested!* Bishop Hnilica shared that this is the same opinion of Pope John Paul II. It is now a matter of public record that Sr. Lucia dos Santos has on numerous occasions stated that the 1984 collegial Act of Consecration by the Holy Father has been accepted. She has said, "It has been accomplished! And God will keep His promise!" testifies also Bishop Amaral of Fatima, Sr. Maria da Cruz, the prioress of her convent in Coimbra, and numerous others, including members of her family. "After the consecration of the world made by the Holy Father in 1984 at her request, she's been saying that she is ready to go to heaven, to be called by God," testifies her close friend and regular visitor, Maria do Fetal, her cousin, adding, "What is going on in Russia now gives her much joy. But the conversion is not complete. The destruction took a long time to happen, and it will take a long time to build things back up," (Denis Nolan, "Fatima — Medjugorje: In The End My Immaculate Heart WIll Triumph", *Our Lady, Queen of Peace,* Pittsburgh Center for Peace, second edition, Winter, 1993).

out arguments supporting his disbelief. Surely it is legitimate for an onlooker to ask both for arguments defending the change of position and for arguments that defend the changed position (there will obviously be a lot of overlap here). When it is known that certain irrelevant external factors were present which could plausibly have motivated the change — for instance, the party in question may be involved in a moral situation that could not be reconciled with adherence to the will of God or he may have suffered a bereavement that resulted in bitterness towards God — it would not be unreasonable to subject the new arguments to rigorous scrutiny and to insist that the burden of proof is with the acrobatic atheist. On analogous grounds, we could hardly be accused of being too picky or pedantic if we sought not just sound arguments from the Bishop for his new position but also sound arguments in support of the sudden and total change in his assessment of the visionaries.

Bishop Zanic's arguments against the apparition are presented in three pronouncements addressed to the general public: the first is "The Present Position (Non-official) of the Bishop's Curia of Mostar With Regard to the Events of Medjugorje" published on October 30, 1984; the second is the text of the Bishop's sermon at the Medjugorje parish Confirmation ceremonies of July 25, 1987; the third is his pamphlet "Medjugorje" released in March, 1990 (at the end of which he asked everyone to read Jones' *Medjugorje: The Untold Story.*)

In a nutshell, the Bishop's chief arguments against the authenticity of the apparitions are the following:

- The misdeeds of the two friars who defied the bishop and who were allegedly encouraged in their wrongdoing by the lady appearing to the visionaries.
- The incident of Vicka's diary which the bishop claims is the "key to the understanding of Medjugorje."
- The fraudulence of claims of healing attributed to the influence of the apparitions.
- Alleged predictions by some of the visionaries that the apparitions would end shortly after they began with a "great sign" scheduled to take place subsequently.
- Claims that Fr. Laurentin is "editing out" inconvenient segments of the messages transmitted by the visionaries.
- Fr. Tomislav Vlasic's alleged role in framing the messages with the visionaries playing the role of "domesticated robots."
- The visionaries' alleged attempts to influence the Bishop through intimidation.

These charges and some other minor charges levelled by the Bishop are addressed in detail in Appendix 1. At this point it would be well to note that the Bishop has not only changed his initial position on the authenticity of the apparition but has also kept changing his assessment of what exactly is happening in Medjugorje. According to Fr. Rupcic, "He has often modified these interpretations himself, whenever he felt the need, because hardly anyone was prepared to accept them. And they were, in fact, unacceptable because they were unreasonable and self-contradictory. The Bishop first claimed that no one had influenced the boys and girls in connection with the visions and messages, later he said that the Friars and especially Fr. Vlasic were behind it all, then he said Satan was responsible and finally, that the whole thing was hallucination. When interpreting the facts, the Bishop has been very emphatic on each separate occasion." (22).

Two preliminary considerations regarding these charges are relevant in this context. The charges that the visionaries are suffering from hallucination or are being manipulated by the priests face a gigantic obstacle that has never been addressed or acknowledged by the critics (some of whom do not even seem aware of it). The regular apparitions ceased for two of the visionaries, Ivanka and Mirjana several years ago after they had both received all ten secrets. For Mirjana the apparitions ceased on Christmas day 1982, for Ivanka they ceased on May 6, 1985. The other visionaries continue to receive the regular apparitions which will cease when each receives all ten of the secrets. Now, this is our question: all the half-hearted theories of manipulation and hallucination fail to address the fact that the purported hallucination or manipulation scenarios ceased for two of the children several years ago but continue to apply to the other four. Have two of the six stopped hallucinating or being manipulated or both as the case may be? If so, the situation is more complex than the current theories admit. What demands an explanation is why the alleged hallucination takes place in such a selective fashion and why the manipulation is not uniform. It is not enough to simplistically say that they are all victims of hallucination or manipulation. For two of the six, at least, this is not apparently the case any more. We would like the critics first to take note of this anomaly and would then like to invite them to give an "explanation" for it that is not as desperate as most of the current "explanations" in circulation.

The second consideration is this. Of all the various charges thrown at Medjugorje, the one that is most incomprehensible is the charge that the apparitions have gone on for too long (a charge which, by the way, ignores the fact that the regular apparitions have ceased for two of the visionaries). Who in his or her right mind would dare to think that the sustained desecration and blasphemy of the modern age does not, at the very least, demand an equally intensive movement of consecration and reparation? After shutting God out of our minds and lives for half a century, do we expect to return to Reality via a swift sequence of sound-bites and prime time spots? The longevity of the apparitions is also a good argument against the fabrication hypothesis. If the whole thing was a fabrication, it would certainly be more prudent and convenient to keep it short because the risk of the fraud being detected grows greater the longer the apparitions continue to take place. A glimpse of the obvious, it would seem, but it is a glimpse the critics refuse to take.

Bishop Zanic's specific critiques of Medjugorje will be addressed in Appendix 1. For now, we end our consideration of his position with a letter sent to Bishop Zanic by the great theologian Cardinal-designate Hans Urs von Balthasar:

Your Excellency,

What a sad document you sent across the world! I was profoundly troubled by seeing the episcopal office degraded this way. Instead of being patient, as it was recommended to you from the high place, you thunder and throw the arrows of Jupiter disparaging the renowned and innocent persons, worthy of your respect and your protection. You come out again with the same accusations which were refuted hundreds of times.

Naturally, I was also extremely troubled with the Episcopal Conference's statement (the exact terms of which I could not read, and which I cannot understand except in the context of the political situation of your country. I hope all the members signed it in good conscience).

I hope that you sincerely pray to the Lord and His Mother to lead this sad drama so important toward the fruitful end for the community of the Church. Join all those who so fervently and devoutly pray in Medjugorje.

Yours in Our Lord,
Hans Urs von Balthasar

From these considerations, we will turn to an overview of some of the other critical positions taken against Medjugorje. Other than His Excellency Bishop Zanic himself, the three main critics of Medjugorje are E. Michael Jones (Editor of *Fidelity Magazine*), Abbe Georges de Nantes, editor of the publication *French Catholic Counter-Reformation,* in which Brother Michael of the Holy Trinity penned a long-running tirade against Medjugorje, and Fr. Ivo Sivric, author of *The Hidden Face of Medjugorje.* All three receive their principal ammunition from Bishop Zanic. At this juncture, one point must be clarified on the import of the former Bishop of Mostar's views on Medjugorje. In an unprecedented move, Rome removed the authority and responsibility for conducting the investigation from Bishop Zanic and transferred it to the Yugoslavian Bishops' Conference. The unofficial text of the statement from the Conference clearly indicates a more or less neutral stance on Medjugorje. Bishop Zanic's current pronouncements on Medjugorje have no specific authority; he is just one member of the Conference.

Michael Jones, the chief antagonist of Medjugorje in America. is author of *Medjugorje: The Untold Story*, a book that attempts to discredit the Medjugorje phenomenon using ridicule and slander rather than polemic. On February, 12 1989 Jones admitted in a speech for Keep the Faith, *The Dangers of Private Revelation*, that he saw himself as the hunter and Medjugorje as a prey that needed to be relentlessly tracked down and dispatched at all costs.

> About a year ago [i.e., three months before his trip to Medjugorje] ...I knew then that Medjugorje was the rhinoceros, and I was the hunter, and I had a gun, and I had one bullet in the gun, and the rhinoceros was heading towards me, and I just better aim right when I'm dealing with this thing because I wouldn't have a second chance.

In *Medjugorje Goes Up in Smoke*, his sequel to *The Untold Story*, Jones uses Joseph Bagiackas as his chief source and quotes him attacking Medjugorje and many people associated with Medjugorje throughout the last seven pages of that thirteen page *Fidelity* article. I received a letter from Mr. Bagiackas (dated March 12, 1991) in which he said "Everything I was quoted as saying about Medjugorje in Mike Jones' article on Medjugorje is totally without foundation and truth.... I, like many other Catholics, support what God is doing in Medjugorje."

In his *Fatima Family Messenger* July-September 1992 issue, Fr. Fox said, "For at least the past two years I stopped taking seriously the journalism produced by the *Fidelity* magazine, which too often has proven itself irresponsible and uncharitable. The magazine too often fosters bitterness which seems to stem from anger and is of no service to the Church. It has become a publication that is a gossip-scandal publication and a witch-hunter. *Fidelity* is not a Church publication. It sets itself up in imprudent positions anticipating judgements of the Holy See. It publishes without facts and too often with misinformation. It is what I call yellow journalism....The uncharitableness in false accusations is most serious."

But before we study Jones' arguments, we will first analyze Fr. Ivo Sivric's critique from which Jones draws much of his thinking. Apart from the Bishop, Fr. Sivric's main sources are his relatives in Medjugorje — who opposed the apparition from the beginning for reasons to be explained below — and the transcripts of purported conversations among the visionaries and the priests. Fr. Sivric's relatives are questionable. One of them, his nephew, had joined the Communist Party in the Seventies and had reached the top tier of the Party in his country. When the apparitions began, his superiors in the Party sent him to Medjugorje to put an end to the whole matter. With this mission in mind, he tried to have St. James Church closed to the public and to have Fr. Zovko transferred from Medjugorje. Fr. Sivric's other source is a cousin of his who was one of the social workers involved in an infamous incident that took place in the early days of the apparitions. As the crowds began to gather every evening at Apparition Hill for the daily apparition, the Government decided to stop the whole thing by spiriting away the visionaries. It sought to do this by having two social workers take the visionaries on a tour of nearby towns. As the hour of the apparition drew near, the social workers refused to take the visionaries back to the village. The visionaries forced them to stop the running car by threatening to jump out and then witnessed the apparition on the roadside.

Needless to say, the villagers did not look too fondly on Fr. Sivric's relatives once their misdeeds became known. We have good reason, therefore, to be suspicious of their reliability as disinterested sources. Moreover, Fr. Sivric's reliance on them raises questions about his objectivity. As Fr. Rupcic writes, "Inasmuch as he [Fr. Sivric] is sentimentally attached to his relatives, he too felt himself a target in the loss of community esteem. For that reason, even prior to his undertaking an investigation of Medjugorje, he held a clearly negative view of the event of Medjugorje. By proving the events to be non-authentic, he, in fact, hopes to demonstrate the correctness of the stance and deeds of his relatives who, supposedly, approached the events in a 'diplomatic' and 'sober' manner (p.364), in contrast to the vast majority of the parishioners and the millions of pilgrims to Medjugorje." (24)

It is odd that Sivric never took advantage of the parish records that were available to him, and that he had been invited to review. The third source of his arguments — the transcripts of alleged conversations among the visionaries — is extremely significant because both Sivric and Jones use these transcripts as the foundations of their conspiracy theories. Michael Jonesstates that the main significance of the Sivric book lies "in the primary documents which can be found in the book's appendices. Now for the first time, the tapes of the interviews between the seers and the priests, primarily Father Zovko, who was pastor at the time, are available. It is as if the entire discussion up until now had been conducted without reference to the primary documents. For unlike what many believe, the so-called messages are not the central documents. The tapes are in effect the first hard evidence in the entire story. In reviewing the tapes one sees not only the crucial role that Fr. Zovko played, but also that virtually the entire trajectory of future events was set in motion by decisions he made within a week of the first apparition." (25)

The climactic chapter of Jones' investigation into Medjugorje, "What Really Happened," follows this melodramatic passage. For Jones the collection of transcripts is the key that opens the door to the mystery of Medjugorje (he uses a psychiatrist colleague to actually put the key in the keyhole). If the transcripts play such a fundamental role in Jones' and Sivric's arguments, they deserve careful attention.

Unfortunately for Jones and Sivric (and for their arguments), closer scrutiny reveals that there is an "untold story" behind the transcripts — a story which dramatically diminishes the usefulness of the transcripts as foundation stones for plausible conspiracy theories. Jones takes the authenticity of the tape recordings from which the transcripts are drawn for granted — and builds his elaborate theory on top of the transcripts. He does not seem to uestion the quality, accuracy or history of the tapes. Are the tapes from which the transcripts were made the original tapes or the end-result of recording after recording? Is there any way to determine whether they are doctored since the tapes have inexplicable gaps and spliced segments? Considering the raging controversies that have surrounded Medjugorje and the fact that almost everyone in authority was ranged against the visionaries, what assurance do we have that the tapes used by Fr. Sivric bear any resemblance to the original tapes which are held by the "authorities"? For an investigative journalist, Jones is surprisingly unconcerned with such critical questions. In his quotes from the transcripts, we notice that he frequently quotes Mica Ivankovic (whom he fails to identify as Fr. Sivric's social worker cousin). Jones pointedly quotes a Mica Ivankovic statement that is intended to throw a cloud over the visionaries: "At one point, Mica Ivankovic tells Father Zovko that a girl asked her, "Is it possible that Gospa would appear to this 'pankerica'?" She then asks Zovko if he knows what the word "pankerica" means. "No, I don't," Zovko replies. "Then I'll explain it to you," Mica says laughing. "It's a girl who is habitually immoral. The people can't identify with them [the seers] because they dress in a fashion that is very liberal. (26)

Before we look at the theories built around these "primary documents," we should first consider their reliability as source material. As usual, Fr. Rupcic has left no stone unturned to get to the bottom of things: "The true sources still today are the living people, the partakers of those events: in the first place, the Seers, their families, and the Pastors and Assistants. The author, nonetheless, relies on a few taped conversations involving some of the direct witnesses. It is important to note here that not all, including the most relevant facts and situations associated with the events at Medjugorje are recorded on tape. Beyond that, the author selects the tape recordings in harmony with the goal he has set for himself. Aside from that, the tape recordings used by Sivric are not the original tapes. The original tapes were entirely clear and complete. The police confiscated those tapes at the time they arrested the pastor, Fr. Jozo Zovko. The Bishop sought to retrieve the tapes so as to make use of them for his Investigative Commission, but was unable to get them. The tapes made use of by Sivric are copies of copies made by individuals for their private use. When the tapes were being copied, often individual parts of the conversations were deleted; thus, the spliced conversations are spread over a period of days and dates. Evidence of this is seen in the transcription of the tapes used by the author in his book. Sivric often notes that the tape has been cut, and notes that the tape recordings are undecipherable in at least 148 instances. Since all the participants in these taped conversations are still living, it boggles the mind that the author does not attempt to fill in or clarify those missing parts. The participants to the conversations were all available to him at the time of his sojourn in Medjugorje. Such tapes, 'documents' for the author, are seventh-hand witness, at best (testes septimae manus), which, by established principles, cannot be recognized as having the strength of proof. Fr. Jozo Zovko, himself, having read the author's transcription of conversations held with him, said: 'This is not my composition.'" (27).

The central framework of Jones' "explanation" of Medjugorje (which is also his argument against Medjugorje) can be most accurately summarized in his own words:

The crucial question is whether the children are telling the truth. If the children are lying or if the priests associated with the apparitions are manipulating them, then any supposed renewal that could come from Medjugorje would be a house built on sand" (28).

It is not a question of adding Marian apparitions to the charismatic renewal, because the authenticity of the Marian apparitions is precisely what is at dispute here. The equation would run more along the following lines: What would happen if you added the charismatic emphasis on signs and wonders and direct contact with the beyond to the powerful techniques known as sensitivity training and applied them to impressionable young people, one of whom had just lost her mother and another who had just read a book on Lourdes, both of whom came from an area known for its Catholic and Marian piety? What effects would you produce if you mixed up powerful elements such as these and let them simmer for a while. Suppose you added in the fact that the Pope had been shot less than two months before, on the anniversary of the first apparition at Fatima? Have we reached critical mass yet? Have we reached a situation which by now explains itself without any recourse to supernatural hypotheses? Psychologist Coulson seems to think so (29).

This leads us to posit a theory about how the apparitions got started. Our hypothesis is simple: the whole thing was a joke that got out of hand. ...What Mirjana and Ivanka hadn't counted on, however, was the reaction of the crowds. Instead of just fooling around and making fun of a few of the locals, the girls suddenly had the entire countryside as well as the police in an uproar over what they were claiming to see. (30)

Although he doesn't cite him as the source, Jones appears to have borrowed this hypothesis from Sivric's book. Sivric contends that the visionaries read a book on Lourdes and this "inspired" them to play a game in which they got so caught up they could not get out of it (the question of why they would bring a restless nine year old like Jakov into such an exercise is conveniently ignored). Fr. Sivric's "Lourdes" connection is subjected to searching scrutiny in his typical "say it like it is" fashion by Fr. Rupcic:

The author explains the happenings at Medjugorje as a false imitation of the apparitions at Lourdes. He maintains that Mirjana Dragicevic read Boze Vuce's book, *Lourdes: Heavenly Apparitions and Miraculous Healings,* between the dates of June 6th and 27th, 1981, which was supposedly given to her by Zdravka Ivankovic, nee Sivric, known as Kovilja (p.169). Meanwhile the document to which the author refers only states that Mirjana read some book about Lourdes, and does not mention its name or author. With neck-breaking logic, Sivric arrives at the title of the book and the author's name (p.193, n.312). He also concludes that Kovilja gave Mirjana the book. Kovilja denies that she ever had any book about Lourdes. Accordingly Kovilja could not give Mirjana a book which she never had. One cannot conclude anything as to the date Mirjana was said to have read such a book. What is at work here, clearly, is a pieced together copy of taped conversations. One cannot conclude from anything in the tapes that all the conversations occurred on the same day. The Pastor, Fr. Jozo Zovko, maintains that he gave Mirjana a copy of Boze Vuce's book about Lourdes but only after his trip, namely, after the 27th of June, 1981, and only after Mirjana, in the course of a conversation, said she never heard of the Virgin's appearances in general, hence, at least a few days after the start of the Virgin's apparition. So too, it is obvious that people spoke to the seers about the eighteen apparitions of the Virgin only after the first apparition in Medjugorje. It is not possible, then, to establish a causal relationship between reading or hearing the apparitions at Lourdes and those in Medjugorje.

The author also falsely maintains that the seers began to have inaudible conversations with the Virgin only after the apparitions were transferred to the Church in January of 1982. Sivric maintains they did so because they read that Bernadette did so (pp.170-171) in Bozidar Nagy's book, Lourdes: *The Meeting of Heaven and Earth*, a book given to them by Grgo Kozina.

Meanwhile, according to the witness of Grgo Kozina himself, who followed the events of the apparitions and the Seers from the very start, the Seers sometimes spoke audibly and at other times inaudibly with the Virgin. They, in principle, always spoke inaudibly with the Virgin. They related the questions of those present in an audible manner. That was the case during the apparitions at Podbrdo. Kozina obtained a copy of Nagy's book only after the 14th of September, 1981, hence, some months later. All in all, nothing confirms the fact that the Seers had the book in hand. The author concludes that they did from the simple fact that the copy he himself saw, was quite worn! It never occurred to him to ask Grgo Kozina or the Seers about it, something he could easily have done. One cannot determine by listening to the tape recordings as to whether there was any inaudible dialogue with the Virgin: it must be clear to the author that inaudible conversations cannot be recorded on tape!

Accordingly, it is not true that the inaudible dialogue began only after the transfer of the apparitions to the church, in January of 1982, nor is it possible to establish a relationship between the inaudible conversations with the Virgin, and the reading of Nagy's book.

Thus, one of the cornerstones in his entire construction falls into the sea as does the entire superstructure of his work, an example of which is his seeking examples of imitation of the Lourdes apparitions by the seers in Medjugorje (p.170). (31)

Another assumption crucial to the Jones hypothesis does not fare much better than the "Lourdes connection." Part of his explanatory framework, as we have seen above, relies on the application of "the charismatic emphasis on signs and wonders and direct contact with the beyond" and "the powerful techniques of sensitivity training" to the visionaries. Jones makes much of the Charismatic prayer group that Fr. Zovko had started in the area. It is his contention that this prayer group used the sensitivity training techniques of encounter groups. "When combined," he continues, "with the normal charismatic tendency of praying for a passage or getting a word of prophecy, especially when this is done under an authority figure like a priest, they can be especially effective in producing what otherwise would be known as mystical experiences in the participants." (32).

After carefully studying the case put together by Jones and Coulson, Paul Vitz, Professor of Psychology at New York University, disputes that the combination described by Jones can produce the kind of experience reported by the visioonaries. It is simply false to associate the techniques of encounter groups with charismatic prayer groups. Jones' only ground for claiming that "Father Zovko was experimenting with an explosive mixture of charismatic prayer and sensitivity training" (33) is the testimony of a hostile witness.

This witness (the only one which Jones cites) is Marijan Pehar, a Croatian who left the Franciscan order, came to America and married. Pehar, says Jones, is accused by the Franciscans of fathering the child who, according to Jones, is actually Vlasic's child. Pehar had apparently attended two of Fr. Zovko's prayer sessions *before* Fr. Zovko came to Medjugorje and this, in Jones' view, gives him sufficient authority to describe Fr. Zovko's prayer group *in* Medjugorje. Pehar admittedly did not sit through the entirety of either prayer session he claimed to have attended. About the first, he says, "Then I left. Me and another guy, we went out and were playing ball." (34). As for the second, "Pehar walked out of a similar meeting in Zagreb for the same reason: he didn't like the manipulative atmosphere" (35). [More light is shed on Pehar's alleged comments to Jones in Dr. Bartulica's interview with Pehar quoted later in this book.]

This whole discussion on the nature of Fr. Zovko's prayer group may seem superfluous when we look at where Jones takes us from there. "When Zovko arrived at the rectory, he found the space in front of the Church full of cars and a huge crowd. Father Zovko, undoubtedly taken by surprise, began interrogating the visionaries" (39). "Judging from the first few tapes, the apparitions took Zovko by surprise" (40). Jones continues by stating "So the encounter/ charismatic prayer group theory needs some modification. There is reason to believe that the children were not in Zovko's prayer group." (41). Anyone following the argument up to this point will find the last statement startling. What we have here is not a question of the theory needing modification since the theory has clearly lost all attempt to hang together. This, of course, is not an issue of psychology but of logic.

If the children were not a part of Fr. Zovko's prayer group before the apparition — and there is overwhelming evidence that they were not and no evidence that they were — then Jones' "what if" scenario combining "the charismatic emphasis on signs and wonders and direct contact with the beyond to the powerful techniques known as sensitivity training" is simply irrelevant. At best, Jones can use this hypothesis to attempt to explain the effect of the apparitions "on the general population of the parish. Having been primed by him [Fr. Zovko] to expect signs and wonders, the village exploded with fervor when they appeared." (42). This bizarre scenario, however, still does not account for the claims of the visionaries concerning the apparitions.

With regard to Jones' hypothesis that it all began as a joke, why, we wonder again, was a restless nine year-old brought into the joke and how could he continue to keep a straight face on the matter for the next ten years? And would Fr. Zovko spend two years in jail defending what he knew (as Jones claims he did) was a joke? In a work of 140 pages, Jones spends 30 pages on personal attacks that have no bearing on the authenticity of the apparition. Another 20 pages is spent slandering Fr. Tomislav Vlasic. The joke hypothesis, which is the fulcrum on which his entire argument turns, is given all of one page.

Fr. Robert Fox, who wrote the foreword to *The Untold Story*, and who has since asked Jones "to discontinue using my name in the advertisement of it" now writes, "I would like to ask you to join me in praying for Michael Jones. In the past couple of years I have come more and more to question the integrity of methodology and journalistic responsibility exercised particularly as it concerns articles in *Fidelity*." [Jones, who is the editor of *Fidelity*, first published *The Untold Story* as a series of articles in the magazine.]

Fr. Fox addressed the 1992 National Conference on Medjugorje. He gave an interview the weekend of the Conference (cited earlier) in which he said, "Medjugorje is fulfilling what Fatima promised.'"

If Jones can be accused of being flippant in dealing with Medjugorje, the same cannot be said about Abbe Nantes and the French publication *Catholic Counter-Reformation*. These are deadly serious, decidedly humorless people (in fact, they are especially upset by the laughter of the visionaries that is [falsely] reported in the Sivric texts). It was the Abbe Nantes who made "the first public pronouncement against the authenticity of Medjugorje for theological reasons." His thesis was that "It may be another of Satan's counterfeits to make us forget Fatima" (43).

Of no one can it be said more truly than of the Abbe Nantes that "he is more Catholic than the Pope." This good priest has for years accused Popes Paul VI and John Paul II of formal heresy. This is no exaggeration as shown in the text below taken word for word from an issue of *The Catholic Counter-Reformation*:

NOTIFICATION

Monsieur l'abbé Georges de Nantes, founder and animator of the movement entitled 'League of the Catholic Counter-Reformation,' accompanied by a delegation of this same movement, came to Rome with the intention of placing in the hands of the Holy Father, 'or any other person delegated by Him' a 'Book of Accusation against Pope John

Paul II for heresy, schism and scandal.' This book, the contents of which are already known in outline from a printed document (no indication of date, by the Contre-Reforme Catholique, Maison Saing Joseph, St. Parres-les-Vaudes), and which mirrors accusations brought over many years against Pope Paul VI and His Holiness John-Paul II, notably in the Bulletin of the 'Catholic Counter-Reformation,' officially request the opening of a trial against the Holy Father himself, before his own tribunal, as 'Supreme Judge of the Faith.'

Despite the character of such a move, and at the request of Superior Authority, M.l'Abbe de Nantes, accompanied by four delegates, was received by His Excellency Mgr. Jerome Hamer, Secretary of the Sacred Congregation for the Doctrine of the Faith, at the Seat of this Dicastery on Friday, 13th May 1983.

At the interview, the Abbé de Nantes was asked to explain his position and the object of his request.

Mgr. Hamer then made the following declaration to the Abbé de Nantes:

1. That he categorically refused to receive his libellum, it being impossible to accept accusations that are unjustified and gravely offensive towards the Holy Father, as were these formulated some time ago against Pope Paul VI in an analogous document dating from 1973.
2. That the publication and broadcasting of this libellum would constitute a grave violation of the Abbé de Nantes' duties as a Christian and still more as a priest, and that the secretary of the Congregation for the Doctrine of the Faith had, by virtue of his office, forbidden any such publication, and had formally notified him of this.
3. That the Sacred Congregation for the Doctrine of the Faith still awaited from him a retraction of his errors and of the accusations of heresy brought by him against Pope Paul VI and the Second Vatican Council — a retraction that had been required of him after the examination of his writings, made at his request, and at his appearances of 25-29th April, 3rd May and 5th July, 1968.
4. That until this retraction has taken place, and whilst attacks of the same nature are made against the person of His Holiness John Paul II, there can be no credence in the seriousness of his desire for reconciliation, which he himself has manifested on two occasions, in 1978 and again in 1981, and which the Holy Father is still disposed to welcome.

Abbé Nantes responds thus to these demands: "To the two lustful old men who condemned the chaste Suzanna to death by stoning, the prophet Daniel announced: 'In truth, your lie will fall upon your own heads' (Daniel 13, 5-59). I announce the same to Cardinal Ratzinger and his entourage who aided or consented to this lie and abuse of authority. ...My 'error' consists in being right against them [Cardinal Ratzinger and Pope John Paul II], their conciliar Reform, against their new Christianity, their New Pentecost and now, they have no fear, their New evangelization" (44).

It is to be expected that someone who presumes to instruct the Pope on matters of doctrine will be even more severe than the Church when setting forth the criteria for discerning authentic apparitions. The *Catholic Counter Reformation* admits its purpose of "'systematically collecting' every objection against Medjugorje. That indeed is our intention, and it is the right method. For it is not a matter of knowing whether the Apparition occasionally says good things or whether good is done at Medjugorje. It is a certainty that an illusory or diabolical apparition is never entirely bad. An authentic apparition, however, has to be true, good and worthy of God in all its parts" (45).

These requirements not only vastly exceed the criteria set forth by the Church, but what is "good or worthy of God" is entirely to be decided by the Abbe Nantes. The CCR claims that there "is reciprocal recognition between the charismatic movement and the Yugoslav Apparition, as they mutually support each other" (46). This bodes ill for the apparition for "it is not the Holy Spirit of the Father and of the Son who is at work at the centre of the charismatic movemen." (47). The CCR cites an "unbreakable link" between the Charismatic Renewal and the apparition simply on the grounds that some of the prominent supporters of Medjugorje are Charismatics. By the CCR's totally arbitrary criteria for authenticity, not only the visionaries but also every one around the visionaries would have to be infallible and impeccable. No apparition in Church history is likely to have passed the stringent trial by fire proposed by this group which is also seeking to put the Holy Father on trial for heresy!

No attempt is made to show that the visionaries are Charismatics, but in this area the CCR treats Bishop Zanic as the primary and only reliable source on the real facts about and behind Medjugorje. According to the CCR, Bishop Zanic's report "published in Italian under the title 'la posizione attuale (non ufficiale) della Curia vescovile di Mostar nei confronti degli eventi di Medjugorje,' is perfectly clear. The facts put forward are beyond dispute. The demonstration is solid. And the conclusion is inescapable: It is not the Virgin Mary who is appearing at Medjugorje. Furious at having been publicly unmasked and denounced, the charismatics of Medjugorje, Laurentin and others, will lambast the Bishop of Mostar with the most odious calumnies, whilst guarding against publishing his text for want of being able to articulate the beginning of a coherent reply. Despite all that could be said in an attempt to annul its demonstrative force, this text by the Bishop of Mostar remains the major document on the question and it provides ample grounds for a negative judgement on the 'apparitions' of Medjugorje" (48).

The Abbé Nantes mounts a passionate defense of Bishop Zanic in an "Open Letter to Cardinal Joseph Ratzinger": "Today the report by the courageous and serious Bishop of Mostar will sufficiently and definitively enlighten any unprejudiced mind. We have the report, therefore you must have it and know it. After this report, it is the policy of wait-and-see that is impious and criminal because it is doing the devil's business. One cannot 'stop God from speaking' you say. But one can and must stop the devil and every liar usurping the sacred authority of God and of His Holy Mother! Your congregation would honor itself by coming to the aid of the Bishop of Mostar to silence this endlessly loquacious 'Apparition' of Medjugorje, the inverted caricature of Our Lady of Fatima" (49).

About this same document by Bishop Zanic, BBC correspondent Mary Craig writes, "It was clear to all but the most purblind that the document revealed nothing so much as Zanic's mounting obsession with the Hercegovina issue. In his view, everything that happened in Medjugorje could be reduced to the simple syllogism: the Virgin of Medjugorje has spoken against the Bishop, who represents the authority of the Church; therefore it is impossible that such a subversive and wrong-headed oracle could actually be the Virgin Mary" (50).

The CCR mode of argument is a sort of rambling stream-of-consciousness commentary on selected events, individuals and statements. They offer no arguments, just opinionss in parenthesis after quoting a given statement or describing an event. An example: "Wednesday 24 June, 1981: First apparition, first grave difficulty! How, in fact, could the sight of the Most Blessed Virgin Mary, the true Virgin radiating beauty, gentleness and motherly mercy, arouse not only an initial movement of fear, as with her authentic manifestations, but the terror and mad [CCR's adjective] panic which the seers afterwards said that they had then felt?" (51). In response to this line of "reasoning," we will only quote two accounts of encounters with the supernatural in the New Testament and leave it that:

> And there appeared to him an angel of the Lord standing on the right side of the altar of incense. And Zacharias was troubled when he saw him, and fear fell upon him" (Luke 1: 11-12).
> And entering the tomb they saw a young man sitting on the right side, dressed in a white robe; and they wer amazed. And he said to them, 'Be not amazed.' (Mark 16: 5-6)
> And the angel said to her, 'Do not be afraid, Mary, for you have found favor with God' (Luke 1:30).

I THANK YOU THAT YOU WILL NOT BETRAY MY PRESENCE HERE.

Predictably, the CCR draws the Vatican into the discussion and accuses the Pope and Cardinal Ratzinger of protecting the apparition. Bishop Zanic, says the CCR, "will have to have the agreement of Cardinal Ratzinger and of the Pope, who very obligingly will risk waiting for the 'apparitions' to end! Saved in 1983 by Laurentin, prolonged in 1984 by Mgr. Franic, the Medjugorje fraud, now protected by the Pope, can last for a good while yet." (52). For the CCR, Church approval of the apparition would actually be proof of its fraudulence! [The entire June 1991 issue of the CCR is a "full-of-sound-and-fury-signifying-nothing" attempt to show that John Paul II, this most Marian of Popes, is committed neither to the Blessed Virgin nor to Fatima!] In fact, in its July 1987 issue, the CCR targets the Holy Father's encouragement of Medjugorje: "For some months now, however, the Pope has not ceased lavishing his encouragement on the seers and the propagandists of Medjugorje. I have in front of me an account of twenty or so of these favors which serve to revive week by week the confidence of thousands of the faithful who continue to go on pilgrimage." The CCR treats the statements of the Bishop of Mostar with utmost deference while heaping ridicule and abuse on papal and other Vatican pronouncements. The CCR has no real arguments against the events in Medjugorje and merely replays the Bishop of Mostar's charges. Their beef is with Church authority and that issue is clearly beyond the scope of this essay.

The same defiant attitude to the Vatican is to be found in Fr. Sivric who writes that Bishop Zanic is still the ultimate authority on the apparitions (p.159) and that the Pope and the Congregation for the Doctrine of the Faith have only sown confusion.

It is obvious that Jones' patience with the Vatican is beginning to run thin because it has not acted soon enough to issue its negative verdict. In *Medjugorje Goes Up in Smoke: The Bishops Just Say No* (*Fidelity,* February 1991), Jones first quotes a bishop who expressed the fear that the Church would lose Medjugorje to the sects if it came up with a negative verdict and then adds, "By spending almost 10 years in coming to a verdict, the Church has all but insured that fear will become reality." (p.28). In the following month's issue of *Fidelity,* he reprints an interview with Cardinal Ratzinger in which the Cardinal, apparently in response to Jones' evident anxiety to get a swift negative verdict on the apparition, tells him on two occasions, "You'll have to be patient."

Jones' reaction to Bishop Zanic's removal as the authority in charge of investigating Medjugorje is extremely revealing: "The Vatican has no authority to do that. Bishop Zanic is the Church in Medjugorje." This is an ironic charge coming from someone whose magazine is published by Ultramontane Associates, Inc. and who has shown little respect for his own Bishop!

Time after time the critics allege that Medjugorje may produce good fruits in the short term but in the long run it undermines Church authority because it encourages an attitude of rebellion. In "Medjugorje Goes Up in Smoke," Jones describes "the diabolical strategy" he sees "behind all phoney apparitions. Behind all of the talk about the 'good fruits' of Medjugorje, one could always discern an attitude of rebellion against Church authority. At first it was directed against the bishop; now that same animosity will be directed against the bishops' commission. It will be directed against Rome too, if Rome chooses to make a pronouncement on the matter. ...The devil [...] has something for everybody. He can even use the most devout piety in the world as his instrument if he can use it to separate believers from the Church." [p.28] After reading the CCR, Sivric and Jones, however, one can surmise that the same quoted criteria of the devil's tactics can also be used in discerning these authors' "arguments."

For these critics, Medjugorje turns out to be an ideal forum in which to pursue their true agendas and Bishop Zanic is a convenient authority figure who lends legitimacy to their pet peeves. Every one of these critics seems to have a gigantic chip on his shoulder (for the Bishop it seems to be "the Hercegovina case," for Sivric it appears to be the defense of his relatives, for the CCR it obviously includes the "errors" of the Second Vatican Council and the "false spirit" of the Charismatic movement and for Jones it seems to be a distaste for the Charismatics, an urge to "defend" Fatima against Medjugorje and a obsessive phobia that just will not go away) — chips which have nothing to do with Medjugorje or the visionaries but which influence the critics' judgment on both. In many ways the best arguments for the authenticity of the Medjugorje apparitions are the desperation and vehemence of the critics. If any stick is good enough to beat the apparition, the critics will use it with a vengeance. Chesterton's classic statement explaining how destructive critical arguments sometimes testify to the truth of the object of their attack has already been quoted. To better understand Jones, Sivric, et. al., we can do no better than to reflect again on the last part of that citation:

> I went over all the cases, and I found the key fitted so far. The fact that Swinburne was irritated at the unhappiness of Christians and yet more irritated at their happiness was easily explained. It was no longer a complication of diseases in Christianity, but a complication of diseases in Swinburne. The restraints of Christianity saddened him simply because he was more hedonist than a healthy man should be. The faith of Christians angered him because he was more pessimist than a healthy man should be. In the same way the Malthusians by instinct attacked Christianity; not because there is anything especially anti-Malthusian about Christianity, but because there is something a little anti-human about Malthusianism. (54).

The venom and the vitriol so characteristic of *Fidelity* and the CCR should serve at least the purpose of planting a seed of suspicion in the minds of those who first hear about Medjugorje in the pages of these publications — suspicion not about the authenticity of Medjugorje but about the objectivity and open-mindedness of the magazines themselves and their editors.

While Jones, Sivric and the *Catholic Counter-Reformation* are the best-known enemies of Medjugorje, they are by no means the only critics who have joined the fray on the side of the opposition. These other critics can be categorized as coming at Medjugorje either from the right or the left.

The critics on the right almost invariably echo the CCR. For instance, Hamish Fraser, the late publisher of *Approaches,* cites the CCR as his main source text in his critique of Medjugorje and accepts the CCR's assertion that Medjugorje is the "anti-thesis" of Fatima. Fraser, who was based in England, found Medjugorje's openness to members of other religions particularly galling. Medjugorje's ecumenism, it must be remembered, is one of inviting members of all religions to conversion and is accompanied by the reminder that "it is intentional that all apparitions are under the auspices of the Catholic Church." He is also enraged by the fact that Charismatics have flocked to Medjugorje and have promoted it in their publications. Many Catholic Charismatics have a very deep devotion to the Holy Mass; does this mean that the Mass must be viewed with suspicion?

Another leading Medjugorje critic in England is Michael Davies. Davies, like Fraser, is also a critic of the Second Vatican Council. Davies cites Fraser, Bishop Zanic and the CCR as his points of reference. In his view, devotees of Medjugorje are motivated by an unhealthy craving for authoritative teaching from alleged apparitions of the present day — and all of these apparitions are spurious. After hurling this "authoritative teaching" at his readers, he goes on to say, "Under no circumstances whatsoever am I prepared to enter into any correspondence upon the subject of Medjugorje." [*The Remnant,* March 31, 1988]. This refusal to discuss the case *for* Medjugorje is characteristic of many of the critics of Medjugorje.

Other than Michael Jones and Fr. Sivric, the major critics of Medjugorje in America are Fr. John O'Connor and Brother James, S.D.B.. Fr. O'Connor contents himself with quoting and endorsing Bishop Zanic's observations and views. He ends with the complaint "But there's no mention of Fatima. There is no mention of Mary's Immaculate Heart." ["Is It Mary Who is Speaking?" An audio tape for Keep the Faith, Inc.]. Both statements, of course, are patently false as can be seen by reading the messages themselves.

Brother James, S.D.B. is America's answer to the CCR — at least in style and tone. His critique of Medjugorje is simply a collection of statements made by the visionaries or by Medjugorje supporters and his commentaries on these statements. The most innocuous statements are turned on their head until they appear positively sinister. Ambiguity is never tolerated. Only the most damning interpretation of any statement is admissible. As in the case of the CCR, this exercise rapidly becomes tiresome because it relies more on scathing sarcasm than on serious analysis. Sometimes the sarcasm is downright mean and petty as illustrated in this sample statement:

> Monthly Message June 25, 1987: *"Dear children! Today I thank you all and would like to call you to the peace of God. I wish that each one of you may experience in his life the peace that God gives. Today I want to bless you all. I bless you with God's blessing, and I ask you, dear children, to follow and live my way. I love you all dear children. That is why I have called you so many times. I thank you for all that you do for my intentions. Please help me so that I may present you to God, save you, and guide you on the path to salvation. Thank you for your response to my call."* Commentary by Brother James: "Let us not deceive ourselves nor attribute these monthly messages to Holy Mary! I had enough of: 'dear children!'" [Critique: *Medjugorje*, p. 25]

In France, the CCR is joined in its opposition to Medjugorje by Fr. Rebut and Fr. Grumel. In *Satan's House of Cards* [1984], a mimeographed pamphlet he produced to denounce Medjugorje, Fr. Rebut predicts that Medjugorje "is a perverse and incoherent work of the devil. It will fall by itself, just as do the fragile card constructions that children make as they play." To date, this prediction has not come true — and few people have described Medjugorje as "perverse and incoherent." Wild charges of diabolic works are apparently not unusual among the French ultra-Traditionalist clergy. Fr. Grumel, "a priest according to the order of Melchisedek" turned out another pamphlet, *The Diabolical Imposture of Medjugorje*, decrying Medjugorje as a "monumental diabolical imposture" because it calls for "peace at any price, extension of the papal fatherhood to the whole world, mad ecumenism" and the like. All the major apparitions of Mary have been dismissed as "impostures of the Devil" at some time or the other.

Theorists are not discouraged by any evidence of "good fruits" or "edifying messages" because they regard these simply as illustrations of the ingenuity of the Devil. These traditionalists may be horrified to find that their same presuppositions and methodologies are applied by Protestant Fundamentalists against all Marian apparitions (which they believe to be diabolic in origin and nature).

Fr. Laurentin's response to critics of this kind is invaluable: "Let us acknowledge the good faith of those who lock themselves in this system. It stimulates their dialectic and, with some, their talent. The ideologies of both right and left have their sparkle and their effectiveness. They are irrefutable and regrettably, incurable. One can only leave them to their good faith and entrust them in prayer to the miracle of God's grace."

A frequent theme in the writings of traditionalist critics is the apparent mania for apparitions that (in their view) have reached epidemic proportions today. They describe Bayside and Necedah and Palmar de Troya in great detail while shaking their heads about the proliferation of claims of apparitions around the world. They lament the reluctance of Catholics to seek sustenance from the Church rather than from an alleged apparition. There is much merit in all this. Our faith is based on Christ and on His teachings as proclaimed infallibly by the Church. There is no substitute for this. Nevertheless we cannot restrain the activity of the Divine. If we have reason to believe that He has sent the Blessed Mother to speak to us at a certain location and at a certain time, we must respond appropriately. Clearly, the message given in any apparition does not add anything new to the public revelation or to the Church's infallible discernment of this revelation. Equally clearly, certain claims of apparitions are false. Simply in terms of the magnitude of its global impact and the significance of its messages, Medjugorje cannot be compared to any alleged apparition taking place today. It must be studied on its own merits. If Medjugorje is authentic then it calls for a response of acceptance from every human person. Most of the traditionalists who complain about the modern fascination with apparitions tend to be devotees of Fatima — and they do not see this devotion as a substitute for their Faith as a whole. The same goes for Medjugorje which is nothing less than a continuation and a fulfillment of Fatima.

Critics of Medjugorje on the left have not been quite as prolific as the critics on the right. Amusingly, Bishop Zanic has proven to be attractive not just to the ultra-traditionalist CCR but also to the Modernist Catholic journalist Peter Hebblethwaite. Hebblethwaite, who is plainly displeased with Medjugorje's traditional theology, uses Bishop Zanics's "facts" and the "revelations" of Fr. Sivric to dismiss Medjugorje as "a pious fraud." [*National Catholic Reporter,* June 3, 1988]. Hebblethwaite's eagerness to accept Sivric at face value apparently overcame his critical instincts as pointed out by Robert Bela Wilhelm [*National Catholic Reporter,* July 15, 1988]. Wilhelm, a theologian who is of partial Yugoslav heritage (a Petrovic) says, "Hebblethwaite places great authority in Father Sivric and his book, *The Hidden Face of Medjugorje.* Hebblethwaite writes,

'Many of the actors in this story are related to (Sivric) ... where nearly everyone is the cousin of everyone else." He later lavishly praises Sivric saying,

'He knows the psychology of his own people' and 'He has performed a service for the church in his native village and the whole church. He has not written a polemical or a passionate book.'

Hebblethwaite is like the anthropologist who has just been hood-winked by his informant and doesn't have the foggiest notion he has just been had.

Yugoslavs are a passionate people and paradoxically both quite individualistic and communal at the same time. Sivric himself is — of course — another actor on the scene, part of the quarreling families of Pavlovics, Vlasics, Ivankovics and Zovkos. The notion of an impartial observer is untenable in the culture of Medjugorje. In this community, personal -subjective knowledge outweighs impersonal-objective knowledge. But Hebblethwaite is oblivious to this reality.

Hebblethwaite's use of outmoded 19th Century dichotomies between 'objective' and 'subjective' religious visions discounts not only Medjugorje, Fatima and Lourdes, but also Guadalupe, Canterbury, Assisi and even the miracle of the resurrection appearances of Jesus.

A more restrained critic on the left is Thomas C. Fox, editor of *The National Catholic Reporter*. In a narrative account of his visit to Medjugorje, Fox reports a conversation that is remarkable for its insight: "Once, in a torn moment, I met an Irish Passionist priest, Father Brian Mulcahy, sitting behind the church. He explained he had come to Medjugorje to offer thanks to Our Lady. 'You find in Medjugorje what you bring to Medjugorje,' he told me. 'Come a skeptic, and you'll leave a skeptic. Come with faith and you'll find faith.'" [*National Catholic Reporter*, October, 1987]. In an interview with Marija, Fox asked her what Our Lady says about feeding the poor and clothing the naked. Marija's response ["Just pray. And the rest will follow."] left him with the feeling that "I had just gone back to a preconciliar time and had listened to religious imagery and theology I had not heard of since the earliest days of my childhood." To those on the right and the left, we can only say that Medjugorje must be taken on its own terms and conditions — not ours.

The most lively critic on the left is Louis Belanger, a French Canadian parapsychologist who edited Sivric's *The Hidden Face of Medjugorje* and wrote the introduction to it. Belanger's introduction is mainly a recitation of the various "facts" uncovered by Sivric. What is of interest here is Belanger's own incredible explanation for the Medjugorje phenomenon which has to be read to be believed:

Tectonic movements of mountains and rocks, which are visible in the form of columns of light and can influence the behavior of a living organism. This electromagnetic light, as it passes through the temporal lobe (...) gives rise to visions which are interpreted according to their culture (...). The children in Medjugorje really saw a luminous phenomenon, which they interpreted, in accord with their culture, as being the Gospa. What else could they possible see, these young people brought up in the faith and cult of Mary, whose month had just finished? (*La Chatelaine,* June 1985, p. 62).

The only response required for this fanciful and thoroughly speculative "theory" that is as philosophically naive as it is theologically amusing is a general comment on the wisdom of making such pompous pontifications. To quote the words of the British philosopher C. D. Broad, this theory belongs to "the numerous class of theories which are so preposterously silly that only very learned men could have thought of them. But such theories are frequently countenanced by the naive since they are put forward in highly technical terms by learned persons who are themselves too confused to know exactly what they mean." In a more colloquial context, an appropriate response to Belanger might be "Give me a break!"

Whether coincidentally or not, almost all the critics coming at Medjugorje from the right and the left tend to have a track record of rebellion against the hierarchy of the Catholic Church. Many of the critics on the right reject the teachings both of the Second Vatican Council and of all popes after Pope John XXIII. Others respect both Vatican II and the Holy Father but show no hesitation in publicly attaching or disparaging bishops, the successors of the Apostles — thus defying the directives to the contrary of the First and the Second Vatican Councils. While the critics on the right reject the current teachings of the Church because they do not consider these teachings to be traditional enough, the critics on the left reject various teachings of the Church because they consider them to be too traditional.

The masters of the spiritual life have warned that disobedience to or disrespect for legitimate authority is a most dangerous form of pride that allows the Devil to gain a foothold in one's soul. Catholics who have decided that they can sit in judgment on their Shepherds are hardly likely to show discretion, prudence or humility when they confront a supernatural phenomenon that appears to transcend their notions of how these kinds of things should behave.

By and large, many of the Traditionalist critics of Medjugorje seek refuge in their own eccentric interpretations of Fatima and use these interpretations as their main arguments against Medjugorje. A favorite presupposition of these Fatima-based critics [CCR, et. al.] is the idea that Russia still has not been consecrated to the Immaculate Heart of Mary as requested by the Blessed Mother at Fatima. They hold to this position despite the fact Sister Lucia dos Santos of Fatima has repeatedly stated that the 1984 collegial act of consecration by Pope john Paul II is a fulfillment of this request ["It has been accomplished"]. Sister Lucia's position has been confirmed both by her Superior and her Bishop.

We should not then be startled to find that these people, who profess to know more about Fatima than the very visionary of Fatima, have determined for themselves that the Virgin of Medjugorje is not the same person as the Virgin of Fatima. It is clear that many of these Fatima experts have formed a certain image of Mary based on their perceptions of Fatima — and it is this image that they set against the Mary we meet in Medjugorje. All too often, these experts lack the sense of history that is required to understand each Marian apparition in its context.

As a footnote introducing some sense of history to the discussion, we might mention that there were many similarities between the ways in which the Fatima and the Medjugorje apparitions were received. At the onset of each apparition, for instance, there were those who attributed the apparition to the deceit of the Devil. With the passage of time, the image of Fatima that often comes to mind is Sister Lucia in her cloistered convent and the fact that the Fatima apparition was actually encountered by simple peasant children is half-forgotten. E. Michael Jones is guilty of this in *The Untold Story* where he compares Sr. Lucia as a nun in a cloister with Ivan in modern-day Medjujgorje.

What Jones fails to realize is that Sister Lucia seventy-five years ago — when she witnessed the apparition at Fatima — was in a different position from the one she is in today. If comparisons are to be made between one visionary and another, we should try to be context-sensitive: both visionaries should be compared in terms of their actions at the time of the respective apparitions they witnessed. If Ivan is to be compared to Sister Lucia, then we would be better served by taking a look at how the peasant girl Lucia responded to the attention she received at the time of the apparition — not seventy-five years later. A good source for historical information of this kind is Sandra Zimdars-Swartz's definitive historical study of Marian apparitions, *Encountering Mary*. Here is what she tells us about Lucia in a context similar to the one in which Jones "catches" Ivan:

> Lucia's sisters, whose normal duties included sewing, working in the fields, and caring for the house, found themselves, after the onset of the apparition, spending a large amount of time dealing with the people who wanted to speak with Lucia and watching the sheep in her place so that she could spend time with these people herself. The

family garden, moreover, which was near the apparition site, was reportedly so overrun by people that both harvesting and replanting had become impractical." [Sandra L. Zimdars-Swartz, *Encountering Mary,* Princeton, New Jersey, Princeton University Press, 1991, p. 86].

In differentiating the Virgin of Fatima from the Virgin of Medjugorje, the critics tend to make their case by playing the messages of one apparition against the other. The critics might as well say that the Virgin of Guadalupe is different from the Virgin of Fatima if these are the rules of the game. We have seen that apparitions of the Virgin Mary do not give us new revelations, but they sometimes do "confirm" a teaching newly defined by the Church. The doctrine of the Immaculate Conception had just been defined when Mary appeared at Lourdes — and the doctrine was strongly expounded at this apparition.

Now Medjugorje is an apparition that is taking place after a Council that has drastically changed us psychologically in terms of openness to all peoples of all religions. There was no change of doctrine at Vatican II; but there was a radical change of attitude. If nothing else, the Council focused on and instilled in us a renewed sense of God's infinite overpowering love. It is this sense of all-encompassing love that inspired the historic Vatican II document on the world religions: a document that recognizes not only the good will of all sincere seekers of God in every religion but also God's desire to bring all men to salvation. While the Catholic Church is seen as a divinely instituted entity, all the major religions are recognized as institutionalized expressions of the human desire for God. To that extent, we must acknowledge and respect all that is good and true in these religions. We are told also that we must always respect the freedom of conscience of every human being and that adherents of different religions should live in tolerance and harmony. This is what the Second Vatican Council tells us. This is what Pope John Paul II tells us. And this is what Medjugorje tells us.

It is precisely this dramatic new awareness of God's infinite love for every human being that many of the critics find objectionable about both Medjugorje and the Second Vatican Council. And it is this which leads them to say that the Virgin of Medjugorje is not the Virgin of Fatima. What Mary says about other religions and members of other religions in Medjugorje is not different from what is said by Vatican II. Since the Church as Teacher is infallible, we must accept the teachings of Vatican II. And since the Vatican II teachings are true, we must not be surprised by the fact that these same teachings are echoed by Mary at Medjugorje. At the same time we realized that these teachings would not be proclaimed by her prior to the proclamation of the Church- and therefore she did not proclaim them in her pre-Vatican II apparitions.

It is worth noting that His Holiness, Pope John Paul II, has been viciously attacked by some of these very same critics of Medjugorje for his courage and compassion in trying to share the love of the Holy Trinity with members of all religions. It does not appear to be a coincidence that Mary announced at Medjugorje (in 1984) that the Holy Father must consider himself not just "the Father of all Catholics, but of all mankind."

At Medjugorje Our Lady says that "this world of sorrows...is without hope for those who do not know Jesus." [November 25, 1991]. And in *The Mission of the Redeemer*, Pope John Paul II proclaims Christ to the religions of the world: "Peoples everywhere, open the doors to Christ!...The number of those who do not know Christ and do not belong to the Church is constantly on the increase...When we consider this immense portion of humanity which is loved by the Father and for whom He sent His Son, the urgency of the Church's mission is obvious...No believer in Christ, no institution of the Church can avoid this supreme duty: to proclaim Christ to all peoples...On the eve of the third millennium the whole Church is invited to live more intensely the mystery of Christ by gratefully cooperating in the work of salvation. The Church does this together with Mary and following the example of Mary, the Church's Mother and model." Vatican II tells us "It is the duty of the Church...in her preaching to proclaim the cross of Christ as the sign of God's universal love and the source of all grace." [*Nostra Aetate,* 4].

What we have here is neither syncretism nor universalism but there is a deep awareness of God's infinite love for every human being and His desire to bring salvation to all. Once one immerses oneself in the teachings of the Second Vatican Council, one finds, first, this sense of God's infinite love and, second, harmony with the messages of Medjugorje. Undoubtedly, the task of understanding and explaining God's love for members of every religion while keeping in mind the unique role of the Catholic Church is not easy. Added to these are complications of linguistics and translation where in certain instances "religion" and "nationality" have been used interchangeabye. The Blessed Virgin's call for religious harmony — in a region riven by ethnic and religious conflict — was reviled by the traditionalists but can now be seen as a prophetic warning.

The very idea that Medjugorje teaches "religious indifferentism" is seen to be false when we ponder the Blessed Mother's dire warnings about Hell and Satan. She is dealing with reality:. Religions [other than the Catholic Church] are human creations but Heaven, Hell and Purgatory are the ultimate realities which matter. As she has said repeatedly, she has come to be with us in Medjugorje to take us to Heaven. Her focus is on human beings as souls who choose for or against God not as member of a particular race or religion. She does not try to sugar coat the options. She makes it clear that she is not offering an easy path: her message is a message of penance and mortification and sacrifice. She makes it clear also that we can easily and freely choose to go to Hell. Systems of religious indifferentism, universalism or syncretism do not require any kind of sacrifice and penance and they certainly do not preach Hell. It is, therefore, preposterous to compare such religious systems to Medjugorje or to even suggest any similarity. Also, Mary's emphasis on the urgent need for confession and the Holy Mass implicitly presupposes the role of the Catholic Church. And it is precisely our awareness of God's infinite love for all our brothers and sisters that inspires our efforts to bring them into the Catholic Church which is God's chosen vehicle of grace. Conversion, however, is inspired not by triumphalism but by compassion, love and humility.

As we study the harsh condemnations of the traditionalist critics, we are reminded time after time of the spite and scorn of the Scribes and Pharisees who hounded Our Blessed Lord as He taught the multitudes. Like the traditionalists who slander the Blessed Mother at Medjugorje, the Pharisees saw only heterodoxy and heresy in the words of Our Lord. His miracles were dismissed as the works of the Devil. The theologians of the time had expected a certain kind of Messiah; when Our Lord did not live up to their expectations He was denounced as an impostor. We have to agree with the traditionalists that their Mary is not the Mary we see in Medjugorje. Certainly, this meek and weeping Queen of Peace does not live up to their expectations of a distant, angry Sovereign. Mary of Medjugorje is the loving Mother of us all who invites all her "dear children" to taste the infinite love of our loving Father in Heaven and who asks each one of us to enter a loving personal relationship with her. This is the Mary we know and love and who comes to us with such overflowing love in Medjugorje.

2. CATHOLIC WRITERS RESPOND TO CRITIQUES OF MEDJUGORJE

In the previous chapter we have addressed the main charges made against Medjugorje. In this chapter we present the response to critiques of Medjugorje by respected Catholic writers. Professor Janet Smith, Dr. Adrian Reimers and Dr. Eugene F. Diamond respond first to E. Michael Jones' *Medjugorje: The Untold Story*. Their responses are followed by a response to Bishop Zanic's critique from Archbishop Frane Franic, a response to the three major critics of Medjugorje by Dr. Nicholas Bartulica and a reflection on the sources of opposition to Medjugorje by Dudley Plunkett.

(i) Professor Janet E. Smith

A Response To *Fidelity* Magazine on Medjugorje

From 1980 - 89 Dr. Janet E. Smith taught in the Program of Liberal Studies at the University of Notre Dame. Presently she is associate professor in the Philosophy Department at the University of Dallas. She is the author of *Humanae Vitae: A Generation Later* published by Catholic University Press of America. She has published on the topics of Plato, virtue, abortion, various bioethical issues, and contraception in such journals as *International Philosophical Quarterly, The Thomist, The New Scholasticism, Phoenix, Apeiron*. She serves on the board of the Fellowship of Catholic Scholars and the American Catholic Philosophical Association. She knew E. Michael Jones when she lived in South Bend. The following article was written in April, 1989, as a response to Jones' articles in *Fidelity,* was submitted for publication there and rejected. It is printed here as it was originally written:

E. Michael Jones finds it unfortunate that so many are wasting so much time and energy in pursuit of spiritual guidance from Medjugorje, since he thinks it cannot truly be enjoying the special supernatural blessing it is claiming. In short, as he makes clear in **Medjugorje: The Untold Story**, he thinks Medjugorje is a hoax. On the other hand, hundreds of thousands, and perhaps even millions of others who have gone to Medjugorje or who have learned of it insist that they have reason to believe the apparitions to be genuine.

Clearly, Mary is either appearing to the young people or she is not. What is at stake in determining the truth about the apparition? Certainly, even if Medjugorje is true, no great harm will necessarily come to us if we do not accept Medjugorje, for all revelation necessary for our salvation is already available to us. Nonetheless if Mary is appearing, it seems fair to assume that she has something important to say to us and it would do us well to heed her counsel. If she is not appearing, then what could be going on? Are the children, or their manipulators, or the devil trying to dupe millions of gullible pilgrims? Perhaps in following the counsels of Medjugorje we may be doing ourselves spiritual harm, for we may be doing the bidding of the devil. We may be setting ourselves up for a disillusionment that would shake our faith. The Church has not yet made a determination about the authenticity of the apparitions and will not do so until the apparitions have ended. Faithful Catholics must be prepared to accept whatever the Church decides. But, in the meantime, it seems appropriate for us to use our own powers of discernment to lead us to a sensible response to the happenings at Medjugorje.

The articles in *Fidelity* are clearly written not with the intent of providing a balanced and thorough reporting of the events of Medjugorje. For, if they were, the author then would have investigated and reported on many different types of evidence, that supporting the claims of Medjugorje as well as that detracting from them. But, as stated, his intent clearly was to expose Medjugorje as a hoax and the articles are crafted to that purpose. This observation is not made with the intent of impugning the motives of Mr. Jones. Indeed, it is fair to attribute the best of motives to him. That is, it seems that Mr. Jones thinks everyone is getting only one side of the story and that there is another side to be told - - indeed the true side. It would not be unusual or even inappropriate for anyone in such a situation simply to bring forward all the information and analysis he thought was being ignored and not to restate any evidence fortifying the beliefs of those who accept the event in question. Still, a disturbing quality of the *Fidelity* articles is their *certainty* that Medjugorje is a hoax. Surely if those who are inclined to believe are best advised to wait for guidance from the Church before they bet their salvation on it, so, too, does it seem advisable for the detractors to show some caution in their opposition to Medjugorje.

The readers of *Fidelity*, then, should keep in mind the one-sidedness of the articles there. Some of them may not have heard the "other" side, the side that finds abundant reason to accept the message of Medjugorje. Anyone wanting to hear the "pro" as well as the "con" arguments about Medjugorje would need to do considerable reading beyond the *Fidelity* articles. A possible place to begin would be the book *A Spark from Heaven* by Mary Clark, a reporter for the BBC. Clark, not inclined to be overly credulous about alleged supernatural events, gives a balanced accounting and in the end remains quite skeptical. Others reading her work may, on the basis of the same evidence, find reason to be much less skeptical; she leaves the door open for such a response. She and others provide discussion of scientific evidence about testing done of the seers during the apparitions and of scientific evidence concerning cures attributed to Medjugorje. It would also be right to learn of the support given by many bishops to Medjugorje, some in Yugoslavia, and to examine the claims of many to have experienced miracles at Medjugorje. Some tell of seeing the cross on the mountain of Medjugorje spin, and of seeing the sun pulsate. Many have had the links in their rosaries turn a golden color. Furthermore, evidence such as the many conversions coming out of Medjugorje and the quality of the sermons and spiritual writings based upon the events must all be taken into account. And, of course, there must be an attempt to assess the messages attributed to Mary. Are they orthodox? Do they have any kind of special urgency or insight peculiarly needed by individuals of our time? Are they likely to lead individuals to a deeper spiritual life and better relationship to God and the Church or are they likely to lead individuals away from God? If they have promised certain signs or predicted certain events, have these materialized?

Here is not the place to attempt the *"Full* Story of Medjugorje" for, as the Church knows, that will not be known for a very long time. The intent of this article is simply to judge the merits of the doubts raised in the *Fidelity* articles. Is it time to cancel our plane reservations; to throw out our videos of documentaries on Medjugorje; to shut our ears to the messages relayed to us from the visionaries? Or do we have reason to continue to respond in the way the Spirit moves each of us to these apparitions, always allowing the final word to the Church?

In response to one of the letters to the editor questioning his interpretation of Vicka's alleged lack of understanding of the feast of the Annunciation, Mr. Jones states: "Based on the quotations, the reader can draw his own conclusions . . . I stand by my interpretation." The incidents which Mr. Jones cites do indeed admit of interpretations other than those provided by him. The "reinterpreter", however, is constrained by the evidence cited, which, understandably was cited in support of a certain line of argument. If further information about these incidents were available, who knows what alternative interpretations might be possible? If and when we know all the facts about different events cited in *Fidelity*, we may think very differently about Medjugorje. This article will attempt to provide some other possible interpretations of some of the incidents cited in *Fidelity*. The length of the *Fidelity* articles makes a complete and detailed response unwieldy but perhaps it will be enough to touch on some of the major points.

Surely there will always be reason to raise doubts about any supernatural occurrence and it will never be possible to eradicate all doubts. But such is the nature of anything accepted on Faith. If it were subject to absolute and certain proof, it would be in the realm of nature not of the supernatural, it would be a matter not of faith but of science. Many elements of the story of Medjugorje are peculiar and certainly give one pause, but such is true about nearly any supernatural occurrence. Furthermore, if the apparitions are genuine, one could expect Satan to try to lead as many away from Medjugorje as possible. The following does not purport to offer an unassailable refutation of facts or interpretations offered by *Fidelity*; indeed, this author allows that Mr. Jones may be correct. Nevertheless, this author believes that his interpretations do have problems that it is fair to point out; he has not yet delivered a death blow to the story of Medjugorje. (Several excellent responses to the articles have been published in *Fidelity* itself; this author recommends particularly those by Mark Miravalle and Rick Guy in the November issue and those by Father Bob Bedard, Bill Reck, and Adrian Reimers in the December issue. Father Laurentin has also written a short response, published by the Riehle Foundation in *Seven Years of Apparitions*.)

Article One

Behavior of Seers

   Fidelity contends that the behavior of the seers is inappropriate for those who have seen a vision of Mary. Their joking with the crowd of pilgrims or fidgeting in Church are cited as examples of troublesome behavior. *Fidelity* laments that the visionaries are not better behaved and do not act like Sister Lucia of Fatima who lived quietly in a convent after her apparitions. Yet, most who have associated with the visionaries have found their behavior exemplary; they are reputed to be kind and gentle and incredibly accessible to the pilgrims day in and day out — in circumstances that most of us would find most trying. There is no evidence that any of them is profiting financially in the slightest from the events — they still live in very humble homes and live very simple lives. *Fidelity's* claim that "the seers at Medjugorje have decided to become part of the tourist industry" hardly seems fair (I, p. 19).

   Still, suppose that on occasion the seers have been observed behaving in ways that can be interpreted as observed behaving in ways that can be interpreted as irreverent. Would this serve to damage their credibility? Perhaps so and perhaps not. Certainly, in reading scripture, one gets the sense that the apostles were not always so wonderfully well-behaved, even after repeated exposure to the miracles and wisdom of Christ Himself. Peter, Christ's chosen head of His Church, lied about his association with Christ. Indeed, most of us even immediately after receiving the person of Christ Himself in the Eucharist are capable of sinful thought and behavior.

Theology of the Seers

Fidelity is not impressed with the theological expertise of the visionaries. For instance, *Fidelity* finds the description of the color (pink, yellow, and grey) of robes worn by those in heaven to be ridiculous. And he thinks it implausible that Vicka does not know what he thinks she ought to know about the Annunciation (i.e., the date) since she says the rosary every day. But what description of hell, heaven, or purgatory doesn't raise questions? Surely any description will be inadequate in some respect. Dante tried to give a description in accord with the best and most sophisticated theology; those who have attempted to teach Dante will know how resistant students are to his work. And how many Catholics get the dates of Marian feasts confused? I do not find it uncommon for very devout Catholics, Catholics who have said the rosary daily, to get the Annunciation, the Assumption and the Immaculate Conception confused both in regard to dates and occasionally in regard to what happened on these feasts.

Fidelity also finds unreasonable the request of Mary, as reported by the seers, that everyone pray for four hours daily. He mocks Ivan who speaks of taking an hour to say the Our Father. But scripture tells us to pray constantly and many spiritual writers recommend lengthy meditation on only a few words of a prayer. The priests at Medjugorje stress the lovingness of Mary and her concern and they teach, it seems rightly, that all of us must learn to pray - - pray better and more. The advice is given to start doing something and to build upon it. The request of Mary is not that we all spend four hours a day in front of the Blessed Sacrament but that we start the day with prayer and that we say the rosary (which can be done at all sorts of odd moments), that we read Scripture, and that we do go to daily Mass if possible. She does not say that we are in a serious state of sin if we do not follow this program. This advice, as all of Mary's advice, is nothing new. The best of spiritual writing throughout the centuries has advised the same - - not as a requisite for salvation but for those who wish to advance in the spiritual life - - for those who seek a complete conversion of heart to the Lord. It seems an odd complaint against an apparition that it requests too much prayer.

Bloody Handkerchief

One of the stories that most disturbs *Fidelity* is that of the "bloody handkerchief." And there is no denying that it is a peculiar story; it is difficult to know what to make of it. Some want to dismiss it altogether and say that it is obviously a case of "miscommunication." Others, such as a writer of a letter to *Fidelity*, attempt to offer an interpretation of it based on the meaning of the symbols in the story. *Fidelity* cites Father Dugandzic as stating "There are also stories in the Bible — I'm a scripture scholar — and similar things that I can't explain either. And anyway things like this are peripheral. I don't have to be able to explain everything." *Fidelity* suspects that this is "misplaced faith" "given the patent absurdity" of the story. But Father Dugandzic's response is not out of line when in the realm of the supernatural. Most of us have trouble with some of the stories in scripture but we do not allow our faith to stand or fall on them alone. Christ's first miracle of changing water to wine at a wedding seems to some a peculiar act for a messiah seeking spiritual conversion of those he has come to save — shouldn't he have done something more spiritual? Many find something unsettling about Christ ordering the devils out of a man into swine whereupon the swine go rushing into the sea. They wonder how the owner of the swine must have felt. No one would want Christ to come around their herds. Others find his telling the tax collectors to "go fish" for a shekel to be a very odd tale. Surely some Fathers of the Church or scripture scholars might offer suitable interpretations for these events but such interpretations are not immediately obvious.

Response of Local Bishop and the Franciscans

Fidelity puts great store in the opposition to Medjugorje by the local Bishop, who after some initial enthusiasm has become Medjugorje's most ardent opponent. Few can feel comfortable reading about the tensions between Bishop Zanic and the Franciscans. Neither "side" seems altogether without fault; certainly it is discomforting to hear messages that suggest that Mary sides with the Franciscans against the Bishop. But then, again, Christ regularly chided the scribes and the pharisees, the leaders of the Jewish Church, and He broke the Jewish laws regarding the Sabbath. Moreover, it is not impossible that bishops can be wrong. Certainly saints have often been at odds with church authorities. The magazine *Thirty Days* featured a most extraordinary article about the life of Padre Pio, not yet a saint but a man whose cause the present pope clearly seems to champion. The story of the official Church response to him is most illuminating. Padre Pio was suspended from exercising his priestly faculties among the faithful for eleven years. An archbishop is cited as having told Pius XI that Padre Pio's stigmata were due to iodine and nitric acid. He swore on his pastoral cross that he saw Padre Pio anoint himself with perfumes to simulate the odor of sanctity reported around him. In 1933 Padre Pio regained permission to carry out his priestly functions, but in 1960 an investigation was ordered because Padre Pio was charged with "immorality, fanaticism, administrative mismanagement" (*Thirty Days* (8 December, 1988, p.77). The report issued after the investigation *confirmed* the charges. Pope Paul VI again restored Padre Pio to his priestly functions. This incident is cited to show that even in modern times there can be a great deal of controversy surrounding alleged supernatural events. Some turn out to be false (this author thinks Bayside has been effectively discredited) but some may be true. Official opposition to an event is no certain guarantee of its inauthenticity.

Illicit Pilgrimages

What is one to make of the claim that the bishops of Yugoslavia have forbidden pilgrimages to Medjugorje? Does this mean that all those who travel there with groups that are guided by priests are acting disobediently? It seems not. The Archbishop of Split, Monsignor Franic, serves as the President of the Doctrinal Commission of the Yugoslav Episcopate. On September 16, 1987 he issued a circular stating some of the conclusions that followed from a meeting of the Croatian bishops. This was subsequent to the publication of a sermon given at Medjugorje by Bishop Zanic in which he denounced the apparitions. Much confusion arose from that sermon, and the Croatian bishops met to clarify some matters. One such matter was the question of pilgrimages. Bishop Franic wrote:

> I hold that the faithful can go freely on a pilgrimage to Medjugorje, individually, or in pilgrimages which are privately organized. That is to say, in pilgrimages not organized by the Church as would be for example, a pilgrimage organized by the priest, the bishop, a convent, or by other similar ecclesiastical entities.

He further states:

> *Priests can go on a pilgrimage to Medjugorje if they go there not as organizers of pilgrimages, but in the goal of assisting spiritually their own faithful, and with the firm intention of submitting themselves to the definitive judgment of the Church.*
> (From *Seven Years of Apparitions* by Father Rene Laurentin; published by the Riehle Foundation).

It would seem, then, that individuals are free to go on the many tours and pilgrimages offered by various groups.

There is a wealth of misinformation being reported about Medjugorje and the views of the local bishops, of the theologians at the Vatican, and of the Pope himself. Those who really wish to do their best to track down these matters might do well to consult the works of Father Rene Laurentin for he prints official documents in their entirety. We at least need to be very cautious when we hear "facts" about Medjugorje, especially when they are reported by those hostile to Medjugorje.

Fanatical Pilgrims

Part of *Fidelity*'s refutation of Medjugorje rests upon the fanaticism of those who are believers. In itself this is certainly a weak refutation for any movement, especially since any movement associated with the supernatural is bound to attract unbalanced individuals. Unbalanced individuals can be found in any Church of nearly any size. It does not seem right to discredit a religion —or event— because of its followers. Catholicism has crazy as well as brilliant and holy adherents. So, too, may Medjugorje.

Charismatic Movement

One of *Fidelity*'s concerns is the connection of Medjugorje with the Charismatic movement. The concerns that *Fidelity* raises are those that can be raised about the Charismatic movement in general — do Charismatics have an excessive interest in signs and wonders and in private communications from God? Yet the charismatic attraction to Medjugorje may also be interpreted as an important corrective to those tendencies. For the charismatics have also been criticized for a hesitancy to cultivate distinctively Catholic devotions and practices - especially devotion to Mary and the Eucharist. But Medjugorje is profoundly Catholic - the messages constantly advise praying the rosary and devotion to the Eucharist and going to confession monthly. Many charismatics have been moved to become more mainstream Catholics as the result of Medjugorje. The priests of Medjugorje seem to be most attentive to the needs of the pilgrims and of their overeagerness for signs and wonders. When I was there the sermons repeatedly stressed that the pilgrims ought not to be seeking supernatural occurrences, miracles or cures, that they ought not to chase after visionaries, or eagerly seek to hear the latest message. Rather, the sermons, both those I've heard and those I have read, stress that we have all the supernatural splendor we need in the Eucharist, that we need to seek conversion of heart and to bear our crosses patiently rather than seek relief from them. And they note that the messages are virtually the same day by day.

Indeed, in its two articles about Medjugorje, *Fidelity* spends almost no time on the messages of Medjugorje. Rather the messages are dismissed as "alternately dire and banal." Others find them hopeful and ringing with the truths Catholicism has always taught. That there is nothing new in the messages is for some a sign of their authenticity not their falsity. Mary seems day by day to be giving the visionaries and the community of Medjugorje the solace and guidance they need to meet the needs of the pilgrims who travel to them to learn how to turn their lives over to God.

Fruits of Medjugorje

Fidelity downplays the fruits of Medjugorje in several ways. It speaks of a kind of fanaticism that comes from Medjugorje and claims that this is a fruit that must be taken into account with all the good fruits. This is true, of course, but, as was argued above, so too is it true that genuine supernatural occurrences also tend to draw their share of fanatics. Few people in their spiritual journeys have not gone through some times of excessive zeal or even superstition. *Fidelity* conjectures that Medjugorje puts God "in a bind" for if He grants the prayers of pilgrims He may be encouraging attachment to a false event; if not, He may be discouraging prayer. *Fidelity* allows that God is more likely to take the risk of answering prayers. A Vatican theologian conjectures that much good may be coming from "the concentration of so much prayer and penance in one place." It certainly occurred to this author on her brief trip to Medjugorje that the effect of the place could as equally well be attributed to its suitability as a terrific retreat center as to its affiliation with extraordinary supernatural events. There are considerable physical mortifications and deprivations to be encountered in traveling and in staying at Medjugorje. All is spartan. While there, all one can do is buy rosaries and pray. There are no newspapers, TV's, movie houses or any other distractions. The place is beautiful - bucolic and restful. One spends a great deal of time either in the church or walking through the lovely countryside. A climb up the mountain with the stations of the cross takes two and a half hours, and one is rewarded with a beautiful vista of the surrounding area. It is hard to arrive at the top and not to experience profound gratitude for the glory of God's creation and the greatness of His mercy. The whole experience is extremely conducive to prayer and concentration on God. Moreover many have observed that sermons (many of them published) are equal in spiritual power to the best spiritual writings.

The Vatican theologian also offers "It is even possible to posit a theory that these good fruits are part of a diabolical tactic where the end-play would be the disillusionment of many thousands of sincere people who have built their faith on the alleged apparitions at Medjugorje." This, admittedly, could be the case. And it would be terribly sad if those who have been led to pray more fervently and constantly, who have begun to go to Mass and to worship in front of the blessed sacrament, and who have experienced great conversion in their lives, would be led to abandon these practices should Medjugorje be determined to be a hoax. But maybe God is using this phenomenon of Medjugorje for the good regardless of its authenticity. The Shroud of Turin seems not to be the genuine item it has long been thought to be by many of the faithful. But many had their faith strengthened by the shroud, and I know none who have had their faith shaken by the latest evaluation of the shroud. I know one young man, a graduate

229

student in philosophy at a top university, who was led to convert to Catholicism upon viewing a documentary about Medjugorje. He recently told me that if Medjugorje were determined to be false, it would not alter his conviction about the truth of Catholicism. Let us hope that others who adopt the program of prayer advised by Medjugorje will adopt this attitude as well.

Article Two

Article Two purports to offer a plausible explanation of what is really going on at Medjugorje. It seeks to answer the difficult question: *If Mary is not appearing to the visionaries, who is lying? What is going on?* The steps in the argument or conjecture are quite difficult to piece together since *Fidelity* mixes together fact, opinion, rumor, testimony from a disaffected former Franciscan priest, analysis from a distant psychologist, the drawing of parallels from such events as the Salem witch trials, and what must also be considered pure conjecture. It involves a theory that the young people started a joke that has been exploited by several priests, one who was desperate to succeed with his Charismatic prayer group and another desperate to find some escape from promises made to a nun he had impregnated. It is difficult to know what to do with the article since it is such a mixture of fact and speculation. One fears that speculation quickly assumes the status of fact.

Let us look closely at a few of the steps in the answer provided by *Fidelity* to the question of what is really going on at Medjugorje.

Joking Punkers

The first conjecture is that the young people who are claiming to have the visions are a group of alienated, disaffected youngsters who pretended to have apparitions in order to mock the piety of some of their more popular peers who belonged to a charismatic prayer group. How does *Fidelity* come to this conclusion? The conjecture begins with the citation of an unknown individual who, shortly after the apparitions began, asked why the "Gospa" (Our Lady) would be appearing to a "pankerica". The priest to whom this question was addressed did not know what a "pankerica" was. He was informed that it refers to "a girl who is habitually immoral. The people can't identify with them [the seers] because they dress in a fashion that is very liberal." *Fidelity* finds this remark "instructive" and from it builds a picture of the likely "position that the seers occupied in Medjugorje at the time of the apparitions." *Fidelity* "after some reflection" is able to determine what "pankerica" means although the three local priests did not know what it means. *Fidelity* determines that it is a Croatian version of "punker" and concludes that "the terms was probably appropriated by the typical small village mentality as meaning citified, trendy, and to some extent at odds with traditional village culture." *Fidelity* may be correct about this "etymology" but *Fidelity* still is clearly conjecturing. Nonetheless the next sentence begins with "This *fact* is significant..." (my emphasis).

This "fact" leads *Fidelity* "to posit a theory about how the apparitions got started." *Fidelity* calls Medjugorje a "joke that got out of hand." Upon the basis of the above reference by an unknown woman to one of the seers as a "pankerica", *Fidelity* conjectures that the seers "were not part of what one would call the young people's 'in crowd' in the parish. Those people were most likely in Father Zovko's prayer group. Unlike those pious young people, the seers seem to have been viewed with some suspicion..." *Fidelity* continues to build its case: "The girls — specifically the two instigators, Mirjana and Ivanka — knew the type of thing that Zovko was doing in his young people's prayer group. Since they were not part of it, and perhaps sensing and resenting the manipulative elements involved in it, they decided to parody it. Mirjana had just read a book on Lourdes, so the vocabulary of apparitions was fresh in her mind. It could have been the revenge of outsiders in the local young people's charismatic prayer group." (II, 30) This is the joke, then, that got out of hand. This is the joke that they have managed to sustain for seven years. This is the joke that has led them to fake seeing apparitions for seven years. This is the joke that has led them and the whole community of Medjugorje and thousands of pilgrims to practice arduous prayer and fasting. If these young people were not alienated and envious, if there was no such joke, this crucial first hypothesis of the theory evaporates. And since it is the cornerstone of the whole theory, the whole theory would evaporate as well.

An Opportunistic Priest

The parish priest, Father Zovko, is portrayed by *Fidelity* as being a somewhat desperate charismatic priest who needed some means to fortify the Franciscans in the battle against the local bishop and some means of vivifying a parish somewhat unresponsive to his charismatic direction. *Fidelity* portrays the priest as having taken charge of the whole phenomenon by moving the children and the apparitions into the church. *Fidelity* reports upon a sermon conducted, in *Fidelity*'s assessment, as a Pentecostal revival. Father Zovko asks the congregation a series of questions:

So you want to accept with love the divine grace and with joy fast on bread and water for three days as testimony to your conversion and to turn back the power of the demon?

"Yes, we do."
"Will you pray the rosary every day in your homes?"
"Yes, we will."
"Will you have your families read the Bible every day?"
"Yes, we will."

Fidelity observes that "It's the type of thing that has happened before." And what comes to *Fidelity*'s mind is the Salem witch trials. (I rather thought the above exchange sounded like the baptismal rite where the congregation is asked to renounce Satan and all his works). We are reminded that in Salem several adolescent girls started acting strangely and a doctor diagnosed them as subject to demonic possession. *Fidelity* tells us that the girls "could either admit that they had been doing voodoo with Tituba, which would almost certainly warrant severe punishment for them and almost certainly death for Tituba, or they could start naming other people as witches. Human nature being what it is, they chose the latter course, and 20 innocent human beings — mostly that society's marginated — were put to death." After explaining how the doctors and the authorities of society all were drawn into this hoax, *Fidelity* concludes: "By now the parallels between Medjugorje and Salem should be apparent. Adolescent girls started both phenomena, but the crucial turning point came when the clergy, influenced by the general atmosphere and the pressure of the crowds — which they in effect helped create — validated the girls' experience as genuine (p.32)." This seems to be a case of overdrawing parallels. After all, there are real similarities between a crowd at a football game and a crowd at a Ku Klux Klan rally, but the differences are more significant than the similarities. Father Zovko asks for more fasting, more saying of the rosary, and more reading of the Bible, whereas the Salem witch trials led to the death of twenty innocent individuals. The differences are more significant than the similarities.

A Pregnant Nun

Fidelity focuses closely on the story of a Father Vlasic who, in 1976, allegedly fathered a child by a Franciscan nun. After the apparitions began in 1981, Father Vlasic became spiritual director for the visionaries. In 1984 letters were written to the Bishop that accused Father Vlasic of fathering the child. *Fidelity* also refers to letters written between the two that are interpreted as indicating an intimate relationship between them. The letters were evidently "discovered" by an elderly man for whom the woman had been a housekeeper. (One suspects she had not given him the letters; what is the propriety of his taking them and of *Fidelity* publishing them? *Fidelity* is not shy about calling people liars; should it be so shy about saying that these letters were probably stolen?) *Fidelity* believes that this pregnancy discredits the visionaries because it understands Vlasic to be manipulating the whole event of Medjugorje to put himself beyond the reach of the local bishop and to get out of the responsibilities of taking care of his child. The same Father Vlasic is now in the process of starting a new religious order with a woman who claims to have experienced a miraculous cure at Medjugorje. *Fidelity*, having decided that there is no doubt that Father Vlasic was responsible for the pregnancy, has no hesitation in understanding Father Vlasic to be romantically involved with his co-foundress.

Determining the truth of the matter is not possible given the evidence we now have. Again, a central issue is the integrity of Father Vlasic and the woman of the child. They both deny that Vlasic is the father. Are both lying? Again, readers of *Fidelity* have no independent access to these individuals, no way of assessing their integrity. But they may wish to read some of the sermons Vlasic has given, published by the Riehle Foundation. They, as nearly all of the sermons published from Medjugorje, are truly moving and inspiring. Father Vlasic at least knows enough about genuine spirituality to imitate it well, if that is what he is doing. Finally, let us note that Father Laurentin, far from repudiating his support of Father Vlasic (as suggested by *Fidelity*), has repeated his defense. (He has also expressed disdain for the interviewing methods of *Fidelity*; see pp. 121-133 of *Seven Years of Apparitions* published by the Riehle Foundation.)

A Priest and a Psychologist

Much of article two involves conversations of *Fidelity* with the man who *Fidelity* believes was falsely accused of fathering the child. This man was a Franciscan priest in Croatia who has moved to the United States where he has married and been laicized. Another key witness is a psychologist from California who interprets at a very long distance some of the events of Medjugorje and the motives of the individuals involved. For instance, on the basis of the testimony of the disaffected priest about prayer groups he walked out on in Medjugorje, the psychologist is able to determine that these prayer groups utilized suspect "encounter group" techniques. The psychologist is also able to determine, on the basis of evidence provided by *Fidelity*, that Father Vlasic and the woman with whom he intends to found a new order are involved in a romantic relationship. Again, *Fidelity* could be right about all these conjectures, but one senses that these "witnesses" are led in their testimony in much the same way that *Fidelity* accuses the priests of leading the visionaries at Medjugorje. The evidence is presented in such a way that it is difficult not to suspect that the interviewer has predetermined what he wants his "experts" to testify.

I THANK YOU THAT YOU WILL NOT BETRAY MY PRESENCE HERE.

Marija lied?

In its November issue, *Fidelity* published a statement issued by Marija acknowledging that she had made statements "that did not correspond with the truth." She is referring to a signed declaration that indicated that Mary had approved the community planned by Father Vlasic and Agnes Heupel. If this author may allow herself some of the speculation freely practiced by *Fidelity*, a rather benign interpretation of what has happened seems quite plausible. It is not unlikely that Marija was affected by Father Vlasic in his enthusiasm for his community. She and he seemed to have understood a message from Mary that "I am blessing the free decision of every one of you..." to constitute a blessing on the new community. Father Vlasic evidently had Marija sign a statement to this effect. Now she says that her statement did not "correspond to the truth", meaning, it seems, that she had not explicitly asked Mary about the group and went beyond proper bounds in interpreting the message to be an endorsement of the community. Many take this statement to be an admission that the visionaries have been lying. This interpretation does not seem warranted to me. Rather, her careful statement and determination to set the record straight seems inconsistent with someone who had been lying all along. What would one more lie be to someone who has told hundreds? Her concern to make certain that the truth is told, her willingness to issue a sworn statement and to incur the embarrassment that this must cost her seem more to be representative actions of an honest person than of a dishonest one.

Suspicion

The events of Medjugorje tend to remind *Fidelity* of the Salem witch trials. The *Fidelity* articles tend to remind this author of the Alfred Hitchcock movie, *Suspicion*. In that movie, Cary Grant plays a charming society gentleman who marries a rich and beautiful, if spinsterish, Joan Fontaine. Months after they marry, Joan discovers that Cary is penniless and begins to suspect that he married her for her money. His protestations to the contrary and his loving ways convince her to cast aside that thought. Yet when Cary begins betting at the race track contrary to his promises and ends up losing a job because he "borrowed" money from the till to pay his gambling debts, her suspicions are again aroused. One of Cary's friends with whom he shared a business venture dies in dubious circumstances, and Joan begins to fear for her own life. Especially when she learns that Cary has been fiddling with her life insurance and when she hears him discussing ways to murder and get away with it with a writer of mystery novels. She works herself into a complete state of anxiety about Cary's motives, although it is clear that a part of her still loves him and believes in him. The reader of *Fidelity* who tends to credit the story of Medjugorje is liable to have a response similar to that of the viewer of *Suspicion*: Is the lovable Cary guilty or not? Is Medjugorje a fake or not? The movie leaves the question unanswered until the end. There, as Cary is driving a car precariously fast near a very high cliff, we see Joan's door swing open and Cary reach for her. It is not immediately clear whether he is pushing her or trying to hold her in the car. When the car stops it becomes clear that he was trying to save her. He finally gets the opportunity to explain that his past peculiar behavior was designed to help him undo the wrong that he had done. He had become so despondent and so convinced that Joan no longer cared for him that he had been inquiring about how to commit murder and get away with it because he was thinking of killing himself. Joan had simply and seriously misinterpreted his behavior.

What is to the point here is that Joan had reason to be suspicious of Cary. His behavior, conversations, and motives all seemed to point to wrong-doing. But his loving ways and her deeper intuitions seemed to point at his innocence. Ultimately, plausible as her interpretations were, they were wrong. All she had were suspicions - some built on facts and some built on conjecture. Yes, Cary did some dubious things but fundamentally he was sound and that was all that mattered in the end. *Fidelity* reports on Medjugorje in such a way that it is difficult not to have one's suspicions aroused at least to some extent. But in the end, if it is a fact that Mary is appearing to the young people, that is the fact that must ultimately determine our response to Medjugorje.

May our Blessed Mother assist us in finding true answers to the authenticity of Medjugorje, and whatever the outcome may be, may none of us harm ourselves or others in our efforts to discover and defend the truth.

(ii) Dr. Adrian J Reimers

Adrian Reimers holds a Ph.D in Philosophy specializing in the thought of St. Thomas Aquinas and Pope John Paul II. Although he had previously published several articles in Fidelity the following letter from him and his wife to the editor was rejected. We print it here in full.

Gisingen-Feldkirch
Austria

Dear Editor,
The first part of your opinion piece, "Medjugorje: The Untold Story" is seriously flawed. Without proposing to address the ultimate question of the validity of the apparitions, we wish here to object to the shortcomings of the article itself. We find it flawed in three general ways. First, it is a slanted and

poorly reasoned piece of journalism. Second, the underlying theological basis is not sound. Third, certain aspects of it constitute a serious offense against charity.

Concerning the quality of the journalism: This is a textbook example of slanted writing. It is fraught with loaded terms - innuendo, guilt by association, and, especially, ridicule - techniques which have but a limited place (if, indeed, any at all) in a publication "as Catholic as the Pope." Thus, for loaded terms, one reads Ivan described as a "modern day oracle" (p.18) and Marijana as "the oracle of the Croatian Delphi" (p.22). No evidence is given that anyone other than the author regards these seers as "oracles." Certainly the pilgrims whose taciturnity he complains about (pp. 18, 21) did not. (One always has questions for an oracle: "Will my husband stop drinking?" "Will I find a husband/wife?") "Oracle" is the author's idea — a loaded term, not a description of what is.

We find innuendo, serious charges or problems, unsupported by the evidence. "The seers at Medjugorje have decided to become part of the tourist industry" (p. 19). A serious charge, but unsupported. On whose payroll are they? The innuendo is that they prophesy for profit, but proof of this charge is not there. We read of "coaching" (p. 20) by the priests and of "the theologian giving an air of learned plausibility" to the seers' statements (p. 23). Indeed, the article ends on a note of innuendo, hinting darkly at sexual improprieties (p. 41).

There is guilt by association. We read of the "Notre Dame types" (p. 39). (A curious comparison, by the way. Which "Notre Dame types" are meant? McInerny or Freddoso of the philosophy department are strong Catholics, faithful to the Church. And what is really the connection to the high school? The most serious problem in its theology department is related more to Berkeley than Notre Dame). Most important is the linking of Medjugorje to Bayside (pp. 30, 40). We will return to this later; here we remark on the guilt by association.

And there is ridicule, a technique which, in fact, Dr. Jones' articles regularly employ. The seer Vicka takes much of the brunt of this. Her vision of heaven is ridiculed (p. 20), as is her "track record on public statements" (p. 21), when, in fact, no such "track record" has been cited. We read elsewhere of the "frenzied seeking after signs and wonders" (p. 31), and we see the normal behavior of visitors to Medjugorje ironically mocked (pp. 18, 21). Ridicule, innuendo and tabloid humor — the verbal tricks described above (and we could easily multiply examples from the article) — are too often substitutes for sound reasoning. And this article, in particular, needs such substitutes, for its thinking is sloppy.

A logic teacher could use this article as a rich source of examples of fallacy and faulty inference: affirming the consequent, contradicting the evidence, proving too much, invalid induction, and petitio principii. Again, we give some examples.

The seer Vicka does not know what Marian mystery is celebrated at the end of March. Anyone ignorant of that mystery would be ignorant of the feast. Therefore, Vicka does not know what the Annunciation is. This is "affirming the consequent." In fact, all that one can conclude from the interview quoted on page 20 is that Vicka does not know the date of that feast. Indeed, her statement, "Really, I thought of that, but I wasn't sure," suggests a different inference than that drawn by Dr. Jones.

Ignoring the evidence: The article tries to characterize the charismatic renewal movement as "in crisis," because of a decline in signs and wonders. There it quotes A. Reimer's article from "New Covnenant" (sic; yes, even *Fidelity* makes mistakes) and the book by Frs. Kosicki and Farrell to illustrate how the transition to a Marian variation of the "charismatic hunger for signs and wonders" (p. 34) came about, rather than an authentic deepening of faith. However, both of the sources cited do themselves refer to a faith that embraces suffering and the cross, which surpasses such a "hunger." This is "ignoring the evidence" on Dr. Jones's part.

Some arguments prove too much. "When the Church finds herself paralyzed, the faithful turn to those who will speak with the authority they once sought from the Church" (p. 31). But this can be said about *Fidelity*, too; indeed, it has been. (Conservative Catholics want a publication to reassure them that they are right, etc., etc.). The "troubled people in confused times" argument can discredit anything.

Indeed, that argument against the validity of the Medjugorje apparitions which is based on the critique of signs and wonders can be applied to other phenomena, such as the alleged miracles of Padre Pio and the apparitions at Fatima and Lourdes. The sign that Jesus refused the Pharisees was given at Fatima.

There is invalid induction. Because there are resemblances between two things, namely, Medjugorje and Bayside, they are the same kind of thing (i. e., fraudulent Marian apparitions). This is flawed! The resemblance alone is not enough; one can find resemblances between the Bayside phenomenon and the New York Yankees (or *Fidelity* magazine). The likeness must be an essential. If a comparison is to be made with Bayside, there must be a parallel figure to Mrs. Lueken to run it, rather than the self-effacing seers and the convinced theologians described in the article. (We note that Dr. Jones acknowledges that these priests really believe the apparitions to be true.) (cf. p. 22) Nor does one see the strident self-assertiveness associated with Bayside. If Dr. Jones wants to equate the two phenomena, then he must bring much more evidence to bear relating to the essence of each.

The overall structure of this first half of the article is a kind of petitio principii, begging the question. The premise, or question, that is begged is this:

The essential reality of the phenomena associated with Medjugorje is a hunger for or fascination with signs and wonders. This is asserted on the first page: "The thirst for signs and wonders is almost palpable," and it runs through the article as its principal connecting theme. In virtue of this premise, the apparitions are discredited, their demonic origin ascribed and the danger that they constitute to the faith and the Church established. Thus, a principal task of the article must be to establish the truth of this premise. But this is not done. To be sure, some anecdotes are provided, such as the story of "Sandy" (pp. 27 ff.), but anecdotal evidence is insufficient. It must be shown that this hunger is the governing factor, overriding any other factors, such as a hunger for holiness, personal conversion, deepening of faith, etc. These factors are not considered. The alleged hunger for signs and wonders is presupposed and, in fact, provides the interpretative framework of the evidence that is cited.

The journalism is poor — loaded terms and sloppy arguments. One looks in vain for a serious consideration of things like the message of Medjugorje, as it is publicized. They are not secret; we receive them quarterly from Vienna; they are translated into perfect German and can be easily understood. Perhaps the second part of the article will consider these. The phenomena at Medjugorje present serious issues for our consideration. The cause of the truth is not well served by the kind of loose treatment offered in the first part of the *Fidelity* article.

The theological basis of the article is not sound. A part of St. John of the Cross's teaching on prayer from *The Ascent of Mount Carmel* is presented as the 'wisdom of the Church' (p. 40). To be sure, St. John has something important to teach the entire Church, even considering that his writing was intended for and is primarily applicable to Carmelites and other contemplatives. However, it is by no means the totality of the Church's teaching on the place of miracles in its life. Jesus himself speaks of the signs that "will accompany those who believe" (Mk. 16:16). "God also bore witness by signs and wonders" (Heb. 2:4). A cursory look at the Gospels and Acts should suffice to show that signs and wonders must have an important role in the economy of salvation. St. Thomas Aquinas, certainly no frenzied fanatic hungering for signs and wonders, writes, "in order to confirm those truths and exceed natural knowledge (the Divine Wisdom) gives visible manifestation to works that surpass the ability of nature" (*S. Contra Gentiles* I 6, 1). Later, after showing that the very existence of the Church itself is such a sign, he continues: "Yet it is also a fact that, even in our own time, God does not cease to work miracles through His saints for the confirmation of the faith" (Ibid. 6, 3).

Dr. Jones's mistake lies in regarding any visible signs or experience supporting faith as a counter to or a substitute for faith (cf. p. 39). This is an inadequate view. The proper object of faith is the Triune God and, after that, what

He reveals. Pentecost need not be an object of faith; the whole point of Pentecost was that it could be experienced. It was a vehicle. Similarly, visions are compatible with faith. The only vision that replaces faith is the Beatific Vision, which no one we know claims to enjoy in this life. The theological distinctions employed by Dr. Jones are too simplistic.

Finally, we turn to the offense against charity which the article constitutes. Here we raise the issues of slander and betrayal of trust. Here we speak of moral fault. As noted above, Dr. Jones takes Vicka, one of the seers, strongly to task for her alleged ignorance of the mystery of the Annunciation. We have already indicated that this conclusion of his is not warranted by the evidence he cites. But more is involved here than logic. Dr. Jones's repeated references to this in the context of Vicka's prayer of the Rosary have the (presumably intended) effect of casting aspersions on her sincerity and the authenticity of her faith. Unless Dr. Jones is prepared to prove with additional evidence that Vicka is ignorant of her faith and insincere, then he has wronged her by his statements.

Here in Austria — and in parts of Yugoslavia as well — one never says the German word for Annunciation while praying the Rosary. Rather, we recite what the mystery means - e.g. "Jesus, whom you conceived by the Holy Spirit". A pious villager here could easily meditate daily on that mystery without ever connecting the reality with its name.

In this connection, we might also mention the alleged ludicrousness of Ivan's remarks on prayer, in particular his claim to need two and a half hours to pray the entire Rosary. In our own village parish, it takes one and a half hours, and we kneel through it all (save the decade on the Resurrection). The piety of simple villagers is not to be sneered at.

Dr. Jones speaks of the former theology teacher at St. Joseph High School, who doubles as a "front man for the Sandinistas." Unless he is prepared to show that this teacher actually represents the government of Nicaragua while using his teaching position to hide this, then this is false. Sympathy and even imprudent advocacy of the Sandinista cause do not themselves make one a "front man." Using these criteria, is it fair to call Fidelity a "front" for the schismatic Pius X Fraternity?

Dr. Jones charges unnamed charismatics with a "substitution of experience for faith." One of them says in his book "We have seen the Lord", and this taken in the most literal — and unfavorable — sense. To represent this author as heterodox or a crude enthusiast in this is unfair.

Last, we come to the grievous offense against Jones' former vice-president, who has been a friend of ours for fifteen years and who has regarded Dr. Jones as his friend for about three. (At least, it was three years ago that he convinced me — AJR — that I ought not prejudge Dr. Jones on the basis of others' remarks against *Fidelity*.) Using the information he obtained under the mantle of friendship, Dr. Jones betrays a fundamental trust that ought to exist between friends, between a host and the guest in his home. Dr. Jones breaks this trust, and thus readers of *Fidelity* are informed about a host of confidential facts and communications. Does the editor of *Fidelity*, a "Catholic" publication, consider this fair or justified? "Even my friend, who had my trust and partook of my bread, has raised his heel against me" (Ps. 41:10).

Even with the confidential information he enjoys and abuses, Dr. Jones's account is often inaccurate, misleading or false. The man's wife travelled abroad against his advice and lost a baby. But her two doctors told her to feel free to go. (By the way, I found my own treatment in an Austrian hospital quite satisfactory. Europe has a fairly advanced civilization.) The former friend refused Dr. Jones's help with his peace and justice class; yes, but he did turn to his friend studying philosophy under an expert in Marxism and liberation theology. His "sin" is not of imprudence, but of turning to specialists rather than to Dr. Jones for advice.

Much more serious than these inaccuracies are the statements about the man's character. We read that "Enthusiasm remained a constant factor in his life" (p. 34), and that he wanted an "apocalyptic jolt" (p. 35). Dr. Jones describes an "obsession with Medjugorje" and a "trajectory of ever-increasing fanaticism." (He is described as a classic enthusiast, preoccupied with signs and wonders.) But this is a calumny. When this man returned from his first trip to Medjugorje, the "miracle" that most moved him was his own conversion to deeper holiness. Dr. Jones does not mention that he has a very sober, theologically sound priest for a spiritual director. Nor does he mention that in the classroom, he always warned the students that, if what he said in the classroom contradicts the parents, they must obey their parents.

Is such a man an enthusiast? Well, he would do anything for God, even risk his job. (The editor of *Fidelity* should respect this; it happened to him.) What is he really like? For our family, a visit with this man's family was always a treat, a time of peace and joyful relaxation. God's love surrounds them. Perhaps that is why so many of his former students keep in touch, come by to talk over problems, show off their new families and — especially — to pray. Prayer is a part of their family life, and they share it with others. Is this extreme? Well, does Dr. Jones presume to dismiss other "enthusiasts" like Bruder Klaus von Flue, (the Patron of Switzerland)? What an expose´ one could do on his imprudence! Or on Maximilian Kolbe's fanatic devotion to the Immaculata, or Anna Maria Taigi's inappropriate (for her vocation) spirituality.

But the journalist must call a spade a spade. Give people straight facts and let 'em decide. S.I. Hayakawa, the noted linguist, comments: Calling "a spade a spade is to provide our minds with a greased runway down which we may slide back into old and discredited patterns of evaluation and behavior." Like reducing a man to a two-dimensional fanatic. St. John of the Cross has a better way:

"Never listen to the weaknesses of others, and if anyone complains to thee of another, thou mayest tell him humbly to say naught of it to thee" (*Spiritual Maxims* II, 61, 7). It is good to listen to the wisdom of the Church.

So what was the point of this expose? Dr. Jones writes: "(The man's) life and subsequent involvement in Medjugorje reads like an illustrated history of the confusion that has reigned in the the (sic: again!) Church for the past 20 years." Is there some evil which must be exposed? Is he defying the Magisterium, promoting some heresy? The article alleges no such thing; there is none to be alleged. No, the whole point of the discussion is to present a graphic instance of a confused, fanatical follower of Medjugorje. This is character assassination for the sake of character assassination. The only reason for exposing (and misrepresenting) the details of a family's private life, for betraying their confidence, is to hold them up to *Fidelity's* readership as an example — a grim version of "Stop crossing your eyes, or you'll wind up looking like Aunt Bertha."

A magazine on family issues that is "As Catholic as the Pope?" No, dear editor, it is not. The ethics of this article are beneath those of the supermarket tabloids. It is disappointing to see an important issue like Medjugorje treated so sloppily or to see a conservative Catholic publication arguing from such a thin theological basis. But the unwarranted attacks on the character, indeed, on the state of soul of an innocent man, are a grave transgression against charity. No matter what the Church may decide concerning the authenticity of the apparitions at Medjugorje, innocent people are defamed to your readers. On this basis, we find the article to be cruel, vicious and wicked.

A book or a magazine article or a news story must tell the truth. E. Michael Jones, in the second part of his article in *Fidelity*, "Medjugorje: The Untold Story" (chapters 4 and 5 of his book by the same name), tells what he believes to be the truth. He believes that the Blessed Mother is not appearing to the six young people in the village of Medjugorje. He also believes that the truth behind the events there has to do with the pranks of local punkers, mass hysteria among the peasantry and serious moral turpitude among the Franciscan priests. E. Michael Jones thinks that he knows the truth and uses his magazine to tell it.

It is never enough for a journalist simply to say what he thinks is true. He has two other responsibilities besides. Before he may publish his belief, he must have good evidence for it, and he must present that evidence. Second, if what he publishes accuses a person of some serious wrong or failing, he must have some good reason for revealing that evil. So, for example, it is acceptable for a journalist to reveal that a candidate for public office is a heavy drinker or a chronic liar (if that is really true), but he may not reveal such things about a private citizen. If he does, he can be sued.

For the Catholic journalist, these requirements are even more stringent. He must be sure of the truth, of course. He has to check his sources carefully and evaluate them charitably. Even more important is that whatever he writes must serve to build up faith, hope and love. This does not mean that negative things may not appear in the Catholic press. There are evils that we need to know about. However, even these things must be placed within the context of hope that the gospel has given us.

The second part of E. Michael Jones's article violates both these principles. He says serious things that he cannot really prove, and he seriously violates the rule of charity. Of course, if the apparitions are a hoax, then Jones does indeed have a responsibility to let the Church know. However, his article consists mainly in innuendo, speculation and unfounded assumption, on the basis of which Jones draws damning conclusions. Let us look at this in detail.

EXPLAINING THE APPARITIONS

If there are no apparitions, then we must look for another explanation of what is going on. Jones' explanation is complicated in its details, but simple in its basic theme: the apparitions are a joke that got out of hand. The visionaries decided to play a prank, to pretend that they had seen the Blessed Virgin, but the villagers responded so vehemently that the children had no way to call off the joke. By itself, this theory is rather far-fetched, so Jones offers a complicated theory of psychological manipulation and mass hysteria to explain how something so far-fetched could come to be. It is worth our while to trace this out.

The explanation depends on two analogies or comparisons which Dr. Jones draws. (It is worth noting here that Dr. Jones holds a doctoral degree in English and not in theology, psychology or sociology. He is not trained to be an expert in any of these fields.)

The first comparison is between the charismatic prayer group at St. James Parish and the encounter movement in Big Sur, California, during the 1960's. Indeed, Jones speaks of the "Californification of Croatia." He explains that — to get his parishioners more excited — the Franciscan pastor at St. James in June of 1981 was using emotionally manipulative and destructive techniques of the Esalen Institute in Big Sur. In particular, the pastor is to have used a "milling around" exercise, by which the normal barriers of reserve between prayer group members was broken down, and they became susceptible to any suggestion which he — the pastor — might offer them.

It is important here to look at Jones's evidence. His source of this information is a former priest who had attended one of these meetings at which the priest leading it did call for participants to get up, mill around and look into each other's eyes. Such an activity may be imprudent or inappropriate for a prayer meeting. However, to support his serious accusation of manipulation, Jones needs to show that this practice was used regularly and that it was part of a pattern of abuse and manipulation. He does not do this. On the basis of one witness, who was present at one (or perhaps two) events, Jones publishes as true his belief that the pastor had adopted the questionable practices of a self-centered, licentious American movement to break down moral inhibitions. This is simply not enough evidence for so serious a charge.

Throughout both parts of his article, Jones characterizes the charismatic renewal in terms of enthusiasm and a hankering for signs and wonders. To be sure, there have been excesses within the movement, and in many places individual or groups have fallen into emotionalistic excess. However, it is also true that many (or indeed most) charismatic groups have been sources of conversion, evangelization, enlivened prayer and renewed faith for many Catholics. This is why Popes Paul VI and John Paul II, along with many bishops, have encouraged the movement and repeatedly offered it direction. Therefore, it is not legitimate to conclude that the presence of a charismatic group is itself proof of religious excess, as Dr. Jones seems to believe. It can also be a sign of rebirth of spiritual vitality.

From his "Californification of Croatia," Jones goes on to characterize the six visionaries. One of the most important facts about them is that they did not belong to the charismatic prayer group. In fact, they were not particularly active in the parish at all, except for normal church-going. (On this point Jones seems to be confused. At first, he hints broadly that the seers — as he calls them — were part of the group, but then he admits that they were not.) Here Jones falls into one of the most blatantly sloppy examples of thinking in his entire article. He argues that the six visionaries, and especially Mirjana, had a reputation as punkers among the local populace. He quotes a villager, who refers to Mirjana as a pankerica. Jones, who speaks no Croatian, could not find a definition of this word. Therefore, he feels entitled to offer his own definition, based on his own etymology, that a pankerica is a punker. This is patently irresponsible. Jones speaks German, a fact that he often alludes to in his article, and he would surely laugh at anyone who would say that Bube means "fool," because it sounds like "boob." (The real meaning is "young boy.") Yet this is precisely what he does with a Croatian word that he does not know.

This language play is silly, especially coming from a scholar and former college professor. Its implications are worse, however, for on the basis of an unnamed villager's casual remark and a definition of his own invention for a word in a language he does not understand, Dr. Jones slurs the reputation of a young woman. If we also consider the coloring of several allusions to drug taking (though without direct accusation), we see that Dr. Jones has deftly painted this young woman in a way that can only be called slanderous. No matter what Mirjana may have done in her life, no matter how good she may have been, the readers of Fidelity will know her first as a punker, a woman of questionable moral character.

Having described the parish as psychologically primed and the visionaries as punkers, Dr. Jones then characterizes the visions themselves as a joke that got out of hand. To attract attention and have some fun, the six young people (who, by the way, did not belong to the same circle) plotted to fake a Marian apparition, and — unexpectedly — the entire town responded enthusiastically. To account for this improbable turn of events, Jones draws the second of his important analogies. He compares the events in Medjugorje with those in Salem, Massachusetts, during the notorious witch-burnings. (We might remark in passing that Jones repeatedly draws his analogies with events in American history — Salem, Big Sur, Bayside — without questioning how much life in 17th or 20th century America is like contemporary Yugoslavia.) His thesis is that, just as a group of young girls in Salem told lies and set off the witch hunts, so in Medjugorje the young girls told some lies and set off a wave of devotion to and excitement about the apparitions of Mary.

We should comment briefly that here Jones falls into blatant and crude sexism. Where the comparison with Salem is drawn, he repeatedly mentions only the girls; the two male visionaries are virtually ignored. It is also important to recognize the coloring that this comparison gives to the article. Any two events will have some feature in common. Hitler's S.S. and the Boy Scouts both had uniforms and marching, but that does not make them alike. In fact, if an author should start to compare these two, we would expect him to show that the Boy Scouts are evil, like the Nazis. This use of comparison between one thing (or person) and some other, notoriously wicked thing (or person) is a common, if reprehensible, trick of smear journalism.

In fact, the comparison between 17th century Salem and Medjugorje does not hold (except in the most superficial ways). The most obvious, and critical, difference is that the girls in Salem set off a wave of evil events. They deliberately took advantage of rivalries and prejudices in their town in order to get them-selves off the hook. The fruit of their deed, together with the poisoned atmo-sphere in the town and a popular religion that was theologically unsound, was a series of judicial murders of innocent people. In Medjugorje, however, the six young people attacked no one and promoted no moral evil in the town. Whether they were lying (as Jones believes) or not, their acts promoted and resulted in a growth in piety, conversion, attendance at Mass and the Sacraments and moral improvement — in short, the good fruits which even Jones does not deny. The comparison is simply too far-fetched. Dr. Jones is pulling it out of his hat.

On the pages of his magazine, Dr. Jones has ridiculed the scientific investi-gations that have been conducted by qualified scientists and medical doctors. He himself, however, has attempted to explain the phenomena in Medjugorje by means of pop psychology and oversimplified historical interpretation. Even if he is right in his belief that the Blessed Virgin is not appearing in Medjugorje, his explanations of what is happening are too superficial and too poorly grounded to deserve serious consideration.

THE ACCUSATION OF IMMORALITY

Far and away the most grievous offense which this article constitutes is its unfounded and unproven accusation that Fr. Tomislav Vlasic is the father of an illegitimate child. From the point in the article where the subject is introduced until its end, Jones does not consider the possibility that Vlasic may be innocent. His character is presented as hypocritical, manipulative and sexually obsessed. This accusation, that Vlasic fathered a child of a nun, has been made before and refuted. Indeed, the late Hans Urs von Balthasar publicly rebuked the bishop of Mostar for repeating precisely this accusation. But Jones claims to present new and conclusive proof of Fr. Vlasic's guilt. Let us look at the case he makes.

To establish the priest's guilt, Jones cites the following facts:

- In 1976, Fr. Vlasic and two other priests lived in a kind of coed monastery with Manda, the mother of the child, and another nun. During that time, Manda became pregnant and delivered a baby boy in early 1977.
- In November, 1984, Bishop Zanic of Mostar received a letter, purportedly naming Fr. Vlasic as the child's father.
- In late 1976 and thereafter, Fr. Vlasic wrote letters to Manda in which he encouraged her not to reveal the name of the child's father.
- In one of her letters, Manda writes, "Don't worry, Tomo, I won't reveal your identity to anyone...at least for now." Elsewhere she tells Vlasic that she loves him and looks upon him as a protector.
- The other likely "suspect," a laicized and subsequently married priest, now living in California, denies being the father.

It is this last point which constitutes Jones's discovery, his new evidence and the so-called proof of Fr. Vlasic's guilt. It is important here to recognize the items listed above are the only points of hard evidence which Jones is able to bring against Vlasic. Everything else is innuendo or part of a psychological profile of Vlasic, which Jones has invented. (The reader does well to note how heavily Jones relies, throughout this article, on such profiles.) Certainly the evidence could support the assumption that Fr. Vlasic was the father. However, they can be explained just as well if Fr. Vlasic was nothing more than a close friend, a counselor, or confidant. The letters do not prove that the priest is guilty. Jones implicitly recognizes this, and therefore his new evidence becomes all important. What is this "new evidence?"

At the time the child was conceived, there were three priests living in the house with the nuns. One of them has subsequently left the Franciscans, entered the lay state and gotten married. He now lives with his family in California. Fr. Laurentin indicates in the French edition of his book, *La Prolongation des Apparitions de Medjugorje*, that this man may be the father. Dr. Jones's reasoning is as follows:

1. The real father is most likely one of the priests living in the monastery at the time.
2. Of these, only Fr. Vlasic and Marjan Pehar, the ex-priest living in California, have been named by anyone as father. Therefore, one of them must be the father.
3. If either of these men can be eliminated, then the other one must be the father.

Jones then sees his task as to prove, by process of elimination, that Vlasic is guilty. He explains that Pehar, the other "suspect," has refused to answer Bishop Zanic's letters to him concerning the matter, and therefore it could not be resolved. Then, in the summer of 1988, Jones himself called Pehar. He writes, "the logjam broke, however, in the summer of 1988 when *Fidelity* reached Pehar, and Pehar categorically denied that he was the father of the child." Now what we have here in fact is a case of one man's word against another's. What Jones finds, however, is conclusive proof against Vlasic. If both men deny it, how does Jones justify taking the word of one rather than that of another? Is it reasonable that the father — whoever he may be — would candidly admit to the press that he is the father, especially when he will not admit it to anyone else? Does Jones really believe that Pehar could have given him any other answer than he did, even if he were guilty? ("Yes, I am the father, but please don't tell my wife.")

E. Michael Jones has, in fact, proved absolutely nothing. It is hard to believe that so intelligent a man as Dr. Jones could be so naive as to believe that the true father in a paternity dispute would voluntarily admit it to the press. Furthermore, Manda, the mother, vigorously denies that Vlasic is the father.

It is very hard to read Dr. Jones's analysis without concluding that he is simply out to get Vlasic and his defenders. The reader will readily notice that, although Jones regularly impugns the motives of Fr. Vlasic, Fr. Laurentin, the visionaries and others who accept the apparitions as authentic and questions their truthfulness, he accepts uncritically and respectfully the testimony of Pehar and Bishop Zanic. Indeed, he is outraged that Fr. Laurentin criticizes the bishop. The matter of this illegitimate birth has been discussed in great detail in other, well-known sources (in particular, Fr. O'Carroll's book). Jones nowhere uses or refers to or addresses the facts presented in these sources. Jones says of his article, "I've never done any work so carefully documented." This is hard to believe. No scholar can earn a doctorate from a school with the standing of Temple University if he does not consider the books and articles that disagree with his position. In fact, the article's sloppy and one-sided research is a disgrace.

Indeed, the entire article and subsequent book are not good investigative journalism. Nor are they good scholarship. Rather, Dr. Jones has written us a kind of novel about religious enthusiasm, repressed sexual guilt and youthful high-jinks. He tried to paint a powerful, compelling, dramatic portrait of weak human beings trying to be more than they are, conniving, sinning, lying to others and to themselves. He paints a picture that some may well find compelling and even convincing. The problem with it is — the entire article proves nothing.

"Medjugorje: The Untold Story" constitutes a serious, clear violation of charity. Dr. Jones blatantly slanders the visionaries and Fr. Vlasic and others. He is perfectly free to hold his opinions. He is entitled to suspect that the apparitions are a fraud and that Fr. Vlasic or anyone else is not what he appears to be. He may certainly investigate and question what others present as true. However, when he begins to publish what he thinks, then he must be sure that he is right. He must be able to prove what he claims when he accuses someone of sexual misconduct or of lying. He must use words according to their true meaning and not according to the meaning he gives them. He must argue according to the norms of logic and sound reasoning and not according to impressions. The journalist who believes something bad about another person may not publish what he thinks, unless he has clear, unambiguous, objective proof. No matter how firmly he may be convinced in his own mind of another's wrongdoing, he violates the rule of justice and of charity if he cannot prove what he publishes.

E. Michael Jones hangs his hat on the peg of orthodoxy. He holds staunchly to the truth as taught by the Magisterium of the Catholic Church. In that he does well. But orthodoxy is not enough. Faith without love, charity, is dead. Authentic faith, St. Thomas Aquinas tells us, is formed by love. And St. Augustine tells us that to violate charity is to wound the Church.

We need to realize — all of us, and not only Dr. Jones — that every act must be an act of charity. To violate charity in one's speech or writing destroys the bond that makes us one in Christ. Our obligation is to build up this unity. This does not mean that we may never say anything negative, critical or accusatory; at times this is necessary so that evil may be rooted out of the Church or so that the innocent may be protected. What is not permitted is the harming of others through slander or through the spreading of suspicions as though they were truth. To do this is always wrong, no matter how good the intentions behind it may be. Being convinced that you have the truth is not enough. You have to know that it is the truth and you must have a sufficiently grave reason for revealing it.

These principles apply to every writer, editor or speaker — to everyone who has the means to address a public audience. They also apply, however, to us as we read or listen. The act of accepting something as true or false is one for which each of us is personally responsible. I am answerable to my conscience and to God for every belief I hold about another person, if that belief is not properly founded in the truth and in love. In this case, I may not judge Fr. Vlasic or the visionaries or Bishop Zanic on the basis of what E. Michael Jones has proposed. And if I repeat this kind of accusation on another's authority — because someone else said it — without carefully evaluating his arguments and evidence, then I too have done wrong. I too have violated charity, harmed my brother and wounded the Catholic Church.

(iii) A Member of the Fidelity Advisory Board

Sometime after Michael Jones' position piece on Medjugorje appeared in *Fidelity*, Dr. Eugene F. Diamond, Professor of Pediatrics at Loyola University Medical Center in Chicago, and a member of *Fidelity*'s Advisory Board, asked Michael Jones to print his article on Medjugorje in "an attempt to inject a tone of moderation into the discussion in *Fidelity*." His request was refused. In granting permission for his article to be reproduced in this book, he has requested that it be prefaced with the following:

Dr. Diamond writes of his experiences at Medjugorje from a personal perspective. He emphasizes that his personal testimony is not intended as a rebuttal to or a refutation of any other published veiwpoint to the contrary. As he states in his conclusion, his belief is that 'the jury is still out on Medjugorje' but that his personal pilgrimage was uplifitng and edifying.

Emile Zola, when visiting the Grotto at Lourdes and seeing the discarded crutches and canes, was said to have remarked, "What, no wooden legs?" Although there is strong evidence that Zola actually witnessed a miraculous cure during his visit, he became a cynical and persistent critic of the alleged healing powers of the Shrine. Alexis Carrell, on the other hand, visited the Shrine out of curiosity and with an open mind. He verified a miraculous cure of tuberculosis peritonitis by actually examining the patient. He reported his findings, as an agnostic, to the French Academy of Sciences, attributing the cure to some poorly understood psychosomatic phenomenon rather than as a miracle. The members of the Academy rose up in righteous indignation to expel him and, ultimately to lead him to emigrate to the United

States. While Carrell was not a believer, he eventually won a Nobel Prize which attested to his scientific skills and detachment.

The fundamental question for any person on pilgrimage to a shrine is "Do you believe in miracles." In other words, do you believe that God, as the author of creation, does in fact intervene to suspend the laws of nature in any particular instance. Some miracles we believe as a matter of obligation. Jesus did, as the gospels tell us, suspend the laws of nature to allow Him to walk on water, heal the leper, cure blindness and deafness, raise Lazarus from the dead and heal the servant of the Centurion, among other things. Were miracles a feature exclusively of Christ's public life or are miracles ongoing through time? The purpose of the miracles performed by Jesus, were apparently intended to increase the faith of the people. Does God intervene in nature now for the same purpose of demonstrating His power and enhancing faith?

In the scientific community, one is likely to find the most outspoken critics of the possibility of miracles. This despite the fact that almost every physician will attest to the fact that he has attended a patient who survived against overwhelming odds from an expected fatal outcome. As my response to such vociferous disclaimers of the possibility of miracles, I usually ask, "If your wife were sick, would you pray for her?" When firmly reassured that they would, of course, pray for a near relative's recovery, I respond "You are praying for a miracle." A person who prays for a sick person is asking that God interfere in nature to alter the course of an illness to convert an unfavorable outcome to a favorable one. One physician friend of mine whose wife had a malignancy, protested that he would only pray that there would be no pain associated with the disease. Even this, however, is a petition for a miracle since what the prayer asks is that the natural course of the disease be altered to spare the patient from painful complications.

During the last century, most of the miraculous occurrences in the Catholic tradition have been associated with Marian apparitions. The inevitable response the huge outpouring of faith occasioned by the few apparitions authenticated by the Church is the proliferation of many unsubstantiated claims fabricated by alleged witnesses for a variety of motives. Some of these are rejected out of hand as transparent hoaxes but others are surrendered with great reluctance by impassioned partisans. Some of these partisans see the disqualification of certain occurrences as part of a grand plot initiated by diabolical forces with certain ecclesiastical authorities as co-conspirators. The painful interlude between claim, counterclaim, and either acceptance of rejection has caused the Church in its wisdom to engage in appropriately cautious evaluation of each now alleged phenomenon. The withholding of official sanction is particularly important in view of the predisposition of the faithful to succumb to what Ronald Knox has called Enthusiasm. The temperate evaluation of alleged miracles is a form of damage control to limit the disenchantment occasioned by revelations of deception or clerical confidence game which sometimes occur.

The alleged Marian apparitions at Medjugorje are currently in this stage of agonizing appraisal. It is obvious that objective evaluation is extremely difficult against a background of literally hundreds of thousands of pilgrimages to the site with innumerable testimonials to personal faith experiences elicited by such pilgrimages. The firm unwillingness of the Holy See to extend official recognition to the apparitions or even to sanction Church sponsored travel is validated by the inescapable ambivalence and strong emotional charge associated with acceptance or rejection of the occurrences at Medjugorje.

The analysis of Franz Werfel has become somewhat of a cliche but it is, nonetheless, highly relevant. As he wrote in the Song of Bernadette, "For those who believe, no explanation is necessary; For those who do not believe no explanation will suffice." As with Lourdes, belief is the key but the credulous are still at risk. The apparitions at Medjugorje are unique in having access to modern scientific technology to help to validate some key points. In the publications of Dr. Henri Joyeaux, written with Rene Laurentin, some factual data emerge. Using the technology of evoked visual response and evoked auditory response, there is scientific evidence from tracings taken on the visionaries during the alleged apparition, that they are in fact hearing something and seeing something. Such evidence would not be available if the visions were a hoax nor would it be present if the young people were hallucinating. Likewise, frame by frame analysis of time lapse motion pictures indicate that the children begin to pray, allegedly in response to an invitation to do so by the Blessed Mother, at the same precisely synchronized moment. This would seemingly rule out the occurrence of joint prayer in imitation of one or the other of the visionaries acting as a leader. The state is described by Dr. Joyeaux as an ecstasy but there is no parallel state described in the medical literature under a different set of circumstances. This scientific evidence is not irrefutable but it would seem to refute, at least, a completely fabricated conspiracy.

Inevitably one must depend on personal first-hand experience to a large extent in evaluating the veracity of the Medjugorje story. It must be conceded that the ambience of the Yugoslavian pastoral countryside is, of itself, an influence to be considered. My own visit came at the urging of five of my sons and daughters who preceded me on pilgrimage. I should emphasize that they are not unsophisticated children but adults with advanced degrees (M.D., J.D., M.S.N., and two M.S.W.'s). I was nonetheless, reluctant and unconvinced until I received an invitation to speak at a meeting in Split, Yugoslavia, close to Medjugorje. Since the invitation was quite unexpected and came from a colleague I had not seen for 15 years, it was problematic for me to deny that I was somehow being summoned to the scene.

It is difficult to capsulate the experience at Medjugorje but I will give what are only personal impressions. First, of all, in all honesty, it must be said that most of what is said by those on the site, would be of dubious credibility. There are always numerous enthusiasts who are anxious to tell you of their personal conversation with the Virgin or an independent sighting in a treetop or on a belfry. I suppose that all of us as pilgrims are longing for such an experience or for the spiritual metanoia which would inevitably follow. Such happenings are mere distractions which do not prove or disprove the authenticity of the revelations described by the visionaries. If these are blocked out, to the extent possible, the central theme and impact of the place is quite extraordinary. The unearthly silence of thousands of pilgrims at the top of Apparition Mountain or Mount Krizevac during the period when the visionaries are said to be engaged in listening to the Blessed Mother is certainly dramatic and unprecedented in my experience.

Some years ago, I was able to march in one of the processions at Lourdes. Physicians who are members of the International Medical Association of Lourdes are privileged to join the procession immediately behind the clergy who carry the Blessed Sacrament to bless the sick and disabled. Even after thirty five years of hospital practice, I have never experienced such a scene of concentrated severely handicapped and pre-terminally ill patients. The benefit of Lourdes to the 99+% who are not cured is surely a new acceptance of their problem and a new access to a spiritual dimension to their suffering.

Likewise, the overriding impact of the scene at Medjugorje is one of profound devotion and prayerful reawakening. There is a fundamental and uncomplicated spiritual message which might be disappointing to those looking for exhilaration or transports of inspiration. Any individual response would obviously be conditioned by one's personal history, expectations, and spiritual readiness. No multiplication of favorable reasons would confirm that Medjugorje is bonafide any more than such experiences could be cancelled out by a plurality of negative responses.

Peripheral to the profoundly moving spiritual experience of the Medjugorje pilgrimage are other events to which differing degrees of significance have been attached. These are the phenomena of the changing color of the rosaries and the so-called "spinning sun". My own rosary did unquestionably change color from silver to gold. I attach no necessarily miraculous significance to this occurrence which could conceivably be related to an environmentally driven chemical effect. The change is factual, however, and not imaginary. I did not witness the sign of the sun. It is said that a quarter of a million people experienced a similar solar display at Fatima indicating that such experiences can be deemed authentic.

Perhaps nothing is more damaging to the credibility of the Medjugorje apparitions than the implacable opposition of the Bishop of Mostar, the ordinary of the diocese in which Medjugorje is located. Bishop Zanic has a long standing incompatibility with the Franciscans who were so actively involved in the early activities of the visionaries. In contrast to the viewpoint of the Bishop of Mostar, Archbishop Franic, the retired Bishop of Split has expressed a preliminary endorsement of the pilgrimages. Marijo Zivkovic, one of the leading Catholic laymen of Croatia has expressed the opinion that disagreement between the bishops had a salutary political effect. The Communist government of Yugoslavia was much less inclined to suppress the activities at Medjugorje as a religious plot in view of the public disagreement between the bishops. Zivkovic has also expressed the viewpoint that the bloodless revolution which now has removed from power the Titoist Communist party is attributed by devout Catholics in Croatia and Slovenia to the intervention of the Virgin of Medjugorje.

Much of what has been attributed to the young seers in their public utterances seems inconsistent and, at times, protective of the political status of their Franciscan sponsors. I suspect that if the statements of the peasant children at Fatima or those of Juan Diego during interrogation were to be subjected to the same scrutiny, similar inconsistencies would have appeared. The Blessed Mother seems to have established a pattern of appearing to simple peasants youths rather than sophisticated intellectuals. It would be unfair to hold them to higher standards of consistency that St. Peter or Doubting Thomas.

My own inclination is to keep an open mind about Medjugorje and to treasure the positive spiritual experiences of my pilgrimage there. At the same time, I do not trivialize the potential scandal of any future exposure of irregularities nor do I minimize the devastating effects of such an exposure on the faithful who have invested much devotional capital in the shrine.

There are many reasons to have confidence in the objective investigating powers of John Paul II and his appointed representatives. In the meanwhile, open discussion and debate should continue and we should not yet be prepared to foreclose either the strong opinions of critics or of advocates alike. The reality of the present situation should be acknowledged honestly, however. The jury is indeed still out on Medjugorje.

(iv) Archbishop Frane Franic

Archbishop Frane Franic is the retired archbishop of Split and Makarska, a diocese bordering the dioceses of Mostar in which Medjugorje is located. Archbishop Franic is a prominent theologian and one of the conciliar Fathers of Vatican II. He is the Chairman of the Committee on the Doctrine of the Yugoslavian Bishops' Conference. Archbishop Franic became convinced of the authenticity of the Medjugorje apparitions almost at the beginning. Below is his response to Bishop Zanic's 1990 pamphlet against Medjugorje.

Your Excellency
Pavlo Zanic, Bishop of Mostar

Your Excellency:

I received your writings of 16 pages about the happenings in Medjugorje. Thank you for your consideration. Allow me, honestly and in brotherly love, to express my humble opinion about your written document. In my opinion, the greatest weakness in your writings is the WRONG METHOD of examining THE TRUTHFULNESS OF THE HAPPENINGS IN MEDJUGORJE. Do not be offended if I say to you that this wrong method is based on your poor knowledge of mystical theology; which today, is a very factual branch of theological science in the Church (by my humble opinion in which I am ready to have further dialogue with you.) Refer to "La Mystica. Fenomenologia e riflessione theologica" 1984. Citta Nuova editrice. Con approvazione ecclesiastica/ISBN 86-311-u213-2/. Due volumi di pp. 668 e 765/

I THANK YOU THAT YOU WILL NOT BETRAY MY PRESENCE HERE.

1. You imagine, in searching for the truth about Medjugorje, some battle between pro and con of Medjugorje. For instance, you are placing me as one of the pillars of Medjugorje in this battle. I, however, was never "fighting" for Medjugorje in the way that you imagine. I always said, however, that Mary belongs, if proven true, in "private revelations" to which no one is obliged to believe the same as that of Lourdes' and Fatima's private revelations. So, the one who believes in private revelations is not holier than the one who does not.

    For that reason, I was always evading the confrontations and arguments and so I asked you that we renew our friendship and love in spite of our differences of opinion about the Medjugorje phenomenon. You, however, answered me that it is impossible; because to accept this phenomenon while the Church did not officially bring a judgment would mean heresy, and that those who accept the Medjugorje messages "deserve to go to the bottom of hell."

    Nothing else was left to me but to withdraw and continue to stay in private opinion about the truthfulness of the Medjugorje message and the supernaturalness of the spiritual fruits which are visible in the pilgrimages of the faithful who come in great numbers from five continents, always ready to surrender to the holy Church.

2. Your method is trying to morally demean the Franciscans, whom you regard as authors of the Medjugorje messages and all other Medjugorje phenomena, such as conversions and unusual feelings. You say, if they are all some "charismatic fortune tellers," as you expressedly ill-named one of them, and as you think now of the rest of them, who are betraying the whole world in gathering money, the "idol" of Medjugorje.

    Further, you hold the visionaries as liars and look for ways on how to prove your thesis about the Franciscans in Medjugorje and the visionaries. All other friends of Medjugorje you try to diminish, as for instance, Fr. Rene Laurentin, for whom you say that he became rich from the books that he wrote about Medjugorje. And among other friends of Medjugorje, you will also count me. In your booklet you didn't give moral judgment about me but in one Italian interview, "Semplice Bugiardo," and in other places, ridiculed me that in my old age I fell into charismatics. Furthermore, in your newsletter, Crkva na Kanemu (Church of the Rock), you allowed articles of the hardest imaginable kind that attack me as a traitor of Church and Faith.

    In spite of everything, I forgive you all this. Furthermore, I wish to forget it. I am offering you a renewal of our friendship on the condition that each one of us continues in our belief.

3. All of the time in your argument about Medjugorje, you bring up the disobedience of the Franciscans about the divisions of the parishes. I think that Our Lady did not come here to divide the parishes between the Bishop and the provincials, because this question belongs to the Church to solve.

    I always said and wrote letters to the Franciscans in Hercegovina to hand over these seven parishes to the Bishop of Mostar, but they insist they will do so when they are allowed to elect the proper guidance of the province. They are also afraid that this would be the first step of the Bishop to chase them out of all parishes. It seems to me that they find themselves "in errore invincibili" regarding solving this question and, so, they need fatherly advice so that they can come to a child's obedience (obedience of a son to a father.)

    I am sorry for this case, but I am confirming that Our Lady is not at all responsible for this; but, I think that this question would be closer to being solved if "Libertas-Cultus" would be allowed in Medjugorje; and not to sharpen this question by insisting that all persons, the priests and the nuns, will be transferred if they accept the Medjugorje happenings.

4. You, Father Bishop, seek and dig out the past life of these individual Franciscans and bring out before the world, the sins which they committed according to your findings. Forgive me if I tell you, as an older brother, that you are making an error regarding your fatherly love. In this, you cannot prove your statements neither against Fr. Vlasic nor against Fr. Jozo Zovko, whom the whole world who comes to Medjugorje regards as a man of God and come to him for spiritual guidance. You bring out accusations against Fr. Jozo which no one believes but you, because there are witnesses to his innocence. You already judged and sentenced Fr. Jozo based on this false accusation. What a persecution...even from the Church...You are doing this, Father Bishop,on the basis of false witnessing against him written by a mentally unstable person. This is a heavy case which is contrary to fatherly and brotherly love to which the Vatican Council II binds us. (L.G. III, 28,)

5. So, you bring out these cases of the sins of the Franciscans who accept Medjugorje. This is not only against a Fatherly Bishop's love, but it is also methodically wrong.

One can answer to you, then that Our Lady appeared to the sinners and not to the righteous as it was with the case of her divine Son.

6. However, the moral behavior of the Franciscans in Medjugorje is highly creditable and rational. Every day they have as much work as the rest of us priests on the biggest holidays. Shouldn't this be acknowledged? Wouldn't this acknowledgement bind us to "iustitis distributiva sub gravi obligatione...?"

7. Regarding the "lies" of the visionaries: Here,too, Father Bishop, you are committing a heavy methodical error.

   A) You are accusing Marija of a lie because she signed in Parma that Our Lady told her to be a part of this prayer group, and later, when she left this prayer group, she signed that Our Lady never told her to belong to this group. From this, you draw the conclusion that she was always lying about the visions of Our Lady from 1981 until today.

      Also, you didn't spare the effort to count how many times the visionaries said that Our Lady said that the Bishop was too hasty in his decision when he forbade the celebration of Mass to two of the Franciscans and that both Franciscans could stay in Mostar. You did not take into consideration any other findings about the Medjugorje phenomenon of other people, but you always hold to your own method; to force the visionaries into a lie, and the message of Medjugorje, you proclaim as heretical because Our Lady could not talk against the Bishop.

      Here, I am also bringing out your public proclamation of the moral fall of Ivica Vego and the nun who entered into civil marriage with him, sacrilegiously,even though they lived in Medjugorje. "How can Our Lady protect such sinners" you exclaim in triumph.

      And Ivan is a liar, because he once said that he wrote about the secret of the "big sign" and that he handed this to the Bishop's ordinary even in the beginning, when he was thinking of becoming a Franciscan. Later, this sane Ivan said that on this paper there was nothing about the "big secret" and that it was, in regard to the "big secret", a blank piece of paper.

      Mirjana from Sarajevo said that all faiths are the same is a heresy that undermines Our Lady. What could be more horrible?

B) To all of this I answer:

Ecstatic prayers, to which one can also add daily ecstatic prayers, are a normal occurrence in our Church. All we are to do is only make sure that these prayers are really ecstatic or not. Therefore, when these prayers cause a gathering of Christian masses, the Church is obliged to carefully examine this through competent specialists. This is being done now in Medjugorje. We should leave these specialists alone, who are responsible to the BKJ (Bishop's Commission of Yugoslavia) and to the Holy See, and not to impose our own conclusions.

Our own opinions should be private ones, only so they can decide in freedom and so they would not bring up conclusions under the influence of the Church officials in fear of offending them.

Ecstasies, as we know, can be a lighter or deeper experience: at first, the visionary remains in contact with the surroundings; secondly, he loses all contact with the surroundings. I know persons who have these light ecstasies, but these people do not draw masses of people to themselves and the Archdiocese is not questioning them, or does not know of them.

So, if lighter ecstasy happens to occur, it is not proof against the validity of the deeper ones (if it happens to the same person.) It is a normal advancement in ecstatic prayer.

It is most significant that the persons in ecstasy can exchange their own convictions with the words of the person they see in ecstasy. Rene Laurentin proved this through examples of persons with ecstasies who are now saints in the Catholic Church. In a deeper ecstasy, they can recognize the WILL OF GOD in a clearer way, and there is no contradiction in these expressions.

Especially, the ecstasies can substitute the inspiration of prayer with the words of the person whom they say they see. This could have happened to Marija in Parma, who was not sure of her decision of whether or not to join this prayer group, and she also did not write the letter by herself—but she signed under the authority of her then spiritual guide; later, she realized that it was not the word of Our Lady — this she realized in deeper prayer.

Therefore, each ecstasy and each apparition should especially be analyzed because in each ecstasy and in each apparition there is, more or less, some human element.

The same rule applies to the interpretation of all God's revelations in the Holy Scripture or the apostles' tradition, so does the public revelation, so that one can come to the meaning which God wanted to reveal. Here, we should separate the FORM from the meaning, as Pio XII taught us in his letter of "Divino afflante Spiritu."

In this way, your method, Father Bishop, with which you interpret "Our Lady's messages" from Medjugorje and find contradiction in them — lies — as you say, so could many contradictions be found in the Holy Scriptures. In fact, some people find such "contradictions" in the Holy Scriptures and then they say that the Holy Scripture is not faultless, and that there are very few words of God in the Holy Scriptures— explicitly "ipsissima verba" — the true words of Christ in the Gospel. We know to what kind of critique the words of God in the Holy Scriptures are subjected in some contemporary exegesis. It is no wonder, then, Father Bishop that the same fate awaited, in my opinion, the words of Our Lady, pronounced to simple children, who did not study theology and who are not recording on a tape. Only they can hear and we who are standing around neither hear nor see anything except the moving lips of the "visionaries."

How many problems were acknowledged in the visions and conversations between St. Bernadette, the children in Fatima and Our Lady, and now we find the same phenomenon in Medjugorje.

I also wish to add, Father Bishop, that Our Lady was appearing in Lourdes and Fatima and, in my opinion, is now appearing in Medjugorje to chosen people, outside of her dwelling surrounding; she is appearing beyond God's substance — extra essentiam divinam — in which substance she lives and where she has her true radiance and life. And when Our Lady comes out of this environment, and she is clothing herself in some garments, she takes some bodily form and appears sometimes as a young girl — to Bernadette as a grown woman , happy one moment, at other times crying real tears, which they gathered in Syracuse and were able to analyze in a laboratory...

Therefore, those who are experiencing Our Lady in this way, as if she is in time and space beyond God's essence(but she is in our time and space in a special way because we do not hear or see her, and if she was in time and space in a material way, we would have to see her in the same way as the visionaries see her)do not see and hear her as she is in reality — in her full splendor.

The conclusion of this mysterious way of looking and listening to the heavenly phenomena is that those who experience it are prone to sin of any kind. Only one who sees God's essence face to face cannot sin without any means and not the one who sees only means of the apparition which is seen beyond God's essence.

Therefore, even great prophets who had inner visions and inner locutions used to sin; Abraham was lying when he came to Egypt and said that Sara is his sister, because he was afraid that the pharoah's people would kill him. Jacob came to be firstborn in the wrong way. David committed adultery and murder to cover his sin. In spite of all this, merciful God forgave His prophets' sins and used them again as His prophets. Also, the apostles lived with Christ and watched His miracles and furthermore, they, themselves performed these miracles; and, anyway, wondered about His Cross and lost faith in His divinity.

Merciful Jesus also forgave them. Only you, Father Bishop cannot forgive the visionary Ivan for once, under pressure and fear not to be taken out of the seminary by you, lied and wrote and gave you a sealed letter in which he consciously lied that the "big secret" consists of the sudden appearance of a great shrine on the Hill of Apparition or on the Mountain of the Cross. He, himself, confessed to this lie and said that he deserved a whipping. What he later said to the commission is that there is nothing there about a big secret and that the paper regarding the secret is blank. This, he could not have disclosed — this was not a lie. You wanted to discontinue the work of the commission, holding this proof to be undeniable...This shows, forgive me, Father Bishop, your poor knowledge of mystical theology.

After all, when a great multitude of believers covers the Hill of Apparitions or the Mountain of the Cross, isn't that, then, the great Church — the great shrine — living Church of God's people. This, perhaps, the visionaries do not understand either, because they simply transmit the words which, I believe, they hear. The Church is called to interpret these words and to separate the chaff, the human words, from the clear grains of God's words. This is not an easy task. Patience and love is needed for this and also much knowledge.

8. Thank you, Father Bishop, that you called me one of the two "pillars" of Medjugorje. I am not in bad company. Naturally, I stand behind and testify to my own conviction and bring out only my subjective religious experience which I had at, for me, a holy place. But you, Father Bishop, insist that in Medjugorje there are no greater spiritual fruits

than any other parish in Hercegovina. For example, your conversation with Fr. Helan from Notre Dame University, USA, which you recently conducted on television. From this, one could conclude that Medjugorje is a mud puddle of sin, heresy, treasons and greed and that all of this is leading to destruction. You, in general, call the pilgrims a fanatic mass with a few exceptions of pious, faithful devoted believers who come here in vain. You repeatedly insist that no miracle has yet happen here, but the "miracles" are evaluated by experts. According to their scientific criteria they are to confirm whether or not certain healings are really overcoming natural forces and then the Church would declare, by religious stance, whether or not it is a miracle. Until then, we who are not experts in this matter can express our own opinions, but not by self-imposing our own views or by despising someone else's opinion. People who obtain sudden healing from terminal illness immediately praise God, not waiting to see whether or not the competent people will proclaim this a miracle. To praise God for special graces, even though there is a doubt whether or not it is a miracle, is a natural trait of God's creatures...

9. Father Bishop, please go sometime, maybe even incognito, to Medjugorje, and begin to hear the confessions of the pilgrims. In this way, I am certain that you can best get to know Medjugorje — by seeing the miraculous conversion of souls, the greatest miracles which are happening in Medjugorje, in far greater numbers and in far greater intensity than in any other parish in Hercegovina and even in Lourdes. Should we bishops be so far from the place where there are so many graces? Satan cannot give even the single smallest actual graces; only God is the Lord of all graces; actual and holy,Lord of all gifts of the Holy Spirit and charisms. This is the correct method of examining the Medjugorje phenomenon: "By the fruits, you should know them."

10. That the visionaries and those who agree with them, those who preach and hear confession in Medjugorje, and those who write, contemplate and testify to their experiences, can also sin and have to struggle daily for their faith, is certainly possible. Your knowledge of mystical theology clearly comes to expression in your letter, when you speak of the subject. Therefore, it would be necessary to postpone arguments as to whether the visionaries see Our Lady or some sign, etc. The freedom of religious expression should be allowed: preaching, hearing confessions, religious instruction, meditating on the Word of God, and allowing the building of necessary religious structures, scientific insti-

tutions and hospitals where we could worthily accept pilgrims and those who are sick and give the freedom to examine unexplainable healings right on the spot.

11. Regarding the declarations of the "visionaries" that Our Lady said that you were too hasty in punishing those two young Franciscans, I would like to note: You were told that Our Lady's reprimand was given to you in confidence, not publicly. You were asked that it stay in confidence as a motherly reprimand. But you, Father Bishop, proclaimed this reprimand throughout the whole world, insisting that Our Lady could not reprimand a bishop. How could a prophet reprimand David?! How did the author of the Apocalypse reprimand the bishops of Asia Minor?! All of these people accepted the reprimand and strived, in their humbleness, to improve themselves. If you did the same, I believe that you could have saved those two young Franciscans for the Church, but as it is, you drove one of them to despair, insisting on heroic obedience from him. To insist on such obedience is not rational. (Forgive me, Father Bishop.) Surely, in numerous cases like these, there will be people who will not obey.

Our Lady said, it is said, that they can stay in Mostar. "Mostar" could simply mean their province. The possibility to even file a complaint was not given to them. I am not sure if the Holy Father, John Paul II, actually wished for such strictness. ...One of those two young Franciscans went to the Dubrovnik Diocese in their monastery, Slano. For him, this was also "Mostar." The Bishop of Dubrovnik, Msgr. Severein Bernek, allowed him pastoral duties. You took this away from him when you became the administrator of the Diocese of Dubrovnik. So, you regard your diocesan decrees as absolutely valid for the whole world.

12. Regarding the declaration of Mirjana from Sarajevo that Our Lady said that "all faiths are the same," we should look at the contexts of these words. From these contexts, Our Lady's motherly regard for all peoples and their beliefs is evident, because the Second Vatican Council declared Our Lady as "Mother of All People." (This expression was nominated by our deceased Fr. Balic.)

In Medjugorje, there is preaching of love and reconciliation between all people, faiths and religions. This is Our Lady's "Equality" in the essence of love as a base. It is something deep and very important for today's world in which COMMUNIST EASTERN EUROPE IS CONVERTING TO HUMANISM. THIS CONVERSION COULD MEAN

I THANK YOU THAT YOU WILL NOT BETRAY MY PRESENCE HERE.

THE FIRST STEP IN THE REALIZATION OF THE FATIMA PROPHECY, interpreted in the Medjugorje messages that this will happen not by the power of arms, not through the power of money, not by the power of politics as some thought before, but rather with the power of faith, love and forgiveness, especially by the merit of so many martyrs in Russia and other Eastern bloc countries, including Yugoslavia. This is, we hope, with Pope John Paul II, the MOTHERLY VICTORY OF MARY which now seeks for forgiveness and NATIONAL, INTERNATIONAl AND INTERDENOMINATIONAL RECONCILIATION. Isn't this Father Bishop, magnificent?! It is not only that we believers would be satisfied with the conversion of atheists to humanists, but we hope that what will follow is RE-EVANGELIZATION, all in the form of the MOTHERLY LOVE OF MARY, and not in the style of oppression and revenge.

For example, Father Bishop, forgive me for being so frank the time, but I think that my age gives me this right and also a Roman decree of "retired Bishops."

I did not wish to lecture you, but only to express to you my own convictions and my own experiences.

Wishing you every good, I greet you as a brother.

Devoted to you in Christ,
Frane Franic

(v) Dr. Nicholas Bartulica

Dr. Bartulica is a Croatian psychiatrist who is the Senior Psychiatrist at the Woodson Children's Psychiatric Hospital in St. Joseph, Missouri. Dr. Bartulica has been investigating Medjugorje almost from the beginning. He interviewed Vicka Ivankovic as far back as October 1981 and has continued his study of the phenomenon of Medjugorje from the standpoint of his specialty, psychiatry. **MEDJUGORJE: Are the Seers Telling the Truth? A Psychiatrist's Viewpoint** [Croatian Franciscan Press: Chicago, Illinois, 1991] is his main contribution to the debate. The excerpt below is taken from the conclusion to his book and addresses the arguments of Bishop Zanic, Michael Jones and Fr. Ivo Sivric.

Finally, we would like to conclude with a reflection on the Medjugorje events.

Regardless of the Church's final verdict, we are certain that Medjugorje will remain in the history of either unusual human behavior or authentic apparitions a unique phenomenon.

262

1. When Bishop Zanic changed his opinion regarding the authenticity of the events, he declared that they were a product of 'collective hallucinations.'

But when we faced six children, who are 'hallucinating' daily and simultaneously for five to ten minutes, experiencing identical hallucinations and the rest of the day they act in a normal manner, then we are dealing with a *psychiatric phenomenon* which has never been described in the psychiatric handbooks, and the psychiatric community ought to study.

2. After the psychiatric profession had rejected the above hypothesis, some researchers suggested a para-psychological explanation.

As we answered above, there are six children in strange state of consciousness, when, according to scientific tests, they lose contact with the surroundings (i.e., they don't hear, see nor feel), but several minutes later they return to the reality reporting similar experiences, then we must be dealing with a *para-psychological phenomenon* where further research and study is imperative.

3. There are suggestions, which include those from the main three critics (M. Jones, Bishop Zanic and Fr. Sivric), that the children are not going through any particular experiences but that they simply pretend. This means they are putting on the act, i.e., they are liars.

But when we find six children who have been lying on a daily basis for ten years and have succeeded in misleading not only experienced researchers, but also have been confounding scientific instruments, then we are dealing with a *deceptive phenomenon* that any criminologist ought to study further,

4. After realizing that a natural explanation was not plausible, some theologians have suggested that the events have been caused by diabolical influence. It might be that Satan is appearing as an 'angel of light.'

But when we find that Satan is causing hundreds of thousands to return to God through repentance and confession, and the multitude of others incited to deepen their spiritual life by forming prayer groups where they daily recite the Rosary, then we are facing a peculiar phenomenon where the *nature of the devil appears to have changed*, and the demonologists should offer a convincing explanation.

5. In view of the fact that the four above-mentioned interpretations are either absurd and untenable, we are compelled to conclude that the events are a result of a higher power's intervention; that is, God's finger must be at work.

Cardinal-designate Hans Urs von Balthasar was considered one of the greatest theologians in this century but passed away on June 26,

1988, two days before he was to receive the red hat from the Pope. He became interested and studied Medjugorje from the beginning and had reached the following conclusion:

'Medjugorje's theology rings true. I'm convinced of its truth. And everything about Medjugorje is authentic, in Catholic sense. What's happening there is so evident, so convincing.'

However, through the history of apparitions we have never witnessed such frequent and lengthy periods of private revelations intended for the visionaries as well as for the world.

In the Medjugorje events there are supernatural interventions of such magnitude and diversity that it appears as if Heaven and earth had come together. A multiplicity of 'signs and wonders,' including physical and spiritual cures and the extended period of apparitions, is confounding to the theologians.

Fr. Albert J. Herbert, the author of several books on prophesies, apparitions and unusual interventions' by God, wrote:

'Nothing like it has ever happened since Jesus walked the earth.'

Therefore, even when the authenticity of the apparitions is declared by the Church, we could say that we will be facing a *unique phenomenon* in the history of the apparitions.

In view of the above, we felt that the Medjugorje phenomena deserved professional interest, and by refuting the unsubstantiated hypothesis with incontestable facts, this writer tried to offer his small contribution to their understanding.

(vi) Dudley Plunkett

Dudley Plunkett is Senior Lecturer in Education at the University of Southhampton and a director of the Medjugorje Network in the United Kingdom. Plunkett, who attributes his conversion to Catholicism to Medjugorje, studies the Gospel message of Medjugorje in **Queen of the Prophets** [Image Books: New York, 1990]. In the excerpt below he reflects on the diabolic and on materialism.

Powers of Evil

It has also been apparent that there is opposition to Medjugorje that is of another order. The frequent references in Mary's messages to the power of Satan in the world, the incidence of exorcisms in Medjugorje itself, and the struggles of those involved in the spiritual work stemming from Medjugorje to maintain peace and harmony in the face of misleading reports in the media, clashes of personality and interpretation, and even disagreements among devotees of different Marian shrines, are all evidence of the extent to which evil influences have deflected the impact of Medjugorje messages on the Church and the wider world. Indeed, the existence of conflict in an apostolic movement which seeks above all to be concerned with peace demonstrates very clearly that Medjugorje is about peace through spiritual warfare, not by organizational means or simply by ignoring the forces of evil. The means selected by Mary are the powers of the Spirit, and where these are deployed so will the contrary forces be in evidence.

Modern rationality, with its sense of civilization as having overcome superstition, inhibited discussion about the existence of powers for evil. It is tolerated in western society to have a belief in God, provided that the implications of this belief are not taken too literally, but it is widely regarded as strange to have an convictions about the existence of an *evil* power. The result of this state of mind in modern secular society is that evil gains power. What we try to explain as social problems, political conflicts, or mental illnesses, need to be looked at more closely. What is going on? The believer wants to know why the plan of God has broken down, why we seem constantly to fall short and go astray in our vocation as the people of God. The answer Jesus gave, the one that modern secular society cannot bring itself to accept, is that his kingdom is not of this world — a world ruled by the powers of darkness that are having their hour. Christian life is a struggle against such powers until they are finally nullified by the victory of the cross.

Part of the reality of evil is that it conceals itself. We are misled if we assume that because we have not directly encountered evil spirits they cannot exist. How else can we explain the fact that, in in spite of all its wonderful powers, talents and virtues, humanity has brought the world to the brink of catastrophe, set upon self-destruction and corrupted in so many ways through individual and social sin? The misuse of body and mind, lovelessness, cynicism and contempt between people, and political oppression and violence, speak not of a rational, humane or holy work, but of a distorted, cursed, obsessed and self-destructive spirit. How could people kill each other of there were no power of evil? How could children be abused or families split? How could there be wars, torture, genocide, ecological destruction and exploitation of poor nations if our nature was uncorrupt? Today we find ourselves polarized as never before, with humanity coming to a frightening clash of values in which there can be no compromise:

godless rationalism against paying the vow to God. One position ignores God, while the other pays him tribute and awaits his relief. Neither side can have empathy with the other, because to understand would be to converted. Christians cannot therefore be surprised if those who implacably oppose them to do so with fierce hatred and disrespect, because that is the nature of evil powers confronted by the evidence of their error.

Modern Idols

Opposition to spiritual phenomenon also comes from those who by the way they live their lives, put their faith and hope primarily in material things including wealth and worldly advantages. With regard to Medjugorje, such opposition is rather to the content than to the fact of the apparitions and messages. Indeed, many of us who accept their authenticity must acknowledge that we resist their implications for our lives because of materialistic concerns. From such resistance develops the direct countering of prophetic truth through sinfulness. This is the consequence to be observed in those modern lifestyles that effectively repudiate any spiritual truth. The ultimate truth is then nothing more than materialistic individualism of the kind that has asserted itself in many western societies today — a puny but cruel philosophy which is gradually being applied to more and more areas of life.

A Verdict on Medjugorje

From what now must be hundreds of personal encounters it is my impression that very few who have visited Medjugorje, and prayed there, appear to have doubt that events of a supernatural character have been occurring. I personally feel a deep gratitude that this has been my own experience. And yet there are others, both inside and outside of the Church, who deny such claims, who can find no place for them in their vision of reality. Such doubters must then provide a convincing alternative explanation for what is happening to the villagers and the pilgrims, but they have not been able to do so. I felt sure that most people I have met through my interest in Medjugorje share a conviction that the Catholic Church will eventually give its endorsement to the supernatural character of these events. When it does, Medjugorje, which is already a world pilgrimage center, seems destined to extend its influence beyond the Catholic Church and to become a focus for Christian renewal, through spiritual conversion and the increase of faith and prayer.

3. CONCLUSION

Polemic is always a painful task: particularly when the object of discussion is a person you love. But in the face of slander and fabrication, there is no choice but to set the record straight if only to remove the obstacles that may be preventing some of her children from responding to Our Lady's call to conversion. We are encouraged in this endeavor by Our Lady's words, "I thank you that you will not betray my presence here."

In Fr. Michael O'Carroll's view, the only relevant testimonies that need to withstand scrutiny in order to establish the authenticity of Medjugorje are "the testimonies of the witnesses about the apparitions as they saw them, when they were seeing them. That's what's essential." All the rest are incidentals. From this standpoint, it is easy to see that every one of the purported critiques entirely misses the mark because each focuses on issues that have nothing to do with these specific testimonies. Nevertheless, in Appendix 1, we respond to each one of the specific critiques in order to clear up the confusion they have caused.

Lest it be thought that he critics have no contribution to make, we would like to point out two things that we found beneficial in their writings. Some Medjugorje proponents have stated that St. Catherine of Sienna wrongly thought that the Blessed Virgin had denied the Immaculate Conception in a private revelation. The *Catholic Counter-Reformation*, however, sets the record straight here: The idea of an erroneous revelation springs from Benedict XIV's "De Canonisatione," L.3, c 53, No. 16. St Benedict's essay, however, explains "that the alleged text is probably apocryphal!" Finally, it is clear from the 'Prayers' of St. Catherine "that the contentious passage, even if really from the saint — as Cavallini, the author of the most recent critical edition, thinks (Rome, 1978) — it is only a theological appendix added to a prayer having nothing to warrant its being interpreted as a revelation received in the course of an apparition! (Le Orazioni, ed. Caterinianae, Rome, 1978, P.185-193). 'It is the almost literal expression of Saint Thomas Aquinas on this point, but the saint nowhere presents it as an oracle of the Virgin Mary against the doctrine of the Immaculate Conception.' (Compl. No.1, p.12)!" [p.50].

The case for Medjugorje is well summarized by Father O'Carroll in **Medjugorje: Facts, Documents, Theology:**

Against these objections, one must align so many reasons for accepting authenticity. Some are mentioned and developed at length by Laurentin, others by Dr. Franic. In summary it may be urged that:

a) the visionaries have survived a systematic drive to nullify their testimony, to subvert their so edifying way of life, to pervert their witness; their tenacity is awe-inspiring;

b) they have, day after day, during five [now over eleven] years, spoken of spiritual realities with entire orthodoxy;

c) thrown suddenly into an existence so different from what they knew and lived with, they show no signs of abnormality. They have, on the contrary, impressed experts by their normal behavior and sincerity;

d) they live exemplary lives of prayer, fasting, detachment form the evils of their age and peers, materialism, pleasure-seeking, waste of time entertainment — pop music and so on, not to mention the terrible addictions which plague their contemporaries.

e) they manifest respect and obedience, true love towards the Church at a time when so many, even Catholics, adopt a critical, irreverent attitude towards it; with which goes their love for the Pope and their fidelity to him. He in turn (and it is noteworthy) has sent them tokens of his favour, autographed photographs with the message "Pax Vobis".

In fine let us adapt the biblical advice: Judge the tree by its fruits. The fruits here have been so overwhelmingly good, in the parish which is transformed, in the lives of countless people who admit that they have been brought back to the practice of their religion or to more serious commitment through contact with this holy place and the prayer movement which is daily in it. The fruits have been miraculous in some cases. These alleged miracles I have not described or discussed in detail, as it would take too much space. I accept the records in a number of cases as reliable. (117).

IV. LOVE LETTERS FROM GOD

We would like here to turn our attention to the call of our Mother.

At Medjugorje, she is concerned not simply with reminding us yet again of the Gospel forgotten and forsaken by a world that has reached the end of its tether. In Medjugorje, she also calls out for personal conversion, for total surrender to God, for a life of holiness and love. She not only wants us to come to the truth and to put the truth into action, but the grace to do so is being offered thorugh her hands. As the Holy Father has said (August 1, 1989) the world that has lost God is finding Him in Medjugorje.

At Fatima, in 1917, Our Lady gave ten-year old Lucia a vocation that would consume the rest of her life, "Jesus wants to use you to make me known and loved. He wants to establish Devotion to my Immaculate Heart in the world." From Medjugorje, seventy years later, Our Lady now calls to the rest of her children: "Dear children, I want you to comprehend that God has chosen each one of you in order to use you for the great plan of salvation of mankind. You cannot comprehend how great your role is in God's plan. Therefore, dear children, pray, so that through prayer you might comprehend God's plan towards you. I am with you so that you can realize it completely. Thank you for having responded to my call," (January 25, 1987).

According to Pope John Paul II, the close of this age has been given to Mary in preparation for a new birth, a new era into which the world is about to enter. In her messages Our Lady now pleads: "You have always asked that I not abandon you. Now I ask of you in turn, not to abandon me ...Medjugorje is a sign to all of you and a call to pray and live the days of grace that God is giving you. ...This is a grace which many people neither understand nor accept. Therefore, dear children, you who have said that you are mine and seek my help, give all of yourself...I ask you to accept and live the messages with seriousness so that your soul will not be sad when I will no longer be with you..."How much time is left? On January 25, 1993 she told us how to "discern the signs of this time," and said, "I am with you and I guide you into a new time, a time which God gives you as grace..." We should remember the teaching of St. Paul: "Working together with Him, then, we entreat you not to accept the grace of God in vain" (2 Cor 6:1).

Our Lady's messages at Medjugorje are truly love letters from God delivered to us by our beloved Mother. When she begins each message with the salutation, "Dear children", she is speaking to each one of us for we are all her children as she has so often poignantly told the visionaries. So each message is personally addressed to you and me and we should read and understand it as such. Each message reminds us both of God's love for us and of His invitation to us to love Him. Praised be Jesus and Mary!

(Space limitations keep us from including all of Our Lady's messages here. We content ourselves with her call from January, 1991 through January, 1993. Her complete messages are readily available through sources listed at the end of the fourth section in the appendices.)

January 25, 1991 Dear children, today like never before I invite you to prayer. Your prayer should be a prayer for peace. Satan is strong and wishes not only to destroy human life but also nature and the planet on which you live. Therefore, dear children, pray that you can protect yourselves through prayer with the blessing of God's peace. God sent me to you so that I can help you. If you wish to, grasp the rosary. The rosary alone can do miracles in the world and in your lives. I bless you and I stay among you as long as it is God's will. Thank you that you will not betray my presence here and I thank you because your response is serving God and peace. Thank you for having responded to my call.

February 25, 1991 Dear children, today I invite you to decide for God, because distance from God is the fruit of the lack of peace in your heart. God is only peace; therefore, approach Him through your personal prayer and then live peace in your hearts, and in this way peace will flow from your heart like a river into the whole world. Do not speak about peace, but make peace. I am blessing each of you and each good decision of yours. Thank you for having responded to my call.

March 25, 1991 Dear Children! Again today I invite you to live the Passion of Jesus in prayer and in union with Him. Decide to give more time to God who gave you these days of grace. Therefore, dear children, pray and in a special way renew the love for Jesus in your hearts. I am with you and I accompany you with my blessing and my prayers. Thank you for having responded to my call.

April 25, 1991 Today I invite you all so that your prayer be prayer with the heart. Let each of you find time for prayer so that in your prayer you discover God. I do not desire you to talk about prayer, but to pray. Let your every day be filled with prayer of gratitude to God for life and for all that you have. I do not desire your life to pass by in words, but that you glorify God with deeds. I am with you, and I am grateful to God for every moment spent with you. Thank you for having responded to my call.

May 25, 1991 Dear Children! Today I invite all of you who have heard my message of peace to realize it with seriousness and with love in your life. There are many who think they are doing a lot by talking about the messages, but do not live them. Dear children, I invite you to life and to change all the negative in you so that it all turns into the positive and life. Dear children, I am with you and

I desire to help each of you to live, and by living to witness the Good News. I am here, dear children, to help you and to lead you to heaven and in heaven is the joy through which you can already live heaven now. Thank you for having responded to my call.

June 25, 1991 Dear Children! Today, on this great day which you have given to me, I desire to bless all of you and to say, these days while I am with you are days of grace. I desire to teach you and to help you walk on the path to holiness. There are many people who do not desire to understand the messages and to accept with seriousness what I am saying. But you are, therefore, called and asked that by your lives and your daily living you witness my presence. If you pray, God will help you discover the true reason for my coming. Therefore, little children, pray and read the Sacred Scriptures, so that through my coming you discover the message in Sacred Scripture for you. Thank you for having responded to my call.

July 25, 1991 Dear Children! Today I invite you to pray for peace. At this time peace is threatened in a special way and I am seeking from you to renew fasting and prayer in your families. Dear Children, I desire you to grasp the seriousness of the situation and that much of what will happen depends on your prayers, and you are praying a little bit. Dear children, I am with you, and I am inviting you to begin to pray and fast seriously, as in the first days of my coming. Thank you for having responded to my call.

August 25, 1991 Dear Children! Today also I invite you to prayer, now as never before, when my plan has begun to be realized. Satan is strong and wants to sweep away plans of peace and joy and make you think that my Son is not strong in His decisions. Therefore, I call all of you, dear children, to pray and fast still more firmly. I invite you to renunciation for nine days so that with your help, everything I wanted to realize through the secrets I began in Fatima may be fulfilled. I call you, dear children, to grasp the importance of my coming and the seriousness of the situation. I want to save all souls and present them to God. Therefore, let us pray that everything I have begun be fully realized. Thank you for having responded to my call.

September 25, 1991 Dear Children! Today in a special way I invite you all to prayer and renunciation. For now as never before Satan wants to show the world his shameful face by which he wants to seduce as many people as possible onto the way of death and sin. Therefore, dear children, help my Immaculate Heart to triumph in the sinful world. I beseech all of you to offer prayers and sacrifices for my intentions so I can present them to God for what is most necessary. Forget your desires, dear children, and pray for what God desires and not for what you desire. Thank you for having responded to my call.

October 25, 1991 Dear Children! Pray, Pray, Pray!

November 25, 1991 "Dear Children! This time also I am inviting you to prayer. Pray, that you might be able to comprehend what God desires to tell you through my presence and through the messages I am giving you. I desire to draw you ever closer to Jesus and to his wounded heart that you might be able to comprehend the immeasurable love which gave itself for each one of you. Therefore, dear children, pray, that from your heart will flow a fountain of love to every person, both to the one who hates you and to the one who despises you. That way you will be able through Jesus' love to overcome all the misery in this world of sorrows which is without hope for those who do not know Jesus. I am with you, and I love you with the immeasurable love of Jesus. Thank you for all your sacrifices and prayers. Pray, so I might be able to help you still more. Your prayers are necessary to me. Thank you for having responded to my call."

December 25, 1991 "Dear Children! Today in a special way I bring the little Jesus to you that he may bless you with his blessing of peace and love. Dear children, do not forget that this is a grace which many people neither understand nor accept. Therefore, you who have said that you are mine and seek my help, give all of your self. First of all, give your love and example in your families. You say that Christmas is a family feast. Therefore, dear children, put God in the first place in your families so that He may give you peace and may protect you not only from war, but also during peace, may protect you from every Satanic attack. When God is with you, you have everything. But when you do not want Him, then you are miserable and lost, and you do not know on whose side you are. Therefore, dear children, decide for God and then you will get everything. Thank you for having responded to my call."

January 25, 1992 "Dear Children! Today I am inviting you to a renewal of prayer in your families, so that way every family will become a joy to my Son, Jesus. Therefore, dear children, pray, and seek more time for Jesus and then you will be able to understand and accept everything, even the most difficult sicknesses and crosses. I am with you and I desire to take you into my heart and protect you, but you have not yet decided. Therefore, dear children, I am seeking for you to pray so through prayer you would allow me to help you. Pray, my dear little children, so prayer becomes your daily bread. Thank you for having responded to my call."

February 25, 1992 "Dear Children! Today I invite you to draw still closer to God through prayer. Only that way will I be able to help you and to protect you from every attack of Satan. I am with you and I intercede for you with God that He protect you. But I need your prayers and your "Yes". You get lost easily in material and human things and forget that God is your greatest friend. Therefore, my dear little children, draw close to God so He may protect you and guard you from every evil. Thank you for having responded to my call."

March 25, 1992 "Dear Children! Today as never before I invite you to live my messages and to put them into practice in your life. I have come to you to help you and therefore I invite you to change your life because you have taken a path of misery, a path of ruin!

When I told you 'Convert, pray, fast, be reconciled,' you took these messages superficially. You started to live them and then you stopped because it was difficult for you. Know, dear children, when something is good you have to persevere in the good and not think 'God does not see me, He's not listening, He's not helping.' And so you have gone away from God and from me because of your miserable interest. I wanted to create of you an Oasis of Peace, love and goodness. God wanted you, with your love and with his help, to do miracles and thus give an example.

Therefore here is what I say to you: Satan is playing with you and with your souls and I cannot help you because you are far away from my heart. Therefore, pray, live my messages and then you will see the miracles of God's love in your everyday life. Thank you for having responded to my call."

April 25, 1992 "Dear Children! Today also I invite you to prayer. Only by prayer and fasting can war be stopped. Therefore, my dear little children, pray and by your life give witness that you are mine and that you belong to me, because Satan wishes in these turbulent days to seduce as many souls as possible. Therefore, I invite you to decide for God and He will protect you and show you what you should do and which path to take. I invite all those who have said yes to me to renew their consecration to my Son Jesus and to His heart and to me, so we can take you more intensely as instruments of peace in this unpeaceful world. Medjugorje is a sign to all of you and a call to pray and live the days of grace that God is giving you. Therefore, dear children, accept the call to prayer with seriousness. I am with you and your suffering is also mine. Thank you for having responded to my call."

May 25, 1992 "Dear children! Today also, I invite you to prayer so that through prayer you come yet closer to God. I am with you and wish to lead you on the path of salvation which Jesus gives. From day to day I am closer and closer to you although you are not conscious of it and do not want to admit that you are connected to me in prayer only a little bit. When temptations and problems arise, you say, 'O God, O Mother, where are you?' And I only wait for you to give me your "Yes" so that I pass it on to Jesus and that He may bestow you with graces. Therefore, once again, accept my call and begin anew to pray, until prayer becomes joy for you, and then you will discover that God is almighty in your everyday life. I am with you and I wait for you. Thank you for having responded to my call."

June 25, 1992 "Dear Children! Today I am happy despite there still being some sadness in my heart for all those who began to take this path and then abandoned it. My presence here is, therefore, to lead you on a new path, the path of salvation. Thus, I call you day after day to conversion. But, if you do not pray you cannot say you are converting. I pray for you and intercede before God for peace: first, for peace in your heart, then around you so that God may be your peace. Thank you for having responded to my call."

July 25, 1992 "Dear Children! Today again I invite all of you to prayer -a joyful prayer -so that in these sad days none of you feel sadness in prayer but a joyful meeting with God, your Creator. Pray, dear children, so that you can be closer to me and feel through prayer what I desire from you. I am with you and everyday I bless you with my motherly blessing so that the Lord may bestow you with the abundance of His grace for your daily life. Thank God for the gift of my being with you because I am telling you: this is a great grace. Thank you for having responded to my call."

August 25, 1992 "Dear Children! Today I wish to tell you that I love you. I love you with my motherly love, and I call upon you to open yourselves completely to me so that through each of you I may be enabled to convert and save the world, where there is much sin and many things that are evil. Therefore, my dear children, open yourselves completely to me so that I may be able to lead you more and more to the marvelous love of God the Creator who reveals Himself to you day by day. I am at your side and I wish to reveal to you and show you the God who loves you. Thank you for having responded to my call!"

September 25, 1992 "Dear Children! Today also I wish to tell you: I am with you in these restless days in which Satan wishes to destroy everything which I and my Son, Jesus, are building up. In a special way he wishes to destroy your souls. He wishes to guide you as far away as possible from Christian life as well as from the Commandments, to which the Church is calling you so you may live them. Satan wishes to destroy everything which is holy in you and around you.

Therefore, little children, pray, pray, pray, in order to be able to comprehend all which God is giving you through my comings. Thank you for having responded to my call!"

October 25, 1992 "Dear Children! I invite you to prayer now when Satan is strong and wishes to make as many souls as possible his own. Pray, dear children, and have more trust in me, because I am here in order to help you, and to guide you on a new path towards a new life. Therefore, dear little children, listen and live what I tell you, because it is important for you, when I shall not be with you any longer, that you remember my words and all that I told you. I call you to begin to change your life from the beginning and that you decide for conversion not with words but with your life. Thank you for having responded to my call!"

November 25, 1992 "Dear Children! Today like never before I invite you to pray. May your life become prayer in fullness. Without love you cannot pray. Therefore, I invite you to first love God the Creator of your life and then you shall also discover and love God in all as He loves you. Dear children, it is a grace that I am with you. Therefore accept and live my messages for your good. I love you and therefore I am with you to teach you and to guide you to a new life of renunciation and conversion. Only in this way you shall discover God and everything which is far from you now. Therefore, little children, pray! Thank you for having responded to my call!"

December 25, 1992 "Dear children! Today, I wish to place you all under my mantle, to protect you from every Satanic attack. Today is the day of Peace, but throughout the whole world there is much lack of peace. Therefore, I call you to build up a new world of Peace together with me, by means of prayer. Without you, I cannot do that, and therefore I call all of you with my motherly love, and God will do the rest. Therefore, open yourselves to God's plans and purposes for you to be able to cooperate with Him for peace and for good. And, do not forget that your life does not belong to you, but is a gift with which you must bring joy to others and lead them to Eternal Life. May the tenderness of my little Jesus always accompany you. Thank you for having responded to my call."

January 25, 1993 "Dear children! Today, I call you to accept and live my messages with seriousness. These days are the days when you need to decide for God, for peace and for the good. May every hatred and jealousy disappear from your life and your thoughts, and may there only dwell love for God and for your neighbor. Only thus shall you be able to discern the signs of this time. I am with you, and I guide you into a new time, a time which God gives you as grace, so that you may get to know Him more. Thank you for having responded to my call!"

EPILOGUE: HOW CAN WE RESPOND

V. EPILOGUE: How Can We Respond?

A PLAN OF ACTION

If Medjugorje is really an authentic apparition of the Blessed Virgin Mary, what difference should this make to a believer? It is true that the public revelation is the touchstone of truth and the source of faith. Authentic private revelation, however, serves the purpose of deepening our appreciation for the public revelation while inspiring us to lead lives of piety. And if a reported apparition is truly an apparition of the Mother of God, then it is rash at best to ignore its message.

The sincere believer who arrives at the conviction that the Blessed Virgin is appearing at Medjugorje must first and foremost contemplate her messages to the world. The primary messages of Medjugorje center on conversion, prayer, fasting, confession, Holy Mass and confession. Specifically, we are asked to pray three hours daily, fast on bread and water on Wednesdays and Fridays, go to confession at least once a month, recite 15 decades of the Rosary daily and "let Holy Mass be our lives." Although these messages may seem rather demanding, they do not differ significantly from the rigorous spiritual regimen recommended by the great spiritual theologians of the past. The practice of fasting on bread and water on Wednesdays and Fridays was common in the early Church.

It is pointless to defend Medjugorje or discuss the "secrets" entrusted to the visionaries if we do not attempt to apply the message of Medjugorje in our lives. As the Blessed Mother said on May 25, 1991: "There are many who think they are doing a lot by talking about the messages, but do not live them." She wants us "to take with seriousness and put into practice the messages which I am giving you." [August 25, 1990]. Also, "I ask you to accept and to live the messages with seriousness...Each day read the messages which I have given you and transform them into life." [December 25, 1989]. The Blessed Mother's primary purpose in appearing at Medjugorje was to "lead you to Heaven." [May 25, 1991]. If we are led to the conviction that Mary is appearing at Medjugorje, then we must at least try to live the messages she gives us there. By God's great grace, hundreds of thousands of pilgrims have tried to transform their lives in the light of the message of Medjugorje ("These days while I am with you are days of grace. I desire to teach you and to help you walk on the path to holiness" [June 25, 1991]).

Once we have lived Medjugorje and experienced its fruits, we must in different degrees do what we can to share Medjugorje with all the children of Our Blessed Mother. The messages of Mary quoted earlier are particularly relevant in this context:

"Let them [visitors to Medjugorje and those who hear about Medjugorje] believe as if they see; believe firmly." [1981] [I wish] "people to know what is happening in Medjugorje. Speak about it so that all will be converted. Tell the whole world, tell it without delay, 'Be converted and do not wait.'" [1985]

"Dear children! You are responsible for the messages. The source of grace is here, but you, dear children, are the vessels transmitting the gifts. Therefore, dear children, I am calling you to work responsibly. Everyone will be responsible be according to his own measure. Dear children, I am calling you to give the gift to others with love, and not to keep it for yourselves." [May 8, 1986]

We can share Medjugorje by our lives, by our words and by our prayers. There is at least one other way in which we can directly participate in the Blessed Mother's mission in Medjugorje: petition appropriate Church authorities to approve the apparition at the earliest possible time. There is ample precedent for sending such petitions. This approach was adopted by devotees of previous apparitions who shared their testimonies with the authorities as the investigation was in progress. Procedures for the canonization of holy men and women also require testimonies and petitions. In the case of the definition of the doctrine of the Assumption, Pope Pius XII received petitions from 113 cardinals, 18 patriarchs, 2,505 archbishops and bishops, 32,000 priests and men religious, 50,000 religious women and 8,000,000 lay people.

If our conscience tells us that the Blessed Virgin Mary is appearing at Medjugorje, then we should not hesitate to pour out our heart on the matter to the Holy Father, the Perfect of the Sacred Congregation for the Doctrine of the Faith and Cardinal Kuharic. Although the Holy Father's sympathies for Medjugorje are well known, in his position as Pope he has to "go by the rules" before allowing the Church to make an official pronouncement on any claim of supernatural phenomena. Even on matters dear to his heart, such as the canonizations of Padre Pio and Sister Faustina, he is letting normal procedures take their course. In the case of Medjugorje, as with other apparitions, the "normal procedure" of investigation requires the data only the faithful can provide — and their perseverance.

She has already made clear that she needs our help. "Dear children, I want you to comprehend that God has chosen each one of you in order to use you for the great plan of salvation of mankind. You cannot comprehend how great your role is in God's plan." (January 25, 1987).

Our desire is to assist our Blessed Mother in her mission of leading her children to her Son. Humble petitions to our shepherds and to the Vicar of Christ with our testimonies will be an act of love to Our Lady and a great service to Holy

Mother Church as she discerns the sensus fidelium. To this end, we recommend that those devoted to responding to Our Lady's urgent call from Medjugorje [religious and lay] send in their testimonies and their petitions for a favorable resolution of the investigation to the following leaders:

His Holiness, Pope John Paul II
00120 Vatican City
ITALY

His Eminence, Cardinal Joseph Ratzinger
Perfect, Sacred Congregation for the Doctrine of the Faith
00120 Vatican City
ITALY

His Eminence, Cardinal Franjo Kuharic
Primate of Croatia
Kaptol 31, p.p. 553
41000, Zagreb
Croatia

APPENDICES

1. REPLIES TO SPECIFIC CRITIQUES OF MEDJUGORJE

Although the critics tend to prefer ad hominem arguments ("He supports Medjugorje because he is a Charismatic" or "Medjugorje cannot be authentic because the Charismatics find it attractive" — instances of these are found in the *Homiletic and Pastoral Review*, November 1990) — in the interests of clarity and consistency we cannot adopt the same approach. The critics have their pet peeves and the chips on their shoulders but they also have arguments. We have already addressed or pre-empted some of their principal arguments in the previous sections. In this section, we will try to address some specific critiques. Before proceeding to the critiques, a few introductory remarks are in order.

As we have noted earlier, the facts of salvation history are founded on the testimony of witnesses. In almost all approved Marian apparitions the witnesses have been peasants or children and their testimonies have generally survived the skepticism and criticism of the authorities and the academics. With the unprecedented outreach of the modern mass media, the "facts" in the Medjugorje apparition are not just the testimonies of the witnesses: there is now an entire "fact"-manufacturing industry funded and directed by friends and foes. Friendly exaggerations and scurrilous fabrications are generated with equal ease by this industry. In this setting, we have to take special care to get to the heart of the matter as we study the apparition without spending too much time or energy on the irrelevant (and there is plenty of this available).

As we have seen, in Fr. O'Carroll's view, the only relevant testimonies are "the testimonies of the witnesses about the apparitions as they saw them, when they were seeing them. That's what's essential." Nevertheless, we will address these critiques if only to better understand the phenomenon of Medjugorje and to clear up needless confusion.

It will be noticed from any survey of their critiques that the critics seem intent on looking at the events in Medjugorje through the rear view mirror. They are not concerned with what is happening now or happened a year ago. Their focus is usually limited to a few isolated events that allegedly took place in the early days of the apparition. The approach of examining the circumstances surrounding the genesis of an event is no doubt a legitimate one but there is something bizarre about keeping one's eyes strictly on the starting line while a race is going on. In addition, the rear view mirror used in studying the events in Medjugorje often seems to be concave or convex and we often find the critics themselves peering at us through the mirrors they provide.

Apart from the attacks on Fr. Vlasic, almost all the heavy artillery has been directed at the three visionaries who have been most accessible to the public, Ivan, Marija and Vicka. Their high visibility has made them marked persons as well as sitting ducks. All three have been accused of lying on at least one occasion and these lies, according to the critics, destroy their reliability as witnesses. The precise charges made against them will be carefully analyzed but it can be said here that the episodes so triumphantly touted by the critics have nothing to do with the actual apparition but concern the responses made by these visionaries in situations where there is clear evidence of manipulation, harassment and intimidation by authority figures. The reactions of the visionaries in these high-pressure situations would not have raised an eyebrow if we were talking of ordinary, normal children responding to such abnormal situations. But the visionaries now are not only expected to be saints but super-men and women as well.

Since it is important to preserve some sense of history when studying an apparition, we will study a similar situation involving one of the La Salette visionaries.

In 1850 there occurred an event which, for a while, put La Salette under a cloud. Some men interested in Maximin thought that he had a vocation to be a Marist religious. They proposed to take him to Ars, so that the celebrated cure there, Jean Baptiste Vianney, might advise him. Maximin agreed to go.

The Curé d'Ars believed the apparition authentic, had a picture of Our Lady of La Salette in his house, and blessed religious articles bearing representatives of the children's experience. But when Maximin came to Ars, he was first received by the curé's brusque and combative assistant, who summarily accused him of being a liar. After listening to considerable railing, Maximin replied, "You'll have it your way. If you suppose that I actually saw nothing, then you'll call me a liar." The assistant informed M. Vianney that the lad had, in effect, admitted being a liar.

The next morning Maximin briefly met the curé, who asked whether he had seen the Blessed Virgin. Maximin said that he had seen a beautiful lady, but did not know whether or not she was the Blessed Virgin. He was, of course, right, since it was for the Church, and not for him, to pronounce on the lady's identity. But the curé seemed disturbed and went on to inquire whether Maximin had ever told lies. The boy admitted that he had, meaning lies of excuse. The curé apparently concluded that Maximin was repudiating the apparition as fraudulent.

For some time thereafter M. Vianney gave up his devotion to Our Lady of La Salette, and this was taken as a sure sign that the apparition had been discredited. But the curé's abandonment of credence in La Salette caused him intense pain. He was constantly disquieted about it. Some years later he said that he determined to put the matter to a test by asking an important favor of Our Lady under the title of La Salette. It was instantly granted. "I am a firm believer in La Salette," he said. "I have been represented as not believing in it. On the contrary, I am a firm believer in it. That boy and I did not understand each other. But I have asked heaven for signs to bolster my faith, and I have had them." (55)

The pressure applied on Maximin in this episode is something the Medjugorje visionaries experience every other day. The controversies involving the three visionaries, however, involved trials by ordeal that went far beyond the episode recounted here. With these introductory remarks, we will turn to the specific critiques. In order to address them fairly and clearly, we will present the critiques as they are presented by the critics followed by appropriate responses. The specific critiques that will be addressed are the following:

(i) Manipulation and Theological Editing?
(ii) Hallucination?
(iii) Croatia on the Couch
(iv) False Predictions of the End of the Apparition?
(v) The "Big Sign?"
(vi) Miracles and Healings?
(vii) Are the Messages Theologically Sound?
(viii) Is the Apparition a Diabolic Phenomenon?
(ix) Ivan and the Letter
(x) Vicka and the Diary
(xi) Marija and the Vlasic Community
(xii) The Vlasic Controversy
(xiii) The Bloody Handkerchief
(xiv) Vicka and Jean Louis Martin
(xv) Jakov's Restlessness
(xvi) The Poem of the Man-God Controversy
(xvii) Vassula Ryden and Medjugorje
(xviii) Was It All A Joke?
(xix) Testimony from a Former Witness against Fr. Jozo
(xx) *Fidelity* Does It Again
(xxi) A Final Word to the Critics
(xie) Miscellaneous
(i) Manipulation and Theological Editing

CRITIQUE

1. The Bishop of Mostar: "The Bishop of Mostar, having personally studied the case and with the help of a suitable Commission, has after all this time, in a responsible way and with moral certainty come to the conclusion that the events of Medjugorje are a case of hallucination. This has been cleverly exploited by a group of Franciscans from

Hercegovina who have made the presumed 'apparitions' and the contents of the messages seem serious, manipulating the sincere desire for the supernatural on the part of the people and their deep love of Our Lady. The greatest responsibility belongs to the mystifier and charismatic wizard Fr. Tomislav Vlasic who, in this affair, risked perjury to defend his position. [...] The presumed visionaries are the ignorant pawns in a game that is way beyond them and by now they behave like domesticated 'robots.'" (56)

2. E. Michael Jones: "One of the fundamental facts of the so-called apparitions of Medjugorje is that the messages are received through a number of filters which the average pilgrim fails to perceive. The message is shaped to a large extent by those surrounding the seers, even if not directly — then by way of explanation and, one might also say, coaching." (57)

3. E. Michael Jones: "The question is crucial if we are to understand what is going on there. Are the seers doing the leading or are they merely being led?" (58)

4. E. Michael Jones: "It reminds one of a clever piece of theological editing. [...] Such, it seems, is the relation between seer and priest at St. James Church. If one switches back and forth fast enough between the improbable statements of the seers and the theologically acute statements of the priests, one tends to forget that one is talking about two separate things." (59)

RESPONSE

1. The thesis that the priests are manipulating the visionaries to fabricate both the accounts of the apparitions and the messages from the apparitions is hard to sustain in the face of the fact that the Franciscan parish priests have been transferred quite regularly after the beginning of the apparitions. In addition, as Jones admits, Fr. Zovko did not know the visionaries before the apparitions began. The most powerful argument against the thesis that the messages are manufactured by the priests is the content of the messages itself. A very controversial element of the Medjugorje messages is the Blessed Virgin's call for reconciliation with the Orthodox and the Moslems. It is simply preposterous to assume that the Franciscans with their centuries-old hostility to the Moslems and the Serbian Orthodox would have fabricated this particular message — especially when the wounds are still so fresh [wounds which have been opened yet again in recent times] and the memories still so bitter. On the contrary, this message appears to be specially directed at them.

2. Fr. Albert J. Hebert: "During the first apparitions, Father Jozo the pastor was away. Later, it took a special revelation to himself to convince him to protect the children. Fr. Zrinko, the other parish priest, treated the children rather severely and said he did better working in his garden than being concerned with apparitions. Later he became convinced of their authenticity. The six children, all their lives in a Communist state, and knowing how their people had suffered and been oppressed for years, would never have 'manipulated' something which would bring down the wrath of a government upon them, which was what happened when the authorities could not in the least make them depart from their account of an actual experience. Various experts have proven that there neither has been nor is any manipulation. You just don't manipulate genuine ecstasies or a world-wide spiritual phenomenon out of a little village. Nor the many cures and all sorts of signs and wonders that have occurred there!" (60)

3. For a change, it may be advisable to hear what the visionaries themselves have to say about this charge. They were asked, "What can you say about the statement of the bishop that it is the priests who are writing the messages which you attribute to the Gospa?"

Marija: "Although the bishop can think that, one day when we are in Heaven he will understand that it was a call from the Gospa to each of us, for all of us. I am distressed that he has been able to establish that. It will cause a panic. Before I used to receive the messages from the Gospa for the people every Thursday, and now I receive them on the 25th of each month. It hurts me that the bishop thinks that the priests are preparing these messages. I say with certainty that this is not true, for the messages have been communicated to me by the Gospa herself."

Ivan: "I would not know what to do other than to make the bishop come, on the 25th of the month, when the Gospa is communicating the messages to Marija. It is indeed she who writes them. That he has been able to have doubts all this time, I do not know what to think of it. It is very difficult to say what it is. It is not true that someone dictates to Marija what she is going to write. That I know, because I am looking when the Gospa communicates the message to her in spite of the fact that I cannot hear anything. It is the truth."

Vicka: "I do not have an answer for that. No one else would have been able to suppose that the clergy would do that. It is a miserable statement for it does not correspond to the truth."

Jakov: "This statement on the part of the bishop does not correspond to the truth."

Mirjana: "It is ridiculous. We are neither stupid nor susceptible to influence. Furthermore, I didn't even know these priests before the Gospa appeared. Father Jozo, I met only afterwards, and when the people came to him to speak to him about the apparitions, he answered in an arrogant manner, and invited them simply to come to pray in the church. I was even upset by his behavior."

Ivanka: "It is inaccurate that the priests did that for us." (61)

4. As for the charges of theological editing, the peasant background of the children coupled with the sustained prolongation of the apparitions makes it more likely than not that the objects of discussion in these encounters are not likely to be restricted to lofty theological themes. When the apparitions started, the visionaries were children. It is well known from the messages that the Blessed Virgin's objective was not just to transmit messages through them but to assist them in their spiritual growth both to bring them closer to God and to make them models for the world.

Fr. Laurentin thinks of this aspect of the apparitions as "a pedagogy." The encounter between the children and the Blessed Virgin "is largely a contact between these adolescents and their mother; doubly a mother in the case of two of them who are orphans. Contact between a mother and child has nothing to do with literature. It is on a different level. At the human level the baby talk between mother and infant, before the child can talk, is what is most fundamental in our initial formation. But no one would ever think of editing it, not even in those families where archives are kept. Tens of thousands of pages would be filled with the 'conversations', liberally sprinkled with babbling from the first one or two years. The result would be insipid and weak, without the smiles, the mimes, the human warmth. It is not always thus with the language of love! And this communication is so true, so formative and so edifying! How these young people are growing in health and holiness! It is pointless to record their daily conversations for they simply repeat a message of prayer, conversion and charity. One could criticize the monotony of all mothers' conversations with their children if we merely spectate from the outside." (62)

He adds elsewhere, "In looking at the meetings of the visionaries with Our Lady during the ecstasies, the lively and simple dialogue which establishes itself, and which culminates in prayer, I understood better and better this formation of the visionaries through the apparition. It is that which has been discussed since Bernadette, and which I witnessed taking place in the daily activity here, slowly, freely, as the daily communication of a mother forms her children. And yet the trials were not lacking, neither external nor internal; the natural faults of each one, and so many physical and theological conflicts. In spite of human frailty, in spite of the struggles and weaknesses inherent in every destiny, it is faith, generosity, good will and holiness which has triumphed." (63)

If the critic finds some of the exchanges banal, he must remember two things: (a) that exchange (this includes all exchanges other than the messages transmitted for public dissemination) was a private conversation between a mother and her child on which he is eavesdropping. (b) the "fault", if there is any, lies with the questioner not with the person who has to respond to whatever question is put to her. The critic is invited to carry on a conversation with a normal Croatian peasant child and to answer all the questions the child may have. Perhaps then he will appreciate better the private exchanges between the children and the Blessed Virgin.

In the three years that Jesus spent with the Apostles, it is unreasonable to think that He only spoke to them of the greatest theological mysteries. And surely, many of their questions to Him would have dealt with local or theologically irrelevant matters. But He dealt with them at all levels because His mission was to form them theologically and spiritually so as to bring them closer to God and to enable them to spread His message to the world. He did not choose the Pharisees as His apostles since their minds were already made up and they already knew the answers to all the questions. The critic concerned with theological editing might as well accuse the Gospel writers of "theological editing" for not including every conversation the Apostles had with Jesus. Even with the "theological editing" that necessarily had to be done in the Gospels, New Testament scholars will testify that the personality of each Gospel writer is reflected in the Gospel he wrote. While recognizing the divine inspiration of the Bible, one also recognizes the imprint left by the human instruments in transmitting the divine Word. The demands laid by critics like the CCR and Michael Jones seem motivated by a Fundamentalist mind-set that cannot comprehend the very real role played by human agents in transmitting divine messages.

5. Archbishop Franic of Split: "There exists in the brain and in the heart of these young seers human imperfections and their relationship with the supernatural depends on the way they master these obstacles at any given moment. These obstacles can also be suggestions they have received from other people. [...] That is why each message should be examined for itself. [...] In this examination, therefore, it is necessary to eliminate human imperfection and find the true kernel, the quintessence of these apparitions. Each message carries its own particular weight which depends on the given moment or

degree of mood. People have their faults, the children remain children, and they can, outside the apparitions, say things that are not right. They can lie or be distracted during prayer. They are not saints." (64)

6. Professor Mark Miravalle: "The Jones article appears unwilling to accept any human error, neither moral nor prudential, regarding the Medjugorje event, and sees any interpretations, explanations or distinctions of 'central or principal' from 'peripheral or incidental' in the Medjugorje message and concurring events that differ from his own individual interpretation as 'theological editing.' This objectively constitutes a literalist, sola scriptura approach applied to the domain of private revelation in general and to the Medjugorje event in specific, bereft of an accurate understanding of the tradition of authentic private revelation, and projects an unjust scrutiny the likes of which many ecclesiastically approved writings and private revelations could never have withstood. This would be analogous to... [claiming] that the Marian apparitions at Lourdes were not authentic because of the incidental event of 50 'fanatical' pilgrims likewise claiming Marian visions immediately following Bernadette's authentic encounter with the 'Immaculate Conception'. Or to judge the authenticity of the Fatima apparitions based primarily on the later moral lives of the 70,000 people who witnessed the solar miracle at Fatima, and at the finding of any having committed serious sin within a few years following the solar miracle, concluding that Fatima was a fraud since Mary always places her 'stamp of approval' upon the complete moral lives of anyone involved in a true Marian apparition." (65)

(ii) Hallucination?

CRITIQUE

"The Bishop of Mostar, having personally studied the case and with the help of a suitable Commission, has after all this time, in a responsible way and with moral certainty come to the conclusion that the events of Medjugorje are a case of collective hallucination." (66)

RESPONSE

1. It must be remembered that the first examiners of the children were materialist Marxists who wished to dismiss the whole event as a hoax. They could not reach a conclusion of hallucination despite their best efforts. Subsequent examinations by competent scientists have elimi-

nated the hallucination hypothesis beyond all reasonable doubt. Collective hallucination over a period of ten years would be more remarkable than the apparition itself from the standpoint of science![1]

2. Father Albert J. Hebert: "Never has any saint, mystic, stigmatist, visionary or seer, or any special instrument of God in all the history of the Church been so extensively, scientifically and thoroughly examined as these six children. These examinations and tests have ruled out anything negative that can be suggested by critics. There is nothing neurotic or hysterical, no epilepsy or catalepsy, no dreaming, hypnosis, suggestion, play-acting, deceit, trance, or 'natural' ecstasy; and no manipulation by priests or anyone else. And, as Archbishop Frane Franic of Split has said, anyone hallucinating for years would have his or her mind destroyed — and this fact would be obvious to experts in this field." (67)

3. Professor Emilio Servadio: "Genuine hallucination (as distinct from optical illusions or mass hysteria), is always peculiar to one individual. It is not possible for a group of people to have repeated identical hallucinatory experiences which they insist are real, without showing signs of psychic abnormality. One cannot but be surprised that a bishop should pronounce a psychiatric diagnosis based on criteria which are psychiatrically unsound." [*Il Tempo*, December 12, 1984].

4. Dr. Nicholas Bartulica, a psychiatrist in the U.S. who is of Croatian origin, has had the opportunity of interviewing the visionaries in their native tongue almost from the beginning of the apparition. In *Are the Seers Telling the Truth?*, he approaches the Medjugorje phenomenon as a psychiatrist and from a psychological point of view and proceeds to refute "the unfounded hypotheses proposed by some Medjugorje opponents who suggest a possibility of 'hallucinations,' 'imaginations', or simply conscious fabrication, that is lying." Here is Dr. Bartulica's analysis of the hallucination hypothesis:

I was able to converse with the seers in their mother tongue. At no time could I detect any symptoms of emotional or mental abnormalities. The hypothesis of 'collective hallucinations' originated from

---

[1] I was in Medjugorje on November 12, 1988. After the evening Mass in St. James Church it was announced from the pulpit: that day the five medical experts of the investigating commission from the Bishop's Conference were also in Medjugorje. They had stated their findings to the priests of the parish: "The visionaries are healthy in every way. No pathological condition can be said to be influencing them. From now we await only the judgment of the theologians on the commission."

Bishop Zanic, who was criticized by several professionals for engaging in a field in which he was not qualified.

Following the establishment of the new Episcopal Commission in January 1987, all seers were again psychologically evaluated by five psychiatrists from different universities in Yugoslavia. Their unanimous conclusion was that all six were presently enjoying perfect mental health, and no symptoms of mental illness could be found. Their findings were submitted to Bishop F. Komarica, the President of the Commission.

As mentioned in the Foreword, I interviewed Vicka for the first time in October 1981. As a psychiatrist, I had a special professional interest in listening to her unusual experience. This young lady appeared of completely sound mind, outspoken and sincere. She was fully convinced of the authenticity of her subjective experience. I was impressed with her natural attitude and of the absence of any tendency toward pretense or fabrication.

A few years later (1985), I observed her during an apparition for about five minutes. She was out of contact with her surroundings and appeared to be conversing with an invisible person.

During the next few years, I periodically interviewed Vicka and the other seers, except Jakov. One has to concur with the observation of the other professional investigators, i.e., that those young people had shown continuous progress in intellectual, emotional as well as spiritual aspect.

An observation of the seers regarding their opinion about themselves is worth being recorded.

While interviewing Vicka, in October 1981, I asked her what could be the reason that she was selected to be a receiver of the apparitions and messages. Without any hesitation Vicka answered, 'We did ask her (Gospa) the same question and she said that she was not looking for the 'best ones'.' The other seers expressed the same attitude; that is, they were puzzled at why they were selected and never displayed any sign of self-conceit or haughtiness for having been the receivers of a special charisma." [*Medjugorje: Are The Seers Telling the Truth?*, pp. 31-33].

5.   Finally, we quote the visionaries themselves again responding to the question, "What do you think of the statements of the bishop when he treats the visionaries as sick people, or when he says that you are liars; that it is the priests in Medjugorje who have incited you to say that you see apparitions of the Blessed Virgin and that she communicates messages to you?"

Marija: "Each one of us holds our position. I am also aware that the bishop likewise maintains his. I am only very sorry that his is negative and that he cites some facts which do not correspond to the truth. We are not sick, nor are we driven by whomever it may be. I am sorry that Satan tries to impede and oppose those who desire to serve the Church; for the Blessed Virgin comes in the name of unity and peace."

Ivan: "To speak in this manner he should have the results of medical exams to support him. As far as it concerns me, I would be of the opinion that it be he who may be the object of a medical exam. It is not true that I am being manipulated by whomever, even less by the clergy, dictating what I have seen and heard on the matter of the apparitions of the Blessed Virgin."

Vicka: "His statements inspire only compassion. I am distressed that such a person can make such statements."

Jakov: "I do not know according to what criteria the bishop can conclude that we are sick. We have not had many contacts together. I ask myself according to what criteria he could conclude that the priests have been instigators. He has never attended the apparitions with us. It is sure that we were not influenced by the priests."

Mirjana: "Number one, I think that these statements are not worthy of a bishop. Number two, he does not have the right to speak in this manner for only once in my life has he spoken to me and after that conversation he stated that everything was true about Medjugorje. By what right can he now verify that I am sick? First it was that, later, everything else. Nevertheless, I think it is necessary to pray for him."

Ivanka: "That does not arouse any interest for me."(68)

(iii) Croatia on the Couch

CRITIQUE

E. Michael Jones:

Father Zovko was experimenting with an explosive mixture of charismatic prayer and sensitivity training. W.R. Coulson, who worked with Carl Rogers doing sensitivity training, recognized the techniques immediately. Coulson, who did encounter work with religious orders including a group of Franciscans in California in the late '60's, has seen the potent effect of combining sensitivity and religion, first hand. He described how it destroyed the Immaculate Heart Nuns in an article in *Fidelity*. ...[Will] Schutz is telling us that encounter groups are extremely effective ways to manipulate people. When combined with the normal charismatic tendency of praying for a passage or getting a word of prophecy, especially when this is done under an authority figure like a priest, they can be especially effective in producing what otherwise would be known as mystical experiences in the participants.... Given the psychic dynamite that is involved in combining encounter groups and charismatic training, it is not surprising. Given that type of combination, anything could happen. People could start seeing visions." (69)

Have we reached a situation which by now explains itself without any recourse to supernatural hypotheses? Psychologist Coulson seems to think so. 'Well it certainly makes the necessity of a supernatural explanation for what they saw unnecessary. I mean certainly any prudent scientific psychologist would say, 'We'd better not run too quickly to heaven for an answer here because we've got something that sounds very much like it's got a naturalistic explanation."

The Californification of Croatia

Coulson now suspects that what claims to be messages from heaven is in reality the Californification of Croatia. 'You know,' he said, 'it's a shame. If the Blessed Mother wants to appear to men today, she had better appear to someone who hasn't been playing the California game because the whole issue is going to be then in doubt.'" (70)

Why shouldn't it [Fr. Zovko's combination of charismatic prayer and encounter group therapy] have the same effect on the general population in the parish? Having been primed by him to expect signs and wonders, the village exploded with fervor when they appeared. The times, it should be remembered, were apocalyptic anyway. (71)

RESPONSE

1. As a careful reading of *The Untold Story* will show, Jones' sudden foray into long-distance psychoanalysis really doesn't touch on what he considers to be the essential issue: "Are the children telling the truth?" He admits reluctantly and grudgingly that the children were not part of Fr. Zovko's prayer group. His only source of information on Fr. Zovko's prayer group, in any case, is someone who is clearly not a disinterested party. At best, Jones' psychoanalysis can be used to show that the villagers had been primed to accept the apparition uncritically. It does not even approach the question of the authenticity of the apparition itself. Nevertheless, Jones' observations on Fr. Zovko's prayer group need to be addressed for one reason: to show his recurrent tendency to leap to gigantic conclusions on the basis of skimpy or irrelevant evidence. In addition, his unkind comments on Fr. Zovko show both lack of comprehension and a definite need for a little sensitivity training. Anyone who has seen or heard Fr. Zovko in

person (or even on a video) cannot fail to be moved and elevated by the depth and power of his call to holiness.

2. What is sauce for the goose is sauce for the gander. If Jones proposes to make a case for his interpretation of events by appealing to the authority of a pliant psychologist, he should at least take the trouble to get a second opinion. Professor Paul Vitz, Professor of Psychology at New York University and author of several major works in psychology of religion, has examined the "psychological" arguments presented in *The Untold Story* and has discussed these with both Jones and Coulson. From his investigation, he has found no persuasive evidence for explaining Medjugorje in terms of encounter group theory.

3. In any case, the issue is not a psychological one but a question of factual evidence for assuming that the visionaries belonged to Fr. Zovko's prayer group. Jones himself, we have seen, admits he has no evidence to this effect although there is reason to believe that he tried to manufacture such evidence [see below]. Dr. Nicholas Bartulica subjects Jones' psychological arguments to searching scrutiny here. In the course of his study, Dr. Bartulica interviewed M. Pehar the Croatian ex-priest whom Jones used as his source in developing the encounter-group explanation. Curiously, Pehar disputes some of the allegations attributed to him by Jones. Dr. Bartulica:

> The reader of *The Untold Story* learned about Fr. Zovko's charismatic background through the information from the ex-Franciscan Pehar. He apparently participated in a 'group session' conducted by Fr. Zovko, that the psychologist W.R. Coulson described as a 'milling-around exercise.'
>
> When this writer talked with M.Pehar on this subject, he confirmed that he attended one such session, which might be characterized as 'sensitivity training'" According to Pehar, Fr. Zovko spent some time in West Germany, where he learned some group techniques. Pehar admits that he did not like the interaction expected from the participants, and he left the session.
>
> While reading the conversation that M. Jones had with Pehar concerning his (Pehar's) opinion about Fr. Zovko influencing the seers, one gets the impression that Pehar agreed that Fr. Zovko could have influenced the visionaries through special techniques.
>
> However, Pehar told this writer that M. Jones talked with him on the telephone several times trying to extract from him a statement that Fr. Zovko had the visionaries in a 'charismatic group' where he (Zovko) could have applied sensitivity training methods. When Pehar explained to M. Jones that, since he left Yugoslavia, he had no further

first-hand knowledge about Fr. Zovko's activities, M. Jones presented a hypothetical scenario, which is described in the above-quoted conversation. It follows that Pehar agreed that Fr. Zovko could have influenced the seers only if they had taken part in his (Fr. Zovko's) prayer groups, but Pehar had no knowledge whether it occurred.

In view of the above, one is moved to raise the question why M. Jones suggested to Pehar that 'the girls (seers) could have gone to one of these meetings' where Fr. Zovko 'could have suggested something to them,' when M. Jones, without checking with Pehar, was aware that none of the visionaries were part of Fr. Zovko's prayer group. In addition, M. Jones, after having reviewed the tapes of Fr. Zovko's interview with the seers, concluded that it was clear that Fr. Zovko 'did not know the seers.'

Furthermore, one wonders why M. Jones, in his conversation, referred to the seers as 'these girls' when it is a well-known fact that among the six seers, there are also two boys, Ivan and Jakov.

The above-mentioned conversation appears as a 'set up' arranged by *The Untold Story* author in which he succeeded in obtaining the answers that he himself suggested. Isn't this a case of intentional manipulation of the facts to prove a point without regard for truth?

As a matter of fact, in the same vein as we mentioned in the case of Fr. Vlasic, M. Pehar disagrees with M. Jones's assessment of Fr. Zovko's manipulative skills.

During the conversation with this writer, Pehar confirmed his dislike for Fr. Zovko's "sensitivity training" sessions, but he does not believe that Fr. Zovko has been involved in "manipulation" of the visions. Without having a final conviction about Medjugorje events, Pehar believes that the visionaries have some unexplained subjective experiences and that they are neither "liars" nor being 'manipulated,' as the author of *The Untold Story* purports.

After being told about Fr. Zovko's 'charismatic' skills, the reader receives a large amount of information on the methods and results of sensitivity/encounter groups and about their combination with charismatic activities.

For instance, M. Jones called such combination 'psychic dynamite' that even can cause visions. In the same vein the psychologist Coulson suggested 'a naturalistic explanation' of seers' experiences, assuming that they participated in the encounter/charismatic groups. The same would apply for Will Schultz's comments about some examples of 'feeling like being in ecstasy.'

However, the reader is at a loss in seeking out the motives for which the aforementioned explanations were given and applied to the Medjugorje seers. As we learned, *The Untold Story* had admitted that the children were 'not in Fr. Zovko's prayer group' and that 'the tapes make it clear that Zovko doesn't know the seers.'

One wonders for what reason have we received such a long lecture on the 'manipulative' character of sensitivity/encounter/charismatic techniques. Perhaps the reader had to be prepared to accept *The Untold Story* assertions that even if Fr. Zovko was not the initiator of the apparitions, he was eager to take control of them by applying his 'manipulative charismatic skills.'" (72)

3. Fr. Laurentin:
A. Fr. Jozo Zovko had only arrived nine months before the apparitions began. He had initiated prayer groups, but they were groups of classical prayer, without the influence of the charismatic renewal. He clearly stated this to me.
B. Fr. Jozo did not know yet the six visionaries of Bijakovici, nor did they attend his prayer group.
C. He was absent from his parish during the days preceding and the first few days of the apparitions, since he was preaching a retreat in Zagreb.
D. Nothing in the first apparitions (which are known to us through multiple testimonies, tape recordings and even a film) shows the least sign of prayer of a wild or emotional kind. The visionaries were familiar only with the arch traditional prayers of the community, particularly the seven Our Father's, Hail Mary's and Glory Be's. They recited them with restrained vigor and peasant conviction, without sentimental coloration. (73)

(iv) False Predictions of the End of the Apparition?

CRITIQUE

1. The Bishop of Mostar: "After the seventh 'apparition' that took place not in Medjugorje, but in Cerno (a few kilometers from Medjugorje, where the 'visionaries' were taken by car by state officials), the boys and girls told the parish priest the same evening that Our Lady had said that there would be three more apparitions: on Wednesday, Thursday and Friday, i.e. on 1,2 and 3 July (1981). The last apparition would be on Friday. Some priests were also present at this last 'apparition' which took place in the parish house of Medjugorje. When the 'apparition' was over, the 'visionaries' said: This is the last apparition! So, how can one explain the fact that the 'apparitions' continued and still haven't finished?" (74)

2.   E. Michael Jones: "Evidently the Blessed Mother was not only unde-
cided, she was also wrong about how much longer the apparitions
were going to last. Or perhaps she changed her mind, or perhaps the
seers are not telling us the truth. The story lacks consistency. [...]
Perhaps they [the defenders of the apparition] can explain why the
children claimed that the Virgin said she was only going to appear for
three more days." (75)

RESPONSE

1.   Anyone who has a supernatural experience will not be able to
comprehend everything about it, especially in the initial stages. This
was only to be expected in the group of peasant children who were
privileged to have the apparition in Medjugorje. They knew nothing
about apparitions in general and after their first encounters, Mirjana
got hold of a book on Lourdes in order to better understand their
own experience. The book talked about how the apparition took
place for a given number of days and then ceased. This Mirjana took
to be a formula for all apparitions and said as much. She expected
the Medjugorje apparition to follow the Lourdes schedule. This,
obviously, did not happen. The incident only shows what we should
have known from the beginning: judgments made by the visionaries
are not infallible.

2.   Fr. Rupcic: The declarations of the visionaries "saying that the
apparitions would last until 3 July 1981, were later interpreted by the
Bishop as doubts, even lies, considering that the apparitions continued afterwards. Previously, even though the Bishop was aware of all
this, nothing had prevented him from saying: 'It is certain, the boys
and girls are not lying.' The accusing statements made about the
visionaries came about in the following way: when the parish priest
Fr. Jozo Zovko, realized that the visionaries were not sufficiently
instructed in the faith and in the problem they were now faced with,
he gave them some prayer books and some rosaries and in addition
to these, he gave Mirjana a book called *The Apparitions of Our Lady*
written by Bozo Vuco and published in Makarska in 1974. As well as
that, he tried to convince the boys and girls to move to the parish
church for the apparitions. In this way, he hoped to discourage
people from roaming on the mountain and lingering around the
visionaries' houses. But the boys and girls were not keen on moving
to the church - in a way, they would have preferred to be alone,
without people. With reference to this, Mirjana said to Fr. Jozo:
"There is no reason for us to move to the church, because the
apparitions will finish next Friday." Fr. Jozo asked if it was Our Lady

who had told her so. Mirjana answered: "It was not she who told me, I read it in the book you gave me. That is what happened in Lourdes and that is what will happen here."

The boys and girls had probably calculated from what they had read in the book that the apparitions of Our Lady would come to an end, and once they were convinced of this, had discussed the matter among themselves. So, on 3 July, after the apparition, they declared that it was all over. But on the following day, a Saturday, even though they had not expected it and did not go up on the mountain, each one had a vision wherever he or she happened to be at the time. So the Bishop was mistaken in saying that it was Our Lady who had spoken about the end of the apparitions. Nor was he right in saying that there were some priests present during the last apparition on 3 July because Fr. Jozo was actually the only one present at that apparition. (76)

3. Fr. Laurentin: "The seers did indeed believe that the apparitions would end July 4. With their weariness and fear of those trying days, that was their mistaken interpretation. On July 4th, they did not meet together and did not expect the apparition, which came and surprised them where they were. But, was it the Gospa who had told them that? Mirjana says so in the (confused) interrogation of June 30th. But she is the only one, and it is only her interpretation. Vicka never said she had heard that and was quite right in saying that she does not remember it anymore. To claim that the Virgin said that to all the seers and repeated it four to five times presents two errors invented to discredit the seers. But this polemic alteration harms rather the credibility of the polemist himself." (77)

(v) The Big Sign?

CRITIQUE

The Bishop of Mostar: "Right from the beginning of the 'apparitions', the 'visionaries' said that Our Lady would leave a sign, visible to all, as proof of her apparitions. In connection with this sign, Vicka wrote the following in her diary: In explaining when the sign would happen, Our Lady said the following: 'It will soon come' [27 August 1981] 'Just a little more patience' [29 August 1981] 'Come on, just a little more patience' [31 August 1981] 'Again, just a little more patience' [3 September 1981]. "Vicka told someone who in turn told the Bishop in confidence that the sign would happen before her Dad came home from Germany. And he was due home in Christmas 1981. This sign, which attracted the pilgrims, was mentioned to the public several times: at the feast of the Immaculate Conception in 1981, at

Christmas during the same year and on New Year's Day 1982. Obviously, when nothing happened, the 'visionaries' said, 'we didn't say anything about it.'" (78)

RESPONSE

Fr. Rupcic: "Vicka, in her notes, in the entry made on 27 August 1981, wrote that Our Lady said the 'big sign' would happen 'soon' and that meanwhile, they had 'to be patient' [29 and 31 August, 3 September 1981]. The Bishop tries to make out that this is a lie, since the promise has not yet come true. But in the case of prophecy, one has to take into account the kind of language that prophets usually use. They express themselves in a literary-prophetic style and sometimes a thousand years can mean just one day. When Vicka uses the word 'soon' this shouldn't create doubt any more than what other prophets have said. Similarly, who would dare to doubt the word of Christ with regard to his coming again 'Yes, I will come soon' [Apoc 22, 20]? The Bishop tries to associate the word 'soon' with the return of Vicka's father from Germany for Christmas or for the feast of the Immaculate Conception in 1981 or for the New Year holiday in 1982, but there is no mention of this in Vicka's notes nor did the visionaries mention this." (79).

(vi) Miracles and Healings?

CRITIQUE

1. The Bishop of Mostar: "The unfulfilled promises concerning the 'healings' make one doubt the authenticity of the apparitions. 'Our Lady" is said to have promised many sick people that they would be healed. Let's give some examples:

   In 1981, there was a promise made concerning a child from Grude suffering from leukemia — that he would get better, certainly and unconditionally. There are written descriptions of the case. But he died towards the end of 1981.

   The Franciscan Brother Ivan Dolan suffered from cancer. His mother went on foot from Rama to Medjugorje to ask Our Lady to heal her son. The 'Visionaries' said that Our Lady promised to heal him. Several months later, the brother died.

   A girl called DB also got cancer. The doctors advised her to have a mastectomy. She went on foot to Medjugorje, to seek health. The 'Visionaries' turned to Our Lady who replied that there was no need for the operation. But the girl died, following terrible suffering, on 24 December 1983.

Amongst the miraculous healings described in the book by Fr. Rupcic, there is the case of Venka Bilic-Brajcic from Split. When her doctor saw the book, he protested outright against the affirmation that she was cured. She delivered her medical certificates on 8 September 1982 and she died in June 1984. And so on.

The last case was that of a heart patient, Marko Blazevic from Buna near Mostar. According to the letter from the Archbishop of Belgrade, Mgr A. Turk, sent to the Bishop's Curia of Mostar on 3 June 1984, Marko was admitted to hospital to the Cardiology Department where the above-named Archbishop was also a patient. Blazevic told the Archbishop that he was due to undergo a risky operation, but that he was sure of the success of this operation, 'since he and his family had asked the boys and girls from Medjugorje where the Holy Mother of God appears and that a boy (he said "boys" to the others) had asked the Virgin Mary whether he should undergo the operation. And the Mother of God replied that he should have the operation and not worry about it because it would certainly be a success as long as prayers were said'. But the patient didn't wake up after the operation; he died.

The Bishop of Mostar sent the letter to Medjugorje, asking for an explanation. Fr. Vlasic made enquiries with the 'Visionaries' about the above-mentioned case. They replied that no one had ever asked them anything whatever. Then the Bishop called the daughter of the deceased man Blazevic. She had probably been instructed by Fr Vlasic and confirmed that she had been to Medjugorje and had asked about her father. But the 'visionaries' replied that it was necessary to pray during the operation, but said nothing as to the success of the operation! So, where does the truth lie!

Diana Basile's 'healing': In mid-August last year, Dr. Luigi Frigerio from the 'Mangiagalli' hospital in Milan came to the Bishop's Curia in Mostar, bringing with him a report on the 'miraculous healing' of Signora Diana Ferro nee Basile. The Lady was supposedly cured of multiple sclerosis and of blindness of the right eye in Medjugorje on 24 May 1984. The world press and especially the Italian press wrote a great deal about this case last summer. Even the Archbishop of Split-Makarsks, Mgr. F. Franic, reported this news in his episcopal bulletin Number 4/1984. Recently we found an article on this case in a magazine called *Giovia* of 29 October 1984.

The Bishop of Mostar thought it was best to send the above mentioned report to the Medical Bureau of Lourdes, the most competent authority for such cases. The president of the Bureau, Dr.

Theodor Mangiapan, replied on 13 September last with a detailed letter. The main points of his letter are:

- Multiple sclerosis is a real challenge to doctors nowadays as far as a positive and objective diagnosis is concerned.
- The President wonders what this Institute Specialisaton in Milan really is. Most of the doctors and 'witnesses' connected with this 'healing' are associated with this 'boutique'.
- In order to judge the permanent nature of this healing, the case required time, i.e. at least 3-4 years.
- We want to let the Medjugorje Commission know our 'reservation in this matter' concerning the 'healing' of Signora D. B. Ferro. Dr Mangiapan advises the Bishop responsible for Medjugorje, not to let himself became too involved, not to accept or refuse this apparent miracle too soon!

This is how the President of the Medical Bureau of Lourdes expressed himself. Time will advise us best." (80).

RESPONSE

1. Fr. Rupcic: "The 'False' Healings" — According to the Bishop's theory on Medjugorje and his false Judgement as regards 'private' revelations, miracles should not and 'could not' happen. Therefore the Bishop rejects them outright. But even here he refers to doubtful witnesses and to cases that were not examined. He refers to a certain child from Grude, in Hercegovina, who suffered from leukemia and whom Our Lady promised to heal but who, instead of getting better, died. This case was not sufficiently examined: we do not really know whether or not the visionaries passed on this message. On the other hand, in no other case, as far as we know, have the visionaries ever promised a healing without conditions. As in the case of young Daniele Setka, from Vukodol, near Mostar, who was cured — his parents were told to believe, pray and fast. It is not certain and it is not easy to believe that things were different in the case of the child from Grude or in the case of Ivan Fzolan, whose mother prayed to Our Lady and asked her to cure him, but he died. Here there are also other reasons for associating Our Lady with the sick; because of this, one would have to examine the above-mentioned cases in an unbiased way, and not merely accept written texts as evidence, especially those written by people who, because of ignorance or ideological reasons, are against the apparitions of Medjugorje. It is possible that the sick children's parents, because they very much wanted their children to get better, distorted Our Lady's promise or overlooked the condition under which such a promise was made.

Even though the above-mentioned cases are not clear, the others mentioned by the Bishop including the case of Desa Busic and of Marko Blazevic are presented in an extremely false way. The Bishop's Curia of Mostar, in its letter addressed to the parish of Mostar (No. 636/84) says that Desa had asked Our Lady if she should undergo an operation or not, and that Our Lady, through the visionaries, replied that it was not necessary, but then the patient died. The deceased woman's sister Maria, who was very attached to her sister especially during her illness, replied to the Bishop's Curia, in connection with this misinformation. These are her words: 'With reference to letter No. 636/84 from the Bishop's Curia dated June 8, 1984, addressed to the parish of Medjugorje, in which my sister's death is connected with declarations made by the visionaries of Medjugorje, I hereby declare that what is mentioned in this report is totally inaccurate'. Despite this, the Bishop continues of his own accord, and claims the contrary, even though he has no evidence relating to the deceased woman Desa Busic.

What happened in the case of Marko Blazevic is almost the same: according to what the Archbishop of Belgrade Alois Turk writes to Bishop Zanic, Mr Blazevic said that he had to undergo a serious operation but that he was sure it would be a success, 'because he and his family had turned to the visionaries of Medjugorje and a boy (to the others he said: the boys) had asked Our Lady if he should undergo the operation. And the Mother of God replied that he should undergo the operation and not be worried because it would certainly be a success, as long as he prayed.

But, with all due respect, Monsignor Turk's declaration does not contain the truth since apparently Blazevic first said 'a boy' had asked Our Lady, and then said 'the boys.' Any way, apart from this, this is what happened: Marko didn't ask either 'a boy' or 'the boys,' neither did his daughter Melania. She merely implored Ivan Dragicevic to recommend the sick man to Our Lady, which he did. This is exactly what happened, but the story continues to be spread. Perhaps we need to ask ourselves, where people like Bishop Zanic are concerned: 'Where is the truth?' One thing is still not clear: why does the Bishop continue to uphold what first-hand witnesses like Ivan and Blazevic's daughter expressly deny? What is the meaning of that sentence that does not prove anything and that is not proved (according to which the daughter of the deceased Blazevic declared to the Bishop that nothing had been said about the success of the operation) other than 'she was probably instructed by Fr Vlasic...?' Obviously anything can be declared as true, the only thing that does not prevail is the truth!

Furthermore, in my book entitled *Apparitions of Our Lady at Medjugorje* I have reported the doctor's diagnosis and the statement made by Venka Bilic-Brajcic, who was suffering from a tumor. The Bishop, in connection with this case, said: 'When her doctor saw the book, he vigorously protested against the declaration that she was cured'. It is not clear to whom the aforementioned statement about the healing is attributed, because in my book I only referred to the doctor's diagnosis and to what the patient had said. Now, after Venka had turned to Our Lady, the diagnosis was as follows: 'The patient has improved, she feels well, there are no signs of changes due to metastasis in the bones and in the organs'. Therefore, if, as the Bishop said, it's true that Venka's doctor protested against something, he could only protest against himself.

With reference to this, I consider it important to draw attention to the false interpretations, some of which are given deliberately, of the extraordinary healings that I have referred to in my book. In this book, I have openly warned that all the cases of healing mentioned are spoken about freely and described personally by those who felt cured. It is simply an account of their own experience and evidence. Likewise, I have clearly stated that this healing like the others (and there are many important healings) are open 'to the researches of natural, medical and theological sciences and to the examination of faith.' So, these healings, instead of being labelled, must be explained, and until they have been scientifically examined in every aspect and in a responsible way (which until now has not been done), no one has the right to judge them 'by appearances' and above all no one has the right to deny personal evidence given in a sincere way, by honest people, as regards these events.

The most interesting case of healing so far is that of Diana Basile from Ferro, near Milan — not only because it is the most important among the healings in Medjugorje but because it is the one that has been most thoroughly examined. Diana suffered from multiple sclerosis. She couldn't get up or move. For a long time she had been treated for her disease in a clinic in Milan but despite treatment from highly qualified specialists, her situation got steadily worse. She had become completely blind in the right eye and for many years had been unable to see with it. For this reason, she had decided to go on a pilgrimage to Medjugorje to where she was accompanied on 23 May 1984; she assisted at the apparition of Our Lady in the church, in the little chapel near the altar. Immediately after the apparition, she was instantly healed, she could see again and she stood up alone. The next day, she went on foot from the Bigeste Hotel in Ljubuski where she was staying to Medjugorje (12 Kilometres) and she went up to the mountain where the apparitions occur. A report on her disease, therapy and healing has been scrupulously drawn up by the same doctors who had treated her. This report was sent by them to the Parish of Medjugorje, to Bishop Zanic and to Archbishop Franic of Split. After this, the Bishop of Mostar says that he asked the opinion of the Medical Bureau, which answered him. Unfortunately, the Bishop doesn't refer to the original reply, so it is not possible to use it as a basis for criticism. Anyway, from what he says we come to the conclusion that as regards this healing, it will be necessary to wait three or four years before being able to give 'a judgment on the permanent character of the healing.' This and everything else referred to by the Bishop is only Mangiapan's opinion, who is really freeing himself from any responsibility, regardless of the truth or otherwise of the healing described. This way of behaving is easier than examining the healing, as is his duty. However, supposing that the answer was made in good faith, we realize that Manigiapan has not a clear concept of what a miracle is, seeing that he gives instructions to the Bishop as to how to behave when accepting a healing as a miracle. A miracle is a special grace from God, and because of this, goes beyond medicine. It can be known only through revelation and faith; thus it has a theological explanation and not a medical or merely scientific one. Its essence and value lie in its capacity to act as a sign, and not in the specific light of its 'supernatural content.' God can make even the things of nature turn into 'signs,' that is to say, miracles; therefore the 'naturalness' is not in itself proof that a thing or event can't also be a miracle, sometimes. But when this really happens, it is not the task of medicine or the other sciences to judge it.

If that is the way things are, medical science can examine every healing but cannot legitimately ascertain if and when any one of these is really a miracle. When medical science has done all that it can, and has reached the limits of its medical aim - that doesn't mean that it has reached the limits of reality and therefore it must remain open to this. We do not understand why it is necessary to wait so long to confirm Diana's healing and that only then can one speak of a miracle. Why three or four years and not more, or less? If this was the criterion used for the healings of Jesus as told to us in the Gospels, then not even one of them could have been proved or could have been recognized as a miracle, at least as long as Jesus remained on earth. Instead the Gospels tell us that the people present noticed and at once recognized these miracles and for this reason were converted. The real meaning of a miracle is this: that it helps men to believe. This is why it is performed and it must therefore be recognizable immediately. At the same time, every science has the right to look at the miracle from its own point of view and to observe the particular aspect that belongs to it.

Even a superficial examination of the many healings that have taken place in Medjugorje show that the people cured and many others, like those of the Gospel, have considered their healings as a message from God and have replied to this with faith, thanking God and Our Lady. Because of this, it is very important to be able to recognize miracles. If we leave all else aside and consider that Diana Basile had been blind in the right eye for years and that in Medjugorje she suddenly began to see again, cannot her case be compared to that of the man born blind in the Gospel (Jn 9:1-28)? If that was noticed and recognized without any moratorium why is such an arbitrary moratorium necessary for this case? I consider that the inconsistency of the request made by Mangiapan concerning a miraculous healing is particularly manifest in the resurrection of Lazarus. Was it necessary to wait years to confirm that Lazarus had really risen from the dead? But, whatever way things are, in the same way in which the man born blind, after his healing, said 'I only know this, I was blind before and now I can see (Jn 9:25), Diana also said: 'I know that I felt condemned for the last ten years and I have had to drag myself round and now I'm well, I'm like everyone else again.' Both of them glorified God immediately after the healing. In this way they show us that they considered the healing as a message from God. And the healing was at the same time a 'sign' (miracle) of the presence of God and his action in them.

From Diana's declaration which has been made known all over the world, we gather that for her, as well as for others, this meant a rekindling of the faith. Diana tells us that her husband who before was almost an atheist, said 'We must go there (i.e. to Medjugorje) to give thanks'. Even here, what Christ said is valid: 'You will know them by their fruits' (Mt 7:20).' "(81)

2.   Mary Craig: "It is hard, if not impossible, to provide satisfactory scientific proof of a miracle. In Lourdes, it has usually taken anything from six to thirteen years for a cure to be authenticated; and over a period of 130 years only sixty four cases were accepted as genuine cures. It may well prove to be the same with Medjugorje. But a balance must somehow be struck - between the necessary patient and hard-headed search for empirical proof, and the actual joy that is brought into the life of a person who believes himself or herself cured. Human beings, despite the scientific advances of the twentieth century, are still more than statistics ...

In Bishop Zanic's judgement, Dr. Mangiapan had rejected all the supposed cures of Medjugorje; and he accused Rene Laurentin of ignoring Mangiapan's report of April 1984. But Laurentin, whose book was published in February of that year, had been sent an advance rough draft of the report by Mangiapan himself, and had incorporated both its positive and negative elements in his own book. He had asked Mangiapan to comment on the list of fifty-four cures originally drawn up by Father Rupcic. Whereupon the doctor had suggested his eliminating all those cases which were not easily verifiable by medical science: as, for example, the curing of persistent alcoholism. He made the fair comment that without exhaustive documentation about relevant medical tests, the cures had no credibility. But, Dr. Mangiapan admitted, thirty-three of the cases were at least interesting and might merit further research. All this Laurentin had duly reported. The bishop, however, had ignored Mangiapan's main directive: that a serious investigation should be undertaken.

In any case, in a later (still 1984) edition of *Is the Virgin Mary Appearing at Medjugorje?* Laurentin had reproduced Dr. Mangiapan's report in full. He adds that one of the doctors on the episcopal commission, and one only, came to Medjugorje in the summer of 1984. He came on his own initiative, somewhat embarrassed that he had not been asked to go there in an official capacity." (82)

3. Fr. Laurentin: "According to Bishop Zanic, Dr. Mangiapan, former director of the Medical Office in Lourdes, is said to have declared all these healings invalid. There again he is slanting. When I sent Dr. Mangiapan the first 55 miraculous healings, very unequal in value, briefly summarized by Fr. Rupcic, he declared with nuance: 'This dossier is worthy of interest, but without value as long as the medical dossiers have not been constituted and studied.' Bishop Zanic omits these specifications and hides the edifying result:

A. The Italian doctors have selected for an on-going examination about twenty declared healings for which they are endeavoring to constitute a dossier.

B. The medical sub-committee of the Yugoslavian Bishops, directed by Dr. Korlyan, has selected two healings for which a complete dossier has already been constituted, greatly equivalent in quality to the best miraculous healings in Lourdes. ...

As Dr. Mangiapan wrote me: 'It is what my predecessor Dr. Saint-Maclou used to call the miracle of the numbers,' a statement of which the bishop is aware but avoids citing. To confuse things, Bishop Zanic, who hides evident facts, ingeniously seeks out the

cases where the sick who had come to pray later died. He mentions
Marco Blazevic. This sick man had gone to Medjugorje to pray for his
hopeless case. After that, he tried to get an operation in Belgrade and
died in May 1984, some six years ago. But we are all mortal. Nobody
had ever declared him healed. This case is therefore unrelated to the
question." (83).

(vii) Are the Messages Theologically Sound?

Criticisms about false ecumenism and religious indifferentism in the messages
are addressed in the earlier sub-chapter on the messages of Medjugorje. We add two
subscripts:

1. Bishop Michael Pfeifer: "If Mary is appearing at Medjugorje, then all
   must heed her message, because she, as the Mother of God, is the
   Mother of truth and goodness. If she is not appearing, then it would
   seem the messages still have a divine source and should receive our
   careful attention. In either case, Medjugorje cannot be disregarded"
   [August 5, 1988, Diocesian Pastoral Letter]. In the letter to his
   diocese the bishop states that his conscience forced him to write the
   pastoral after having conversed with the Holy Father about Medjugorje
   during his ad limina visit in Rome.

2. Fr. Jozo Zovko: "The journey which I undertook before the
   anniversary...ended with the Pope in Rome [June 17, 1992]. I said:
   'Holy Father, I am Father Jozo. I come from Medjugorje.' He said: 'I
   know.' I continued: 'I am inspired by Our Lady's message of peace,
   the Queen of Peace in Medjugorje, and have set out on a mission of
   peace to tell heads of state what Our Lady says. I want to end this
   mission with you.' 'Thank you,' he said, 'I know of this mission. They
   told me.' I continued: 'My people suffer but we are united in prayer
   around the world.' The Pope then said: *Tell Medjugorje that I am
   with you. I bless you. **I beg you: protect Medjugorje, protect
   Our Lady's message**. Persevere. I am with you, I pray with you,
   I am blessing you. Convey my greetings and blessing to the people
   of Medjugorje and to all the Croatian people.* '" Today, on this 11th
   anniversary, we have to remember these words: Protect Medjugorje,
   protect the grace which God, through His mother sent here and gave
   to His Church.

   Brothers and sisters: It would be a great tragedy if we did not
   live the message. When the Pope says: 'Protect Medjugorje,' he
   mentions the messages first of all. Do we pray the rosary every day in
   our families? Do we live the message of prayer? Our Lady has been

teaching us for 11 years: Pray, and through prayer you will achieve everything. As much as we pray, that much we will win. We will enjoy as much freedom as we win with our weapons - prayer, fasting, Scripture, conversion, Mass, Confession. These are the steps along the way called Peace. (*Mary's People,* Twin Circle Publishing Company, August 30, 1992, p.8).

(viii) Is the Apparition a Diabolic Phenomenon?

CRITIQUE

Fr. Rebut: "Medjugorje is a perverse and incoherent work of the devil. It will fall by itself, just as do the fragile card constructions that children make as they play." (84).

RESPONSE

1. The strategy of pointing to the Devil as the source of a supernatural phenomenon is most commonly used by Protestant Fundamentalists who lack a credible "theology" of the diabolic; their scattershot approach in this area and in exegesis in general has been (and continues to be) charitably but logically dissected and decimated in publications like *This Rock* and we need not concern ourselves with them here. For Catholics, the accusation of Satanic inspiration is one which is most clearly studied in terms of the soundness of doctrines and the nature of the spiritual fruits. The recurrent emphasis in Medjugorje has been prayer and penance, the Mass and the confessional. These are the means most highly recommended by the Church to Catholics seeking to resist the wiles of the world, the flesh and the devil. If someone suggests that a message of this nature could come from Satan in order to achieve some greater goal, surely the burden of proof is on him to show that this indeed is the case.

2. Fr. Albert J. Hebert: "What is diabolical is this charge or allegation. Who would profit from it except Satan? Where God is most active on this earth (e.g. Calvary) Satan is too. But he is there attacking what is good, not promoting it. Satan blinds some people into attacking or discrediting Medjugorje, just because it is a tremendous spiritual threat to him. If the apparitions were false Satan would let them ride without interference because the fruits would be evil. Satan influences opponents of Medjugorje to prevent pilgrims from going there and being converted. Satan is experienced in springing many false

apparitions on us. Mary said early at Medjugorje: 'God exists!' Satan's fight against her in that place is an admission that God really exists. Mary said there: 'I want Mass to be celebrated every evening.' Does that sound like Satan? People who talk about Satan as the cause of these apparitions had better beware of blasphemy. Does Satan think that people go to Hell through good confessions — they conquer Sin and Satan himself! Satan hates to see Redemption in action! Don't join him!" (85).

3. Fr. Laurentin: *Satan disguised as an angel of light:*

We might well ask, 'Should this be a cause of scandal?' No, because Satan can, according to St Paul, disguise himself as an angel of light (2 Co 11:14) and two thousand years of Christian history bear witness to this. Bernadette considered this hypothesis, probably suggested in the family circle, after the first apparition. For this reason she brought a bottle of holy water to the second apparition and sprinkled Our Lady with it. The visionaries at Medjugorje did the same thing and were reassured by the same smile.

Saints who have been favoured with particular tangible graces, together with their spiritual directors, have retained a certain skepticism with regard to exceptional phenomena, situated as they are on that ambivalent frontier which is subject to illusion and temptation. It was proper that the hypothesis should be considered.

We do not wish to enter into a polemic with the protagonists of the hypothesis. It would merely serve to exacerbate the situation and increase the unhealthy preoccupation with the spirit of darkness. It is better to adopt the humorous attitude of St Therese of Lisieux who pictured herself chasing the devil in the family cellar where he hid himself behind the barrels. I will respect the anonymity of the three protagonists (all independent) knowing that a polemic can wound the adversary and stifle debate. I respect the intelligence and even the integrity of those who have developed this thesis; at times I have to admire the dexterity with which they can highlight even the smallest detail.

What is lacking is first-hand knowledge of the facts: the visionaries, the ecstasy, parish life, the admirable movement towards conversion, the innumerable attestations (oral and written) of these conversions, which are the principal elements in this debate according to the Gospel saying, 'a tree is judged by its fruit'. It is illusory to attempt a second-hand examination of Medjugorje, purely at the level of dialectical argument and without any critical examination of the sources.

Another weakness in these intelligent studies is their systematic and polemic nature. This leads them to discover in the slightest detail, in the smallest complaint, dark and infernal indications that do not make sense in the light of the facts. I do not claim that there have not been mistakes and weaknesses at Medjugorje; I fear in fact that these weaknesses may be aggravated in the tense situation of a parish that is not only not helped by episcopal authority but is constantly placed in impossible situations that multiply the risks of error and deviation. In such conditions I have great admiration that up to now such good sense has prevailed or, at least, that mistakes have been rectified.

Finally, the dialectical method used to discover the Devil at Medjugorje consists of stringing together a number of most unusual studies, all guided by the initial hypothesis, thus trying in minute details to suit the pre-established position. The method is attractive, but artificial.

Where it is said that Fr Laurentin does not quote such and such a statement, recall such and such a fact, why does he hide them? (for what subterfuge, what dishonest motives? etc.) — usually it is because I had no definite proof or, indeed, because the fact or statement was of a secondary nature: I retained only the essential in a book of 198 pages. It was not a book of 1000 or 2000 pages and yet it dealt with over 1000 apparitions. Discernment comes through contact with people and the places that is why I returned so often to Medjugorje....

In order to take a more accurate measure of the diabolical interpretations of Medjugorje I have endeavored to develop a counter-position. Were we to apply the same method to Lourdes, La Salette, Fatima: seek out the worst, exploit every ambiguity or implication, Lourdes would have been much more vulnerable than Medjugorje. Bernadette's penitential gestures: kissing the ground, eating grass, would certainly have scandalized the devotees of the apparition and embarrassed the commission. 'You have eaten grass like animals,' they said to Bernadette. 'This sordid gesture is not worthy of the Mother of God and (not in keeping with) human dignity.' 'But we eat salad,' she answered ingenuously." (86)

(ix) Ivan and the Letter

CRITIQUE

1. The Bishop of Mostar: "Regarding the 'great sign,' in the spring of 1982, I asked the 'seers' to write down everything they knew about the sign without making the 'secret' public. The way I suggested they

do it was to write down information on paper in duplicate. Then this would be sealed in an envelope, and one copy would remain with them and one with the bishop. When the 'sign' occurs, then we would open the envelopes and see whether or not the 'sign' was predicted... Two members of the first Commission Dr. M. Zovkic and Dr. Z. Puljic (now bishop of Dubrovnik) went to visit Ivan in Visoko. They gave him a sheet of paper which was somewhat greenish in color with questions typed on it. Ivan wrote down the content of the 'sign,' dated the document and signed it in their presence without a word or any sign of fear. A few years later, Laurentin wrote that Ivan told him personally that he wrote absolutely nothing on that sheet of paper and that he tricked the Commission. On March 7, 1985, three members of the Commission went to ask Ivan if what Laurentin wrote was true. Ivan said it was true and that they could freely go ahead and open the envelope in the Chancery office because in it they would only find a white sheet of paper. They came back to Mostar where the Commission was having a meeting and before all the members, they opened the envelope. In the envelope on a greenish piece of paper they found written the content of the sign: 'Our Lady said that she would leave a sign. The content of this sign I reveal to your trust. The sign is that there will be a great shrine in Medjugorje in honor of my apparitions, a shrine in my image. When will this occur? The sign will occur in June. Dated May 9, 1982. Seer, Ivan Dragicevic.'" [*Fidelity* p.12,1/91].

RESPONSE

1. Mary Craig: At last the scales tipped in the bishop's favor. On 9th May, the Commissioners went in search of Ivan in the seminary at Visoko. Nobody could give Ivan any advance warning, said the bishop triumphantly, since the seminary phone was controlled by the local authorities. So poor demoralized Ivan, confronted by visiting Commissioners and his own intimidating Prefect of Studies, 'described everything without the least hesitation.' There is, to say the least, some confusion about Ivan's action; and he has not helped matters by going to pieces and contradicting his own testimony. Probably the boy panicked; and there was nobody at hand to help him out of his difficulty. Ivan was miserable at the seminary, not least because his fellow students made fun of him and poured scorn on the apparitions, which had continued after his first week there. The Commissioners found him in a state of utter wretchedness and self-doubt: he had just — to nobody's surprise — failed his first exams, and his future was very uncertain. The bishop claims that when ordered to

divulge the secret of 'the sign' the boy did so. But Ivan tells a different story — or, rather, two different stories at two different times. At first, he told the Franciscans that he simply wrote 'nothing at all' on the paper he was given. Later in 1985, when the Commissioners opened the envelope, he admitted that he had written 'something,' but that it had nothing to do with the sign. The affair Ivan inevitably reduced the boy's credibility, an outcome no doubt desired by the bishop and from which he would make considerable capital in the months ahead. [p.106-7]. ...

On 7th March 1985, three members of the episcopal Commission asked Ivan directly if what he had written on the paper in the sealed envelope really concerned the Sign. 'No,' said Ivan. They then opened the envelope and found the paper headed: 'Declaration of visionary concerning the sign to be given by the Blessed Virgin at Medjugorje.' 'What sign will the Virgin leave?' went the question. And Ivan had clearly replied: 'The Blessed Virgin has said that she will leave a Sign... There is to be a great shrine dedicated to her in Medjugorje in honor of her apparitions there.' 'When will this Sign come about?' Answer: 'In the sixth month.' Signed, Ivan Dragicevic. There was no escaping the disgrace. Fra Slavko Barbaric went to investigate. ...Ivan was at home working on his family's farm. ...'I know why you're here,' he said when Fra Slavko found him, standing in front of Vicka's gate. 'The Commissioners have opened the envelope and found something there. But it isn't the Sign, and I didn't reveal the date.' 'How do you know that's why I've come?' demanded Slavko. 'Because the Lady told me you were coming,' Ivan replied. 'She was angry with me for what I did.' And the boy wept with shame. 'Only prayer will undo Ivan's silly mistake,' the Lady reportedly told Vicka. 'He should have written nothing, and told everyone so. Then there could have been no doubt.' ...Appearing to Mirjana on her birthday on 18th March, the Madonna said, 'It wasn't Ivan's fault. I've scolded him enough now. Let him alone.' (87)

2. Fr. Laurentin: Will the sign come? Will it be gratifying or disappointing? I simply do not know and I have certain reservations as to this future event, for the seers are not infallible. But no objection is possible as long as the secrets remain secret. As for the subterfuge of the timid Ivan when he was ordered by two members of the Commission, Zovkic and Puljic to write this sign, I clarified this complicated affair in 'Latest News #4.' Ivan wrote just anything out of fear, and he admitted this subterfuge to me. His fearful peasant dodge was a sin. He repented it in tears. He should have refused to write as the other seers did. But he was alone and threatened with dismissal from the seminary for academic difficulties. He gave in to his fear, writing

those lines and placing them in an envelope which was to remain sealed. (88)

3. Archbishop Frane Franic: The case of Ivan Dragicevic is held by certain members of the Commission to be proof positive that everything that happens in Medjugorje is pure fantasy. We must distinguish Ivan the seer from Ivan the human being. Ivan the human being can fall into error, as the patriarch Abraham was mistaken when he asked his fair wife Sara to tell the Egyptians that she was his sister, not his wife, to avoid being killed by the Egyptians, or when the patriarch Jacob misled his father to take the place of the elder brother (instead of Esau). Ivan the human being was under duress from authority. As a seminarist he had a reverential fear of his superiors and of the Bishop, while on the other hand he knew that he could say nothing about the great sign, as Our Lady had forbidden him to do so. He deceived, because he wrote a lie, through fear of being expelled from the seminary if he wrote nothing. That was a mistake on his part, but he wrote nothing about the secret. With this proviso, he could say that he had written nothing, that there was nothing on the paper, that he had written nothing on it, all the time in the context of the secret. The other seers testify that Ivan wrote nothing on the secret of the great sign. Ivan admitted his fault to me to me on 11 April 1985, and told me that he should be punished for it. (89) [p.206]

4. The whole Ivan and the letter incident has nothing to do with the veracity of the visionaries' experience of the apparition which is the only issue that is of relevance in studying the authenticity of the apparition. The importance of the incident is in revealing two things: (a) The readiness of the authorities to use intimidation; (b) The fact that any human being can crack given the right amount of pressure.

(x) Vicka and the Diary

CRITIQUE

E. Michael Jones: Over the next year the bishop had a series of meetings with Vlasic and Vicka during which they alternately told the bishop to publish the journal excerpts and then denied that they existed. At one point Vlasic swore on the cross that there was no journal. Finally, he handed over his own 'Chronicles of the Apparitions' to the bishop after the bishop went to St. James and demanded it from him. Upon reading this chronicle, the bishop came across a passage dated March 16, 1982 in which Vlasic mentions talking to Vicka about the journal which he swore on October 16, 1983 never existed. Vlasic, in other words, lied. So had Vicka. (100)

RESPONSE

1. Fr. Rupcic: The 'diary of the apparitions'
    Among the alleged arguments against the apparitions of
Medjugorje, 'Vicka's diary' is of special importance. This diary is
absolutely non-existent. But the Bishop insists that 'The Friars have
hidden it, and now they say it does not exist. They are afraid of
something'. This is what he wrote on 12 December 1983 to Fr.
Radogost Grafenauer, a Jesuit, adding that some articles in the
Chronicle and in the diary constitute 'the key to the understanding of
Medjugorje.' Later, when he spoke to Fr. Vlasic, who swore on the
Cross that the 'diary' was not in his house and did not even exist, the
Bishop did not change his mind and called Fr. Vlasic a perjurer and
liar; later he spread this version of his both in written form, and
orally, all over the world. In connection with the existence of the
'diary', he first refers to Fr Grafenauer. But Grafenauer, in a letter to
Fr. Ljubicic dated 7 October 1984, writes: 'You know what he (the
Bishop) has been telling everyone about this diary, and how he has
publicly put Fr. Tomislav to shame... This same person swore on the
Cross that he had not even seen the diary, but he says that Vicka
showed it to me. He considers me a witness against Vlasic. I have
heard all this from Mate Zovkic, who sent me the Bishop's circular
letter. I immediately let the Bishop know, through Zovkic, that I had
not seen Vicka's diary. He cannot consider me a witness against
Tomislav in this affair. I also sent a photostat copy to Tomislav. In this
letter I explained to the Bishop in what way I had spoken about and
written about Vicka's diary. The Bishop did not take into account my
extracts about Tomislav in the chronicle, because he does not believe
in the chronicle. He only believes in the diary.... Alas, at that time, I
had not the courage to write and tell him that I had never seen the
diary. At least from then onwards the Bishop knew how things
stood...Even though I communicated these events to the Bishop, until
now, from what I am told, he has not withdrawn what he originally
declared. And he continues to write in foreign newspapers and refer
to me as a witness as regards Vicka's diary. I am sorry that people are
getting confused ideas about the Medjugorje apparitions and that the
Bishop is impugning the honesty of Our Lady's witnesses'.
    In the same letter Grafenauer goes on to say that in connection
with all this, he has drafted a letter to an important German person,
whom he asks to inform the Pope or Cardinal Ratzinger himself:
'With reference to all this, I have prepared a letter — writes Grafenauer
— though in the eyes of the Lord, it honestly appears to me that the
bishop is getting an undue amount of importance. But why say

nothing when the Bishop is making his "honest" opinion — the only one — heard all ever the world? Why can not people use this "corpus delicti" to show what kind of honesty is underneath the whole thing? It is time for everything to be brought out onto the open. Many people have suffered because of the Bishop's haste, but he himself does not consider that he has been hasty, let alone dishonest'.

At this stage, there is little else to add. We are faced with the logic of facts; The Bishop refers to Vicka, Grafenauer and Vlasic as the only witnesses to the fact that the hidden 'diary' exists, whereas the witnesses Vicka, Grafenauer and Vlasic - who even swore before God - all claim 'it does not exist'! And now the Bishop, on the basis of their collective witness, comes to this conclusion: Vicka wrote the diary, Vlasic hid it and Grafenauer saw it and copied some of Our Lady's massages from it. No matter how muddled this seems, the Bishop sees as 'key to the understanding of Medjugorje' things that don't exist and considers as 'key' witnesses people who witness the non-existence of such things; He considers the whole thing to be the result of 'collective hallucination' and this whole thing actually cannot even exist. So, he does not judge Medjugorje from what is happening there, but on the basis of things that have been invented, and things that have been fabricated elsewhere and that he has wanted, at all costs, to include. (91)

2. Mary Craig: Vicka reported that since 7th January 1983 the Virgin Mary had been telling the story of her life to the five remaining visionaries. ...Vicka transcribed the 'Life' into three large exercise books which were carefully hidden from view and shown to nobody. The question of whether or not Vicka had, in addition to these, secret notebooks in which she recorded what was said during the apparitions, would soon be triggering off a spectacular and unpleasant row. Father Radogost Grafenauer, a Jesuit from Slovenia, was persuaded by Bishop Zanic to visit Medjugorje. According to the bishop, once Fr. Grafenauer reached Medjugorje, he was 'got at' by Tomislav Vlasic, and that as soon as the friars realized what a valuable conquest they had made, they allowed him a privileged look at Vicka Ivankovic's 'secret diary' and at the detailed chronicle of events kept by Vlasic. According to Father Grafenauer, however, all he saw were five sheets of paper, four of them in Vicka's handwriting, the other in Mirjana's. He denied and continues to deny the existence of a secret diary. Whatever it was that he saw, it is undeniable that he returned from Medjugorje [16th February 1983] with his own verbatim copies of various messages said to have been transmitted by the Lady for the bishop, by way of Vicka. Messages concerning the two

expelled Franciscans which could and did raise Bishop Zanic's blood pressure several degrees. ...The messages bore all the hallmarks of Vicka's choleric and uncontrolled temperament, and the outraged bishop set off in pursuit of the 'secret diary', the existence of which the Franciscans firmly denied. There were, they said, one notebook belonging to Vicka's sister, Ana, describing the events of 25th June to 5th July, with written comments by Vicka herself; a second notebook belonging to two other sisters of Vicka, Mirjana and Zdenka, briefly recording the apparitions of 18th October to 14th January (1982); and a third, in Vicka's own hand relating to those of 6th February to 25th March 1982. To write anything at all at the end of such long and exhausting days was too arduous for Vicka; and after 25th March 1982 even her random jottings ceased, despite urgings from the friars who wanted her to continue. Ignoring all this, the bishop ordered the offending 'diary' to be handed over to him without delay. ...It may well have been a question of semantics, of when is a diary not a diary? That Vicka kept some kind of record is not open to doubt; but what the bishop had in mind was something much more sinister. As he wrote to Father Grafenauer, 'The friars have hidden it and now they say it doesn't exist. They're afraid of something.' ... 'Do you, in fact, have a secret (a fourth) notebook which you don't want anyone to know about?' Fra Janko Bubalo asked Vicka in 1986. 'No,' she replied. 'I have no secret notebook except the one where I record the story of the Virgin's Life. I will, if you wish, swear that on oath.' (92)

3. Dr. Nicholas Bartulica: In Chapter V on Bishop Zanic's opposition, we mentioned on several occasions the controversy regarding Vicka's secret diary. As we wrote this issue was one of five factors which contributed to Bishop Zanic's suspicions in regard to the Franciscans, and finally he became confirmed in his belief that the apparitions were a result of a 'conspiracy.'

    According to the Bishop's statement, he learned of a diary in February 1983 when Fr. R. Grafenauer sent to him some copies of additional messages concerning the two expelled friars. Bishop Zanic apparently was under the impression that Fr. Grafenauer had seen Vicka's diary from which he made the copies, and the Bishop's 'Present Position of the Bishop's Curia' had a special chapter on this subject.

    It is evident, as we previously said, that the existence of this 'hidden' diary almost became Bishop Zanic's obsession, and from February until December 1983 he made several efforts to get hold of this item. He wrote several letters to Medjugorje asking for the diary (in April, May, June) requesting either Vicka or Fr. Vlasic to bring it to him, and in November he went to Medjugorje to obtain the diary himself.

Finally, Fr. Vlasic, trying to dissuade the Bishop of the diary's existence, on December 14, 1983, swore on the cross in the presence of the Bishop that 'he has not ever seen the hidden diary which the Bishop talks about,' but instead of persuading the Bishop of the diary's non-existence, from this moment Bishop Zanic has been branding Fr. Vlasic a 'perjurer.'

As a proof, Bishop Zanic claimed Fr. Grafenauer as a witness, and in addition, he (the Bishop) quotes Vicka's letter to him of May 7, 1983, in which she protests that some parts of her diary have been copied and distributed (by the diocese), and she considers her writings are for her private matter and not for public consumption.

Later, the Bishop quotes Fr. Vlasic's Chronicle of Apparitions in which on March 16, 1982, he (Fr. Vlasic) wrote that he talked with Vicka for a long period of time 'since she has not brought her diary of the apparition.' A little later Fr. Vlasic allegedly wrote, 'She (Vicka) records everything chronologically)'

From the above evidence Bishop Zanic had reached the conclusion that there was a special Vicka's diary, but for some unexplained reason, Vicka and Fr. Vlasic had kept it 'hidden' from him.

The Untold Story refers briefly to Fr.Vlasic's swearing on the cross that Vicka's journal never existed, and then M. Jones commented: 'Vlasic in other words had lied and so had Vicka,' but one has the right to ask what is the evidence that 'special journal' existed? *The Untold Story* is not offering any proof to the reader, and the only evidence is Bishop Zanic's statement.

What are the available facts on this matter? We have already quoted some parts from the diary by Vicka's sister Ana which contains about 26 entries over 75 days, from June 24 to September 6, 1981. This whole 'diary' was published in Fr. Sivric's book *The Hidden Face of Medjugorje*. After reading the first two entries for June 24 and June 25, it becomes clear that the entries were written a few days later and the fact that those documentations were made by Vicka's sister demonstrates that Vicka was not a person who 'keeps a diary in chronological order.'

In her conversations with Fr. Bubalo, Vicka admits having in her possession the following written records about the apparitions:

1. The diary already mentioned from June 24 to Sept. 6, 1981, that was written by her sister Ana, an account of Vicka's and some other visionaries' statements.

2. The diary containing events between October 18 to December 14,1981 (57 days), recorded by two of Vicka's sisters, Mirjana and Zdenka.
3. The diary containing events February 6 to March 25, 1982 (48 days). The recording was made by Vicka herself.

Fr. Bubalo commented that on March 25, 1982, Vicka had ceased to make any writings in spite of his advice to make the recording. He had several interviews with Vicka between 1982 and 1983, in preparation for the book *A Thousand Encounters With The Blessed Virgin Mary...*, and at the end of 1983 he wrote that out of 900 days, that is, from the beginning of the apparitions till the end of 1983, there are only 137 days when the apparitions were recorded, which is contained in the three above-mentioned diaries.

4. There is an additional diary where Vicka has recorded the life of the Blessed Virgin Mary, which she wrote from Jan. 7, 1982, until April 10, 1985. She will reveal the contents when she obtains the Gospa's permission.

To Fr. Bubalo's question about the existence of an additional 'secret' diary, Vicka answered: 'I don't have any secret notebook except the one where I record the story of the Virgin's life. I can, if you wish, take an oath to the effect.'

On account of these facts it is clear that when Bishop Zanic quotes Vicka's letter about a 'diary,' she (Vicka) was talking about one of those notebooks. The same would apply to Fr. Vlasic's comments in regard to Vicka's diary, which was quoted by the Bishop as proof of the existence of a 'secret' diary.

Finally, Bishop Zanic's claim that Fr. Grafenauer in February 1983 had seen and made copies from a special Vicka's diary, was disavowed by Fr. Grafenauer himself. He (Grafenauer) wrote a letter to Fr. P. Ljubicic, a Franciscan in Medjugorje, dated October 7, 1984, in which he wrote: 'I immediately let the Bishop know... that I had not seen Vicka's diary. He can not consider me a witness against Tomislav (Fr. Vlasic) in this affair... and he continues to write in foreign newspapers and refer to me as a witness as regards Vicka's diary' (*Medjugorje Facts, Documents, Theology*, by Fr. Michael O'Carroll, CSSp., p. 118).

Fr. L. Rupcic, a former professor of Theology in Sarajevo, wrote (1985) an answer to Bishop Zanic's 'Present Position of the Bishop Curia' on Oct. 30, 1984. After investigating all facts on the controversy about the diary, he succinctly summarized the unsoundness of Bishop Zanic's claim:

'The Bishop refers to Vicka, Grafenauer and Vlasic as the only witnesses to the fact that the hidden 'diary' exists, whereas the witnesses, Vicka, Grafenauer, Vlasic - who even swore before God -

all claim it does not exist. And now the Bishop, on the basis on their collective testimony comes to this conclusion: Vicka wrote the diary, Vlasic hid it and Grafenauer saw it and copied some of our Lady's messages from it.... The Bishop sees as 'key to the understanding of Medjugorje' things that don't exist and considers as 'key' witnesses, people who witness the non-existence of such things' (*Medjugorje: Facts, Document, Theology*, p.119).

We would like to end this Chapter with a question: 'Would any jury on this earth pass a guilty verdict of being 'liars' on Vicka or Fr. Vlasic on account of such evidence?'

But, this is exactly what Bishop Zanic has been maintaining and *The Untold Story* keeps repeating. (93)

(xi) Marija and the Vlasic Community

CRITIQUE

E. Michael Jones: As you probably guessed by now, God has asked Father Vlasic to form a religious community... with a German woman by the name of Agnes Heupel. ...Marija Pavlovich, late of Medjugorje and now of Parma, endorsed it in a communique of her own dated April 22, 1988. Not only that, she now says that the Blessed Mother has endorsed it as well and suggested that Marija now follow the lead of Father Tomo and Agnes. It seems that Marija and her prayer group prayed for 'a light that we might understand the program which the Madonna had given through Agnes Heupel and Fr. Tomislav Vlasic.' No sooner had the group prayed than The Madonna arrived. She was joyful. She prayed over us all and said: 'Dear children! Today I am offering you a special gift, a gift of freedom that you may opt for God. I am blessing the free decision of every one of you.' In that way it became clear to me that I may accept this way since I have been waiting for an opportunity that I may withdraw into solitude and prayer.

...In a surprise announcement issued in both Italian and Croatian (the Croatian version bears her signature) on July 11, 1988, Marija Pavlovic stated that 'my first declaration,' referring to what she had written on April 21, 1988, 'does not correspond to the truth.' She goes on to write that I have never asked the Madonna for any approval for this undertaking begun by Father Tomislav V. and Agnes Heupel.' It seems that she wrote the first statement as a result of pressure put on her by Vlasic. 'I personally,' she testifies in her July statement, 'had no desire to give any sort of written declaration. Father Tomislav V. kept suggesting to me, stressing over and over again that I as a seer should write the declaration which the world was waiting for.' ...By the fall of 1988, the situation had changed dramatically. Marija's attempt at dissociating herself from Vlasic had damaged her own credibility and revealed Vlasic's behind the scenes manipulation of at least one seer. (94)

RESPONSE

1. Despite Jones' editorializations, it is clear from the text of the message from the Blessed Virgin quoted by him that she is not endorsing Fr. Vlasic or asking Marija to join the community: she is only blessing their free decisions. It seems clear too that Jones is trying to extract as much capital as he can out of the situation by implying some sort of change of mind on the part of the Blessed Virgin regarding Fr. Vlasic's community. The text simply does not support such an implication. It may help to quote Marija's second statement at greater length than Jones does: "I state that I never asked the Gospa for any confirmation for the work undertaken by Father Tomislav and Agnes Heupel. I never asked her explicitly and I never received any instructions from the Gospa with respect to the group, except that each one should be free to choose his own life [...] I repeat that I never received from the Gospa, nor gave Father Tomislav or anyone else, a confirmation of the program of Father Tomislav and Agnes Heupel. The testimony which was published in Italian does not correspond to the truth [...]. Personally, I had no desire to make a written statement. Father Tomislav had suggested to me insistently to write as a visionary, a testimony which the world was waiting for [...]. I must state on the matter of the publication such as it was presented. All that is perceived as confirmation or explicit approval of the work of Father Tomislav and Agnes Heupel, by me, on the part of the Gospa is absolutely foreign to the truth; as well as the idea that I would have had the desire to write this testimony."

    Father Laurentin rightly notes that "There is a common denominator in the testimony of Marija which was published by Tomislav, and in her protest against this same testimony. In both she proclaims the freedom which must guide all commitments inspired by Medjugorje.

    Freedom: so that you may be able to decide for God. I bless the free choice of each one. [Marija's testimony, published by T. Vlasic, April 21, 1988].

    Each one must be free to choose his own life" [denial of July 11, signed by Marija, and disseminated by her friends]. [p.61]. (95)

2. Father Laurentin: According to Jones, Maria followed Tomislav Vlasic through manipulation and blind dependence. On this matter he cites the diagnosis of a psychologist who did not see Marija (no more than Jones himself): He claimed she would 'probably be a victim, certainly an obedient young person'.... He does not realize that 'the obedient young person' suffered greatly in leaving Tomislav's com-

munity and from the openly published reasons for the disagreement. For goodness sake, let us end with this claim of manipulation, hurled from Mostar, and the attribution of this 'manipulation' to Tomislav Vlasic! The apparitions began without him. ...Medjugorje, which was deemed not to be able to survive without Tomislav (they thought in 1984, seeing his gift and his spiritual authority), continued perfectly after his departure (September, 1984). (96). Father Laurentin also notes that Jones claim that Marija is susceptible to manipulation is contradicted by the fact that she left Fr. Vlasic's community with an open letter of protest. He gets himself out of this fix, says Fr. Laurentin, by implying that "women are fickle.

3. The girl whom Jones considers so manipulable was a source of consternation for Louis Belanger, the skeptic whom Jones quotes as an authority. "Ah, Marija," sighed Professor Belanger. "That extraordinary girl — she defeats any thesis I can propose." (97)

(xii) The Vlasic Controversy

The nature and import of this controversy have already been discussed in the previous section and it will be treated here only in a summary fashion and with reference to some additional material from Dr. Bartulica.

CRITIQUE

E. Michael Jones: Now the fact that the seers' spiritual advisor was involved in serious sexual immorality as well as lying, calumny and a cover-up (the latter involving Medjugorje's chief propagandist) does not speak well for the authenticity of the apparitions. However, there are undoubtedly those who will claim that this still leaves the principal actors in the drama untouched. (98)

RESPONSE

1. Mary Craig: The unfortunate man at the centre of this scandal was not summoned to Mostar until 12th December. Laurentin does not actually mention him by name, so I will refrain from doing so. Nevertheless, his identity was left in little doubt, since Bishop Zanic then accused the friar directly, inviting him to confess 'that the Virgin is not appearing and that the whole Medjugorje was your idea in the first place.' The accused man on whose head Bishop Zanic had so often heaped so many choice insults demurred. 'The Virgin is appearing, how can I possibly say she is not?' he demurred. 'As for what you accuse me of, why am I the last person to be told of the charge?' For the rest, he lapsed into silence.

According to Laurentin, the ex-nun in question had indeed given birth to a child in 1977; the putative father — a Croatian Franciscan but a different one — had left the Order and gone to live in America where he had subsequently married. The ex-nun had gone to keep house for an nonagenarian widower in exchange for a home. The man whom Bishop Zanic was now charging with the offence had been with the offence had been the nun's Father Superior and had continued to keep contact with her at Christmas and Easter, with an occasional affectionate letter besides. These tokens of affection had been enough to start the rumors and suspicions. (99)

2. Father Laurentin: The next chapter in his book is a formal defamation against Father Tomislav Vlasic, who was the person mainly responsible for looking after the happenings in Medjugorje from August 15, 1981 to September 1984. Jones accuses him of being the father of a child born to an ex-nun in 1976. As we have stated in *Seven Years of Apparitions*, the mother of the child has denied this paternity. And she has denied it to her detriment, for she had found a useful and secure job as a housekeeper in the home of a fine deserving German widower, Mr. Ott. He was visited by Monsignor Zanic in November 1984, and the additional defamation which resulted compelled her in conscience to leave him. She thus lost her security and comfortable position at the home of this honorable man, who was apparently satisfied with her services and was concerned with assuring her future and that of her child, whom he had taken in affectionately like a good grandfather. She left him out of pure integrity in order to protect against an 'error' and to break away from a defamation. Her new employment, as a waitress, separated her from her child, nine years of age, during the day. Jones blames her for it. But she had to make a living. And in addition, he finds nothing better than to ridicule her for her 'broken German'. This Croatian woman, who suddenly emigrated to Germany, speaks (as Jones says) 'abominable German.' Would it not have been better for truth, justice and charity, to respect the discretion desired by this woman, and her dignity, instead of adding to her misfortune? I shall not come back to this dossier in which Jones takes great pleasure, even to the extent of including some letters (without references to the source) which she protests not to be in her handwriting. Little does it matter. The facts with which we are dealing took place five years prior to the apparitions of Medjugorje. They are, in every assumption, foreign to the origin of the apparitions. It does not relate to the events, according to the criteria of discernment established by the Congregation of the Faith in 1978. The liveliness with which Jones is dead-set against the personal reputation of esteemed men (Denis

Nolan, then Father Tomislav Vlasic) to discredit a cause, is a well-know polemic process, but unworthy of *Fidelity* which claims to be 'As Catholic as the Pope.' (100)

3. Dr. Nicholas Bartulica: Some *Fidelity* readers have described *The Untold Story* as a 'thorough investigation,' but M. Jones's reporting of the alleged correspondence between Fr.Vlasic and Manda has left several questions unanswered. For instance:

I. Manda had been living for seven years a as a housekeeper in a house of a 94-year-old man (Mr. Ott) who must have known something about her past, in particular that she bore an illegitimate child. What prompted Mr. Ott "to do some investigating of his own" and why should he begin "wondering about the past of the woman"?

According to M. Jones, the reason for Mr. Ott's behavior was the visit of Bishop Zanic, which M. Jones describes as a "mysterious appearance." There is no explanation why the bishop's visit was "mysterious" and what caused Mr. Ott to "start an investigation."

II. In defending Mr. Ott against the accusation of forgery, M. Jones wrote that "the accusation is preposterous" and he (Jones) raised the question, "How is an almost blind 94-year-old German, who by his own admission speaks no Croatian, supposed to forge a series of letters in that language in two separate hands? The ideas impossible and ridiculous."

But as we saw above, it was M. Jones who suggested that Mr. Ott did "some investigating on his own" and then discovered the letters. Since the letters were written in Croatian and Mr. Ott is "almost blind" and could not read Croatian, how did he learn of the content of the letters?

Furthermore, M. Jones wrote that Mr. Ott published the letters in a student newspaper. Isn't it "preposterous" to suggest that Mr. Ott "on his own" found the letters written in a foreign language, translated them and published them?

Who was the person (or persons) who assisted him in his 'investigation' and in translating the letters and for what purpose?

III. If Mr. Ott had found the letters from Fr. Vlasic to Manda, who found the letters from Manda to Fr. Vlasic? It is certain that it was not Fr. Vlasic who supplied Manda's letter to Bishop Zanic. (It is likely that it was the Bishop who gave the letters to M. Jones.)

In answering a letter to a *Fidelity* reader, M. Jones offered the hypothesis that Manda probably had copied her letters, which is the only plausible explanation, but it remains only an unproven speculation.

IV. Why did Manda remain silent for seven years and finally in November 1984 write a letter to bishop Zanic revealing the father's identity?

M. Jones explained that according to Pehar, maybe she wanted the Bishop to "kick out" Fr. Vlasic, but why had she waited for seven years?

V. Furthermore, as we learned, she wrote a letter to the Bishop denying that she ever wrote the first letter of accusation. According to M. Jones, both letters are written in the same handwriting, but since they contradict each other, it means that at least in one letter, Manda was lying. Therefore, any statement from Manda, either written or oral, had lost its credibility.[2]

The above are only a few puzzling questions that *The Untold Story* left unexplained.

Anyone reading the respective letters can ascertain that the letter's writer is not admitting his paternity but only offering some advice. Therefore, M. Jones is not using the letters' content to prove the paternity case but, as we mentioned earlier, to reveal the "manipulative" traits of Fr. Vlasic.

In addition, M. Jones, while reading the letters, discovered some of Fr. Vlasic's secret intentions that are not explicitly mentioned in any excerpts of the published letters. For instance, M. Jones wrote, "The impression one gets is that Vlasic will soon leave the priesthood and marry Manda." Since there is nothing of this sort contained in any letter, it appears that this is merely fruit of M. Jones's imagination.

What does one actually find in those letters?

M. Jones had to admit that the letter of December 1976 was 'full of reassurance;' that is, the letter's writer was emotionally supportive when he wrote, 'Don't be so afraid. I'm sure that God will help you and we will take care of you.... I will not desert you even if all efforts fail.'

However, after scrutinizing the letters carefully, M. Jones felt that he 'caught' the letter's writer in advising Manda 'to lie' and 'to live a lie as well.' Consequently, such an attitude is interpreted as a 'manipulative side' of Fr. Vlasic's character.

---

2 Daria Klanac, from Montreal, Canada (born in Croatia), had an interview with Bishop Zanic on October 14, 1986. During this interview the Bishop showed to her an alleged letter from Manda to Fr. Vlasic, written in 1976 after she went to live in Germany. On the Bishop's desk, D. Klanac noticed another letter that Manda allegedly wrote to the Bishop in November 1984, naming Fr. Vlasic as the father of her child. In the transcription of the tape recorded interview, D. Klanac made a remark: "Another letter allegedly from the same person (Manda) was in totally different hand-writing." (This writer [the author of the article quoted, Fr. Laurentine] has a copy of this interview.)

For this purpose, the reader is referred to the part of the letter where the writer advises Manda on how to handle the people pestering her with questions about the child's father. There is the following advice: 'I think that is best to say that you met someone passing by and that he gave you a false name.... It is best to say that you don't know him, because they won't bother you...'

When one considers the situation of a pregnant, unwed woman who refuses to discuss the father's identity and looks for the most simple way to turn away a curiosity seeker, some moralist might argue that, under the broad interpretation of mental reservation such a statement (I don't know him) is not a lie in a strict sense.

However, it appears that the advice is imprudent, since it implies her conceiving a child by an unknown man, and thus, the woman would declare herself to be of loose moral character. Therefore, the advice might be criticized as being inappropriate.

But, on the other hand, there is nothing "manipulative" in such a suggestion, and one wonders in which manner was Manda "manipulated?"

Here again we find M. Jones's subjective interpretation which is a product of a far-fetched imagination. As he 'discovered' in the letters Fr. Vlasic's plans of leaving the priesthood, which were never mentioned, now in the same vein, in imprudent advice, rediscovered a 'manipulator.'

As we said before, such misinterpretation serves M. Jones's main purpose, i.e., to denigrate the character of Medjugorje principal participants. Any detached observer, after reading the letters, would conclude that the writer is a caring, concerned person trying to reassure a woman in a difficult situation. Some advice was not prudent, but the total letter's content does not reveal any flaw in the writer's character as *The Untold Story* leads us to believe.

Finally, M. Jones interpreted the intent of the letter's writer 'as an attempt to save himself from unpleasant consequences of his selfish behavior.'

It is obvious that M. Jones is after Fr. Vlasic's scalp. Don't we hear the echo of an incident of about 2,000 years ago when the accusers brought to Jesus a woman caught in adultery, and in their self-righteous indignation, they asked Jesus whether He agreed with 'the consequences' as written in the Law of Moses?

Would M.Jones tell the reader which 'unpleasant consequence' Fr. Vlasic (assuming that he is the child's father) should suffer?

Isn't the continuous defamation of his reputation since 1985, started by Bishop Zanic and propagated by *Fidelity*, a 'sufficient punishment?'

It appears that this issue requires some additional comments, which we will discuss in the following chapter.

Detraction: Through the previous discussion we tried to demonstrate that *The Untold Story* evidence for F. Vlasic's fatherhood was not convincing and that the letters allegedly written by Fr. Vlasic did not reveal a 'manipulative' person.

But, assuming that *The Untold Story* had enough evidence that the child was fathered by Fr. Vlasic, M. Jones still would be guilty of engaging in a case of blatant detraction against a Catholic priest of good standing. This is a serious violation of the precept on justice and Christian charity.

Let us briefly review a summary of suggested facts.

In 1976 Fr. Vlasic was living in coed monastery and allegedly was involved in an illicit affair with a nun, who gave birth to a child in January 1977.

In the letters that he allegedly wrote, he displayed a caring and supportive attitude, but apparently decided not to leave the priesthood.

In August 1981, Fr. Vlasic was assigned as the Assistant Pastor in Medjugorje, where six children, beginning June 24, 1981, were claiming the apparition of the Virgin Mary. He then became the spiritual adviser of the seers, and through his sermons and writings, he spread the messages that the children were claiming to receive during the apparitions.

In September 1984, he was transferred out of Medjugorje. At the time *The Untold Story* was written (May 1988), he was in Italy with a small community which he founded.

While nobody would claim that the priests in Medjugorje represent a paragon of holiness, one is entitled to raise the question of what *The Untold Story* tried to accomplish by revealing publicly some alleged past personal faults of a priest.

In the Catholic dictionary, detraction is defined as 'revealing something about another that is true, but harmful to that person's reputation.' It is considered to be a sin against justice, unless there is 'proportionate good' involved.

The only 'good' that we can think of would be that by revealing Fr. Vlasic's past faults, the author of *The Untold Story* tried to undercut the veracity of the Medjugorje apparitions.

Does M. Jones consider that this reason represents the 'proportionate good'? Shouldn't the authenticity of the apparitions depend upon other criteria than on the 'sinless life' of a priest associated with the visionaries?

Could the history of any apparition produce such a priest?

Does the *Fidelity* editor consider himself faultless and entitled to 'cast the first stone?'

Finally, couldn't the same *Untold Story* be written fourteen centuries ago, if the apparitions had been taking place in Carthage, Africa, and the spiritual adviser of the visionaries had been St.Augustine? He himself confessed that he had fathered a child out of wedlock.

It is obvious, as we mentioned earlier, that M. Jones, through the character assassination, tried to discredit the credibility of the principals associated with the events of the Medjugorje apparitions.

But, could Fr. Vlasic be one of the "initiators" of Medjugorje events, as Bishop Zanic and The Untold Story author contend, when he (Vlasic) was not even stationed in Medjugorje when the apparitions began?

We will consider this issue in the following chapter.

Fr. Vlasic's impact on the apparitions: If *The Untold Story* reader tried to pay any attention to Fr. Vlasic's presence in Medjugorje, he would learn from its last part that Fr. Vlasic 'rushed to Medjugorje on June 29 and we must assume had lengthy discussions of the situation with Zovko.'

While *The Untold Story* does not claim Fr. Vlasic's presence in Medjugorje from the beginning of the apparitions, that is, on June 24, 1981, the reader is left under the impression that Fr. Vlasic remained at St. James Parish after June 29, 1981, which is simply not true.

In June 1981, Fr. Vlasic was the pastor in the parish of St. Francis of Assisi in Capljina, which is about sixteen miles from Medjugorje. It is certain that after the apparitions began, he must have heard about the events. For instance on Sunday, June 28,1981, it was reported that the crowd of about 15,000 gathered on the apparition hill and many members of the clergy were also present.

For the next one and a half months, Fr. Vlasic remained stationed at his parish at Capljina. After Fr. Zovko's arrest, which took place August 17, 1981, he (Fr. Vlasic) was assigned as the assistant Pastor to Medjugorje effective on August 18, 1981; that is, 54 days after the apparitions started.

In July 1991, this writer questioned Fr. Vlasic about the frequency of his visits to Medjugorje during the period of June 24 and

August 18, 1981, when he assumed the role of Assistant Pastor. According to Fr. Vlasic, he visited Medjugorje, in addition to June 29,1981, on two other occasions, that is July 16, when he replaced Fr. Zovko for evening service, and on August 2, but Fr. Sivric in his book *Hidden Side of Medjugorje* imputes, without any proof, that Fr. Vlasic probably was coming to Medjugorje on a daily basis.

One has the right to ask what influence he could have exercised over the visionaries from June 24, 1981, until August 18, 1981, while he was serving as a pastor sixteen miles from Medjugorje? The author of *The Untold Story* should have been informed about this fact.

As we demonstrated, *The Untold Story*'s author first engaged in slander and detraction. He then accused Fr. Vlasic of 'manipulative' behavior, by suggesting that he advised Manda to lie; and yet most of his advice is morally defensible.

However, even if all accusations from *The Untold Story* could be proven to be accurate, Fr. Vlasic was not present in Medjugorje during the first 54 days of the apparitions and with all alleged "manipulative skills" was not able to exercise any influence over the visionaries.

We must conclude that the tarnishing of his character had only one purpose; that is, to discredit the authenticity of the apparitions by insisting that even if the apparitions did not start under Fr. Vlasic's influence, the Medjugorje "hoax" needed somebody's "manipulative" qualities for its continued existence. (101)

(xviii) The Bloody Handkerchief

CRITIQUE

1. The Bishop of Mostar: Toward the end of 1981 and during 1982, various 'miracles' and absurd things happened. People spoke about them a great deal. Some of the gossip was even put into writing. [In Vicka's diary we find]: "Friday 4 September, 1981. Today, we waited for our Lady at Marija's house. Marija, Ivanka, Jakov and I (Vicka) were there. We started to pray at 6:20 p.m. Our Lady immediately appeared. We asked her about the Friars and nuns from our parish. We asked about the man who saw Jesus along the road when he took the people in his car. He met a man who was covered in blood — this man was Jesus — and he (Jesus) gave him a handkerchief soaked in blood and told him to throw it into the river. Driving on further, he met a woman, it was the Blessed Virgin Mary, and she asked the driver for the blood-soaked handkerchief. The man gave her a

handkerchief that belonged to him, but Our Lady asked for the blood-stained handkerchief. When the man gave her the blood-stained handkerchief, Our Lady said: 'If you hadn't given it to me, it would have been the last judgment for everyone!' Our Lady said that this was true. This is what Vicka writes in her diary and this is also what the 'visionaries' have said in various interviews. (102)

RESPONSE

1. Professor Mark Miravalle: The presence of appropriately-termed peripheral events, such as occasional pilgrim fanaticism or human error in transmitting an individual message, has unfortunately always accompanied authentic, Church approved private revelation. Hence, to conclude Medjugorje a fraud by overlooking more than 1,000 messages which are doctrinally orthodox in order to focus on one obviously miscommunicated 'bloody handkerchief' story; or to represent the worldwide spiritual fruits of Medjugorje by citing occasions of pilgrim fanaticism or the moral lapses of two pilgrim Franciscan priests would be a grave injustice, one seriously wanting in true Catholic scholarship. (103)

2. Father Laurentin: The strange story of a bloody handkerchief which supposedly Jesus had returned to a taxi driver and which the Blessed Virgin picked up in order to stop a threat on the world. I will not go back on this story which has been badly attested. I had suggested to Father Bubalo to eliminate this confusing and insignificant event from his book. This mythical account seems to me to come from the apocalyptic expansion which blazed in 1981 in Medjugorje (and which had come to Lourdes in April-May 1858, according to the mechanisms which I studied in *Lourdes Authentic Documents* Volume 2). These transitory extrapolations of fervor do not discredit either Lourdes or Medjugorje, and to reduce Vicka to these details does not show any discernment. (104)

3. We conclude our discussion of the Bloody Hankerchief story by quoting from an interview with Dr. Radogost Grafenauer, S.J. on February 12, 1992 by the head of Medjugorje Gebetsaktion. In the course of the interview Dr. Grafenauer, a Jesuit from Maribor, for the first time clarified publicly statements not previously made known:

Father Grafenauer has been familiar with the Medjugorje phenomena from the very beginning of these events. Through the years he has remained silent regarding the serious accusations of the bishop against him, which he had published worldwide. Now Father Grafenauer sees the time has come at which an answer should be given. Some confusions on

Medjugorje are obviously founded on misunderstandings and on the deviousness of certain persons.

FATHER GRAFENAUER: The first time I came into a connection with Medjugorje was through a soldier, who had already been in Medjugorje in 1981. He came to me to confession, and he told me about the events there. I didn't know at that time: Should I believe him or not? The whole thing sounded very peculiar to me.

Then in 1982 I was in Medjugorje for the anniversary. That time I spoke with Mirjana and with Vicka. What most amazed me was that, although a drought had been going on for several months, neither of the two said that they prayed for rain. They said this was not the most important thing for them. Then I recognized that the most important thing for them is to pray for souls.

At the end of 1982, Most Reverend Pavao Zanic, Bishop of Mostar, invited me in writing to Medjugorje, so that I could be myself convinced whether God or Satan was behind it all. Earlier Bishop Zanic had made it possible for me to be able to listen to twenty cassettes.

Now the bishop was talking as though by listening to these cassettes I would have been in agreement with them and in conclusion he said: "Thank you!" — But in fact, I had rejected everything on these cassettes! (Grafenauer, Point #1, 2/19/92 in Vienna.)

I wrote to Bishop Zanic what I thought the Blessed Mother would like to say to him. Something terrible can be caused or unleashed, perhaps even a war — perhaps this war that is raging in Yugoslavia. I am afraid that it has come to this confrontation precisely for this reason, just exactly as it stands written in the previous issue of your magazine. Really, I feared this even before I read it in your magazine. Well — now I would like to tell something:

"When I first came to be bishop of Mostar," he told me when he first was named a bishop by the Pope, he felt "like a chauffeur who reads the road signs and follows them."

At the time I understood it thus: He meant by this the "signs of the times." Already from the previous bishop he took over the problems of the Church in Hercegovina. Like a dirty piece of clothing or filthy rag, which represents the mark of shame of the Mostar diocese and is a mark of shame for him, as he told me. It would be particularly important to make this filthy rag clean!

And then the bishop told me of an occurrence which later, in his essay, "The Truth about Medjugorje", he described as follows:

It was then related that a taxi driver met a man all covered with blood. The man gave him a bloody handkerchief and said, "Throw this in the river!"

He went on and then met a woman dressed for mourning. She stopped him and said that he should give her his own, but she answered, "Not his one, but that bloody one!"

He gave it to her and she spoke, "If you had thrown it into the river, it would immediately have been the end of the world."

"We asked Our Lady," so wrote Vicka Ivankovic in her diary, "if this were true, and she answered that it was true, and 'That blood-soaked man was my Son Jesus, and the woman in mourning garments was I, the Mother of God."

Comment: In the above-mentioned essay by the bishop, he added: "What kind of theology is this supposed to be? Jesus will annihilate the world if a bloody handkerchief is thrown in the water, and the Mother of God saves the world from him."

A CLARIFICATION OF THIS: The Croatian expression "smak sveta" means not only "end of the world", but can also mean "catastrophe", "war".

This taxi driver then returned and asked the children whether they could ask Our Lady what this might mean. And she answered the children, and they also then told this, although they were laughed at by all the members of the commission because of these statements: The Blessed Mother said that the blood-soaked man had been her Son and she was the woman in mourning.

The bishop then stopped the cassette and asked me, "What do you think about this affair? — I answered him and it was a bit unpleasant for me to tell him this: "You know, this taxi driver really could be you," — He asked me, "Why me?" — I said, "Look, there are often such prophetic images in the Bible — with Ezekiel, for instance. You yourself have said that when you were named bishop you felt like a chauffeur, who pays attention to the traffic signs, the signs of the times. And look: Who gave you — as the children too have said — this bloody handkerchief? Jesus gave it to you! Mary is asking you to hand this bloody cloth to her!"

The bishop responded, "For God's sake, it won't be the end of the world just because I don't hand over this handkerchief to the Blessed Mother."

I said to him, "You know, Bishop, the Church is the sign of peace, a sign of peace in the world, a Sacrament of peace, as the Council says. And especially the shepherds are a sign of peace. This is something that pertains to the shepherds! When you bring about such a confusion among the shepherds that one is against GOD, so can it actually come to pass that the end of the world is caused by this or — translated otherwise — a great catastrophe can be brought about."

We have all seen that such a catastrophe has come upon Croatia. And I presume — unfortunately I must say this — that Bishop Zanic is to blame, too, because he has so negatively influenced precisely the shepherds, the bishops with things that I will present more exactly later. These were things that simply were not correct and which the Yugoslavian bishops believed much too readily. They had the task of investigating it, as I have investigated it. Really they have examined nothing exactly! They carelessly believed Bishop Zanic in just everything, an unreliable person in this respect, who not one single time has correctly presented a sentence by me to the bishops.

Also, with regard to journalists, he has not presented a single correct sentence about me, and indeed in matters that were strictly confidential and of which he ought to have spoken to no one.

He said it however, and said it falsely, as for example to the correspondent from Herder for the newspaper for pastoral workers. Mr. Hanauer told me expressly concerning this, "Bishop Zanic sent me this." Such things, about me too, has Bishop Zanic spread all over the world. This is a great injustice."

In his July, 25, 1987 homily at Mass in Medjugorje, Bishop Pavao Zanic said, "...It is a well-planned enterprise to lead naive people from all over the world around by the nose. They will wait for secrets and great signs until the end of the world. If the Madonna leaves behind the sign, about which the "visionaries" have spoken, I will walk from Mostar on my knees to Medjugorje and ask forgiveness of the Franciscans.

To the following message from Our Lady given on June 21, 1983, Bishop Zanic, who of course regarded the apparitions as not authentic, added the comment, "Fr. Tomislav Vlasic brought me this. Most probably he composed it in a state of exaltation:"

'Tell father the bishop that I request of him right away a conversion in relation to the events in Medjugorje; otherwise it will be just too late. Let him approach these events with much understanding, love and great sense of responsibility. I would like him to create no tension between priests and not to emphasize their weaknesses. The Holy Father has entrusted tasks for their dioceses to all bishops, for example even to settle problems and disputes. Father bishop is the high priest for all the parishes in Hercegovina. Therefore I request of him his conversion regarding these events. With this I am sending him the next to last admonition. If he does not do what I am communicating to him, my judgment and my Son's judgment await him; this means that he has not found the way of my Son

Jesus.' The Madonna ordered me to direct this message to you. I greet you warmly.

(xiv) Vicka and the Jean Louis Martin Incident

CRITIQUE

E. Michael Jones: Fuerhoff attributes that more to the experiment carried out by the Frenchman Jean Louis Martin than to his own observations. After hearing that the children were out of space and time during the apparitions, Martin approached Vicka during one of the apparitions and made as if he were going to poke her in the eyes with his two fingers. Vicka jumped back instinctively and was quickly led out of the room by Father Vego. A little while later she returned and explained that while she had been watching the Blessed Virgin, the infant Jesus looked as if He were slipping out of her arms. The reaction that Martin saw as her avoiding being poked in the eye was in reality her attempt to catch the falling Baby Jesus, at least according to Vicka's explanation. (105)

RESPONSE

1. As usual, Jones will clutch at any straw to discredit the Medjugorje phenomenon. Anyone critical of Medjugorje with a sensational story gets a hearing, no questions asked, no references checked. In describing incidents reported by Martin and Fuerhoff, all we are told about them is that Walter Fuerhoff is a photographer from Munich and that Jean Louis Martin is a Frenchman. Their testimonies are accepted without question and with no inquiries at all about their reliability as witnesses.

2. From Mary Craig, we find out that "Jean-Louis Martin, an opponent of the apparitions, spent seven months in Medjugorje and many times saw strange phenomena. And he continues to search for a natural explanation." [p.132]. Here we have the epitome of the dogmatic skeptic who will not believe even the testimony of his senses if it contradicts his presuppositions. It may well be the case that his story about Vicka jumping back in reaction to his gesture is true. But it doesn't prove anything one way or another because there are definite variations on different occasions in the degree to which the visionaries are dissociated from the material reality around them. When Professor Belanger told Fr. Slavko that Vicka's reaction proved that she was not "in a true trance," Fr. Slavko replied, "Of

course she wasn't. She was not in a trance but in ecstasy: a state in which the person is only partially disconnected from reality." (106). As for the story about Vicka explaining her motion as an attempt to catch the falling Baby Jesus, we have only Martin's word for it. Those who know about the incident deny that any such explanation was offered. Martin is not just a dogmatic skeptic but a creative one too. With respect to Jones and Medjugorje, we are reminded of the saying, "He who stands for nothing falls for everything."

3. The notion that a witness to an apparition will necessarily be disconnected from everything and everyone around him or her is entirely fallacious as can be seen by reference to both Fatima and Lourdes [although it is true that such disconnection does take place at times]. In *Encountering Mary*, her major historical study of Marian apparitions, Sandra Zimdars-Swartz recounts some details of the Fatima apparition that are relevant here:

Lucia dos Santos, the only one of the three Fatima seers to grow up to adulthood... has played a particularly important in defining the character and the meaning of the Fatima apparition. It has not simply been Lucia's longevity, however, that has lent her significance, for it is clear that she played the leading role in the scenario of the apparition itself. All accounts agree that she was the only one of the three seers to interact with both her vision and with the crowd, carrying on conversations with both while her cousins stood by silently. (107)

Clearly, Lucia (like St. Bernadette before her) did have interaction with those around her even during the apparition. So why should it be relevant that Vicka allegedly reacted to a stimulus during the apparition?

(xv) Jakov the Restless

CRITIQUE

E. Michael Jones: 'Last night Jakov was there too, as he frequently is. He acted silly, teasing Marija during the Mass.' Is it 'normal' for 14 year-olds to misbehave in this fashion at Mass? When my oldest son was 14, he didn't act that way; in fact, he hasn't acted that way at Mass since he was two. But the question is in a way miscast. The real question here is not whether such behavior is normal for 14 year-olds. The question is whether such behavior is normal for a 14 year-old who within the past 24 hours entertained a visit from the Blessed Virgin Mary. (108)

RESPONSE

1. Even little Jakov does not escape the wrath of Jones' pen. The smugness with which he compares his son's behavior with Jakov's cuts to the quick because Jakov is an orphan who does not have a father to ensure that "he didn't act that way." But he does have a spiritual Mother who spares no effort to straighten him out. And, by all accounts, she hasn't found it easy. There is some irony in Jones paying attention to Jakov because Jakov is the wild card that wrecks all the insipid theories — including Jones' — that seek to debunk Medjugorje. The incongruity of someone so earthy being mixed up in something so ethereal is striking enough to make nonsense of all the sophisticated "explanations" for the Medjugorje phenomenon that are currently in circulation.

2. Mary Craig: Jakov arrived wearing a bright orange singlet covered by a check shirt. He had left his rosary beads at home, and had to keep borrowing Marija's. ('Jakov is my cross,' she would sigh later in mock protest.) The two visionaries led the Rosary prayers in turn, but after a while Jakov got tired of kneeling upright and went and squatted on his haunches in a corner. In contrast to this restlessness, the total silence and absorbed concentration in which, at six-forty-five, both visionaries knelt before what to the rest of us looked like a blank wall, were electrifying. (109)

(xvi) The Poem of the Man-God Controversy

CRITIQUE

E. Michael Jones, *Fidelity*, May, 1992:

Caritas of Birmingham, one of this country's leading Medjugorje promoters, announced in its bulletin of that month (June 1989) that 'Vicka asked Our Lady about the book, *Poem of the Man God*, and Our Lady is reported to have said, "It makes for good reading."...There is only one small problem here. It seems that the Blessed Mother enjoys reading works that were previously on the Index of Forbidden Books. (On a talk show in March 1991, Marija Pavlovic was asked) 'What exactly did Our Lady say regarding the *Poem of the Man God*?' Marija who spoke Italian, responded by saying that she had asked the Blessed Mother about the book at the request of 'some lay brother,' and that the Blessed Virgin responded by saying,'It can be read.' 'Si puo leggere,' is what she said in the Italian, which was translated, 'You can read it.'...We now have two seers confirming the fact the the Blessed Mother recommends reading books condemned by the Church."

Paul Likoudis, *The Wanderer*, June 4, 1992:

One of the hottest-selling books in Catholic stores today is Maria Valtorta's multivolume *Poem of the Man-God*, a book placed on the Church's Index of Forbidden Books in 1961. ...The book is selling like hotcakes, because it is part of the Medjugorje phenomenon, promoted among Medjugorje enthusiasts as endorsed by the Blessed Virgin herself. (Terry Colafrancesco, director of Caritas of Birmingham) said interest in the book was 'sparked' when Marija Pavlovich, one of the Medjugorje seers, asked the Virgin Mary - at the request of a seminarian friend - if it was okay to read the book. In Colafrancescio's recollection, Mary said, 'One could read it.'

RESPONSE

Always on the lookout for a stick with which to beat Medjugorje, Jones thinks he's found a plausible candidate in the Blessed Mother's alleged endorsement of *The Poem of The Man-God* by Maria Valtorta, a narrative of the life of Jesus that Valtorta claims to have received from Our Lord. Unfortunately, the intensity of Jones' obsessive quest for a clinching argument against Medjugorje will not allow him to calmly and dispassionately apply the principles of sound inference and judgment. Guilt by association arguments, ad hominem arguments, reductionist arguments: almost every one of the textbook fallacies in logic are recklessly deployed by Jones in his Long March against Medjugorje.

Since none of his other arguments seem to have had much effect, he has now tried to make an argument out of the *Poem* issue. As with his other arguments, the pattern here seems to be one of making a mountain out of a molehill. And as often before, the whole basis of the argument is a report of an obscure, disjointed report of a private exchange between one or more of the visionaries and the Blessed Mother. We have seen that the messages to be considered should be the public messages of the Madonna. Inevitably, the potential for misunderstanding and miscommunication is multiplied when the visionaries bring their own questions or the questions of onlookers to the Blessed Mother: her message is clearest when she is instructing them on specific actions such as prayer and fasting or when she is giving them messages for the world: she appeared to them for this latter purpose not to answer questions about the Bishop and the friars or the red handkerchief story or *The Poem of the Man God*. When a mother is responding to random questions put to her by her small children, it is quite possible that they may misunderstand her answers: this is a result of their limitations and not hers. If she, however, is teaching them lessons of her own that are adapted to the level of their mental development, then there is less likelihood of their misunderstanding her.

In his usual shoot-from-the-hip style, Jones has mixed five entirely distinct issues that should be studied independently:

1. The authenticity of *The Poem of The Man-God*
2. The authenticity of Medjugorje
3. The authenticity of the Blessed Mother approving *The Poem of The Man-God*
4. The authenticity of the report of the visionaries saying that the Blessed Mother approved *The Poem of The Man-God*
5. The activities of Medjugorje enthusiasts in promoting *The Poem of The Man-God*.

All five issues must be studied separately. If the answer to (1) is that the Poem is not authentic, this negative verdict has no logical bearing on (2), the authenticity of Medjugorje. Once one has reached definite conclusions on each one of the five issues, it is possible to try to determine if and whether any of them are related to the others. This is the bare minimum of "due process" that must be adopted in any rational investigation of the question raised by Jones. But "due process" is a road less travelled in *Fidelity*'s judicial environment.

If only to humor him, let us grant Jones his worst case scenario. Suppose the Blessed Mother did indeed tell Vicka that the *Poem* "makes for good reading" and suppose she did tell Marija "It can be read," what are we to infer from such recommendations? Clearly, neither statement specifies or even implies that the *Poem* can be taken to be a historically accurate rendering of the life of Jesus. At this point, Jones will triumphantly spring his trap and announce that we have just made the Blessed Mother recommend a book that has been placed by the Church on the Index of Forbidden Books.

Here Jones betrays his simple ignorance of history. Books that have been placed on the Index have subsequently been taken off. A prominent example that almost exactly parallels the Poem is *The Mystical City of God* by Mary Agreda. Venerable Mary Agreda claimed to have divine revelation too in writing about details concerning the life of Jesus in *The Mystical City of God*. Like the Poem, *The City of God* too was accused of being childish and implausible (as well as "pompous and strained"). But *The City of God* was later taken off the Index and Mary Agreda subsequently became Venerable Mary Agreda. Does this mean that *The City of God* is a "true story"? By no means - although Agreda claims that God told her, "I do not intend that thy descriptions... shall be mere opinions or contemplations, but reliable truth." We can reasonably assume that Mary Agreda, and Maria Valtorta for that matter, were pious women who sincerely believed that they were receiving divine revelation in writing about the life of Jesus. If either of them were deceiving themselves, then what we have are pious speculations that could be edifying. If they were receiving some kind of divine guidance, we need not look at the fruits of their labors with the Fundamentalist criteria favored by Jones and his like. Without question, anything written by them would reflect their personalities, their flaws, their predilections: only a Fundamentalist assumes that writings receiving divine guidance do not reflect the human agent. So we can well expect both works to tell us a great deal about their authors — even if they had some measure of divine truth to them. By no means should we look at any such work as a papal bull or a Gospel. In fact, many of the writings of medieval saints and mystics on the "secret" lives of Jesus and Mary may seem implausible and may only be bursts of piety. But even in the latter category they "make for good reading."

Now even if the *Poem* were not placed on the Index, an alleged endorsement by the Blessed Mother of the kind reported here would not automatically guarantee its veracity. There is too much obscurity in the partial exchanges reported by Jones. If Valtorta had no malicious motive in writing the *Poem*, surely we cannot expect the Blessed Mother to condemn it in the strongest terms. Her alleged comments in fact seem to reflect Marija's and Vicka's own interpretations more than anything else. As to the charge that the Blessed Mother was recommending a book placed on the Index, we simply have to say that the Index does not exist any more. Yes, it retains its moral authority in a general sense but it is not infallible and it is not now canonically binding. So even if the Blessed Mother endorsed a book that <u>had</u> been on the Index — and there is certainly no evidence that she did — she is in no way undermining the canonical authority of the Church.

The question of the Blessed Mother recommending a book that had been on the Index and the relevance of this recommendation to the moral authority of the Church requires a little further exploration — especially the question of moral authority. When an issue involving disciplinary rules of the Church is under consideration, the first question must be whether the rule is still in effect. If it is not in effect then legitimate exceptions to the rule are permissible without any express or implied infringement of the moral authority of the Church. The Church's disciplinary rule forbidding meat on Fridays is no longer in effect. That rule has now been taken "off the books," so to speak, but it still retains its moral authority. Nevertheless, a Catholic can now eat meat on a Friday in circumstances where no other food is available without violating the moral authority of the rule. Similarly, in general, books on the Index must remain forbidden to the Catholic but it is quite possible that a book that had been placed on the Index may turn out to be innocuous. Even when the Index was in effect this has happened. Today the Index does not continue to have the same disciplinary authority on the Catholic: given legitimate reasons (and this is a critical condition), it is permissible for a Catholic to study a book that had once been on the Index. In any case, the infallibility or the authority of the Church is nowhere at stake. In all fairness, we must also bear in mind the claim of proponents of the *Poem* that Pope Pius XII expressly sanctioned publication of the work in these words; "Publish this work as it is. There is not need to give an opinion about its origin, whether it is extraordinary or not. Who reads it will understand. One hears of many visions and revelations. I will not say they are all authentic; but there are some of which it could be said that they are." This purported endorsement of Pope Pius was nevertheless followed in 1959 by the placing of the *Poem* on the Index of Forbidden Books.

Returning to the crux of our discussion, the logical fulcrum remains the same: the authenticity of Medjugorje should be judged on its own terms and not by reference to extraneous allegations (no matter how colorful these may be). The *Poem* too must be judged on its own terms: in terms of its theological content and the mental soundness of its author. Obedience to the Church and adherence to the public revelation granted in Scripture and Tradition, of course, come first. These are the litmus tests against which the *Poem* should be judged — although we must not ignore the complexities and subtleties that have already been discussed with reference to historical precedents.

We would like to end this discussion by reiterating a point made earlier: acceptance of the authenticity of Medjugorje by no means commits one to acceptance of any other supernatural phenomenon. It is well known that a number of adult women claim to have had apparitions "back at the ranch" in places like Denver, Colorado, Atlanta, Georgia and Scottsdale, Arizona; also claims of messages directed by Jesus have come from Vassula Ryden. These claims should be examined on their merits and not in the same breath as Medjugorje. The authenticity of Medjugorje in no sense serves as an endorsement of any one of these claimed apparitions although most of them do make reference to Medjugorje. Self-deception, hallucination and even occult explanations of such claims are not to be ruled out until they have been closely studied. In Medjugorje, as at Lourdes and Fatima, we are dealing with peasant children; in addition, in all these three cases, the messages themselves have been clearly orthodox and there has been no question of moral impropriety with regard to the visionaries. In the history of the Church, the most reliable cases of older women witnessing apparitions that have been approved involved women religious (the Sacred Heart, the Miraculous Medal and Akita are three examples): the constraints of authority, obedience and discipline tend to separate the wheat from the chaff.

(xvii) Vassula Ryden and Medjugorje

> Many *Fidelity* readers will note the similarity in spirit between [Vassula Ryden's] 'ecumenical' outpourings and some of the messages attributed to Our Lady by the Medjugorje 'visionaries'...Amongst Medjugorje enthusiasts, the Church often seems to be viewed in practice as 'our denomination' — one amongst others — and no longer as the one true Church." [Fr. Brian Harrison, *Fidelity,* May 1992, p.39.]

> Vassula Ryden is a superstar, a supernova in Catholic circles today, the hottest property in that growing galaxy of visionaries spinning off the Medjugorje phenomenon." [*The Wanderer,* January 28, 1993].[3]

Although from the very first sentence, the Wanderer article sounded like the usual type of "reporting" in *Fidelity*, we have noted earlier that some of the worst enemies of Medjugorje are its friends. It must readily be admitted that some devoted to Medjugorje are little better than sensation-seekers who pursue the latest apparitions and visionaries much as New Age enthusiasts sniff out gurus and channelers. We have seen earlier that the multiplication of false claims of apparitions is not an uncommon tendency after an authentic apparition takes place. This was definitely the case at Lourdes where numerous false apparitions were reported at the time of St. Bernadette's apparitions — one such false apparition even overshadowed Lourdes for a time.

In this book, we have tried to show that Medjugorje is one of the two greatest apparitions of this century, the other being Fatima. And the Holy Father, among others, has recognized a definite connection between Fatima and Medjugorje. Simply in terms of global impact, Medjugorje is comparable to Fatima and Lourdes. As a result many would-be visionaries seek their inspiration from Medjugorje.

Anyone who compares Medjugorje to any of the recent purported apparitions cannot fail to notice some drastic differences. Global impact is one major hallmark of Medjugorje. In addition, Medjugorje fits in with the general pattern of previous Marian apparitions [the visionaries are peasant children, the messages echo familiar themes, etc.]. Then we must consider the unparalleled scientific analyses of the visionaries carried out during the apparitions. Finally, we cite the "fruits" of Medjugorje: the many cures and healings and supernatural phenomena associated with Medjugorje and the conversion and return to the sacraments of hundreds of thousands. None of the other recent claims of apparitions even remotely resemble the splendor of this phenomenon. And Medjugorje will not tolerate those who simply seek "signs and wonder". "I invite you to change your life because you have taken a path of misery, a path of ruin. When I told you to convert, pray, fast, be reconciled, you took these messages superficially," warns Our Lady [March 25, 1992].

Having said all this, we must admit that there are probably other authentic apparitions taking place. We should remember that in Medjugorje Our Lady responded "If it is necessary I will appear in each home," when told, "People are surprised that you are appearing in so many places," (Spring, 1982). But none of

---

[3] In fairness we should point out that Fr. Michale O'Carroll clearly refuted, point by point, the "erroneous" charges made in the *Wanderer* article. "The person who wrote it has obviously never read any of Vassula's writings." Fr. O'Carroll sent his rely to this writer. It is to be published in the future.

her apparitions can claim the kind of pre-eminence enjoyed by Fatima and Medjugorje. And we should not accept every claim of apparitions uncritically. Each claim should be weighed against the criteria given to us by the Church and in particular in the context of the teachings of the Church.

Now it is simply preposterous to suggest that Medjugorje teaches a kind of false ecumenism. The charges of religious indifferentism and syncretism have been answered in great detail earlier in this book. We have seen that Medjugorje's teachings on other religions are in full accord with the teachings of the Second Vatican Council and of Pope John Paul II. The proof of the pudding is in the eating: many non-Catholics have converted to Catholicism as a direct result of Medjugorje. A prominent example is the Lutheran writer, Wayne Weible.

The attempt to attack Medjugorje by pointing to the flaws of other alleged visionaries is obviously fallacious from a logical standpoint. It is similarly fallacious to criticize Medjugorje because some of the proponents of Medjugorje also endorse more dubious phenomena: if you are right on one matter you will not necessarily be right on everything else. In particular, Medjugorje cannot be held responsible for the pronouncements of Vassula Ryden, a Greek Orthodox lady. Her claims and pronouncements must be evaluated on their own terms.

We must point out here that the kinds of claims she is making cannot even be compared to the claims of Medjugorje. She does not claim to witness an apparition of the Blessed Virgin and she has not been scrutinized by scientists in the same way as the visionaries of Medjugorje. And clearly she cannot be compared to Medjugorje in terms of impact.

Vassula Ryden claims to be writing messages given her by Jesus and Mary. Some have raised concerns about her particular mode of revelation. The content of Vassula's messages must also be scrutinized carefully.

Such concerns have no bearing whatsoever on the authenticity of Medjugorje. Additionally, those devoted to Our Lady's call from Medjugorje should not assume that the authenticity of Medjugorje guarantees the authenticity of Vassula Ryden. The two are radically distinct phenomena and, as we have said, should be studied on their own terms.

(xiii) Was It All a Joke?

Jones' extraordinary "thesis" that the whole Medjugorje phenomenon can be explained as a joke that got out of hand has already been reviewed and rejected. For some comic relief after this tedious exercise in point by point refutation of egregious error, it might be helpful to apply the "joke" thesis to the events in Medjugorje to see if it takes us anywhere.

CRITIQUE

E. Michael Jones: This leads us to posit a theory about how the apparitions got started. Our hypothesis is simple: the whole thing was a joke that got out of hand. ...What Mirjana and Ivanka hadn't counted on, however, was the reaction of the crowds. Instead of just fooling around and making fun of a few of the locals the girls suddenly had the entire countryside as well as the police in an uproar over what they were claiming to see. (110)

RESPONSE

Dr. Nicholas Bartulica:

As it was previously mentioned, the author of *The Untold Story* is of the opinion that all started as a "joke which got out of hand."

We already wrote that there are many who subscribe to such a possibility, and therefore in this chapter, we will examine whether the visionaries' actions are compatible with the behavior of one who plays a 'joke.'

Let us therefore assume that the "joke hypothesis" might be right, and we will try to seek out whether it is possible to understand and explain the visionaries' behavior as a result of a 'joke,' that is, pretense without having any real subjective experience.

Ivanka probably was the first of six future 'jokers' who started the 'joke'; that is, to claim that they had an apparition. Her friend Mirjana apparently agreed, and those two girls were soon joined by Milka Pavlovic, 13, to whom they confided their plan, and she consented to it.

The first person on whom they played their 'joke' was Vicka Ivankovic, who come and noticed her three friends 'staring at something,' and they shouted, 'look there is the Gospa.' Vicka, not knowing that it was a 'joke,' got scared, took off her shoes and ran away. The three jokers, realizing that their 'joke' was successful, must have had a good laugh together.

Vicka soon returned with two Ivans, one 16 and another 20, and all three approached the three girls. They started to look at the appointed direction, but since it was a 'joke,' they obviously could not see anything. At this moment the three 'instigators' must have admitted to Vicka that this was only 'a joke' and knowing Vicka's choleric character, we must assume that she probably did not hide her displeasure with this kind of play. However, somehow she changed her attitude, decided to join them and became the fourth 'joker.' From this time on she herself started to play a 'joke' by claiming that she also saw 'an apparition.'

Now the explanation of the visionaries' behavior by the 'joke hypothesis' becomes a little complicated. When Vicka turned back to ask Ivan

(Dragicevic) if he saw something, she saw him jumping over the stone fence and dropping his apples. He must have heard the three girls explaining to Vicka that all it was "only a joke," and since there was nothing to be seen, it is puzzling what Ivan got scared of and why he was running away.

The other Ivan (Ivankovic) apparently accepted the first day to be part of the group, and later he said he saw something 'light and turning.' However, he did not return to Apparition Hill, he stopped playing the 'joke,' but he never publicly admitted that the incident was 'joke.'

Milka Pavlovic also did not return the second day and in the future did not continue to be one of 'joke players,' but neither did she admit that she was 'joking.'

Her older sister, Marija, 16, after hearing her story and being curious, told Vicka to call her on the second day if she saw something. When Marija joined the other three girls and found out that this was only a 'joke,' she must have felt deeply disappointed. However, she decided to join the 'play,' and she become a permanent member of six 'jokers,' who continued to put on an act in the future. She was accompanied by her little cousin Jakov, 10, who must have been persuaded to become a member of the 'jokers club.'

On the second evening, there were about fifteen onlookers, and the children must have enjoyed acting in front of an audience. They behaved as if they were seeing an 'apparition' and knelt down and started to pray. The onlookers noticed that the children became upset and cried, but they were not aware that this was only a well played performance. As we already wrote, after the "apparition" was over, little Jakov kept repeating, 'I would not be sorry if I would die right now, since I have seen the Gospa,' and during the apparition he was observed grabbing Vicka saying, 'Look at her. She is beauty itself.... She is beautiful like an actress.' The onlookers were probably impressed without being aware that they were watching a polished actor, who was only pretending as if he were really experiencing an apparition.

When the children returned from the hill, they appeared distressed and crying. Marinko Ivankovic, cousin of some of the children, later affirmed that Ivanka cried bitterly, embraced her grandmother, telling her that she asked the Gospa about her dead mother, but he was not aware that this was only an 'act' since Ivanka neither saw Gospa not could she have asked about her mother, and all along her tears were part of her acting to appear more convincing.

Marija on returning home also pretended to have seen the Gospa. She was telling her parents 'ten times' how the Gospa looked. That is, she was repeating the lies, until her parents had to believe. She apparently was successful in her deception while repeatedly describing the Gospa whom she never saw. Two days later she would tell Fr. Cuvalo, 'I was scared, I wasn't able to eat, my hands were completely white and cold like ice water.'

Here again we have another sophisticated liar who would not only lie about seeing Gospa, but in order to convince Fr. Cuvalo, she was describing her (Marija's) emotional state, and by inserting the physiological changes (i.e. white and cold hands), one is at a loss looking for the performing school which she must have frequented.

Ivan came home and, apparently not able to put on an act in case they would question him extensively, made a few laconic statements. At the interview with Fr.Cuvalo he said, 'When I entered the house, I said I have seen, have been, have prayed in front of her, knelt, said the Our Father and seen her, the Gospa.' As we mentioned, his parents in the beginning were skeptical but later started to believe him.

On June 26, Ivan was back on the Apparition Hill with the other 'jokers,' and he pretended that he saw 'a little figure of a woman.' When he was interviewed by Fr. Cuvalo in June 27, he insisted that he even heard her voice. Since some of his statements did not appear convincing, Fr. Cuvalo challenged him with a question, 'Do you lie?' but Ivan defended his "joke" with a categorical denial: 'I don't lie.' He even gave a more elaborate statement about the Gospa, who allegedly told them the reason why she was appearing. According to Ivan, the Gospa said, 'You are the best faithful.' Since Ivan was only pretending that he heard the Gospa's voice, this last statement attributed to Gospa was pure fabrication.

But here the 'joke hypothesis' runs again into a problem. Ivan was not present during the morning interview when Fr. Cuvalo questioned Ivanka, Marija and Vicka. During this interview Ivanka also 'pretended' that they asked Gospa, 'Why did you come right here?' and she (Gospa) allegedly replied, 'Because there were a lot of faithful ...'

Assuming that none of the visionaries had an apparition an all was only a 'pretense,' it becomes puzzling that four different children during separate interviews gave almost identical answers. Could this be pure coincidence? This explanation is not only implausible but absurd. Thus, there is only one logical explanation; namely, that the visionaries somehow got together before the interview and concocted the answers. It means that we are not only dealing with a simple, childish prank but with a well-planned plot to deceive the clergy and the faithful. But then we must ask the question, 'when did the children get together?'

We know that little Jakov was not present on the first day, June 24, and Ivan was absent the second evening on June 25. Both of them were together for first time during the 'apparition' on June 26 when they supposedly heard the Gospa talking of a 'lot of faithful.' It follows that Jakov and Ivan must have gotten together sometime after the apparition of

June 26 but before the interview the next day June 27. In addition, Ivanka and Mirjana, who gave similar answers, must have also attended the meeting.

We have not read from any opponent of authenticity of apparitions any existing evidence that the visionaries had such private and secret meetings. If we want to consider the 'joke hypothesis' to be plausible, the meetings must have taken place because besides the statement of 'lot of faithful,' there are many other identical answers from the visionaries, and the only logical explanation is that several well-planned rehearsals must have taken place.

For instance several visionaries during separate interviews said that they heard the Gospa say before leaving, "Go in God's peace" (Ivanka, Vicka, Mirjana, Ivan and Jakov). Ivanka mentioned another statement from the Gospa that "we must be together, that people should reconcile." Similar statements were heard by Marija, Jakov and Ivan.

On the second evening Ivanka allegedly asked about her mother, and on the third evening she received a 'a message' that her mother wanted her to obey her grandmother. The same Gospa statement is confirmed during separate interviews by Mirjana and Ivan.

The visionaries are in total agreement in describing several items regarding the Gospa's appearance. For instance, they said that she is about 20 years old, has blue eyes, black hair and a crown of stars around her head. She wears a white veil, gray-bluish robe, and nobody was able to see her feet. She is hovering above the ground on a white cloud, and she speaks with a "singing voice." Since there is no contradiction on their description, the only explanation is that the children were attending some meetings when they prepared themselves for their unusual performance. It would be up to the proponents of fraud to produce the evidence when and where such meetings were taking place and who was the organizer. As we learned, the two principal "manipulators were not present. Fr. Vlasic had not been assigned to Medjugorje until August 18 while Fr. Zovko was absent from June 17 to June 27.

On the third day the 'jokers' continued to put on their act. There were several hundred people present, and Vicka was given holy water to sprinkle on the "apparition." In view of the fact that Vicka was not seeing anything, she was sprinkling the empty space "pretending" that she was seeing and talking to the Gospa. The onlookers heard her saying, 'In the name of the Father, and of the Son and of the Holy Spirit, Amen. If you are the Gospa, remain with us. If you are not, get lost!' Vicka then victoriously reported that the Gospa had remained, but Vicka's whole performance was only a 'joke.'

On Sunday, June 28 the crowd reportedly reached 15,000 people, and the 'jokers' gave a new performance. As we already described, a man

(G. Kozina) brought a tape recorder and recorded the visionaries' voices. They were given the question to ask the 'alleged apparition.' Vicka was selected as the spokesperson, and when the Gospa 'appeared,' Vicka asked loudly the questions. After allegedly receiving the answers, which only the visionaries heard, she transmitted those answers for the benefit of the onlookers. Both the questions and answers were recorded. Among the questions there is one regarding appearing in the church. For instance, Vicka asked, 'Gospa, why don't you appear in the church so that all can see you?' To which, according to Vicka, the Gospa replied: 'Blest are they who don't see, but believe.'

Since all was a pure performance and Vicka was not seeing a vision, it means that she was quickly concocting the answers. One must admit that this young peasant girl, 16 at the time, was not only an excellent performer, but a smart theologian as well.

Bishop Zanic later suggested that the visionaries had the answers prepared by some Franciscans, in particular Fr. Vlasic. However, Fr. Vlasic was a still a pastor in Capljina, 16 miles away, and his first recorded visit after the apparitions had started took place the next day on June 29 1981.

Between June 27 and June 30 the children were subjected to rigorous interrogation by the skeptical clergy, first Fr. Zrinko Cuvalo and then the parish priest, Fr. Zovko.

We have previously discussed those interviews during which the priests tried to get the seers to contradict themselves and to admit that they had concocted the whole story. However, the 'jokers' withstood the attack and did not retreat an inch. When they were threatened by God's punishment, they declared that they were not afraid because they were not lying.

Little Jakov, 10, was challenged by his pastor, Fr. Zovko, who called his bluff with 'you did not see her.' In spite of knowing that he was telling a lie, Jakov had the audacity to say, 'I saw the Gospa. I saw her as if she were in front of me. I saw her like I see you.'

Ivanka and Mirjana added a special performance to their pretense when Fr. Zovko commented that the visionaries' claim of 'seeing' was not convincing to others who cannot have similar experiences. At this moment the two girls pretended that they were empathizing with other people who were not able to have the same experience. For instance, Mirjana said, 'It would not be convincing to me either thus I would not believe so easily of I did not see her.' And a little later, 'I experienced a terrible sorrow... I would like it if all of them could see her.' Ivanka in the same vein said, 'If people would see her and I would not, I would not believe either.' And again, 'My most ardent desire would be that the crowd could see her.'

Here we have again difficulty with 'joke hypothesis' because liars are regularly self-centered and unable to empathize with others. The only explanation for Mirjana's and Ivanka's attitude is that we are facing here highly sophisticated liars who are pretending to be empathic in order to confound further the interrogator.

An additional problem for 'joke hypothesis' is Vicka's dream talk which was reported to Fr. Zovko by Mirjana during the interview on June 30. According to Vicka's cousin, she (the cousin) could not sleep because 'when Vicka sleeps she keeps saying in her sleep, 'Leave us a sign.'' Assuming that Vicka had no experience of 'seeing an apparition' but was simply lying, one wonders what she was dreaming of? It looks as if Vicka kept 'pretending' and playing a 'joke' even in her sleep. But there is a rule regulating dreams, and that is, there can be nothing in a dream that was not sometime perceived. One wonders whom Vicka was seeing in her dream while asking for a sign. Or perhaps Vicka is such a polished and compulsive liar that she keeps lying even in her sleep?

When Fr. Zovko commented that the visionaries were becoming popular and questioned their feelings regarding the big crowds, almost all of them declared that they would prefer to be alone with the Gospa and that they were bothered by the crowds.

Here again there is a puzzle for the 'joke hypothesis.' We have six young 'actors' who don't care to have any audiences and would prefer to put on an act without having anybody present.

As we heard before, on June 29 the little 'jokers' were taken by police to a psychiatric ward and subjected to psychiatric examination. In front of the psychiatrist they continued to insist that they witnessed an 'apparition,' which they knew that was 'a lie.' The psychiatrist told them that if they continued claiming to have 'apparitions' and going to Apparition Hill, they would risk being committed to a mental hospital.

Now this was no longer a 'joke.' Mirjana openly admitted the next day to Fr. Zovko that she felt 'petrified.' The same feeling was experienced by Marija and Ivanka. However, the "jokers" for some unknown reason continued playing the 'joke,' which might have resulted in a confinement in a mental institution. The 'jokers' motivation for continuing such risky behavior remains to be explained by the proponents of the 'joke hypothesis.'

The same evening (June 29) the 'jokers' during the 'faked' apparition asked the 'Gospa' for the cure for young Daniel. Mirjana and Ivanka in separate interviews talked about this incident, and Mirjana even pretended that she was certain that the boy would get better because 'she (Gospa) looked at him so mercifully.' In accordance with the 'joke hypothesis,' this additional fabrication illustrates again that we are dealing with a very 'sophisticated liar' who was describing the special look of the Gospa to camouflage the fact of 'lying.'

A particular problem for the 'joke hypothesis' is the visionaries' behavior during the apparition on July 3 in the rectory, which was described in the diary of Fr. Loncar. He wrote that during the apparition Jakov was moving his lips and nobody could hear a sound. After the apparition Ivanka asked him, 'Why you were asking for that,' and she explained to Fr. Loncar that Jakov was asking for a sign. Since Jakov was only moving his lips, what sound did Ivanka hear? Was the whole event only a performance to confound further the onlookers? The previous day the children were mistreated by the police and were hiding in the rectory. Did they have any time for a rehearsal for the above act?

From the above discussion we saw some of the ordeals that the children brought on themselves by 'joking,' but they persisted with their claim that they had been seeing, hearing and even touching 'the Gospa.' What is behind this stubborn persistence?

The Untold Story offers some explanation: 'Once the shock settled in and the seers were faced with the possibility of admitting that they had made the whole thing up, they got scared; thus there was a good possibility that the police might become involved.'

Here the author of *The Untold Story* contradicts his own findings, since in the beginning of the same chapter, 'The reaction of the crowds,' he wrote: 'Instead of just fooling around and making fun of a few of the locals, the girls (had two boys disappeared? N.B.) suddenly had the entire countryside as well as the police in an uproar over what they were claiming to see.'

Since it was a fact that the police got heavily involved, the claim that the visionaries got 'scared' about the possibility of police involvement does not make any sense.

The second explanation, that the visionaries were facing the possibility of admitting that they were lying, does not appear logical either.

For example, if somebody is 'joking' about a nonexisting experience, that is, lying, and the 'joke' becomes a source of a serious problem, he simply stops joking. There was no need for the visionaries to admit that they 'made the whole thing up.' Once in trouble, they could have simply said, 'We don't see any more,' and the whole affair would have been over, and nobody would have bothered to make them admit that they only 'pretended.' The psychiatrist told them directly, 'Stop talking about the apparition and going to Apparition Hill or else you might end in the mental hospital.' She (the psychiatrist) was not insisting that 'the visionaries should admit they were lying from the beginning.'

We know that Milka Pavlovic claimed seeing the first apparition on June 24, 1981, but did not return the second day. Since that time she never again claimed to have apparition, but she never faced the situation that she had to admit that she had 'lied,' and until today she maintains that she really saw the Gospa but just on the first day.

Another visionary, Mirjana, ceased to claim the apparition on Dec. 25, 1982, but she still insists on having the same experience once each year on her birthday (March 18).

Ivanka had her last apparition on May 7, 1985, but since that time she claims an annual experience on June 25.

Neither one of those two girls ever retracted their previous experience, and they did not suffer any punitive or unpleasant consequences after they said that their daily visions had come to an end.

The remaining four visionaries continued to claim almost daily visions which, according to them, will cease after they receive the tenth secret message.

The above examples demonstrate that the "fear" cannot explain the continuation of a 'joke,' and since the behavior, which according to *The Untold Story* is a 'pretense,' continued on spite of external threats, logic postulates another explanation.

One flagrant example of the implausibility of the 'joke hypothesis' was the already described incident on July 2, 1981. The visionaries were chased by the police through the fields, and at the door of the church they met Fr. Zovko, who hid them in the rectory. They were obviously in panic and apprehensive that plans were made to commit them to the mental hospital where they were examined three days earlier. While they were still hiding in the rectory, they claimed again having an apparition.

Is it logical to assume that after having experienced a scare by the police and facing a possibility of confinement to a mental hospital for their playing a 'joke,' they engaged again in the same behavior; that is, they 'pretended' to have an apparition which was the cause of the whole ordeal in the first place? Such behavior one might find in an insane person with masochistic traits, traits which no one has yet established in six Medjugorje visionaries.

During the above discussion we have tried to expose the illogicality of the 'joke hypothesis.' We are aware that multiple scientific tests had excluded the possibility of a pretense and lying, but since there are still many who are willing or consider the "joke" as a plausible explanation, we felt that the untenability of such theory should be directly exposed.

If it was not a 'joke,' what have we been witnessing?

From the beginning it was clear that the children have been having an unusual subjective experience and that they were not pretending. Many scientists have been investigating and have offered different hypotheses to such phenomena. On the other hand, millions believe that the children's experience is authentic and of supernatural origin. The Church authorities will have the final say, but we can be certain that the whole thing was not just 'a joke.' (111)

(xix) The Testimony Against Fr. Jozo

THE TESTIMONY OF A FORMER WITNESS AGAINST FR. JOZO, TIHOMIR KARACIC. (*Nasa Ognijista*, MARCH, 1991)

What was told to us by the former witness against Fr. Jozo Zovko?
The Public Confession of a Perjured Witness:

Almost ten years ago the former Medjugorje Pastor, Fr. Jozo Zovko, was put on trial and convicted. The reason being the words from Holy Scripture which he used in his sermon. At that time the government officials gave a completely different meaning to his words. They also hired a fraudulent witness who was to speak out against Jozo the precise words ordered by UDBA (Secret Intelligence Agency). The conscience of this man was long ago awakened because of this deceitful witnessing, and more and more it bothered him through the years. And he has been seeking an opportunity to offer Fr. Jozo an apology. Recently, he did precisely that, and afterwards he came to our newsroom and gave us his confession with the intention that it be printed publicly in this newspaper, *Nasa Ognijista* (*Our Hearth*). So now, in his own words let his story be told —

My name is Tihomir Karacic. I was born in Donji Crnac, not far from Siroki Brijeg, on July 19, 1962. My mother died in 1969. My father is still living. My family was very poor and this was my main reason for attending, after my graduation from grammar school, the School of Internal Affairs in Sarajevo which was free. The school program was 4 years and after I completed studies I worked for 6 years in Listica. Generally speaking, I was a Traffic Policeman. Three years ago I left that position, and after that I could find work nowhere. Now I live with my father, and occasionally I go to work in Germany for a month in order to make ends meet. My fraudulent witnessing against Fr. Jozo came about in this way:

During the year 1981 I completed my third year at the School in Sarajevo. It is customary that after completing three years each candidate goes for practical experience, and I was assigned to my own area, Listica. Around that time the Gospa began to appear in Medjugorje. One day the local police chief of the area ordered me to go to Medjugorje with Branko Pinjuh, who was the President of the Youth Organization in Listica at that time. We were told to listen to Fr. Jozo's sermon and to remember as much of it as possible, and that's what we did. That was July 11, 1981. When I returned to Listica I told the police officers all that I remembered, but I got the distinct impression that they had already made their decision against Jozo's sermon. So obviously, my going there was just a formality.

In the Fall I returned to Sarajevo for my fourth year of studies. One day I received an order to report to the Mostar SUP (Contra Intelligence Service) because I was to act as a witness at Jozo's trial. At Sarajevo the director of the school encouraged me not to be concerned about anything, that all would be fine and that it had to be this way. In Mostar the main investigator of the Mostar SUP, a man named Augustin Gaspar (whom I believe later became the main chief of the Mostar UDBA) immediately upon our meeting recommended that I not go home, but instead take a room somewhere in Mostar not far from the SUP Institution, so that nothing would be noticed and I would be nearby for the trial. I went to stay at my aunt's home in Ilico. Soon after I was settled in at the house, Gaspar came to me. He told me to take a pen and paper and to write down what he would dictate. I complied. When I finished he told me to memorize it by tomorrow because I'd have to relate this at the trial against Jozo Zovko. I arrived at the trial at the appointed time and was waiting in the corridor. When they called me into the courtroom I testified what I had learned by heart.

After my testimony I returned to Sarajevo to continue my last year of studies. During this time I noticed they were very kind to me, showing me special attention because of my so-called 'merits' - because I had testified falsely against this innocent man. After I completed school they even offered me a free apartment in Sarajevo so that I might progress quickly through the ranks. I refused it. This is my great consolation, that I did not accept reward for my fraudulent testimony. According to my father's wish I returned to Listica and, as I mentioned before, I remained for 6 years as a Traffic Policeman. At Listica my supervisors were not so pleasant towards me, almost an animosity was shown. They even plotted against me, showing that I was not their friend. Obviously it was clear to them that I was not their friend and because of this I was looking for an opportunity to leave this job. Then on one occasion, when they wanted to send me to Sarajevo for a special course, I refused to go. Soon after that I left the job as a policeman and since that time, 3 years already, I've been without a job. But they were following me constantly. I have obvious proof of that. For example, after I left the job I went to Germany to work illegally. I soon realized they were following me. They reported me to the authorities and I had to go back home. At the same time in Listica and the neighboring areas, already the rumors were circulating that I was a spy and a dishonest man and that I was to be avoided. Even though this is an ugly label I felt I had no need to defend myself because my conscience was clear as far as I was concerned since I'd been forced to make false statements. If I were really a spy and a dishonest man certainly I wouldn't be without a job for

3 years. It's well known how those who are involved in this type of work live, never lacking anything.

But let's put all this aside. As a convinced Catholic believer and one who wants to live honestly, for me throughout all these years the greatest pain was in knowing that I as an immature youth believed UDBA, and in one weak moment I gave false testimony. Because of UDBA I inflicted an injustice upon this innocent man, Fr. Jozo Zovko. From year to year my conscience was bothering me more and more. Because of my remorseful conscience I have not been to confession for almost ten years. And that, for a believer, was too heavy a burden. And, conscientiously, I could not go to confession until I first went and asked forgiveness of the man upon whom I had inflicted this injustice, Fr. Jozo Zovko. Also, because of this I had no desire to marry. I remained single. Through these many years I have been seeking an opportunity to approach Jozo, but there were many obstacles on the road. First my job, second my reluctance to approach, without an intermediary, the person to whom I had caused much suffering due to my false testimony. Fortunately, not too long ago, I found some people — a priest and a friend of mine — who acted as mediators and paved the road enabling me to reach Fr. Jozo. Fr. Jozo accepted me as a friend is received. Immediately from his heart he forgave me, and through my own desire he gave me confession. After that we embraced and kissed each other. In that moment, from my heart was lifted a great burden which had been crushing me all these years. Fr. Jozo even promised to personally perform my wedding ceremony. I'm grateful to God for this great grace which he has given me.

The greatest pain in all this, the most difficult, is in knowing that I consciously lied about Jozo. Even though I didn't do it through my own will, but through the imposed will of those whom I simply could not refuse. And in this the main role was played by the agent Augustin Gaspar, who dictated the fraudulent testimony and even drove me to Fr. Jozo's trial. But I would not say that he was the only guilty participant in my case. Another guilty participant was Viktor Rezic from Crnic, who personally sent me to listen to Zovko's sermon. But really, the true guilt should be attributed to the political system which continually uses the weak people and those who desire to achieve certain career goals. The system hid behind these people.

Now, thank God, this is ended. Not only in our country, but in a great part of Europe. And I believe this is God's work in action, above all in our country — and also the work of Our Lady in Medjugorje.

I am not a person who harbors resentment, and I know that ill-will cannot exist in the hearts of Christians. That is why I have forgiven everyone as Jozo forgave me, and also as God has forgiven me through confession. And from now on I want to live as an honorable man, a True Croat, and a True Christian.

(The editor said Tihomir Karacic poured forth his story in one breath.)
The exact text of the fraudulent testimony, as dictated by the agent Augustin Gaspar, to the witness Tihomir Karacic:

I was in Mostar purchasing some materials. When I reached the bus station, with the intention to return to my home, I noticed a group of people who were discussing the apparitions of the Blessed Mother in Medjugorje. They were planning to go to Medjugorje that day. I had heard of the apparitions of the Gospa in my own village and that made me decide to go on that day to Medjugorje. I boarded the bus which travels from Mostar to Ljubuski leaving at 3:30 pm. Since I had never before been to Medjugorje I asked some people in the group where I should exit the bus. They said I should get off when they do. Our bus stopped at an intersection about 2 or 3 kilometers past Citluk. This group of people got off and I got off with them. Then we walked left of the road and kept on by foot. Masses of people were walking on foot, and also on busses. Since I was thirsty I stopped to have a soda before I went to the church. When I arrived at the church I stood in the shade of a tree because it was very hot and humid. The church was quite full when the Mass began. I noticed the loud speakers outside so I had no reason to go into the church. From some people who were standing nearby I heard that Pastor Zovko was saying the Mass.

During one point of his sermon, which was of a religious character, I noticed that Jozo in one moment was mentioning 40 years of life in chains, in pain, in darkness, in fear. He was calling the light to this darkness. And also he was saying how we have to be free. He was calling God to unfasten these chains and shackles. He was saying that there are some who are afraid to be seen going into the church during the daytime, afraid to marry, afraid to have children because this society offers no chance to feed them, no opportunity for a livelihood. And because of a desire to strengthen the Catholic faith Jozo was, at one point, calling upon God to awaken the Christian people who were asleep. To get rid of darkness and fear so that Christians would rise to power and not those who didn't believe in God. He was mentioning that Christians have no rights at all, not even in the United Nations. But that the power of Christians is on their knees and in their might.

I cannot remember all the details of his sermon but I understood that he wanted to tell the faithful that the Catholic Faith is being suppressed because he questioned "Is the Catholic Church in Herzegovina and in Croatia unstable?"

"Is this moment for the Catholic Church Good Friday or Easter Sunday?" He was encouraging the faithful not to be afraid of anything because for the Catholic Faith one must be willing even to give his blood. And also that the future belongs to those who believe in the Catholic Church. I understood that Fr. Jozo was speaking these words because, at that time, our press was writing about cleric - nationalism and that some misuse their positions as priests. It is known to me that this year, 1981, marked 40 years since the uprising of our nation against fascism and I'm convinced that Jozo was speaking about 40 years of slavery, darkness, and shackles.

Taken from *Nasa Ognijista*
March '91 Issue

[Translated Croatian to English by Fr. Chris Coric and Marie Leman]

(xx) *Fidelity* Does It Again!

Fidelity's penchant for slander and calumny reached another of its lowest points in the February 1993 issue with a cowardly attack on one of the bravest champions of Mary of our generation by two anonymous authors [who are described as "two well known Catholic journalists" — although the article curiously and consistently talks about "I saw," "I had come," "I had been impressed," etc., never about "we"]. For some twisted reason, this magazine and its editor have thrived on the misfortunes and the maladies of fellow Catholics. With spiteful glee they gloat over the sufferings of their victims and rub salt in the wounds inflicted by the enemies of the Faith.

Coincidently, the February issue is accompanied by a letter to subscribers from Michael Jones appealing for $100 donations from them and warning that *Fidelity* is on the verge of closing down. We say "coincidently" because the blatant sensationalism of the cover story may well have been designed to re-awaken interest in the magazine by giving new life to its pet obsession: Medjugorje-bashing. Jones, we should remember, was able to wage his crusade against Medjugorje only because his magazine provided him with a captive audience. Articles submitted to *Fidelity* in response to his slanderous attacks on Medjugorje were summarily rejected. Nearly half of *Fidelity's* readers, however, voted with their feet by cancelling their subscriptions.

We return now to the main subject of the February *Fidelity*. The cover is adorned with pictures of Bishop Pavao Hnilica, Roberto Calvi, Agostino Cardinal

Casaroli and Vicka Ivankovic with two captions: "What Do These People Have in Common?" and "Bishop Hnilica Goes on Trial." The dramatic question on top is neither answered nor explained in the body of the article but the cover certainly serves the purpose of slyly suggesting that Medjugorje is somehow linked to an infamous banking scandal — although no such connection is even remotely pointed out in the article itself.

Bishop Hnilica is well known throughout Eastern Europe as a champion of the Pope, the Church and the Blessed Virgin. This is what Fr. Robert Fox, "the Fatima Priest," says about Bishop Hnilica in *The Fatima Family Messenger* [July-September 1992]: "A personal friend of the Pope, he spent years in a Communist prison work camp...Bishop Hnilica, titular bishop of Russado, born in Slovakia, entered the Community of Jesus and is in a special way Mary's Bishop as Pope John Paul II is the Marian Pope. Paul Hnilica was imprisoned in 1950 in a labor camp as a seminarian with members of other religious orders. At the age of 29 he was secretly ordained as a priest and three months later secretly as a bishop. He built up the catacomb church in Czechoslovakia. He participated in 1963 in the Second Vatican Council and was the first to publicly inform the Vatican of the situation of the Christians in the totalitarian countries. In 1968 he founded Pro-Fratribus, an organization for the spiritual and pastoral care of the persecuted church and for the evangelization in atheist countries." The *Fatima Family Messenger*, October-December 1992, adds, "His consecrating Bishop told him his mission field was 'Peking, Moscow and Berlin.' This meant to help those brothers and sisters persecuted under Communism. After having consecrated a new bishop (the present Cardinal Korec) to guarantee the survival of the underground Church, Bishop Hnilica flew to Rome to bring this and other information to Pope Pius XII. Pope Pius XII asked Bishop Hnilica to remain in Rome, as a representative of the persecuted Church. Pope Paul VI asked Bishop Hnilica to found the Pro Deo et Fratribus Association. In all the following years the Bishop has travelled throughout the world to give witness to the needs of the Eastern European Church. Simultaneously, he promoted the consecration of Russia to the Immaculate Heart of Mary."

It is against this holy martyr for the Faith — as simple in his idealism on behalf of the Church as he is dedicated to his Mother — that *Fidelity* has launched its trademark barrage of toxic insinuations. So what does *Fidelity* have "on" Bishop Hnilica? Simply this: in the eyes of *Fidelity*, he is guilty of one unpardonable act: he champions not just Fatima but Medjugorje, too [the article, in fact, highlights Bishop Hnilica's support for Medjugorje while pointedly ignoring his well-known association with Fatima and Sister Lucia].

Fidelity's primary strategy in its war against Medjugorje is to discredit champions and defenders of the apparitions. By championing Medjugorje, Bishop Hnilica has earned *Fidelity*'s wrath. In trying to discredit the Bishop, *Fidelity* relies entirely on "unnamed sources;" sources which are acceptable to *Fidelity* because they are hostile to Medjugorje and Bishop Hnilica

Fidelity's critique of the Bishop centers on his alleged attempt to extricate the Vatican from the Banco Ambrosiano scandal. On this issue, even the strongest critics of Bishop Hnilica say that at worst he was imprudent and counter-productive in his enthusiasm for the Church.

During his years in a concentration camp, Bishop Hnilica found out that the primary enemy in the eyes of his Communist captors was the Papacy. He was offered his freedom if he would renounce the Pope and accept the Patriarch of Moscow — an offer he immediately rejected. Bishop Hnilica's vision of the Vicar of Christ as the primary "sign" of the Church in the world made him especially sensitive to attacks on the Papacy and the Vatican.

According to *Fidelity,* Bishop Hnilica's loyalty led him into a series of rash actions on behalf of the Vatican. The gist of the *Fidelity* account is given below. When the media reports on the alleged links between the Vatican and the failed Banco Ambrosiano began, Bishop Hnilica saw in these attacks an attempt to subvert the Papacy. Driven by a desire to "clear" the Church's name, he located Roberto Calvi's assistant Flavio Carboni. Carboni expressed his willingness to supply Bishop Hnilica with documents that would prove the Church's innocence with regard to Banco Ambrosiano and the Bishop used these documents to defend the Church in the media. As time passed, Carboni told the Bishop that he was undergoing financial difficulties and needed money. In gratitude to Carboni for his work on behalf of the Church, the Bishop gave him five blank checks. Carboni wrote checks for nearly a million dollars but the Bishop's account did not have the funds to cover such large transactions. Eventually, the Italian Government's investigations into the Banco Ambrosiano led them to the discussions between Carboni and the Bishop — as a result of which, the Bishop has been asked to stand trial.

The motives behind Bishop Hnilica's actions were worthy — the defense of the Church — although the results did not match initial expectations (Bishop Hnilica says, however, that "he would do the same thing again if he could"). The history of the Church is full of stories of holy men and women who have risen to defend the Papacy against its enemies. On some occasions, the passion and dedication of these lonely martyrs led them to pursue courses of action which in retrospect turned out to be well-intended but ineffective and even counter-productive. One is reminded here of St. Peter Damian and the holy monk Hildebrand.

Upon reaching this stage of the discussion the *Fidelity* analysis suddenly takes a bizarre turn. Medjugorje enters the picture and we are treated to the same kind of tortuous, strained speculation that we are given in Jones' "joke hypothesis." To begin with the retired Bishop of Mostar is quoted as saying that Bishop Hnilica was "conducting himself...as if he were more important than I was." Then the author proceeds to speculate that some of the money that poured into Medjugorje was used "to purchase favorable articles on Medjugorje in the press throughout the world" and some "also used to purchase weapons for the Croatians." Someone has to be the conduit for all this activity and who better to perform this function, says the anonymous author(s), than Bishop Hnilica? After making such serious charges, one would expect the author to offer at least the slightest shred of evidence. This, however, is simply not offered. The whole weight of any speculation rests on the veracity and credibility of its source. This is what we are told about the source or sources of the slanderous speculation in this article: "according to one source close to the Franciscans in Medjugorje", "according to that source", "according to this same source", "according to one source". What we have here is an anonymous author with anonymous sources. With such thick veils, any war can be won and any enemy slain.

In its many personal attacks, *Fidelity* has often been guilty of the sin of detraction. In this truly vicious assault against a great man of God, against "Mary's Bishop," *Fidelity* has committed the far graver sin of calumny. We quote below the nature of the sin of calumny as explicated in the *Catholic Encyclopedia* [edited by Fr. Peter Stravinskas, Our Sunday Visitor, Huntington, Indiana, 1991, p. 158]:

"The uttering or publishing of statements or making claims about another that are not only unjust but also false. Calumny is the most serious form of detraction because it does the most serious harm to the reputation and good name of others that one can do. Calumny is so serious and grave that it demands retraction and restoration of the good name of the person harmed by it; it sins against the virtues of charity, truthfulness and justice."

We invite the editor of *Fidelity* and the author of the article to prayerfully reflect on this passage and then repent of their actions.

(xxi) A Final Word to the Critics

All the frontal assaults against Medjugorje have failed. The critics have now been reduced to sniping at straw men and pursuing victims who have at best an indirect connection to Medjugorje. The hot-button issues in the anti-Medjugorje in the anti-Medjugorje movement today are the Poem of the Man-God and Vassula Ryden. We have seen why neither issue has any bearing on Medjugorje . Even an novice in logic can see that the authenticity of Medjugorjje is in no way affected if it is shown that the Poem is merely a fabrication and Vassula Ryden is a fraud: the evidence for Medjugorje does not in any sense derive from either the Poem or Vassula Ryden. For that matter, there are advocates of Medjugorje who are critics of the Poem and of Vassula Ryden. To say that Medjugorje is false because some of its adherents have pursued "false prophets" is like saying that Christianity is false because Jim Jones of Jonestown and David Koresh of the Branch Davidian claimed to be Christians.

We have more or less come full circle now. In the Introduction to this book we have shown that Medjugorje does not fit any agenda: it does not fit in with the Charismatic agenda, the anti-Charismatic agenda, the pre-Vatican II agenda, the post-Vatican II agenda, the static view of Marian apparitions and the fluid view of

Marian apparitions. Once we take off these "agenda" blinkers we can appraise Medjugorje on its own terms and perhaps come to realize its truth. It is possible, however, to exchange one set of blinkers for another. If we do not wear "agenda" blinkers we might still be viewing Medjugorje with "fallacy" blinkers. Too often critics of Medjugorje trap themselves in logical fallacies and analyze Medjugorje within the framework of these fallacies.

By far the worst offender in this regard is E. Michael Jones. In his contribution to this book, Dr. Reimers has documented some of Jones' errors in logic: "A logic teacher could use this article [Jones' "Untold Story"] as a rich source of examples of fallacy and faulty inference: affirming the consequent, contradicting the evidence, proving too much, invalid induction, and petitio principii [begging the question]." Reimers gives graphic examples of these fallacies in Jones' first work on Medjugorje.

Unfortunately, Jones' fallacies did not stop there but have been running riot in every one of his subsequent articles on Medjugorje. In recent issues of *Fidelity*, he has tried to undermine Medjugorje by trying to link it to the Poem of the Man God and to Vassula Ryden. He is clearly pleased by the divergent approaches to both issues taken by various proponents of Medjugorje. Citing these divergences he says, "The [Medjugorje] movement itself is now full of the same cacophony of competing and contradictory claims that made the movement so appealing in the first place." ["Money Talking: In Vassula We Trust", Fidelity, March 1993]. This is hardly a credible critique of Medjugorje: adherents of Fatima have had fierce battles on their respective interpretations of the Fatima messages and on other issues: but no one suggests that such differences of opinion undermine the authenticity of Fatima. There is no Medjugorje "party line" on every possible issue precisely because Medjugorje is not a cult; if this comes as a disappointment to Jones, so be it. In the same article, Jones links Medjugorje to an alleged contemporary mania for apparitions: "By now what I said in my book on Medjugorje almost five years ago has become commonplace. The phoney apparition mania sweeping the country is a function of the vacuum in authority created following Vatican II." There was a "phoney apparition mania sweeping the country" when Lourdes took place as well. But, as we have said, the existence of counterfeit currency hardly disproves the existence of genuine currency.

We will end our survey of critiques and critics of Medjugorje by clarifying the issue yet again. Just as Medjugorje must not be appraised in terms of the various agendas listed earlier, it cannot be analyzed in the light of events or individuals that are not a direct part of the phenomenon itself. Let us be specific here. The critics have tried to discredit Medjugorje by trying to discredit a variety of individuals or events associated with Medjugorje:

- Fr. Tomislav Vlasic
- The Charismatic Movement and the alleged enthusiasm of Charismatics for miraculous phenomena

- The Franciscans and their conflict with their Bishop
- The "phoney apparition mania" and the associated "thirst for signs and wonders"
- The "false ecumenism" of denying differences between the major religions
- The Poem of the Man God
- Vassula Ryden
- Prominent proponents of Medjugorje like Fr. Rene Laurentin who have also endorsed less reliable phenomena

Just by listing the issues above, we see for ourselves that none of these has any actual bearing on the authenticity of Medjugorje. None of these issues will give an answer one way or another to the question of whether or not the six young visionaries are actually witnessing the Blessed Virgin Mary. This is the only relevant question - and no one has denied that the children are sane and sincere.

Our final word to the critics is this: focus on the issues: the issue is Medjugorje: stay away from side-issues. To appreciate Medjugorje, we must have not just purity of soul but clarity of mind: this means taking off all blinkers: agenda blinkers and fallacy blinkers. Perhaps then we can perceive Medjugorje in all its shining splendor.

Napoleon is said to have once told a cardinal that he was going to destroy his church. The cardinal simply laughed at him and said he did not stand a chance because clerics and bishops have been trying to destroy the church for centuries and even they have not succeeded. This little story can just as accurately be applied to Medjugorje. It should also serve as a warning to Medjugorje devotees: they should beware of trying to hook their own agendas to Medjugorje.

In conclusion it can be said that this survey of the specific critiques only confirms the fact that none of these critiques touch on the essential point at issue. This basic datum, as Fr. O'Carroll has said, is "The testimony of the witnesses about the apparitions, as they saw them, when they were seeing them." He adds that, "The problem is what is the bearing of those messages on the message of salvation. How do they accord with the truths of faith? How do they accord with the present life of the Church? How do they accord with previous apparitions? How do they accord with the reliable character, not necessarily saintly, in regard to the truthfulness on the part of the witnesses? How does it accord with the normalcy of the witnesses? Are the witnesses normal? They have been tested scientifically more than any other witnesses of apparitions in history. Scientists have tested them over and over again and have found them totally normal. The issue is they are tested about what they see and how that is relevant in the life of the Church."

We have tried to present here all the main evidence that so undeniably testifies to the truth of Medjugorje while confounding the critics. Where we have addressed the arguments of the critics, we have sought to show that their critiques illuminate the obviousness of the fact that we are dealing with something extraordinary. Great

Mariologists and great men and women of God, we have seen, are convinced with good reason that the evidence for the authenticity of Medjugorje is overwhelming. But now, dear reader, it is your turn. It is your turn to make a decision about Medjugorje. This whole book was inspired by Our Lady's message of May 8, 1986: "Dear children!" You are responsible for the messages. The source of grace is here, but you, dear children are the vehicles transmitting the gifts......I am calling you to give the gift to others with love and not to keep it for yourselves." With this in mind, we call on you to accept the invitation of the Queen of Peace. For reasons so memorably spelt out by Bishop Paolo Hnilica (a close advisor to Pope John Paul II), we are convinced that acceptance of this invitation is acceptance of a gift of God:

> When signs like Medjugorje take place before our eyes it is the obligation of every Christian to take a stance concerning them.
>
> ...Messages like Fatima, Lourdes or Medjugorje say nothing new, but only repeat what is in the Gospel. They are an actualization, a realization, an urgent prod, encouragement and warning for everyone who accepts them of his own freewill.
>
> The story of poor Lazarus and the rich man, which Christ Himself taught us (Luke 16:19-30), can help us to understand. The rich man, suffering with great pain in the underworld after his death, begs Abraham to let Lazarus, who is now in heaven, go to the house of his father. The rich man still has five brothers, and he wants them to be warned so that they do not suffer the same fate as he. Abraham, however, answers him: "If they do not listen to Moses and the prophets, they will not repent even if someone should rise from the dead.
>
> Here is what this means for us today: In the same way, those who do not believe the Gospel will not believe the messages - for example - of Fatima, Lourdes or Medjugorje (only a few Christians know their contents at all anyway). Apparently the Fatima message was accepted in practice and taken seriously by only a minority of the faithful, although it goes back more than 70 years and was already officially recognized by the Church after onlly 13 years. The Church allows the faithful the freedom, for God does not force us. He 'only' invites us.
>
> For the faithful, signs like Medjugorje are a new encouragement, a spur to be more open to God. [*Medjugorje Gebetsaktion*, 1986, #4]

(xxii) Miscellaneous

A few more critiques will be considered in this sub-section but in less detail because they are obviously less important.

1. The Bishop of Mostar claims that there are forty seven people who claim to be 'visionaries' outside Medjugorje.

Fr. Rupcic: "The Bishop tries to use the great number of 'visionaries' as proof that the apparitions of Medjugorje are not authentic. The forty-seven 'visionaries' that he claims to have discovered outside Medjugorje in other parishes, and that have had similar 'visions' are, the Bishop would have us believe, all false. ...It remains a fact that none of the visionaries, outside Medjugorje, mentioned by the Bishop, has ever been examined scientifically. Therefore they cannot be used to prove anything against the visionaries and apparitions in Medjugorje be they authentic or otherwise. ...If some visions were found to be false, that would be no reason to reject them all: as one false pearl doesn't exclude the real ones, neither do false apparitions exclude authentic ones. It is known that along with the apparitions at Lourdes recognized as authentic, in the vicinity of Lourdes and even in places further away, about fifty other apparitions were registered. However, they did not undermine the authenticity of the recognized apparitions and visions. (112)

Fr. Laurentin: The most serious problem at Lourdes was the epidemic of false visionaries who invaded the Grotto of Lourdes from 11 April to 11 July, 1868. Bernadette was forgotten. ...It is true that the Bishop of Mostar claims to have forty-seven visionaries in his diocese. To my knowledge, none of them operates in public. Priests have had to dispel one or other illusion either in the confessional or through spiritual direction. There are no others in the chapel of the apparitions or with the visionaries, as there were in the grotto at Lourdes. (113)

2. Fr. Ivica Vego, one of the two Franciscans who had the initial confrontation with the Bishop is reported to have gotten a nun pregnant.

Fr. Laurentin: In fact, if Friar Ivica Vego left the priesthood, it was after having been deprived of the exercise of his priesthood for seven years and for reasons prior to Medjugorje. In this debilitating situation, Friar Vego came to Medjugorje just to pray; he did not live there. Along with his companion in misfortune, Friar Ivan Prusina, he repeatedly requested normal judgment procedures, for they had been condemned by administrative measure without having been heard and judged. Their case was finally submitted to the supreme court of the Church, the Tribunal of the Apostolic Signature, in 1986. But the trial was suspended by a new administrative intervention. Discouraged and scandalized that the highest tribunal of the Church should be subject to such influence for the convenience of government, Ivica Vego, depressed and discouraged, became disoriented. A nun, who was very caring for anyone in distress, went too far in her compassion. Ivica Vego admitted his sin, committed in Mostar, where he was still living in the provincial house. He wanted to confess it publicly, but they talked him out of it. It would be desirable that those by whom scandal came should repent of it rather than triumph; rather than forcing another friar, who had remained faithful in spite of the shock, out of the priesthood, in which he courageously remains steadfast. ...The two Franciscans being punished had protested when they had been excused from their vows of poverty, chastity and obedience. It is strange that, by getting married, Ivica Vego is conforming to this forced dispensation from the vow of chastity, which had been inflicted on him without a hearing and judgment. The serpent whose head Our Lady crushes in Medjugorje, struggles to find other heels which it can wound. Let us pray for those thus wounded (including Bishop Zanic, for he suffers in this affair) and let us not heap scorn on them. (114)

3. The Bishop of Mostar claims that the reasons given by the visionaries for taking their first walk before the apparitions are contradictory.
    Fr.Rupcic: The Bishop's method of argument is full of cleverly constructed doubts and is utterly worthless. For example, he tells us that the visionaries do not agree as to the reason for their going to the Podbrdo district just before the apparition. ...It is quite obvious to anyone with a minimum of common sense that these statements made by the visionaries do not represent any contradiction at all. These reasons fit together very well; they prompted the visionaries to go out for a walk or for recreation. (115)

4. Fr. Ivo Sivric has contended that Medjugorje is a copy of Lourdes. Here Dr. Bartulica responds to this charge.

    Is Medjugorje "A Copy of Lourdes"?

    In the last chapter of his book *The Hidden Face* of Medjugorje, Fr. Sivric tried to offer 'a plausible' and natural explanation of the Medjugorje events.

    First, he mentioned an opinion of some 'highly educated' people, who from the beginning were acquainted with the visionaries, and they felt that some manipulation was behind the visionaries' behavior. However, according to this speculation, the visionaries later continued to pretend as if they really have been having an extraordinary experience, which was explained as 'autosuggestion, imagination, or obstinacy.'

    Fr. Sivric disagrees with the above explanation and offered his own hypothesis. He wrote, 'One day, they might have been at loose ends, looking for something to do to relieve their frustrations.... On their own initiative they might have wanted to try something 'for the greater glory of God and the spiritual well-being of the people.' They might have decided to try to shake the people up spiritually'.

But, since the visionaries' behavior reminds Fr.Sivric of St. Bernadette of Lourdes, believes that the visionaries' behavior postulates a recent reading about the Lourdes apparition.

Consequently, Fr. Sivric speculates that the Medjugorje visionaries actually tried to imitate the behavior of St. Bernadette, and he concludes that the Medjugorje is 'a copy of Lourdes.'

In order to support his hypothesis Fr. Sivric enumerates several points which allegedly illustrate a similarity between Medjugorje and Lourdes events.

For instance, St. Bernadette and Medjugorje visionaries would exclaim, after noticing the apparition, 'Here she is' and both used holy water for sprinkling the apparition.

Furthermore, the description of the apparition is 'similar'; that is, both said that she was 'beautiful and smiling.'

Both were attracted to some place e.g., St. Bernadette to the grotto and Medjugorje visionaries to the Podbrdo (Apparition Hill).

We heard that Fr. Sivric is certain that the visionary Mirjana had read a book on the Lourdes apparitions sometime between January 6 and 24, 1981; that is, before she started to claim having her own apparition and that she also must have shared her knowledge with the other visionaries.

According to Fr. Sivric, a special case of similarity was the visionaries' imitation of St. Bernadette by conversing with the Gospa in inaudible sounds, that is, by only moving their lips. The behavior they allegedly learned form another book, and Fr. Sivric writes that to his 'surprise and joy' he found out that Grgo Kozina, a friend of the visionaries, had purchased a book in September 1981 (Lourdes: Where Heaven and Earth Meet, by B. Nagy, S.J.) which described St. Bernadette's seventh apparition during which she was speaking with Madonna in an inaudible voice. Fr. Sivric, speculates that G. Kozina gave the book to the visionaries, who subsequently read about St. Bernadette's behavior and tried to imitate her during their apparitions.

Is there any substantial evidence or plausibility on Fr. Sivric's hypothesis?

Did he offer a significant and striking similarity between the two phenomena?

Fr. Rene Laurentin, who wrote several books on Medjugorje and Lourdes, commented that 'Medjugorje is not a copy of Lourdes in any way. These young people did not look for a grotto or for water... The message is not an imitation of the messages of Lourdes' (Seven Years of Apparitions, p.49).

Let us examine some of Fr. Sivric's 'proofs' for similarity.

To his (Sivric's) assertion that the Medjugorje visionaries would exclaim as St. Bernadette, 'Here she is,' Fr. Viktor Nuic, in his book (Vatru Vjere u Medjugorju Potpalila je Gospa - The Fire of Faith in Medjugorje Was Lighted by the Gospa) in which he criticized Fr. Sivric's book, remarked incisively, 'As if they should have exclaimed, 'Here she is not.'

What is to be said about Fr. Sivric's claim that the Medjugorje visionaries were imitating St.Bernadette when they described the Gospa as 'beautiful and smiling'?

Did Fr. Sivric expect that he Madonna in Medjugorje should have been different from the one in Lourdes, for instance, instead of being beautiful would be 'ugly' and 'unsmiling.'

What is similar between St. Bernadette's being attracted towards the grotto and the Medjugorje visionaries towards the Podbrdo? Do a grotto and a Podbrdo (Apparition Hill) look alike?

However, the whole hypothesis of Fr. Sivric is contingent on his assumption that the Medjugorje visionaries had read two books on Lourdes, one in June and the second in September 1981.

As we already have demonstrated in subchapter 3 (Mirjana and the Book on Lourdes), Fr. Sivric could not offer any evidence for his assertion, and therefore, we are dealing here with his pure speculation. Mirjana and the other visionaries deny not only reading any book on Lourdes, but according to them, they never heard about the Lourdes apparition until some persons told them about the events, and that happened after June 24, 1981.

Fr. Sivric then comes out with another speculation that the visionaries had read a second book on Lourdes after September 1981, from which they allegedly learned about St. Bernadette's inaudible conversation.

Here again we have another case of Fr. Sivric's speculation, and he does not offer any conclusive evidence, except that the book 'passed through many hands.'

However, even if one could prove that the Medjugorje visionaries have read the book mentioned by Fr. Sivric, he is mistaken in his belief that they started to converse with the Gospa in an inaudible voice after September 1981.

G. Kozina, who tape recorded the visionaries during the apparition on June 28-29, 1981, asserts that the visionaries usually were conversing with the Gospa in a silent manner (Vatru Vjere u Medjugorju Potpalila je Gospa — The Fire of Faith in Medjugorje was Lighted by the Gospa, p. 58.)

We already wrote about the apparitions of June 28-29 when they were repeating the questions which they had received from the audience and then they would repeat loudly the Gospa's answers. It is obvious that the inaudible part of the conversation could not be recorded.

In addition, in chapter IV while describing the apparition of July 3, 1981, we mentioned an excerpt from Fr. U. Loncar's diary of the same day when he recorded his answer to Ivanka, who asked them to leave the room. He wrote, 'We said that anyhow we don't hear anything while they converse with the Gospa.' A little later the remarks, 'They knelt down and were staring at one point and they were moving their lips. ...Little Jakov started to tell something to Gospa (we saw his lips moving), then some of the children said loudly, 'ode' (she is gone).'

In summary, Fr. Sivric's hypothesis is a form of pure speculation and the fact is that a) the Medjugorje visionaries before June 24, 1981, have never read any book on Lourdes, and therefore they could not imitate something that they even did not know had ever taken place; b) there is no striking similarity between the behavior of St. Bernadette and the Medjugorje visionaries; and c) Fr. Sivric's assertion that the Medjugorje visionaries started to talk in an inaudible voice after September 1981 is totally inaccurate and cannot be supported with available testimony. According to several witnesses, the Medjugorje visionaries from the beginning were conversing with the Gospa in a silent manner.

In conclusion, the Medjugorje as a 'copy of Lourdes' might exist in somebody's fantasy but is without any foundation in reality."
[Medjugorje: Are the Seers Telling the Truth?, pp. 204-208]

5.   One critic thinks Medjugorje can be explained in terms of a peasant syndrome.

Fr. O'Carroll: Fr. Sivric's book entitled was based like Beranger's publication, on the archives of Dr. Zanic, the Bishop of Mostar. The written product is not impressive and has been respectfully demolished by Fr. Laurentin and Fr. Sivric's brother in religion, Fr. Rupcic, for years a student on the spot of all the happenings in Medjugorje.

Fr. Rupcic gives an account of the family complications which are a sad background to the friar's study. He relies for his knowledge not on direct contact with the witnesses but on his own relatives, who have been in the five percent of parishioners antipathetic to the apparitions. Much has been made of Fr. Sivric's study of peasant culture in his native Croatia and this, we have been assured by a reviewer, is a determining factor in the visionaries.

We've had 'hallucination' as an explanation until serious scientists told the proponents of the theory to stop talking nonsense. We've had 'manipulation' but this was difficult to sustain with millions of people streaming in and out of the village, and thousands of us at one time or another present during the apparitions. So now it's the peasants!

Here a little history may serve. Practically every recognized Marian apparition has been granted to peasants: Guadalupe, the Miraculous Medal, La Salette, Lourdes, Knock, Fatima, Beauraing, Banneux. How right Oliver Goldsmith was: "A bold peasantry, its country's pride, when once destroyed, can never be supplied." Who is the heroine depicted in picture or sculpture in every church in France, the one who inspired three dramatic masterpieces by Schiller, George Bernard Shaw and Jean Anouille, and moved a great sculptor, Fremiet, to a miracle in bronze, her statue in the Rue de Rivoli? The peasant girl of Domremy, Joan of Arc. Anyone who believes that these alert, happy, upright, devout children whom we have watched in ecstasy, were acting out some peasant syndrome, would believe anything. (116).

In closing, we might examine the charge that Medjugorje calls for excessive, impractical piety. Our Lady's request to recite fifteen decades of the Rosary every day and to fast on bread and water on Wednesdays and Fridays may seem excessive to those who are trapped by the hustle and bustle of the modern world. But she is trying to turn our minds to our eternal destiny. As for the charges of excessive piety and discipline, let us look at orthodox Moslems as they prostrate themselves five times a day in prayer and go through one month a year with nothing to eat or drink during the day.

In conclusion it can be said that this survey of the specific critiques only confirms the fact that none of these critiques touch on the essential point at issue. This basic datum, as Fr. O'Carroll has said, is "The testimony of the witnesses about the apparitions, as they saw them, when they were seeing them." He adds that, "The problem is what is the bearing of these messages on the message of salvation. How do they accord with the present life of the Church? How do they accord with previous apparitions? How do the accord with the reliable character, not necessarily saintly, in regard to the truthfulness on the part of the witnesses? How does it accord with the normalcy of the witnesses? Are the witnesses normal? They have been tested scientifically more than any other witnesses of apparitions in history. Scientists have tested them over and over again and have found them totally normal. The issue is they are tested about what they see and how that is relevant in the life of the Church."

We have tried to present here all the main evidence that so undeniably testifies to the truth of Medjugorje while confounding the critics. Where we have addressed the arguments of the critics, we have sought to show that their critiques illuminate the obviousness of the fact that we are dealing with something extraordinary. Great Mariologists and great men and women of God, we have seen, are convinced with good reason that the evidence for the authenticity of Medjugorje is overwhelming.

But now, dear reader, it is your turn. It is your turn to make a decision about Medjugorje. This whole book was inspired by Our Lady's message of May 8. 1986: "Dear children! You are responsible for the messages." With this in mind, we call on you to accept the invitation of the Queen of Peace. For reasons so memorably spelled out by Bishop Paolo Hnilica, we are convinced that acceptance of this invitation is acceptance of a gift of God:

> When signs like Medjugorje take place before our eyes it is the obligation of every Christian to take a stance concerning them.
>
> ...Messages like Fatima, Lourdes or Medjugorje say nothing new but only repeat what is in the Gospel. They are an actualization, a realization, an urgent prod, encouragement and warning for everyone who accepts them of his own free will.
>
> The story of poor Lazarus and the rich man, which Christ Himself taught us (Luke 16:19-30), can help us to understand. The rich man, suffering with great pain in the underworld after his death, begs Abraham to let Lazarus, who is now in heaven, go to the house of his father. The rich man still has five brothers, and he wants them to be warned so that they do not suffer the same fate as he. Abraham, however, answers him: 'If they do not listen to Moses and the prophets, they will not repent even if someone should rise from the dead.'
>
> Here is what this means for us today: In the same way, those who do not believe the Gospel will not believe the messages — for example — of Fatima, Lourdes or Medjugorje (only a few Christians know their contents at all anyway). Apparently the Fatima message was accepted in practice and taken seriously by only a minority of the faithful, although it goes back more than 70 years and was officially recognized by the Church after only 13 years. The Church allows the faithful the freedom, for God does not force us. He 'only' invites us[4]

The urgency of the invitation Our Lady is giving us through her apparitions in Medjugorje is only too clear: "These apparitions are the last for humanity." [May 31, 1985] "It is necessary for the world to be saved while there is still time." [Novemeber 29, 1981] "God has chosen each one of you in order to use you for the great plan of salvation of mankind. You cannot comprehend how great your role is in God's plan. Therefore, dear children, pray, so that through prayer you may comprehend God's

---

[4] Quoted from *Medjugorje Gebetsaktion.*

plan towards you. I am with you so that you can realize it completely. Thank you for having responded to my call." [January 25, 1987]

2. GOD RENEWS THE WORLD THROUGH MARY

Bishop Paolo Hnilica, S. J.

What impressed me the most this year (1989) in my visits to Medjugorje: The many young people whom I have seen there! I was there at the beginning of August and spoke on the eve of Our Lady of the Snows for the German-speaking group that had come to the international youth gathering. It is a joy to see these young people, who are really seeking something — youth cannot remain neutral: but many seek happiness in entirely worldly things. In Medjugorje I have seen their search for God.

Two worlds. For example, I have observed this: Many, many young people — hundreds — sat there in the afternoon before the church. They were not very properly dressed, if we measure by the usual standards (in August it is hot: perhaps they came from the sea), which is typical of youth, but with rosaries in hand for hours on end in little groups, deep, deep in prayer. This is what I have seen: Mary seeks her children in the "world," among human beings, who therefore live as before, but she draws them to herself and then comes the transformation. In Medjugorje the atmosphere of the world comes together with that of heaven and then is taken into this supernatural atmosphere, in God's atmosphere.

Prayer, fasting, confession. I remember a very nice testimony on Medjugorje by the Holy Father. On August 1 (1989), he spoke to Italian doctors who stand up for the defense of the unborn. He thanked them heartily for this — it is his heart's intention to save life, unborn life. These doctors, however, also work hard for Medjugorje. They have scientifically studied the ecstasies of the visionaries and now they are analyzing all of the miracles of healing that happen in Medjugorje. As the discussion came to Medjugorje on this occasion, the Holy Father said something very beautiful: "Yes, today the world has lost the supernatural. Many people sought it and found it in Medjugorje through prayer, fasting and through confession." These words of the Holy Father are the most beautiful testimony! The world has virtually lost God, the sense for God, for the supernatural. Many are seeking it and finding it in Medjugorje through these means, which the Gospel, too recommends: prayer, fasting and penance.

Renewal. God wants, to lead the people through Mary, again to himself, as he does in every Marian apparition — in Lourdes, in Fatima, in every sanctuary. In his address in Kevelaer, during his visit to Germany two years ago, the Pope said that the decisive centers of world — and salvation — history are not the bustling capital cities; the true center points of history are in the quiet places of human prayer. Where there is prayer, there one decides — not only about our life after death, but also about the events of this world.

The mercy of God. The people come to Medjugorje out of conviction and with great — and still with great — sacrifices, in order to pray. And really, God is renewing the world today through Mary and through this place Medjugorje.

In Fatima, the Mother of God committed herself to converting Russia. I have often said to her in prayer here: "Why don't you appear in Russia, in Moscow?" But this is what is new and beautiful in her apparitions here in Medjugorje: It is a step in this direction — she is appearing in a socialist country, where pilgrims from socialist lands can also enter easily. And what they said about Fatima cannot be said about Medjugorje, that it is a capitalistic enterprise against communism. Now the Blessed Mother is appearing in a communist country, so they can't accuse her on account of politics. And really, so many have come here from Hungary, from Czechoslovakia, from Poland, Romania, even from Russia.... I believe that the conversion of Russia is a desire of Mary's heart. In Fatima she has committed herself to doing this; she has solemnly spoken about it. One cannot understand the entire message of Fatima — Pius XII even said this 50 years ago — if one does not know what is going on in Russia.

Sister Lucia (of Fatima) once told me: "When Mary spoke the first time about Russia, we children believed that 'Russia' was the name of a woman, a sinner for whose conversion we should pray." Therefore Mary spoke repeatedly about this "woman" Russia, in her messages, and she solemnly obligated herself to convert Russia. **"IN THE END MY IMMACULATE HEART WILL TRIUMPH."** What is the most important thing to a mother? To save the children! Above all, those who are in danger. Mary's maternal concern certainly applies to the entire world, but above all to those who have most need of God's mercy — these are the godless, those who are in danger of being lost for eternity.

Sodom and Gomorrah. Once as I spoke with the Holy Father, he asked me: "So when can Russia be converted?" I said to him that Padre Pio (an Italian priest-stigmatist who died in the odor of sanctity) had said that Russia will be converted when one can find as many Christians as there are godless ones. And I said that this would be nothing other than the message of Fatima: to believe, to love, to hope for those who do not believe... above all for those who are most in need of God's mercy. Then I said to the Holy Father: "Perhaps regarding the number we can be more optimistic than Padre Pio, for we have a biblical example: Sodom and Gomorrah (Gen. 18, 23-33), where ten righteous persons could have saved a city that had perhaps ten-thousand inhabitants." The Holy Father asked: "Yes, and how many righteous ones are necessary today in order to save the world?" This is a very great and serious question for God's representative on earth.

When God wanted to punish Sodom and Gomorrah, he revealed it beforehand to Abraham. He did not want to conceal it from the one whom he had chosen as his co-worker and as a father of many descendants. Why? God wanted Abraham to plead for the salvation of Sodom and Gomorrah. Had Abraham found the ten righteous ones or had he shown even more trust in God and bargained down to five or three righteous persons, the destruction of Sodom and Gomorrah might have been prevented.

Today this instruction is given to Mary. Mary — the Mother of God and our Mother — does not lack for trust. However, this is the minimum; she needs a certain number of souls, of righteous ones. Now Mary is seeking the "ten righteous ones" for the salvation of the world, to save others, even for the conversion of Russia. And this is how we can explain the appearing of our Blessed Mother for over eight years. Some people say to me: "Now this is really incredible! Has the Blessed Mother nothing better to do than to appear to little children every day." I have said: "And don't we need it? Is the world really so holy that the mother can remain idle?" My mother would do the same thing, if she knew that her own children were in danger. She would not sleep; she would not rest. This is the nature of a mother! This is her first task: to save the children.

Helping one another. Mary turns to the good children — for this is in God's plan — so that they will intercede for the others: As I have already indicated, we are responsible for others. For example: If a flood is coming, who can save himself? Only those who can swim well and they can also save some others. So is it also with moral floods.

To those who are "living Christians" — and they are those who believe, who hope, who love and adore God — to them the appeal goes out to intercede for those who can no longer swim. And this I see in Medjugorje: There Mary is seeking and calling many children, not only for the sake of their own salvation, but really to plead for others as well. This is something that we see in Medjugorje: people who come out from Medjugorje are restless; restless in the sense that they want to do something for God, for others.

Cardinal Siri too — he died just this year — told me this, when I was in Genoa (he was cardinal there at that time) for a Medjugorje meeting. At dinner he said to me: "I have noticed that the people who come from Medjugorje become apostles. They renew the parishes. They form groups in which they get together — prayer groups — and they pray before the Blessed Sacrament. They hold lectures, lead discussions and bring others to Medjugorje. And these circles, these prayer groups spread out more and more. They renew the church." This was one of the greatest cardinals who gave this testimony about Medjugorje.

Unfortunately, it so happens the case that Baptists, Adventists, Jews stand together like a family much more than we Catholics do. We fall short here. In Medjugorje, however, the people who go there receive a new family spirit; they feel like one family. I see this when I am in America or anywhere else: When I speak there — even when I am not speaking about Medjugorje but about Fatima or some other theme — people who have been in Medjugorje come up to me, and immediately I feel like a family with them. Through this one recognizes the power of the Holy Spirit. Mary is the mother of all, and if we recognize her as mother, as truly mother, then it is obvious that we also recognize each other as her children, whether black or yellow or of this or that language.

Prayer and sacrifice. Sister Lucia said to me that the most important thing that Mary called for, from the children in her first apparition at Fatima was the following: Whether they were ready to accept the daily crosses and sufferings — everything that the Lord sends — for sinners. Through this Mary challenged them to co-redemption. Just as Mary suffered under the cross and so became co-redemptrix, so should all Christians become co-redeemers. Today Mary is mobilizing her generation. Her primary task is set out in the Bible, in the Old Testament: "I will set enmity between you and the woman, between your offspring and her offspring." (Gen. 3, 15). If today Satan is mobilizing as never before — he has millions who serve him — so too is Mary mobilizing her generation, that is, those who serve her, so that they will immediately intercede consciously for the others, for the salvation of sinners — for those who are most in need of God's mercy.

What can we do? This concerns Mary's honor, her credibility, that we all intercede consciously for this triumph of Mary. This will be the greatest victory of all time! For the first time we see what history has never seen before - the banner of Satan lifted directly against God and against everything holy. When one analyzes the different appeals of the popes, one can say that in the year 1917, Satan challenged God as never before in history to an open battle through the Russian revolution. And Mary - this was her task - accepted this challenge; she took up the gauntlet. And her triumph, which she foretold at Fatima, is God's triumph, the mercy of God. The mother's heart has become a symbol of mercy.... And now it has to do with this duel between Satan and Mary.

So, what can we do? Firstly, that which Fatima and also Medjugorje say: **PRAY, FAST, SACRIFICE** for those who have most need of God's mercy. Secondly: BIBLES. Several years ago when I was in Russia and the faithful there learned that I came from Rome, they said to me: "Greet the Holy Father for us!" I asked them: "Yes, and what do you need, what do you expect from the Holy Father?" The answer was, "Bibles, Bibles, Bibles — but in our language!"

When I told him this, the Holy Father was impressed and said: "You see. They do not require gold, nor money, not even bread to eat, but the word of God." The Holy Father himself, however, cannot provide ten or fifteen million Bibles, which is what the great family of the Russian people would need. This cry from Russia, this appeal to the Pope is a plea to all Catholics. It would really be a mission, for Mary's children especially, to make it possible for each brother and each sister who is without a Bible to get one.

And Orthodox priests - they are truly priests too - have, for example, said to me: "During baptism it was our custom to press a simple cross onto the child's chest, and we then also gave him the cross. Now the priest cannot give it away, for he only has but one, and he must take it back again from the breast of the child." But would that not be very symbolic - I have already said this to so many priests, that it would be also lovely for us, at the baptism of a child, to give a cross as was the practice in Russia. For the Orthodox priests, such SIMPLE CROSSES - one costs maybe $1.25 — would be a great gift. Also, MEDALS AND ROSARIES are asked for by so many. But who will give a rosary or a Bible or a cross? Only someone who reads and treasures the Bible, who prays and treasures the rosary, who treasures and honors the cross will have the understanding. It is, for example, much easier to gather bread for the hungry than bibles, for those Christians who read and treasure the Bible are perhaps ten per-cent.

Almost too late. These aids will be necessary very quickly, for what we let slip today in Russia can be too late tomorrow. The developments in the east from day to day are so fast. In my visit to Russia, I feared that we arrived late with our pastoral mission train to Russia. We are perhaps only at the end of the train; everything is already fully occupied with Baptists, Adventists, Jehovah's Witnesses, Pentecostals. They have prepared millions of books, thousands of apostles — lay people who speak Russian — and they send them now as technicians, technologists, etc., into the east.

Our only hope is again God's help. Mary wants, in a certain way, to educate and challenge us to intercede through our prayer, through our sacrifice, through the crosses that are laid upon us also through donations for Bibles and through pastoral help.

Another example: In Russia, hundreds of churches are now being opened, which until now had been turned into warehouses, some to municipal toilets, etc. The Christians, if they need these churches, must fix them up quickly, within a prescribed time, to be permitted to use them. There is no help from the state. The Christians are making efforts to clean and repair these as soon as possible. But they need, for example, CHALICES, VESTMENTS, MONSTRANCES, ALTAR LINENS.

And then the PRIESTS: Some are already seventy, eighty years old, and for the first time they can again officially celebrate. They are turning to us with the appeal for MASS STIPENDS so that they can again put their churches in order. Or in Rome, I have already looked around with a Polish cardinal for the cheapest chalices, etc. The Holy Father, too, has already given away many he has received, but they are always too few.

And then the SEMINARIES. Russia — there the earth is drenched with the blood of martyrs; there will be many vocations to the priesthood, and they are there already. In Innsbruck, Austria, for instance, three Russian seminarians who want to study in Rome are waiting. And there are yet many others who will need support, in Russia, in Poland... Here in the west, either the family or the bishop pays for the seminarian; there, however, there is no support for those who want to be priests. This too would be a contribution to the evangelization of Russia, and the help of all Christians would be necessary.

Being ready to sacrifice. Even if not everyone can give money, each can nevertheless GIVE HIS HEART. This is the most important thing: TO OFFER ONE'S

SELF for the salvation of Russia. One can, for example, spiritually adopt so many atheists and say: "Mary, I am ready to pay for this through suffering, through prayer. You must tell me how much is needed for the conversion of one or ten atheists." Mary will tell us this for sure.

Every donation, no matter how small, should be a fast, a sacrifice of something. For example, when I speak to children I say, "Do you want to sacrifice for a Bible for a child in Russia? But you may not ask for it from your father or your mother, because then the Bible would not be from you. You must give up ice cream, chocolate or a toy!" The children then write me: "Dear Father Paolo, I have already given up ice cream ten times!" and they send their donations. This year, for example, because of a call during Lent, ten thousand children have saved enough for at least one Gospel. They received envelopes from us, on which was printed, "A Gospel for a Boy in Russia," and they then brought these on a pilgrimage together, organized by themselves to the Holy Father - ten thousand children. The children did it really with such great joy. So should we educate our children: to give up, not always to need to have everything, and above all to sacrifice for evangelization, for the salvation of souls.

Land of Icons — Mary's Land. Reports are coming out of Russia daily on TV and in the newspapers, but they are more political and economical reports. Less is reported to us of the Christian Russia with its Christian needs and Christian duties. Therefore, it would be good to write REPORTS about this. Russia is really Mary's land; she always has been honored there. Many Russian poets and writers have said that this is Mary's land. There has always been an icon in every family there. Nowhere was Mary so honored as in Russia, nowhere, not even in Italy or Poland.

Sometimes I think that Satan has made a strategic mistake when he chose Russia as the showplace for his final battle with Mary — there he will lose. Mary will not be able to give up Russia, and he will lose (and he has already as good as lost against her). Mary has not committed herself so solemnly for any other land than for Russia. We should take that seriously! Those who honor Mary will save the world today.

[Medjugorje Gebetsaktion thanked Bishop Hnilica for his remarks, given in Vienna on October 14, 1989, published in their fall quarterly, 1990.]

In February, 1990, I spent an hour and a half with Bishop Paovo Zanic, ordinary at the time of the diocese which includes Medjugorje. (Our discussion was video taped.) In answer to my plea, "It would show great openness on the part of Your Excellency if you would come to Medjugorje and pray during a reported apparition." he responded, "I've seen them on video tape. I don't need to go to Medjugorje!" Such an attitude stands in sharp contrast to that of Bishop Hnilica, S.J. At that same time he was saying in *Medjugorje Gebetsaktion* (4th quarter, 1990):

When I speak with people who doubt about Medjugorje I always counsel them, 'Come and see!' This is the answer that the Savior also once gave. I myself have often been in Medjugorje for I see it as my obligation to form my own judgment. Concerning no other pilgrimage site do people speak so much about today as Medjugorje. Both sides, for and against, can have certain reasons. As bishop, in order to know where the truth is I must scrutinize it closely, all the more so because the church has not yet spoken any judgment concerning it officially, and already millions of people from all over the world are making pilgrimages there. Therefore, I, myself, go there, for when one sees a thing from up close he can better judge concerning it. I find that each bishop (who, of course, is the guardian of the faith), should go there in order to form for himself a judgment, with all the possibilities of checking and investigating, 'Is it true, or not?' When he is there with the heart and the eyes open, then he has to come to the conclusion: It is genuine!

Bishop Zanic's attitude toward Medjugorje was made embarrassingly clear during an interview with reporter Gabriel Meyer (published in the April 1, 1990 *National Catholic Register*):

'What do you as a bishop want to have happen in Medjugorje? What could the Franciscans and the parishioners there do to work with you?' Zanic leaned back in his chair. 'Simple. I want Medjugorje destroyed.'[5]

3. On August 23, 1992 Bishop, Paolo Hnilica sent the following appeal to all the faithful in the Church:

"Summons to live the message of Medjugorje *more seriously!*
The cruelties that are happening daily in former Yugoslavia encourage us to direct this appeal to all the faithful in the Church, so that more than ever we become aware of the importance of the messages of Medjugorje. In this unknown country of Hercegovina, people have been praying and fasting for eleven years for peace, for reconciliation and forgiveness; a forgiveness that became tangible among all the inhabitants of Medjugorje and that was also experienced by 30 - million pilgrims there.
The war that has been raging for a year in this area shows us more deeply how very much we share responsibility for these horrible events when we take these messages with too little seriousness or even reject

---

5   Mr. Meyer later admitted to this writer that he had added, out of charity to the Bishop, the phrase, "As a phenomenon" in parenthesis, at the end of his statement.

them. If one had thought before that Medjugorje could develop like any other shrine, he now becomes aware very quickly that the invitation to prayer really was intensely acute and, in the first place, concerned exactly this region that used to appear outwardly calm and peaceful.

But today in Mostar as well as in the surrounding villages, thousands of people who have heard this message of forgiveness and reconciliation have been met with pain and sorrow, because family members were cruelly slaughtered before their eyes.

Many Croatian soldiers report about their frequent prayers of the Rosary while under heavy fire in the trenches at the front.

Who can now help these persons to grasp new hope again to begin a new life, while forgiving their attackers and persecutors? Precisely this forgiveness, however, is the basis and content of the messages of Medjugorje which, slowed by authority and reluctance, have penetrated into the hearts of the people of this region torn by suffering and into the hearts of numerous pilgrims from all the world. No one ought, especially now, to take away this invitation and this help that was communicated through the messages.

For us to withhold this help from them would make us share responsibility for the cruelties that are still occurring through the typically human craving for revenge and through the understandable want to bring about justice by taking things into their own hands.

The Holy Father John Paul II said we can resolve this conflict with spiritual weapons. The Blessed Mother has been offering them to us for eleven years.

Cardinal Kuharic, Primate of the Croatian church, was asked about this by the head of Gebetsaktion-Vienna and stressed: 'People who believe and are convinced in conscience that with these messages they can stimulate people to the good — to conversion, to peace — they should do it! This is a matter of conscience!'

4. Recommended Reading List

Apologias for the Authenticity of Medjugorje

1. Michael O'Carroll, *Medjugorje: Facts, Documents, Theology,* [Dublin: Veritas, 1989].

    One of the most balanced and fair treatments available on the controversy over Medjugorje by a great Mariologist. Should be read in conjunction with his later supplement, *Is Medjugorje Approved?*

2. Rene Laurentin, *Nine Years of Apparitions* [Milford, Ohio: The Riehle Foundation].

An analysis of some of the most recent polemical works on Medjugorje by a great scholar who is both a pre-eminent Mariologist and a singular authority on Medjugorje.

3. Rene Laurentin and Henri Joyeux, *Scientific and Medical Studies on the Apparitions at Medjugorje* [Dublin: Veritas, 1987].

   Another great work by Laurentin written in collaboration with Professor Henri Joyeux of the University of Montpellier who headed one of the medical teams that examined the visionaries. Contains a wealth of fascinating scientific data on the physiological patterns of visionaries during an apparition.

4. Ljudevit Rupcic, *The Truth About Medjugorje* [Ljubuski-Humac, 1990].

   A particularly pungent contribution to the debate that is notable for its painstaking concern for "the facts". The author has tracked the phenomenon from the very beginning.

5. Nicholas Bartulica, *Medjugorje: Are the Seers Telling the Truth?* A Psychiatrist's Viewpoint [Chicago, Illinois: Croatian Franciscan Press, 1991].

   A psychiatrist who has continued to interview the visionaries in their native tongue from the first days of the apparition here responds to and refutes Jones' book almost word for word!

6. Albert J. Heber, *Medjugorje: An Affirmation and Defense* [Paulina, Louisiana: 1990].

   A very readable exposition of the evidence in favor of Medjugorje that is accompanied by a powerful and insightful defense against common criticisms.

Explorations and Reflections on the Medjugorje Phenomenon

1. Medjugorje Gebetsaktion
   P.O. Box 18
   A-1153 Vienna, AUSTRIA

   English and Spanish editions are available through:
   Florida Center for Peace
   P.O. Box 431 306
   Miami, Florida 33143

2. Mark Miravalle, *The Message of Medjugorje* [New York: University Press of America, 1986].

For those who wish to understand the doctrinal content of the messages of Medjugorje, this is the book to read. The author's doctoral dissertation, successfully defended at the Pontifical University in Rome, concerned the subject of this book - that the messages of Medjugorje are orthodox and edifying.

3. John DeMers, *Invited to Light* [Trinakria Press, 1990].
   The best-written account of the meaning of the Medjugorje apparition. Its author is a veteran journalist who was initially skeptical but later convinced about the authenticity of Medjugorje.

4. *Live The Messages*
   There is no substitute for reading the actual messages of Our Lady issued to the world for over the last 11 years. For a copy, write:

-D.R. Golob, Box 23351, Harahan, LA 70183; or
The Riehle Foundation, PO Box 7 Milford,OH 45150

NOTES

1. Michael O'Carroll, *Theotokos* [Wilmington: Michael Glazier, 1982], 48.
2. Michael O'Carroll, *Medjugorje: Facts, Documents, Theology,* [Dublin: Veritas, 1988], 11.
3. Ibid., 11.
4. *Decreta authenticaa Congregationis rituum,* III, 1900, 79; cited in Medjugorje: Facts, Documents Theology.
5. Mary Craig, *Spark from Heaven* [Notre Dame, Indiana: Ave Maria Press, 1988], 141.
6. Rene Laurentin and Henri Joyeux, *Scientific and Medical Studies on the Apparitions at Medjugorje* [Dublin: Veritas, 1987], 34.
7. Rene Laurentin, *Eight Years* [Milford, Ohio: The Riehle Foundation, 1989], 116.
8. Mark Miravalle, *Response to: Medjugorje: The Untold Story, E.Michael Jones, Fidelity Magazine, September 1988.*
9. *Declaration on the Relation of the Church to Non-Christian Religions,* Vatican II, Nostra Aetate, 28, October, 1965, cited in Vatican Council II: The Conciliar and Post Conciliar Documents, edited by Austin Flannery [Northport, New York: Costello, 1975], 738-740.
10. Rene Laurentin, *Report to the National Conference on Medjugorje, May 12-13, 1990* [Milford, Ohio: The Riehle Foundation], 6.
11. Craig, op. cit., 105.
12. Michael O'Carroll in *Mary's People,* January 27, 1991, 4.
13. Mark Miravalle in *Mary's People,* January 27, 1991, 4.
14. Rene Laurentin in *Mary's People,* January 27, 1991, 5
15. Bishop Michael D. Pfeifer, O.M.I., "The Gospel, Mary and Medjugorje", San Angelo, Texas, August 5, 1988.
16. Ljudevit Rupcic, *The Truth About Medjugorje* [Ljubuski-Humac, 1990], 70-75, 100-101.
17. Craig, op. cit., 101.
18. Ibid., 102.
19. Rene Laurentin, *Report to the National Conference on Medjugorje, May 12-13, 1990* [Milford, Ohio: The Riehle Foundation], 1-2.
20. Ibid., 5.
21. Rene Laurentin, *The Apparitions of the Blessed Virgin Mary Today* [Dublin: Veritas, 1990], 47.
22. Quoted in Michael O'Carroll, *Medjugorje: Facts, Documents, Theology,* 113.
23. E. Michael Jones, *Medjugorje: The Untold Story* [South Bend, Indiana: Fidelity Press, 1988], 99.
24. Ljudevit Rupcic, *The Great Falsification: The Hidden Face of Medjugorje by Ivo Sivric,* 3.

25. Jones, ibid., 99-100.
26. Ibid., 118.
27. Ljudevit Rupcic, *The Great Falsification: The Hidden Face of Medjugorje by Ivo Sivric,* 4.
28. Jones, ibid., 80.
29. Ibid., 11.
30. Ibid., 119-120.
31. Ljudevit Rupcic, *The Great Falsification: The Hidden Face of Medjugorje by Ivo Sivric,* 5-6.
32. Jones, ibid., 108.
33. Ibid., 105.
34. Ibid., 104.
35. Ibid., 105.
36. Ibid., 105.
37. Ibid., 105.
38. Ibid., 105.
39. Ibid., 102.
40. Ibid., 112.
41. Ibid., 118.
42. Ibid., 121.
43. *The Catholic Counter-Reformation in the XXth Century,* Number 191, June-July 1986, 13.
44. Ibid., 3.
45. Ibid., 10.
46. Ibid., 10.
47. Ibid., 11.
48. Ibid., 30.
49. Ibid., 36.
50. Craig, op. cit., 149.
51. *The Catholic Counter-Reformation in the XXth Century,* op. cit., 11.
52. Ibid., 47.
53. Jones, 44.
54. G.K.Chesterton, *Orthodoxy* [Garden City, New York: Image Books, 1959], 88-91.
55. *A Woman Clothed with the Sun* edited by John J. Delaney [Garden City, New York: Image Books, 1990], 104-105.
56. Quoted in *Medjugorje: Facts, Documents, Theology,* 102.
57. Jones, ibid., 8.
58. Ibid., 12.
59. Ibid., 17-18.
60. Albert J. Heber, Medjugorje: *An Affirmation and Defense* [Paulina, Louisiana: 1990], 174.

61. Rene Laurentin, *Eight Years*, 114-115.
62. Rene Laurentin and Henri Joyeux, *Scientific and Medical Studies on the Apparitions at Medjugorje*, 124-125.
63. Rene Laurentin, *Eight Years*, 98.
64. Interview with Bishop Frane Franic, *Glas Koncila*, December 1985.
65. Mark Miravalle, *Response to Medjugorje The Untold Story.*
66. Quoted in *Medjugorje: Facts, Documents, Theology*, 102.
67. Hebert, ibid., 11-2.
68. Rene Laurentin, *Eight Years*, 13-114.
69. Jones, ibid., 105, 107-109.
70. Ibid., 11-12.
71. Ibid., 120-121.
72. Nicholas Bartulica, *Medjugorje: Are the Seers Telling the Truth?* A Psychiatrist's Viewpoint [Chicago, Illinois: Croatian Franciscan Press, 1991], pp.67-70.
73. Rene Laurentin, *Eight Years*, 42.
74. Quoted in *Medjugorje: Facts, Documents, Theology*, 80-81.
75. Jones, ibid., 115.
76. Quoted in *Medjugorje: Facts, Documents, Theology*, 110.
77. Rene Laurentin, *Response to the Most Recent Objections of His Excellency Bishop Zanic Against Medjugorje* [Milford, Ohio: The Riehle Foundation, May 1990], 3.
78. Quoted in *Medjugorje: Facts, Documents, Theology*, 83-84.
79. Quoted in *Medjugorje: Facts, Documents, Theology*, 116.
80. Quoted in *Medjugorje: Facts, Documents, Theology*, 110, 111.
81. Quoted in *Medjugorje: Facts, Documents, Theology*, 122-127.
82. Craig, op. cit., 159, 162.
83. Rene Laurentin, *Response to the Most Recent Objections of His Excellency Bishop Zanic Against Medjugorje*, 2.
84. Abbe Rebut, *The House of Cards of Satan.*
85. Hebert, op. cit., 174-175.
86. Rene Laurentin and Henri Joyeux, *Scientific and Medical Studies on the Apparitions at Medjugorje*, 123-124.
87. Craig, op. cit., 152-153.
88. Rene Laurentin, *Response to the Most Recent Objections of His Excellency Bishop Zanic Against Medjugorje*, 3.
89. Quoted in *Medjugorje: Facts, Documents, Theology*, 206.
90. Jones, op. cit., 27.
91. Quoted in *Medjugorje: Facts, Documents, Theology*, 117-119.
92. Craig, op. cit., 110-113.
93. Bartulica, op. cit., 200-208.
94. Jones, op. cit., 132, 134, 139-140.
95. Rene Laurentin, *Eight Years*, 61.

96. Ibid., 43.
97. Craig, op. cit., 140.
98. Jones, op. cit., 94.
99. Craig, op. cit., 171.
100. Rene Laurentin, *Eight Years,* 40-41.
101. Bartulica, op. cit., 54-61.
102. Quoted in *Medjugorje: Facts, Documents, Theology,* 83.
103. Mark Miravalle, *Response to Medjugorje: The Untold Story.*
104. Rene Laurentin, *Eight Years,* 38.
105. Jones, op. cit., 98.
106. Craig, op. cit., 139.
107. Sandra L. Zimdars-Swartz, *Encountering Mary,* Princeton, New Jersey, Princeton University Press, 1991, p.68.
108. Jones, op. cit., 6.
109. Craig, op. cit., 189.
110. Jones, op. cit., 119-120.
111. Bartulica, op. cit., pp. 128-140.
112. Quoted in Medjugorje: **Facts, Documents, Theology,** 121.
113. Rene Laurentin and Henri Joyeux, **Scientific and Medical Studies on the Apparitions at Medjugorje,** 123.
114. Rene Laurentin, **Response to the Most Recent Objections of His Excellency Bishop Zanic Against Medjugorje,** 1-2.
115. Quoted in **Medjugorje: Facts, Documents, Theology,** 106-107.
116. Michael O'Carroll, **Medjugorje: Facts, Documents, Theology,** Fourth Edition, 1989, 261-262.
117. Michael O'Carroll, **Medjugorje: Facts, Documents, Theology,** 198.